Nobel

A CENTURY OF PRIZE WINNERS

SECOND EDITION

Nobel

A CENTURY OF PRIZE WINNERS

Selected and Edited by
MICHAEL WOREK

FIREFLY BOOKS

A FIREFLY BOOK

Published by Firefly Books Ltd. 2010

First printing

Publisher Cataloging-in-Publication Data (U.S.)
Worek, Michael.
    Nobel : a century of prize winners / Michael Worek.
2nd ed.
Originally publisher: Lisbon, Portugal: QuidNovi, 2007.
[336] p. : photos. ; cm.
Includes index.
Translation of original Portuguese book.
Summary: Profiles of over 180 Nobel Laureates, 1901-2009.
ISBN-13: 978-1-55407-780-9 (bound) ISBN-10: 1-55407-780-X (bound)
ISBN-13: 978-1-55407-741-0 (pbk.) ISBN-10: 1-55407-741-9 (pbk.)
1. Nobel Prizes. 2. Nobel Prize winners. 3. Biography – 20th century – Dictionaries. I. Title.
303.6/6 dc22   AS911.N9.W6745   2010

Library and Archives Canada Cataloguing in Publication
    Nobel : a century of prize winners / selected and edited by Michael Worek. -- 2nd ed.
Includes index.
Translation of original Portuguese book.
ISBN-13: 978-1-55407-780-9 (bound) ISBN-10: 1-55407-780-X (bound)
ISBN-13: 978-1-55407-741-0 (pbk.) — ISBN-10: 1-55407-741-9 (pbk.)
1. Nobel Prize winners – Biography. 2. Nobel Prizes – History.
I. Worek, Michael
AS911.N9N63 2010   001.4'4   C2010-901871-0

Published in the United States by
Firefly Books (U.S.) Inc.
P.O. Box 1338, Ellicott Station
Buffalo, New York 14205

Published in Canada by
Firefly Books Ltd.
66 Leek Crescent
Richmond Hill, Ontario L4B 1H1

Printed in Canada

Cover and interior design: Jacqueline Hope Raynor
Page production: Tinge Design Studio
Idiomatic English translation: Jordan Worek

Photo Credits

All photographs and illustrations courtesy of Quid-Novi except for the following:

Corbis
Page 165 Bettman/CORBIS; 184 CORBIS; 304 Molly Riley/Reuters/CORBIS; 306 Bjorn Sigurdson/epa/CORBIS; 308 Colin McPherson/CORBIS

Reuters
Page 309 REUTERS/Chip East; 310 REUTERS/Bob Strong; 312 REUTERS/Alex Grimm; 313 REUTERS/Bobby Yp; 314 REUTERS/Larry Downing; 316 REUTERS/Kimberly White.

Getty
Page 226 Time & Life Pictures/ Getty Images

Alfred Nobel:
Promoter of Peace

Life

1833: Born October 21, 1833, in Stockholm, Sweden.

Discovery: In 1866 he combined nitro-glycerin with Kieselguhr to create an explosive which he called dynamite.

After the discovery: He became one of the richest men in the world. He made other discoveries such as Balistite, synthetic rubber, and synthetic silk. He registered 355 patents and set up factories in about 20 countries.

Literature: Nobel was passionate about literature. He wrote novels, poetry and plays and owned a vast library, featuring Swedish and foreign writers.

The fund: A significant part of his fortune went to creating a fund that is used for awarding annual prizes.

1896: He died December 10, 1896, in San Remo.

Nobel Prizes

Objective: To recognize individuals who make a valuable contribution for the good of humanity.

Categories: The five initial Prizes included Physics, Chemistry, Physiology or Medicine, Literature and Peace. The sixth Prize, Economic Sciences, was awarded for the first time in 1969.

Attribution: Four institutions are responsible for awarding the Prizes: the Royal Swedish Academy of Sciences; the Karolinska Institute; the Swedish Academy.

First award: Held in 1901.

Ceremony: On the 10th of December every year, on the anniversary of Alfred Nobel's death, ceremonies are held in Stockholm to award all prizes with the exception of the Nobel Peace Prize, which is awarded in Oslo, Norway.

Laureates: Over 800 Nobel Prizes have been awarded.

Prize: A medal with the head of Alfred Nobel, a diploma and approximately 1 million euros.

Alfred Bernhard Nobel (1833-1896)

Contents

1920–1929 Selected Profiles of Nobel Laureates

1930-1939 Selected Profiles of Nobel Laureates

1940–1949 Selected Profiles of Nobel Laureates

1950–1959 Selected Profiles of Nobel Laureates

1960–1969 Selected Profiles of Nobel Laureates

1970–1979 Selected Profiles of Nobel Laureates

1980–1989 Selected Profiles of Nobel Laureates

1990–1999 Selected Profiles of Nobel Laureates

2000–2009 Selected Profiles of Nobel Laureates

Introduction

Since 1901, the first year the award was given, until the present day, nearly 800 individuals and organizations have been recognized with the Nobel Prize. This group includes some of the greatest scientists, writers, economists and peacemakers in the world.

The five original Nobel awards were expanded in 1968 to include the Economic Sciences (normally known as the Nobel Prize in Economics). Prizes are awarded every December 10th to coincide with the anniversary of Alfred Nobel's death. Often controversial—as was Alfred Nobel himself—and at other times a nearly unanimous choice, the winners chosen by the Norwegian Nobel Committee (Peace), the Swedish Academy (Literature), the Royal Swedish Academy of Sciences (Physics, Chemistry and Economics) and the Karolinska Institute (Physiology or Medicine) don't make history, but they do help write it.

On the October 21, 1833, Alfred Bernhard was born in Stockholm, Sweden, third son of Immanuel and Andriette Nobel. Although in the coming years the young Alfred was pampered by his older brothers, the instability of the family's financial situation was always apparent, and a threat of prison hung over Immanuel Nobel because of his debts. In 1837 Immanuel Nobel moved to Finland and then to the Russian city of Saint Petersburg, where he was finally able to rebuild his capital and the family's honor.

Alfred Nobel's father found his son had a melancholic, idealistic side, and he ordered him at just 17 to embark on an extensive educational journey to expand his horizons and increase his interest in business. He also intended to expose his son to developments in the field of engineering, and explosives in particular. Alfred certainly benefited from studying abroad, meeting the brightest scientific minds of his day. In Paris he spent time with the inventor of nitroglycerin, the Italian Ascanio Sobrero, and in the United States he received lessons from the Swedish engineer John Ericsson.

In 1852 his father called him home to become more involved in the family business, which was booming at the time because of orders from the Russian military. Immanuel Nobel had first come into contact with the world of explosives through civil construction and believed that his future in Russia lay in this rapidly changing field. His inventions include deadly land and sea mines, and he was responsible for the most important Russian armaments factory during the Crimean War. The end of this conflict, however, brought another wave of difficulties to Immanuel and, in 1863, facing bankruptcy once again, he left his elder sons, Robert and Ludvig, to run the Russian businesses and returned with his wife and two younger sons, Alfred and Emil, to Stockholm.

While the family industries experienced a boom during the Crimean War, Alfred had devoted himself to studying explosives, particularly nitroglycerin. This compound was as dangerous as it was powerful, since its explosion could be set off by shock or heat. Nobel knew that if he could somehow "tame" nitroglycerin, it would become an unbeatable commercial product.

One of the first experiments, performed in 1864, went horribly wrong and several people died in the explosion, including the young Emil Nobel. The Swedish authorities put an immediate stop to any new experiments within Stockholm, but neither this, nor the loss of his brother, could stop Alfred Nobel. He moved his research center to the banks of Lake Malaren and went back to producing nitroglycerin, experimenting with different types of additives as a way of taming it. He finally achieved his goal in 1866 by mixing nitroglycerin with kieselguhr, thus producing a malleable and safe paste. Months later, on September 19, 1867, Alfred Nobel registered a patent for the new explosive, which he named "dynamite."

Nobel's first factories were in Krümmel, Germany, and very remote, allowing him to experiment without risk to the local population. Between 1865 and 1873 Nobel lived in a simple house between Krümmel and Hamburg, where the family's offices were located. During World War I Krümmel, with 2,700 employees, supplied the German army's gunpowder needs. The Versailles Treaty put an end to this contract, however, and during peace the factory was used to produce artificial silk. With the arrival of World War II, Krümmel was once again at the service of the German war interests, with more than 9,000 workers. The facilities were destroyed in 1945 by an Allied air raid, with bombs based on the inventions of Nobel himself.

Dynamite was, without a doubt, Alfred Nobel's most famous invention, but the list of his other accomplishments is long. In 1887 he created ballistite; known as smokeless gunpowder, this compound is made of 40 percent nitrocellulose and 60 percent nitroglycerin. The explosive was originally intended for the mining industry, but its appearance coincided with a tumultuous period at the end of the 19th century, when governments were scrambling to acquire new military technology. When the patent was made public, Alfred Nobel offered his product to the French government, but they turned the proposal down. When he offered ballistite to the Italians, however, they did not hesitate in accepting, and a large production facility was built near Turin.

Through more than 30 productive years of experimentation and developments carried out in Sweden, Germany, France, Italy and other nations around the world, Alfred Nobel never stopped applying himself to the tasks he undertook, whether it was to produce artificial silk or the most powerful explosives of the day. When he died he had put his name to no less than 355 patents, many of them now applicable to the fabrics industry and used in more than 20 countries.

Although just before his 30th birthday Alfred Nobel decided to rejoin his parents in Stockholm, the city had not been his primary residence for some time. Until the end of his days at the age of 63, Alfred Nobel was a constant pilgrim. He kept a house, ready to be lived in, in six different countries. "My home is where I am found working," he wrote, "and I work anywhere." He also kept completely equipped laboratories in Stockholm and Karlskoga (Sweden), Hamburg (Germany), Ardeer (Scotland), Paris and Sevran (France) and San Remo (Italy).

Alfred Nobel lived and died as one of the earliest citizens of the world, and this lifestyle was a deeply interwoven part of his personality. He can be considered one of the founding fathers of multinational corporations. Many of the companies he founded still exist today and are at the forefront of their industrial field, including companies like Imperial Chemical Industries (ICI), Société Centrale de Dynamite and Dyno Industries.

Alfred Nobel's Will

When he reached the age of 60, Alfred Nobel began to make arrangements for his vast fortune after his death. He wrote his will himself, without any legal assistance, and signed it on November 27, 1895, in a room of the Swedish-Norwegian Club in Paris, witnessed by four friends.

Nobel gave part of his inheritance to his nieces, nephews and closest collaborators, and he left lifelong pensions to his most dedicated employees, but the amounts he bequeathed to these individuals were smaller than expected (considering the size of his fortune) and criticized by many.

The excerpt from the will below deals exclusively with establishing the annual prizes.

The whole of my remaining realizable estate shall be dealt with in the following way: The capital shall be invested by my executors in safe securities and shall constitute a fund, the interest on which shall be annually distributed in the form of prizes to those who, during the preceding year, shall have conferred the greatest benefit on mankind. The said interest shall be divided into five equal parts, which shall be apportioned as follows: one part to the person who shall have made the most important discovery or invention within the field of physics; one part to the person who shall have made the most important chemical discovery or improvement; one part to the person who shall have made the most important discovery within the domain of physiology or medicine; one part to the person who shall have produced in the field of literature the most outstanding work of an idealistic tendency; and one part to the person who shall have done the most or best work for the fraternity among nations, for the abolition or reduction of standing armies and for the holding and promotion of peace congresses.

The prizes for physics and chemistry shall be awarded by the Swedish Academy of Sciences; that for physiology or medical work by the Karolinska Institute in Stockholm; that for literature by the Academy in Stockholm; and that for champions of peace by a committee of five persons to be elected by the Norwegian Storting. It is my express wish that in awarding the prizes no consideration whatever shall be given to the nationality of the candidates, so that the most worthy shall receive the prize, whether he be a Scandinavian or not.

Nobel finished his will with a list of his assets, including his properties in Paris and San Remo, an endless list of activities in banks and other credit institutions, and the income from his patents, whose registers he stated were guarded in his safe. The immense fortune was calculated at the time to be worth about 31 million Swedish Krona, and interest with careful management by the Foundation has been swelling the coffers for more than a century.

The Prize

The idea of creating prizes to award individual artists and scientists for their efforts is rooted in the French Revolution. Throughout the 19th century there were plenty of awards given to academies, clubs and administrations, but it wasn't until the second half of the century that private foundations began to bestow their own prizes.

What is it, however, that makes the Nobel Prize different from others and grants it the recognition and support it has today? First of all, as is very clear in Alfred Nobel's will and contrary to other contemporary examples, it is a universal award, and there was no intention of benefiting a specific nation. Also to be noted is that Nobel did not create one prize but five (the sixth, for Economic Sciences, was only created in 1968.) The recognition offered by the prizes is, therefore, more complete, bringing together a diverse group of talents from fields that usually have little interaction. The most important point that distinguished the Nobel Prize from other awards, however, was the large sum given to the laureates. In addition to the prize money, a diploma and medal were also presented, which was not specified in Nobel's will.

Although there is great importance in a scientist, writer or pacifist seeing their work published in consequence of being given an award, the Nobel means much more. For the first time there existed a prize with which scientists could continue their investigations without traditional economic limitations, writers could avoid commercial temptations and follow their more creative desires, and pacifists could, against powerful forces, maintain campaigns that could only be kept alive with financial support.

The first people to receive the Nobel Prize took home approximately 150,000 Swedish Krona. In 1923, as a result of an increase in taxes, smaller quantities were awarded, and each

The Nobel Award Ceremony.

laureate received 115,000 Swedish Krona. In 1946 the Nobel Foundation was finally guaranteed an exemption from taxes, which led to the prizes increasing in worth. In 2006 each of the six laureates was given the highest amounts ever: 10 million Swedish Krona, equivalent to about US$1 million.

On December 10th of every year, to coincide with the anniversary of Alfred Nobel's death, the award ceremonies for five of the six Nobel prizes are held in Stockholm, Sweden; the exception is the Nobel Peace Prize, which is presented in Oslo, Norway. The laureates present Nobel lectures several days before the ceremonies in Stockholm and on the day of the event in Oslo. These ceremonies are attended by Their Majesties the King and Queen of Sweden and Norway, respectively, in addition to the laureates, their families and other distinguished guests. Lavish banquets follow the event.

The honors are conferred in physics, chemistry, physiology or medicine, literature, peace and economics, unless no laureate has been chosen in a given field. As with almost any event, the work that takes place beforehand is of vital importance. The selection process for the people, or institutions, as is sometimes the case with the Nobel Peace Prize, to be awarded are meticulous and performed with a great sense of responsibility since the world will scrutinize every decision.

Candidate selection is carried out by four Nobel Committees that are based within the institutions Nobel's will made responsible for attributing the awards. Each of these committees is composed of five elected members, the majority of whom are of Swedish origin, with the exception of the Norwegian Nobel Committee. Every year the six committees send invitations to hundreds of scientists, academy members and university professors from around the world to nominate an individual for a Nobel Prize; former laureates are also encouraged to put forward a name. There are differences in the rules regarding nomination for the individual prizes, but they are accentuated with the Nobel Peace Prize, which can be recommended by members of national assemblies, the Inter-Parliamentary Union, Hague Permanent Court of Arbitration, the International Law Institutes and governments themselves. According to the statutes of the Nobel Foundation, however, no one prize can be attributed to more than three people in the same year. Additionally, no scientific community, academic institution or organization may receive a prize on their own, except in the case of the Nobel Peace Prize. Since 1974, a Nobel Prize cannot be attributed posthumously.

Royal Swedish Academy of Sciences

During the first half of the 18th century a remarkable group of Swedish scientists were active in the country, and in 1739 the Royal Swedish Academy of Sciences was established to help advance their work. Based on the Royal Society in London and the Académie Royale des Sciences (Royal Academy for Sciences) in Paris, it first began to encourage research in the areas of mathematics and the natural sciences. Among its founders were the renowned naturalist Carl Linnaeus, the mercantilist Jonas Alströmer, the mechanical engineer Mårten Triewald and the politician Anders Johan von Höpken, who was the first permanent secretary of the organization.

Although it had modest beginnings, the Royal Swedish Academy of Sciences soon began to develop important contacts with other scientific institutions across Europe. It developed a major program to publish scientific findings and began promoting more applied fields, including agriculture, ship building and mining. At the beginning of the 19th century the chemist Jacob Berzelius was appointed secretary-general. He reorganized the Royal Swedish Academy of Sciences, making it an institution with strictly scientific objectives.

The academy continued developing, and, at the beginning of the 20th century, it took on an important role in relation to the Nobel Foundation. Physics and chemistry were two subjects that Alfred Nobel knew well and expected much from in the coming years. He specified in his will that a prize should be awarded in both fields, and he chose the Royal Swedish Academy of Sciences to attribute the awards.

In 1968 the society was made responsible for attributing the Sveriges Riksbank Prize in Economic in Memory of Alfred Nobel, commonly known as the Nobel Prize in Economics. It was awarded for the first time the following year. Economics is the only prize not referred to in the will of Alfred Nobel but the Bank of Sweden, on its 300th anniversary, established a considerable financial commitment to the Nobel Foundation in perpetuity. This commitment has allowed those who have made contributions to mathematic formulation, financial economics, game theories and macroeconomics to be recognized. Some have challenged whether the Sveriges Riksbank Prize in Economic in Memory of Alfred Nobel fairly mirrors current tendencies in economic analysis, but most accept that decisions are stimulated by the multidimensional nature of economic investigation.

The Royal Swedish Academy of Sciences has approximately 350 native members and half that number again from foreign countries. Each member is part of one of the following 10 divisions: mathematics, astronomy and space sciences, physics, chemistry, geosciences, biological sciences, medical sciences, engineering sciences, social and economic sciences and the humanities. These members work within their divisions and permanent committees, contributing to their respective fields of research and presenting conferences and seminars.

Current social and environmental issues are also monitored by the Royal Swedish Academy of Sciences. It continues to promote innovative studies, and the Environmental Committee is dedicated to questions regarding sustainable development, natural resource use and maintaining biological diversity. The society's journal *Ambio* is recognized as a leading forum for environmental issues. Two other committees in the society are those for Science Education and Human Rights, demonstrating the diverse nature of its work. The Royal Swedish Academy of Sciences also runs the Observatory and Berzelius museums, which have impressive collections of scientific artifacts and other resources.

The Karolinska Institute

At the end of the 19th century, Alfred Nobel recognized the pressing need for humanity to develop its medical knowledge, products and procedures. He had himself suffered from ill health for much of his life and experienced the primitive help available at the time. Accordingly, he specified in his will that a prize was to be set aside for this field, and in 1901 the first Nobel Prize in Physiology or Medicine was conferred by the Karolinska Institute. The first winner was the German Emil von Behring, who was distinguished for his "work on serum therapy, especially its application against diphtheria, by which he has opened a new road in the domain of medical science and thereby placed in the hands of the physician a victorious weapon against illness and death."

The difficult mission of choosing up to three people annually for this prize is still in the hands of the Karolinska Institute, located in Solna, just outside Stockholm. It initially entrusted the selection process of the nominees to its teaching staff, but nowadays the Nobel Assembly of the Karolinska Institute is composed of 50 elected members of the Faculty of Medicine.

The organization continues to train doctors, dentists, physiotherapists, speech therapists and toxicologists. It also maintains a strong academic research department responsible for nearly 40 percent of such work in the country. According to the 2007 Academic Ranking of World Universities, it is the best such department in the country and 11th in Europe. Besides its close ties to the Nobel Foundation, the institute also preserves valuable relationships with the Swedish government and health organizations, businesses and other universities worldwide.

Swedish Academy

Since 1901 the Swedish Academy has had the responsibility of attributing the Nobel Prize in Literature. The academy was established in 1786 by King Gustaf III. He personally wrote most of its statutes, having been inspired by the French Academy; he also conferred on the institution its motto, "Snille och smak" (Talent and good taste). The main objective drawn up for the academy by Gustaf III was to work for the "purity, vigor and majesty" of the Swedish language. In the monarch's understanding, the academy had a patriotic duty to elevate the country's language and literature, as well as commemorate great national events of the past.

With the turn of the century, and after much debate, the academy accepted a task that was not a part of its initial mandate: to spend a considerable portion of its capacities to annually attribute the Nobel Prize in Literature. Erik Axel Karlfeldt, who, during the time he was permanent secretary between 1913 and 1931, revitalized and modernized the Swedish Academy, opened its doors to new writers and electing the first woman to its team.

Norwegian Nobel Committee

In accordance with the wishes of Alfred Nobel, the laureates for the Nobel Peace Prize are chosen by an independent committee composed of five people elected by the Norwegian Parliament and have been since 1901. These vague directions, however, have been controversial and sparked some degree of change.

The challenge for the Norwegian Nobel Committee is to be impartial in their decisions; many claim that this was far from true in the early years, when most members selected by Parliament were influential politicians. Over the decades this committee has also achieved a certain status, since it does not work in the favor of public opinion or political authorities.

In contrast to the other categories, the Nobel Peace Prize can be attributed to institutions and organizations as well as individuals. The Norwegian Nobel Committee does not receive outside orders of any nature and, in accordance with the statutes of the Nobel Foundation, should not reveal anything that takes place within the meetings that lead to the selection of the laureates. To such ends, the members do not take part in the debates that follow the announcement of the decision.

The Norwegian Nobel Institute was created in 1904 and, in 1905, it moved into a classic mansion in the centre of Oslo. At the time the site was completely renovated, and the Nobel Foundation was criticized for spending too much money on the work. The main obligation of the Norwegian Nobel Institute is to support to the Norwegian Nobel Committee during the selection process of laureates, as well as to organize events in Oslo dedicated to the Nobel Peace Prize.

As a way of showing its status as the center of knowledge related to peace and world questions in general, the institute has created a library with approximately 175,000 volumes. The works available in the library are principally concerned with peace, international relations, law, economics and political history. The library is open to the public and has a pleasant reading room. The institute also organizes seminars, meetings and conferences with specialists from around the world.

They laugh at me, the man of dynamite as a man of peace. But, since men don't listen to reason, it is necessary to invent an instrument of death which, through fear, will make Humanity move to peace. Alfred Nobel

Selected Profiles of Nobel Laureates

1901–1909

Sully Prudhomme

In special recognition of his poetic composition, which gives evidence of lofty idealism, artistic perfection and a rare combination of the qualities of both heart and intellect.

René François Armand Prudhomme, better known by his literary pseudonym Sully Prudhomme, did not begin his career with the world of letters in mind. The son of a storekeeper, he intended to study science and enrolled in a polytechnic institute. An eye disease, however, forced him to change his plans. The disappointed young Frenchman soon turned to literature and took pleasure in the study, recording his thoughts and reading avidly. Nevertheless, Prudhomme was not able to make a living from his writing, so he accepted a clerical position in a factory. Understandably dissatisfied, he left the factory in 1860, determined to study law, and he soon began working in a lawyer's office.

During this time he was a member of the distinguished student society "Conférence La Bruyère," and it was here that Prudhomme heard the first words of encouragement for his literary pursuits. In 1865, at just 26, he published his first work, *Stances et poèmes (Stanzas and Poems)*, a collection of fluent, melancholic poems inspired by a passionate dissatisfaction with life. Sainte-Beuve, a writer and influential French literary critic, gave the book a favorable review, which helped Prudhomme's reputation. One of these early poems, "Le vase brisé" ("The Broken Vase"), remains popular today.

In 1866 *Les Épreuves (Trials)* was published and, three years, later came *Les Solitudes*. These works, similar in style and content to *Stances et poèmes*, are dominated by romanticism and emotionalism. It was not long, however, before this early lyrical phase of his writing evolved. This change is credited to the influence of the Parnassian school, of which he would go on to become a preeminent member. Presenting philosophical concepts in verse dominated Prudhomme's latter poetical works, particularly *La Justice (Justice*, published in 1878) and *Le Bonheur (Happiness*, 1888).

Prudhomme's literary career was characterized by intense activity, as can be seen by his vast bibliography. Besides his best-known works listed above, he wrote *Croquis italiens (Italian Notebook, 1866–68)*, *Impressions de la guerre (Impressions of War, 1870)*, *Les Destins (Destinies, 1872)*, *La Révolte des fleurs (Revolt of the Flowers, 1872)*, *La France (1874)*, *Les vaines tendresses (Vain Endearments, 1875)* and many others.

In 1881, aged 42, Sully Prudhomme was elected a member of the prestigious French Academy, which demonstrated his peers' respect and admiration for him. His highest level of recognition came when he was awarded the 1901 Nobel Prize in Literature.

Jean Henry Dunant

*For actions developing the organization of the Geneva
Conventions of 1863 and 1864 and the International Red Cross,
created by these conventions.*

Jean Henry Dunant seemed destined to dedicate his life to others. The son
of a respected and prosperous couple, he grew up in Geneva, Switzerland,
admiring his parents' philanthropic efforts within their community. At the
age of six, he went with his father, Jean Jacques, on a visit to a penitentiary
in Toulon, France. For the little Dunant, the sight of the chained prisoners
was shocking and had lasting effects. Later in life, this memory led him to
dedicate his Sunday afternoons to visiting prisoners.

Entering the world of business, Dunant first went to Algeria, where he managed an
estate. A number of difficulties arose for him in the French territory, however, due to his
Swiss citizenship. He decided that the best hope of resolving his problems was to speak
personally with Emperor Napoleon III and convince the Emperor to grant him concessions
to explore new lands. When news arrived that Napoleon III was leading French troops in Italy
to expel the Austrians at what was to be the Battle of Solferino, Dunant made his way north
to meet the Emperor.

When he arrived at Solferino, however, his intentions were shattered upon witnessing the
violence of the fighting. When the battle was over, one of the bloodiest of the 19th century,
Dunant put his own concerns aside and began ministering to the needy. In 1862 he published
A Memory of Solferino. The book brought him fame and presented a detailed plan to create a
structure aimed at supporting the wounded in times of war. This effort led to the formation
of the International Red Cross, which he established in 1863. It was recognized a year later
by the Geneva Convention, and the idea was worthy of the first Nobel Peace Prize.

Dunant set aside his business concerns to dedicate himself to helping others, and it is no
surprise that he went bankrupt in 1867. After his setbacks in business, which also involved
some of his friends in Geneva, Dunant was no longer welcome in his hometown. Instead he
chose to live in Heiden, a small Swiss town, where he lived mostly in obscurity. He fell ill in
1892 and was transferred to the hospital in Heiden, where he would die 18 years later.

After 1895, while Dunant remained hospitalized, he was recognized more frequently and
was honored with various prizes, including the Order of Christ in 1897, awarded by Portugal.
Dunant, who never married or had children, maintained his generosity to the end, giving
the money from his prizes to those who cared for him in the hospital and to humanitarian
institutions in Norway and Switzerland.

Frédéric Passy also received half of the prize.

Emil Fischer

In recognition of the extraordinary services he has rendered by his work on sugar and purine syntheses.

Hermann Emil Fischer always possessed an excellent memory, a fascination with scientific problems and a rare determination to prove hypotheses. These characteristics were essential for someone who would go on to become one of the greatest scientists of all time. Against his father's will, who would have liked his son to continue the family timber business in Cologne, Germany, Fischer pursued the natural sciences, especially physics, and was rewarded for his dedication.

After three years with a private tutor, the young German attended the local school. He also studied in Wetzlar and Bonn, where he passed his final exam with distinction in 1869. Faced with his son's insistence on studying science, his father decided to enroll him in the University of Bonn to study chemistry. What Fischer really wanted, however, was to dedicate himself to physics. One year later, accompanied by his cousin, Otto Fischer, he left for the University of Strasbourg. There he met Adolf von Baeyer, whose influence finally persuaded him to return to chemistry.

In 1874 he took his doctorate and was also appointed assistant teacher at Strasbourg. He continued his studies and discovered the first hydrazine base, phenylhydrazine, and showed its relationship with hydrazobenzene and sulphonic acid. In 1875, Adolf von Baeyer went to the University of Munich, and Fischer accompanied him as his assistant in the subject of organic chemistry. Later Fischer taught at the universities of Erlangen and Wurzburg, and in 1892 he was invited to the University of Berlin where he stayed until his death.

Fischer left his mark on research in every university in which he worked. In Munich he continued his studies in the field of hydrazenes and, along with his cousin Otto, formulated a new theory on the constitution of dyes derived from triphenylmethane. In Erlangen he studied the active ingredients of tea, coffee and cocoa and established the constitution of a series of components in this field. His work on sugars between 1884 and 1894 were significant, particularly his synthesis of glucose, fructose and mannose and his studies of glycosides.

His research into purines and sugars was recognized with the 1902 Nobel Prize in Chemistry, and Fischer also contributed to the study of proteins, enzymes and other chemical substances. His dedication to chemistry was further acknowledged with the Hofmann Medal from the German Chemical Society in 1906, the Elliot Cresson Gold Medal from the Franklin Institute in 1913, and many other distinctions. After his death, the German Chemical Society initiated a prize in his name, the Emil Fischer Memorial Medal.

Svante Arrhenius

In recognition of the extraordinary services he has rendered to the advancement of chemistry by his electrolytic theory of dissociation.

The Swede Svante August Arrhenius, father of the ionic theory that explains the movement of electric currents in solutions, was born in Vik to a family of farmers. When he was only a year old his parents moved to Uppsala, where he first attended school; he demonstrated a rare facility for solving mathematical problems and an unusual interest in physics and mathematics.

In 1876 he entered the University of Uppsala, the oldest university in Sweden, to study mathematics, chemistry and physics. In 1881 he moved to the Academy of Sciences in Stockholm. After working as an assistant to a professor he developed his doctoral thesis on the galvanic conductivity of electrolytes. Arrhenius concluded that electrical conductivity was possible in a solution due to the presence of ions. He was to later say that "the idea occurred on the night of the May 17, 1883, and I could not look at anything else until I had solved the problem."

The relationship between electricity and chemistry was rejected by the scientific community at the time. However, while jury members raised many doubts about the new theory, Arrhenius obtained his doctorate in 1884. He lectured in physical chemistry at Uppsala, the first Swede to lecture in this branch of science, and, in 1895, he became a physics professor at the Stockholm Högskola (the "High School of Stockholm," a private foundation that was the equivalent of a university science faculty). Arrhenius managed to win over many scientists in diverse fields and, in 1903, was awarded the Nobel Prize in Chemistry, his theory for electrolytic dissociation having been widely accepted by that time. Two years later, despite being made various offers from universities, he stopped giving classes and became chief of the Nobel Institute for Physical Chemistry, newly created by the Academy of Sciences.

Arrhenius accumulated various distinctions, including being the first foreigner to be elected to the Royal Society and receiving a medal from the Chemical Society, among other prizes. He also published many popular books that could be understood by a non-scientific public. His interests in astronomy led him to propose a new theory on the formation of the solar system, based on the collision of stars, and he did valuable research into the use of chemical serum in fighting diseases.

Both in his professional and private life, Arrhenius was a quiet but happy man. During World War I he showed great bravery, successfully freeing and repatriating German and Austrian scientists. He married twice, first in 1894 to Sofia Rudbeck, with whom he had a son, and then to Maria Johansson in 1905, with whom he had three children. He died in Stockholm in 1927 and was buried in Uppsala.

(1852–1908)

Henri Becquerel

In recognition of the extraordinary services he has rendered by his discovery of spontaneous radioactivity.

Antoine Henri Becquerel was one of the most renowned physicists at the end of the 19th century, and his work is still widely recognized today. He grew up in a world where physics was a popular subject of conversation and a part of everyday life. His interest in physics began with his grandfather, Antoine César, and his father, Alexander Edmond Becquerel, was a scientist and professor of applied physics. Aware of the enormous work he would have to do to become a respected physicist, Henri Becquerel began his career at the Paris Polytechnic in 1872. He also distinguished himself at the École Nationale des Ponts-et-Chaussées (National School of Bridges and Roads), where he became an engineer and later received his doctorate. Along with these achievements he advanced his professional career by teaching at both the Department of Natural History at the Paris Museum and the Paris Polytechnic.

An extremely hardworking man, Becquerel dedicated himself to physics, dividing his days betweens the demands of teaching, studying and scientific research. He did, however, marry twice, first to the daughter of a civil engineer. Their son became a physicist, ushering in a fourth generation of scientists into the Becquerel family. This marriage ended after four years with the death of his wife, and he remarried a decade later, in 1890.

Among the daily bustle, Becquerel continued his research, strengthening his family's reputation and maintaining his own high profile. In 1896 he demonstrated the phenomenon that would overshadow his previous work. His discovery of spontaneous radioactivity brought him the 1903 Nobel Prize in Physics, which he shared with Marie and Pierre Curie, who extended his research into the phenomena. Showing that not all atomic nuclei are stable has proven to be one of the greatest scientific revolutions of our age.

Becquerel published many papers about his discoveries, mainly in the *Annales de physique et chimie* (*Annals of Physics and Chemistry*) and the *Comptes rendus de l'Academie des Sciences* (*Proceedings of the French Academy of Sciences*). Called the "father of radioactivity," he was elected a member of the French Academy of Sciences, where he remained a prominent figure. Further important posts he held during his life include those in the Accademia dei Lincei and the Royal Academy of Berlin. After a life marked by achievement, Becquerel died in Le Croisic.

Pierre and Marie Curie also each received one-quarter of the prize.

Pierre Curie

In recognition of the extraordinary services they have rendered by their joint researches on the radiation phenomena discovered by Professor Henri Becquerel.

Working with his brilliant wife, Marie, Pierre Curie proved he was a man with a fierce intelligence and great capacity for work. He not only shared the task of "investigating the phenomenon of radiation discovered by Becquerel" with his wife — for which they received the 1903 Nobel Prize in Physics — the two also shared an intimate personal life.

Pierre Curie was born in Paris on the May 15, 1859. His father, a doctor, educated him at home until he entered the faculty of sciences at the Sorbonne. In 1878 he obtained a licentiate degree and continued at the Sorbonne as a demonstrator in the physics laboratory until 1882, when he became supervisor of all practical work in the Physics and Industrial Chemistry Schools. Finally obtaining his doctorate in sciences in 1895, Curie started lecturing in physics, and five years later he became a professor at the Faculty of Sciences. In 1904 he took on the role of titular professor.

Curie made his first discovery two years after obtaining his licentiate degree. In 1880, working with his brother Jacques, he discovered piezoelectric effects, the name given to a phenomenon observed in anisotropic crystals. The studies he carried out on the properties of crystals then led him to reflect on the general symmetry of physical phenomena, and in 1894 he formulated what is now known as the Curie principle, a symmetry principle that allowed scientists to predict the possibility or impossibility of numerous phenomena. A year later, Pierre discovered that below a certain temperature, which is still known as the Curie point, ferromagnetism is transformed into paramagnetism.

In 1895, after repeated proposals, Maria Sklodowska, a woman who had a great love of physics, finally accepted Pierre's hand in marriage. From then on the couple did all their research together. Deeply interested in Becquerel's discovery of radioactivity, the pair went on to discover polonium and radium after separating and measuring all the elements contained in pitchblende. The world recognized this achievement in 1903 with the Nobel Prize in Physics. Unfortunately, due to Pierre and Marie's ill health, which they blamed on the effects of prolonged exposure to radiation, the couple was unable to attend the ceremony. The monetary value of the Nobel Prize was important in helping the Curie family with their expenses and allowed them to offset the high costs of their research.

The Curies had two girls, Irène and Eve, the first of whom followed in her parents' footsteps and, along with her husband Frédéric Joliot, received the 1935 Nobel Prize in Chemistry. Pierre Curie was struck and killed by a horse-drawn carriage on April 19, 1906, in Paris.

Henri Becquerel also received half the prize, and Marie Curie one-quarter.

Ivan Pavlov

In recognition of his work on the physiology of digestion, through which knowledge on vital aspects of the subject has been transformed and enlarged.

Ivan Petrovich Pavlov was born in Ryazan, Russia, into a religious family. Following in the footsteps of his father, a parish priest, and his grandfather, a sacristan, the young Pavlov began his studies in the church school and continued them at the local seminary. However several influential teachers, including a renowned Russian physiologist, inspired the young Pavlov with a passion for scientific knowledge. Under their influence, he abandoned his religious studies in 1870 to study science.

After obtaining a bachelor's degree in the natural sciences, Pavlov decided to pursue his interest in physiology and enrolled in the Academy of Medical Surgery in Saint Petersburg, where he graduated with distinction. Pavlov remained in the institution on a fellowship while also acting as director of the physiology laboratory. In 1890 he was invited by the Institute of Experimental Medicine in Saint Petersburg to administer the Department of Physiology, a position he accepted and held until the end of his life.

Pavlov contributed to the understanding of the heart and circulatory system, but it was his work in the physiology of digestion that earned him the 1904 Nobel Prize in Medicine. To this day his work is associated with the concept of the conditioned reflex, which he demonstrated through an unconventional experiment; having previously associated the ring of a bell with the appearance of food, he trained a hungry dog to salivate at its sound.

Pavlov also enjoyed a fulfilling private life with his family. In 1881 he married a teacher who was a friend of the famous writer Dostoyevsky. A woman of firm character, she was admired by her husband and dedicated her life to the home, their four children and religion.

Pavlov was not afraid of defending his ideas, even when his words were directed at the most important figures in his country. In 1922, as Russia struggled with its revolution, Pavlov asked Lenin's permission to transfer his laboratory abroad. Lenin refused and instead offered to increase the amount of food available to him, to which Pavlov boldly responded, "I will not accept these privileges unless they are given to all my collaborators as well."

Two years later he again brought himself into the spotlight when sons of parish priests were expelled from the Military Medical Academy in Saint Petersburg, where he lectured on physiology. He resigned from his post saying, "I am also the son of a priest, and if they are expelled, then so am I!"

Throughout his life, Ivan Pavlov received numerous honors, among them an honorary doctorate from Cambridge University and acceptance into the Order of the Legion of Honour from the Medical Academy of Paris.

Physiology of digestion

The Russian physiologist Ivan Pavlov dedicated much of his study to understanding the physiology of digestion. It was as a result of his work in this area that he was awarded the Nobel Prize and not, as many believe, for the discovery of the conditioned reflex.

Based on his observations that irregular secretions are produced in non-anaesthetized animals, the physiologist formulated the laws of the Conditioned Reflex. Pavlov (pictured with the famous dog) used saliva secretion as a quantitive or subjective measure of brain activity in the animal. He trained the dog to eat immediately after the ring of a bell. After a period of time it was enough for the dog to hear the bell to start salivating. In this way he demonstrated his theory of the Conditioned Reflex.

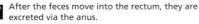

NORMAL DIGESTION

1 Food is introduced. In the mouth the tiny channels of the salivary glands release saliva, which makes sure the food is lubricated and is easier to chew and swallow.

2 The bolus reaches the stomach and is mixed with gastric juice. The stomach stores, mixes and starts the digestion of proteins and fats.

3 Bile, which is produced by the liver and stored in the gallbladder, helps in the digestion of fats. Bile contains minerals that help emulsify fats to make their absorption easier.

4 The pancreas, an organ situated behind the stomach, produces secretions rich in enzymes which deal with carbohydrates, proteins and in particular fats.

5 It is in the small intestine, which is about seven meters long, where most of the digestion takes place. In this part of the digestive system substances are absorbed into the blood.

6 In the large intestine, water and minerals are also absorbed. Unabsorbed materials are transformed into feces.

7 After the feces move into the rectum, they are excreted via the anus.

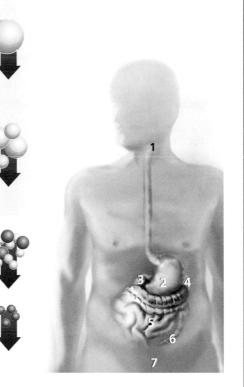

Robert Koch

For his investigations and discoveries in relation to tuberculosis.

Born in Clausthal, Germany, Robert Heinrich Hermann Koch was expected to become a shoemaker, but he showed methodical persistence and intelligence from a very early age. To the surprise of his parents, at five he taught himself to read by studying newspapers, and it became evident that he was destined to be more than a shoemaker. Koch's distinctive drive and ambition led him to study medicine in the hope of becoming a doctor.

In high school he showed a great aptitude for biology and developed a desire to travel, which confirmed his early ambitions. In 1862 he enrolled at the University of Göttingen to study medicine. When he finished his studies four years later he practiced medicine in various places around Germany until 1870, when he volunteered for the Franco-Prussian War.

After the war Koch realized that his vocation lay in a different field, the natural sciences; although abandoning his career as a doctor, a resolve to help the needy was still foremost in the young German's mind. Researching the causes of disease and their prevention soon occupied his time.

Koch was in Wollstein when an anthrax epidemic attacked the farm animals in the district, and he immediately decided to analyze the disease. His wife had given him a new microscope for his 28th birthday, which greatly enriched the poorly equipped laboratory in the couple's apartment. Koch worked without other adequate scientific equipment, access to libraries or contact with other scientists.

Around 1880 his studies on the anthrax bacteria earned him a job in the Reichs-Gesundheitsamt (the Imperial Health Bureau) laboratories in Berlin. Initially he was given a small, insufficient laboratory but soon was moved into better surroundings, where he worked with assistants. A few years after arriving in Berlin, Koch discovered tubercle bacillus, now known as Koch's bacillus. This research was of such importance to the scientific field that it earned him the 1905 Nobel Prize in Physiology or Medicine.

Although perhaps best known for his work on tuberculosis, Robert Koch dedicated valuable research time to a number of human and animal diseases, including cholera, leprosy, bovine plague, bubonic plague and malaria. These studies allowed him to realize his early dreams of traveling, and he spent considerable periods in Egypt, India, Africa and Italy doing research.

Tuberculosis

In the years since Robert Koch discovered the tuberculosis bacillus in 1882, many advances have been made in the fight against this disease. For centuries suffered from against tuberculosis without knowing its cause and how to treat it. Throughout the 20th century great strides were made in the fight against tuberculosis, but in recent times new cases have appeared particularly in those infected with the HIV virus.

Some Peruvian mummies contain bacteria related to tuberculosis.

How tuberculosis attacks the lungs:

1 The person with tuberculosis coughs and releases droplets of mucous infected by the Koch bacillus into the air.

2 Another person inhales the bacillus.

3 Some bacilli reach the lungs.

tuberculosis mycobacteria

4 The macrophagic cells, which are part of the body's immune system, absorb the tuberculose bacteria.

5 Macrophages and white blood cells transform the bacteria into granuloma. If the person has a strong immune system, the tuberculosis is blocked and no symptoms appear.

Sanitoriums: Patients were isolated here and forced to rest and attention was paid to diet.

In the 1940s (see right) treatment consisted of injecting air into the thorax to collapse the lungs.

Testing for tuberculosis: A substance derived from the bacillus is injected under the skin (see below). A papule forms if there is contact with the bacillus (active or inactive tuberculosis).

6 If the immune system is weak, for example in the case of HIV, the granuloma ruptures and the bacteria are spread throughout the body.

Symptoms of active tuberculosis: Fever, cough with mucous or blood, nighttime sweats, loss of weight and difficulty breathing.

8th c. Skeletons from this period have been found showing bone deformations caused by tuberculosis.

17th c. Tuberculosis spreads quickly through European cities. Many Europeans have tuberculosis, which was called "consumption."

18th c. Tuberculosis spreads to the colonies of European nations.

19th c. Doctors take blood from patients with tuberculosis as a form of treatment.

1882: Scientists, among them Robert Koch, identify the bacteria which cause tuberculosis.

1920s: Rest and fresh air are indicated as the treatment for tuberculosis.

1940s: Isoniazide is used for the first time.

1950s: Streptomycin is used to treat advance tuberculosis.

1960s: Scientists develop a new skin test (see left) to detect tuberculosis (tuberculin test).

1980s: The weakened immune system of people infected with HIV increases the risk of developing tuberculosis.

1999: 33% of the world's population is infected.

2000-2020: According to the World Health Organization, about 70 million people will die of tuberculosis.

Physiology or Medicine 1905

Bertha von Suttner

For her activities in favor of peace, both for her writings and her active presence in peace societies and international conferences.

Baroness Bertha Sophie Felicita von Suttner, born Countess Kinsky von Chinic und Tettau, always said that Alfred Nobel, an intimate friend, wanted her to be the first person to receive the Nobel Peace Prize. This was not to be the case, however; the first female peace activist of the modern age had to wait four years, until 1905, while seeing her male friends and fellow pacifists receive the award.

A native of Prague, at the time Austrian territory, von Suttner was educated by her mother in accordance with aristocratic perceptions and traditions she accepted for the first half of her life. These early years were very difficult for her. At the age of 30 she accept a position of teacher-companion to a Mr. Suttner's four daughters. It was then, however, that she fell in love with her pupils' brother.

His parents opposed the marriage, refusing to accept her as a daughter-in-law, but the marriage went ahead in secret. The newlyweds were forced to move to the Caucasus, where they lived in precarious circumstances, surviving by writing and giving music and language lessons. Only after nine years did the Suttners accept their daughter-in-law and invite the couple to live in the family castle in Austria, where days were filled with parties, writing and studying.

In the winter of 1886, Bertha von Suttner became deeply interested in the new International Arbitration and Peace Association. This organization was established in England and was working to establish a court of international arbitration, the headquarters of which would act as a stage for nations to air and resolve their differences. Suttner's emergence on the global stage started with the publication in 1889 of her book *Die Waffen nieder (Lay Down Your Arms)*, in which she showed the true horror of war. She reached the pinnacle of her fame during the Hague Peace Conference in 1899.

The much sought-after Nobel Prize was awarded to her for her activities in the name of peace as well as for her writings and active presence in peace societies. She was the second woman to receive a Nobel Prize, but, unlike Marie Curie, Bertha von Suttner did not share the honor. Her newspaper articles were also important in preserving peace, and von Suttner was recognized as the first woman to write political journalism of exceptional quality.

Two months before the outbreak of World War I, Bertha von Suttner, now a Baroness, died in Vienna, apparently of cancer; she was thus spared witnessing the beginning of a war she had so tirelessly fought against.

Santiago Ramón y Cajal

In recognition of their work on the structure of the nervous system.

Santiago Ramón y Cajal was born in the village of Petilla de Aragón, Spain, the son of an anatomy professor at the University of Saragossa. Although a quiet and intelligent boy, Cajal did not dedicate himself to his studies, preferring the arts, and his father did nothing to encourage his son's emerging vocation. Justo Ramón Cajal, in fact, did everything he could to take him away from the world of the pencil and the paintbrush, even forcing the boy to apprentice to a barber and a shoemaker.

However, Cajal went on to study medicine at Saragossa, where his drawing skills served him well in anatomical studies, and in 1873 he joined the expeditionary army as a doctor. Sent to Cuba, where the Spanish were fighting against an independence movement, he contracted several serious diseases, including malaria and dysentery, which almost cost him his life. On his return to Spain he quickly recovered and, encouraged by his once skeptical father, decided to continue his studies. Cajal failed twice before becoming a professor of descriptive anatomy in 1883 at the University of Valencia, where he began a career as a researcher in the field of histology.

In 1887 he entered University of Barcelona as professor of normal histology and pathological anatomy, but he did not lose his enthusiasm for research and concentrated on the study of the nervous system. By showing that nerve cells are independent units and are related to each other through their long fibrous extensions, Cajal lay the foundation of modern neuroscience. This theory led to the theory of polarization, which describes how the nervous impulse is transmitted in one direction only, passing through the axon to the dendrites and then to the rest of the cell body.

Cajal transferred to the University of Madrid in 1892, which marked the beginning of a new stage in his research — a concentration on the interior of nerve cells and the brain. This exhaustive research was published in his most important work, the *Textura del sistema nervioso del hombre y de los vertebrados (Textbook on the Nervous System of Man and the Vertebrates)*, which is still considered the most complete neurohistological portrait ever published. At this time he was already considered a highly respected researcher by his foreign colleagues, having received the Moscow Prize, established by the Congress of Moscow, from the International Congress of Medicine in Paris in 1900 and the Helmholtz Medal from the Royal Academy of Sciences of Berlin in 1905.

He died in the Madrid Laboratory for Biological Investigation, which was created for him in 1901.

Camillo Golgi also received half of the prize.

Theodore Roosevelt

For his intervention in the Russo-Japanese War at the Peace Conference in Portsmouth, New Hampshire.

Theodore Roosevelt was a controversial and important president, as well as a historian, biographer, hunter, naturalist and orator. He was as independent and remarkable as his nation. The descendent of a Dutch family who came to America in the 17th century, Roosevelt was born into a wealthy Manhattan home on October 27, 1858. His father was a merchant and philanthropist in New York City who, politically, was strongly Democratic until the mid 1850s, when he joined the Republican Party; during the Civil War he had been a noted supported of President Abraham Lincoln and the Union Army. Roosevelt's mother was the daughter of an affluent, slave-holding family from the South and held Confederate sympathies.

Fragile and asthmatic but still known as mischievous and excitable, the young Theodore Roosevelt was educated by a private tutor in his youth. In 1876 he entered Harvard University and divided his time between books and sport. Although a dedicated student with a photographic memory, Roosevelt also became a fan of the cowboy and the adventurous lifestyle — what he referred to as the "strenuous life."

Leaving Harvard Phi Beta Kappa and magna cum laude in 1880, he married Alice Hathaway Lee and took his first step into politics by joining the New York Republican Party. Four years later Roosevelt experienced a tragic year: a few hours after losing his mother, his wife died after giving birth to their only child, a daughter. Distraught, he sought refuge on his ranch in North Dakota, where he spent his time outdoors and writing. His *The Naval War of 1812* became a classical history text for the next two generations. In 1886 Roosevelt was remarried in London to Edith Kermit Carow — a childhood friend with whom he would have five children — and returned to Oyster Bay, New York, and political activity.

He was director of the New York City Police Department from 1895 to 1897 and dramatically reformed the corrupt department. Roosevelt then served as Assistant Secretary of the Navy until 1898, when he enlisted in a regiment of cavalry volunteers known as the Rough Riders, which had been created to fight in the Spanish-American War. As a lieutenant colonel he fought in Cuba, showing great bravery, and he was posthumously awarded the Medal of Honor in 2001 for his actions in the Battle of San Juan Hill.

He also continued to dedicate himself to literature, and his most influential work was his four-volume history *The Winning of the West* (1889–1896), in which he explains on an evolutionary model how "the conquest and settlement by the whites of the Indian lands was necessary to the greatness of the race and to the well being of civilized mankind." Although he believed in the superiority of his race, Roosevelt always insisted that jobs and education should be available to all without discrimination. Later works include *An Autobiography* (1913) and *Rough Riders* (1898).

Roosevelt was elected governor of New York at the end of 1898, and in 1900 he accepted the Republican nomination for vice president, helping William McKinley to an overwhelming victory. In September 1901 McKinley was assassinated and Roosevelt became president. At 42 years old he is the youngest person to become president in the history of the United States.

Roosevelt's presidency from 1901 to 1909 (he was elected to a full term in 1904) was marked by a foreign policy based on the phrase "speak softly and carry a big stick," which he first used during the 1901 Minnesota State Fair. He invested heavily in the navy to support an imperial strategy, defended the right of the United States to intervene in any conflict in the Americas and obtained American influence over the Panama Canal Zone in 1903. He would later criticize President Woodrow Wilson's foreign policy as weak during World War I.

His mediation in the Russo-Japanese war, which ended in the signing of the Portsmouth Treaty, brought him the 1906 Nobel Peace Prize, the first American to be awarded the honor. At home Roosevelt fought against large industrial trusts, mediated in conflicts between companies and workers, pushed Congress to pass the Pure Food and Drug Act of 1906, reserved 194 million acres (over 785,000 sq. km) for national parks and nature preserves and began large irrigation projects.

Never loosing his interest in the so-called strenuous life, in 1909 Roosevelt left on an African safari that killed a total of 11,397 creatures, from insects to hippopotamuses and elephants, and he sent many specimens back to museums in Washington, DC. He also held numerous conferences with native and colonial leaders there. From 1913 to 1914 he was a member of a scientific expedition through South America that traced the 400-mile (644 km) River of Doubt, later renamed Rio Roosevelt, but he nearly died from malaria and other infections that would affect him until the end of his life.

While campaigning in Wisconsin in 1912, Roosevelt was shot in the chest by John Schrank, but the bullet first passed through his steel eyeglass case and a thick copy of his speech; he stoically finished while blood seeped through his shirt. Theodore Roosevelt died on January 6, 1919, after living out his belief that "Far better is it to dare mighty things, to win glorious triumphs even though checkered by failure than to take rank with those poor spirits who neither enjoy much nor suffer much because they live in the gray twilight that knows neither victory nor defeat." He is commemorated alongside George Washington, Thomas Jefferson and Abraham Lincoln at the Mount Rushmore National Memorial in South Dakota.

Rudyard Kipling

In consideration of the power of observation, originality of imagination, virility of ideas and remarkable talent for narration which characterize the creations of this world-famous author.

Kipling was born in Bombay, India, into a family of artists and literary figures. His father was a conservationist at the Lahore Museum, his mother came from a family of good social standing — two of her sisters were the wives of the painters Sir Edward Burne-Jones and Sir Edward Poynter, and a third sister was mother to Stanley Baldwin, who would later become prime minister of Great Britain.

Despite the family's good standing, Kipling, at just six years old, was sent to England, where he was to stay with relatives in Southsea for five years. This somewhat traumatic experience served as inspiration for the story "Baa, Baa, Black Sheep," published in 1888. He next attended the United Services College, a boarding school he regarded with some disdain.

Returning to India in 1882, he was a professional journalist for six years and started to publish his prose and verse in the newspapers he worked for. Many of these writings were influenced by his observations of the Anglo-Indian high society of which his parents were a part. Between 1886 and 1889, Kipling published various collections of stories, including *Departmental Ditties and Other Verses*, *Plain Tales from the Hills*, *Soldiers Three*, *The Phantom Rickshaw and Other Tales* and *Wee Willie Winkie and Other Child Stories*. During his time as a journalist, Kipling also had the opportunity to travel extensively throughout India; these journeys helped him develop an accurate insight into Hindu customs, beliefs and sentiments, which he went on to present in his writing. It was later said that these reflections on Indian life helped to bring the country nearer to his readers in England than did the Suez Canal.

The Light That Failed, a novel, was published in 1890, and after publishing Barrack Room *Ballads and Other Verses* in 1892, Kipling saw his reputation established almost immediately. Back in England in 1892, Kipling married Caroline Balestier, the sister of an American writer and publisher. The couple moved to the United States and stayed there for several years, during which time *Captains Courageous* (1897), *The Jungle Book* (1894) and *The Second Jungle Book* (1895) and *Kim* (1901) were published. During these busy years in America, Kipling's international popularity was widely confirmed. When he took seriously ill in 1899, the American newspapers immediately began to print daily updates of his condition, and the German Emperor sent a telegram to Kipling's wife expressing his deepest sympathy.

His *Jungle Books*, particularly, have retained their popularity with children of all ages around the world. Mowgli, the young jungle boy, Bagheera, the black panther, Baloo, the bear, and Kaa, the rock python have been lovingly portrayed in print and film for more than a century. *Kim*, about a curious Buddhist priest on a pilgrimage, shows Kipling's deep interest in the Indian culture.

The poet of the British Empire was declared by the Nobel Committee in 1907 to be "the greatest genius in the realm of narrative that that country has produced in our times."

Ernest Rutherford

*For his investigations into the disintegration of the elements
and the chemistry of radioactive substances.*

Ernest Rutherford was the fourth child in a family of seven boys and five girls. His father, James Rutherford, was a carpenter who immigrated to New Zealand in 1842, just as his mother, Martha Thompson, would later do as a young English teacher. The two married in New Zealand and lived in Spring Grove, where they gave up much of their own comfort so that the children could receive a good education.

In his early years, Ernest Rutherford attended state schools. At the Nelson Collegiate School he was a popular boy noted for his talent in sports. With a state scholarship he started his academic life at the University of New Zealand, and in 1893 he graduated with honors in mathematics and physics. The following year he was given the opportunity to go to Trinity College, Cambridge, England, as a student investigator at the Cavendish Laboratory. Here he would be under the guidance of J.J. Thomson, the renowned scientist who had won the 1906 Nobel Prize in Physics.

Before leaving for England, Rutherford became engaged to Mary Newton. When he was in Cambridge he never stopped writing to her and his mother, who lived until the age of 92. Both religiously kept his correspondence, which reveals the many traits of this man who, despite loving his work, possessed a wide variety of interests and concerns. Rutherford was a passionate reader, loved to golf and was fond of the quiet home life. He listened attentively to others' points of view and tried to be fair in his judgments.

In 1898, Rutherford was recommended for the physics chair at McGill University in Montreal, Canada. At the time he wrote to his fiancé that the salary he had been offered was not abundant but enough for them to start a life together. Finally, after another two years, he went to New Zealand to marry Mary Newton and visit his parents.

Rutherford was awarded the 1908 Nobel Prize in Chemistry for his research in the disintegration of elements and the chemistry of radioactive substances. Two years later he would come to the forefront of the field again with theories on the nucleus of the atom. In 1919 he accepted an invitation to succeed Professor Thomson at Cambridge and, despite the fact that his research was not as extensive as in earlier years, his influence on students was enormous, and he quickly won their esteem and affection.

In 1931 he was invested as First Baron Rutherford of Nelson, New Zealand, and Cambridge. When Rutherford died a few years later in Cambridge, England, his ashes were deposited in the nave of Westminster Abbey in London, near Sir Isaac Newton's tomb.

Chemistry 1908

Guglielmo Marconi

In recognition of their contributions to the development of wireless telegraphy.

Guglielmo Marconi, Italian by birth, was the second son of Giuseppe Marconi, an Italian landowner, and Annie Jameson Marconi, descendent of a respected Irish family. Privately educated in Bologna, his birthplace, Florence and Leghorn, he showed an interest in physics and electrical experiments at a young age.

Marconi was about 21 years old when he conducted his first successful experiment by sending wireless signals between two rooms in the attic of his father's property on the outskirts of Bologna. He spent the following months developing the invention. Unable to find financial backing for his discovery in Italy, Marconi went to England in 1896. In the same year he took out a patent for his wireless telegraphy, and in 1897 he formed the Wireless Telegraph & Signal Company Limited, the name of which was changed in 1900 to Marconi's Wireless Telegraph Company Limited.

At noon of December 12, 1901, he achieved what the public regarded as a remarkable feat: Marconi sent a signal by wireless telegraphy from Poldhu, Cornwall, England, to Saint John's, Newfoundland, Canada. This accomplishment was a turning point in Marconi's life, and the moment when the world acknowledged this man who had diligently worked unnoticed for years. Soon many young physicists were following in his footsteps.

What few know today about this inventor is that he was also a distinguished soldier. Marconi left the army with the rank of Captain in the Navy, and in 1917 he served as a member of the Italian government mission to the United States. Two years later he was a delegate at the Paris Peace Conference. His military and government service, however, never stopped his experiments with shortwave technology.

Inventiveness and persistence sum up the character of this Italian who was at first ignored and then made famous and granted the highest honors, including the 1909 Nobel Prize in Physics. Marconi shared the prize for contributions to the development of wireless telegraphy with Karl Ferdinand Braun.

Marconi's personal life was nearly as dramatic as his discoveries, beginning in 1905 when he married Beatrice O'Brien, the daughter of the 14th Baron Inchiquin. This marriage was annulled in 1927, the same year he married the Countess Bezzi-Scali of Rome. Despite living the high life and mixing with aristocrats, Marconi was a simple man who enjoyed hunting, cycling and automobiles. The Marchese Marconi, the title he received in 1929, died on July 20, 1937, in Rome.

Karl Ferdinand Braun also received half of the prize.

Wireless telegraphy

Guglielmo Marconi was one of the main figures behind wireless telegraphy. The skepticism which initially greeted his invention disappeared when Marconi sent a wireless signal from Poldhu, Cornwall to St. John's, Newfoundland on the 12th of December 1901. He was vindicated and his position as the "father of radio" secured.

Marconi

Marconi immigrated to England seeking investors for his invention, which he patented in 1896. One year later he formed the Wireless Telegraph and Signal Company, Ltd., whose name was changed in 1901 to Marconi's Wireless Telegraph Company, Ltd. This company supplied the first equipment to the BBC.

Small spheres transmit electricity

Electromagnetic waves

Copper parabolic reflectors

Ebonite support

Marconi transmitter

In 1894 he started working with electromagnetic waves. An early successful experiment led to a transmission between two attic rooms and led him to develop the invention. He tried to concentrate the waves by using a curved reflector. This transmitter, dating from 1896, could send signals more than three kilometers.

How the transmitter works

Energy is emitted in all directions simply by using a simple aerial. As a result only a small quantity reaches the receiver. To ensure that the waves don't lose much energy a reflector is used in the transmitter.

The last SOS

Marconi's work became a lifesaver at sea. The wireless requests for help sent by the ships the *Republic* (1909) and *Titanic* (1912) made these events less tragic. Marconi's name was once more acclaimed around the world. Radio still saves life, but is now adapted to modern times. The Inmarsat satellites establish communications between ships and coastal stations. The emergency messages indicate the ship's position and are captured by the Cospas-Sarsat satellites, which are in polar orbit.

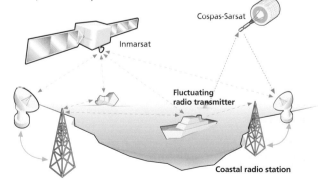

Cospas-Sarsat

Inmarsat

Fluctuating radio transmitter

Coastal radio station

Nobel Laureates

1901-1909

1901

Nobel Prize in Physics
Wilhelm Conrad Röntgen
Born March 27, 1845, in Lennep, Germany, and died
February 10, 1923, in Munich.
In recognition of the extraordinary services he has
rendered by the discovery of the remarkable rays
subsequently named after him.

Nobel Prize in Chemistry
Jacobus Henricus van 't Hoff
Born August 30, 1852, in Rotterdam, Netherlands, and
died March 1, 1911, in Steglitz, Germany.
In recognition of the extraordinary services he has
rendered by the discovery of the laws of chemical
dynamics and osmotic pressure in solutions.

Nobel Prize in Physiology or Medicine
Emil Adolf von Behring
Born March 15, 1854, in Hansdorf, Prussia, and died
March 31, 1917, in Marburg, Germany.
For his work on serum therapy, especially its application
against diphtheria, by which he has opened a new road
in the domain of medical science and thereby placed in
the hands of the physician a victorious weapon against
illness and deaths.

Nobel Prize in Literature
**Sully Prudhomme, pseudonym of René
François Armand Prudhomme**
Born March 16, 1839, in Paris, France, and died
September 7, 1907, in Châtenay.
In special recognition of his poetic composition, which
gives evidence of lofty idealism, artistic perfection and
a rare combination of the qualities of both heart and
intellect.

Nobel Peace Prize
Jean Henry Dunant
Born May 8, 1828, in Geneva, Switzerland, and died

October 30, 1910, in Heiden.
For actions developing the organization of the Geneva
Conventions of 1863 and 1864 and the International Red
Cross, created by these conventions.
&
Frédéric Passy
Born May 20, 1822, in Paris, France, and died June 12,
1912, in Paris.
Fighting for the Peace Movement for more than 50
years, becoming known as the Apostle of Peace.

1902

Nobel Prize in Physics
Hendrik Antoon Lorentz
Born July 18, 1853, in Arnhem, Netherlands, and died
February 4, 1928, in Haarlem.
&
Pieter Zeeman
Born May 25, 1865, in Zonnemaire,
Netherlands, and died October 9, 1943, in Amsterdam.
In recognition of the extraordinary service they
rendered by their researches into the influence of
magnetism upon radiation phenomena.

Nobel Prize in Chemistry
Hermann Emil Fischer
Born October 9, 1852, in Euskirchen, Prussia, and died
July 15, 1919, in Berlin.
In recognition of the extraordinary services he has
rendered by his work on sugar and purine syntheses.

Nobel Prize in Physiology or Medicine
Ronald Ross
Born May 13, 1857, in Almora, India, and died
September 16, 1932, in London, England.
For his work on malaria, by which he has shown
how it enters the organism and thereby has laid the
foundation for successful research on this disease and
methods of combating it.

Nobel Prize in Literature
Christian Matthias Theodor Mommsen
Born November 30, 1817, in Garding, Germany, and
died November 1, 1903, in Charlottenburg.
The greatest living master of the art of historical
writing, with special reference to his monumental
work, *A History of Rome.*

Nobel Peace Prize
Élie Ducommun
Born February 19, 1833, in Geneva, Switzerland, and
died December 7, 1906, in Bern.
Tireless as the director of the Peace Bureau in Berne,
heading the work of all peace societies in the world.
&
Charles Albert Gobat
Born May 21, 1843, in Tramelan, Switzerland, and died
March 16, 1914, in Bern.
Efforts for peace and his activity as president of the
IV Conference of the Inter-Parliamentary Union, in 1892.

1903

Nobel Prize in Physics
Antoine Henri Becquerel
Born December 15, 1852, in Paris, France, and died
August 25, 1908, in Le Croisic.
In recognition of the extraordinary services he has
rendered by his discovery of spontaneous radioactivity.
&
Marie Curie, née Maria Sklodowska
Born November 7, 1867, in Warsaw, Poland, and died
July 4, 1934, near Sallanches, France.
&
Pierre Curie
Born May 15, 1859, in Paris, France, and died April 19,
1906, in Paris.
In recognition of the extraordinary services they have
rendered by their joint researches on the radiation
phenomena discovered by Professor Henri Becquerel.

Nobel Prize in Chemistry
Svante August Arrhenius
Born February 19, 1859, in Vik, Sweden, and died
October 2, 1927, in Stockholm.
In recognition of the extraordinary services he has

rendered to the advancement of chemistry by his
electrolytic theory of dissociation.

Nobel Prize in Physiology or Medicine
Niels Ryberg Finsen
Born December 15, 1860, in Thórshavn, Denmark, and
died September 24, 1904, in Copenhagen.
In recognition of his contribution to the treatment of
diseases, especially lupus vulgaris, with concentrated
light radiation, whereby he has opened a new avenue
for medical science.

Nobel Prize in Literature
Bjørnstjerne Bjørnson
Born December 8, 1832, in Kvikne, Norway, and died
April 26, 1910, in Paris, France.
As a tribute to his noble, magnificent and versatile
poetry, which has always been distinguished by both
the freshness of its inspiration and the rare purity of
its spirit.

Nobel Peace Prize
William Randal Cremer
Born March 18, 1828, in Fareham, England, and died
July 22, 1908, in London.
Intense work in favor of the peace movement and the
growth of international arbitration as a means of
achieving world peace.

1904

Nobel Prize in Physics
Lord Rayleigh (John William Strutt)
Born November 12, 1842, in Langford Grove,
England, and died June 30, 1919, in Witham.
For his investigations of the densities of the most
important gases and for his discovery of argon in
connection with these studies.

Nobel Prize in Chemistry
William Ramsay
Born October 2, 1852, in Glasgow, Scotland, and died
July 23, 1916, in High Wycombe, England.
In recognition of his services in the discovery of the inert
gaseous elements in air, and his determination
of their place in the periodic system.

Nobel Prize in Physiology or Medicine
Ivan Petrovich Pavlov
Born September 14, 1849, in Ryazan, Russia, and died February 27, 1936, in Leningrad (now Saint Petersburg). In recognition of his work on the physiology of digestion, through which knowledge on vital aspects of the subject has been transformed and enlarged.

Nobel Prize in Literature
Joséde Echegaray
Born April 19, 1832, in Madrid, Spain, and died September 4, 1916, in Madrid.
In recognition of the numerous and brilliant compositions which, in an individual and original manner, have revived the great traditions of the Spanish drama.
&
Frédéric Mistral
Born September 8, 1830, in Maillane, France, and died March 25, 1914, in Maillane.
In recognition of the fresh originality and true inspiration of his poetic production, which faithfully reflects the natural scenery and native spirit of his people, and, in addition, his significant work as a Provençal philologist.

Nobel Peace Prize
Institute of International Law
Founded in 1873 in Ghent, Belgium.
Efforts so that the law between nations is the result of the action of a scholarly institution, which aspires to be the legal conscience of the world.

1905

Nobel Prize in Physics
Philipp Eduard von Lenard
Born June 7, 1862, in Pressburg, Austria-Hungary (now Bratislava, Slovakia), and died May 20, 1947, in Messelhausen, Germany.
For his work on cathode rays.

Nobel Prize in Chemistry
Johann Friedrich Wilhelm Adolf von Baeyer
Born October 31, 1835, in Berlin, Germany, and died August 20, 1917, in Starnberg.
In recognition of his services in the advancement of organic chemistry and the chemical industry, through his work on organic dyes and hydroaromatic compounds.

Nobel Prize in Physiology or Medicine
Robert Koch
Born December 11, 1843, in Clausthal, Hanover, and died May 27, 1910, in Baden-Baden.
For his investigations and discoveries in relation to tuberculosis.

Nobel Prize in Literature
Henryk Sienkiewicz
Born May 5, 1846, in Wola Okrzejska, Poland, and died November 15, 1916, in Vevey, Switzerland.
Because of his outstanding merits as an epic writer.

Nobel Peace Prize
Baroness Bertha Sophie Felicita von Suttner, née Countess Kinsky von Chinic und Tettau
Born June 9, 1843, in Prague, Austrian (now Czech Republic), and died June 21, 1914, in Vienna, Austria.
For her activities in favor of peace, both for her writings and her active presence in peace societies and international conferences.

1906

Nobel Prize in Physics
Joseph John Thomson
Born December 18, 1856, near Manchester, England, and died August 30, 1940, in Cambridge.
In recognition of the great merits of his theoretical and experimental investigations on the conduction of electricity by gases.

Nobel Prize in Chemistry
Henri Moissan
Born September 28, 1852, in Paris, France, and died February 20, 1907, in Paris.
In recognition of the great services rendered by him in his investigation and isolation of the element fluorine, and for the adoption in the service of science of the electric furnace called after him.

Nobel Prize in Physiology or Medicine
Camillo Golgi
Born July 7, 1843, in Corteno, Italy, and died January 21, 1926, in Pavia.
&

Santiago Ramón y Cajal
Born May 1, 1852, in Petilla de Aragón, Spain,
and died October 17, 1934, in Madrid.
In recognition of their work on the structure of the
nervous system.

Nobel Prize in Literature
Giosuè Carducci
Born July 27, 1835, in Val di Castello, Italy, and died
February 16, 1907, in Bologna.
Not only in consideration of his deep learning and critical
research, but above all as a tribute to the
creative energy, freshness of style and lyrical force
which characterize his poetic masterpieces.

Nobel Peace Prize
Theodore Roosevelt
Born October 27, 1858, in New York, New York, and
died January 6, 1919, in Oyster Bay, New York.
For his intervention in the Russo-Japanese War at the
Peace Conference in Portsmouth, New Hampshire.

1907

Nobel Prize in Physics
Albert Abraham Michelson
Born December 19, 1852, in Strelno, Prussia
(now Poland), and died May 9, 1931, in Pasadena,
California.
For his optical precision instruments and the
spectroscopic and metrological investigations carried
out with their aid.

Nobel Prize in Chemistry
Eduard Buchner
Born May 20, 1860, in Munich, Germany, and died
August 12, 1917, in Munich.
For his biochemical researches and his discovery of
cell-free fermentation.

Nobel Prize in Physiology or Medicine
Charles Louis Alphonse Laveran
Born June 18, 1845, in Paris, France, and died May 18,
1922, in Paris.
In recognition of his work on the role played by protozoa
in causing diseases.

Nobel Prize in Literature
Rudyard Kipling
Born December 30, 1865, in Bombay, India, and died
January 18, 1936, in London, England.
In consideration of the power of observation, originality
of imagination, virility of ideas and remarkable talent
for narration, which characterize the creations of this
world-famous author.

Nobel Peace Prize
Ernesto Teodoro Moneta
Born September 20, 1833, in Milan, Italy, and died
February 10, 1918, Milan.
Distinguished for the foundation of the Unione
Lombarda [Lombard Union of Peace] in 1887, the
conferences for peace in Italy and presidency of the
1906 International Peace Congress in Milan.
&
Louis Renault
Born May 21, 1843, in Autun, France, and died February
8, 1918, in Barbizon.
Principal mentor of the Hague Peace Conferences in
1899 and 1907.

1908

Nobel Prize in Physics
Gabriel Lippmann
Born August 16, 1845, in Hollerich, Luxembourg, and
died July 13, 1921, at sea, returning to Paris, France.
For his method of reproducing colors photographically
based on the phenomenon of interference.

Nobel Prize in Chemistry
Ernest Rutherford
Born August 30, 1871, in Nelson, New Zealand, and died
October 19, 1937, in Cambridge, England.
For his investigations into the disintegration of the
elements, and the chemistry of radioactive substances.

Nobel Prize in Physiology or Medicine
Paul Ehrlich
Born March 14, 1854, in Strehlen, Germany, and died
August 20, 1915, in Bad Homburg.
&
Elie Mechnikov, née Ilya Ilyich Mechnikov
Born May 16, 1845, in Kharkov, Russia (now Ukraine),

and died July 16, 1916, in Paris, France.
In recognition of their work on immunity.

Nobel Prize in Literature
Rudolf Christoph Eucken
Born January 5, 1846, in Aurich, Germany, and died
September 14, 1926, in Jena.
In recognition of his earnest search for truth, his
penetrating power of thought, his wide range of vision,
and the warmth and strength in presentation with which
in his numerous works he has vindicated and developed
an idealistic philosophy of life.

Nobel Peace Prize
Klas Pontus Arnoldson
Born October 27, 1844, in Gothenberg, Sweden, and
died February 20, 1916, in Stockholm.
He has fought for peace for 35 years, especially through
his writings, which were important for the founding of
the Swedish Arbitration Society.
&
Fredrik Bajer
Born April 21, 1837, in Vester Egede, Denmark, and died
January 22, 1922, in Copenhagen.
[For] political activities and writings in support of peace.

1909

Nobel Prize in Physics
Guglielmo Marconi
Born April 25, 1874, in Bologna, Italy, and died July 20,
1937, in Rome.
&
Karl Ferdinand Braun
Born June 6, 1850, in Fulda, Germany, and died April
20, 1918, in Brooklyn, New York.
In recognition of their contributions to the development
of wireless telegraphy.

Nobel Prize in Chemistry
Wilhelm Ostwald
Born September 2, 1853, in Riga, Latvia, and died April
4, 1932, in Grossbothen, Germany.
In recognition of his work on catalysis and for his
investigations into the fundamental principles
governing chemical equilibrium and rates of reaction.

Nobel Prize in Physiology or Medicine
Emil Theodor Kocher
Born August 25, 1841, in Bern, Switzerland, and died
July 27, 1917, in Berne.
For his work on the physiology, pathology and surgery of
the thyroid gland.

Nobel Prize in Literature
Selma Ottilia Lovisa Lagerlöf
Born November 20, 1858, in Östra Emterwik,
Sweden, and died March 16, 1940, in Marbacka.
In appreciation of the lofty idealism, vivid
imagination and spiritual perception that
characterize her writing.

Nobel Peace Prize
Auguste Marie François Beernaert
Born July 26, 1829, in Ostend, Belgium, and
died October 6, 1912, in Lucerne, Switzerland.
[For] tireless efforts for peace in the last 30 years of
his active life.
&
**Paul Henri Benjamin Balluet d'Estournelles
de Constant, Baron de Constant de Rebecque**
Born November 22, 1852, in La Flèche, France, and died
May 15, 1924, in Paris.
[For] services rendered to the international cause of
peace and solidarity.

Selected Profiles of Nobel Laureates

1910–1919

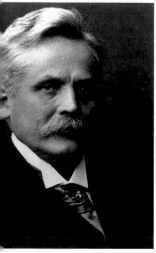

Wilhelm Wien

For his discoveries regarding the laws governing the radiation of heat.

Wilhelm Carl Werner Otto Fritz Franz Wien was the son of a rural landowner in Fischhausen, East Prussia, and seemed likely to follow in his father's footsteps until an economic crisis forced the family to uproot their lives. They moved to Drachstein in 1866, where the young Wilhelm attended school for the first time. Not long afterward, he transferred to The City School at Heidelberg. As Wien's fascination with science grew, so did his ambitions of studying at university.

In 1882 he entered the University of Göttingen and the University of Berlin to study mathematics and the natural sciences. Between 1883 and 1885 he worked in the laboratory of Hermann von Helmholtz, a noted German physicist, while continuing his studies. A year later, in 1886, Wien presented his thesis on experiments on the diffraction of light on sections of metal and the influence of materials on the color of refracted light and received his doctorate.

When his father became ill, however, Wien was obliged to return home to help run the household. Despite this professional setback, he did not break his ties with the scientific world and managed to spend some time experimenting with Helmholtz. After a number of years the family estate was sold, allowing Wien to return to Helmholtz's laboratory.

Wien served as a professor of physics in Aix-la-Chapelle in 1896, and there he met Luise Mehler. The couple married in 1898 and had four children together.

Wien's scientific work during his life did not offer solutions to all the questions that science asked at the time, but his contributions were undeniable. In 1893 he proved that the length of a radioactive wave emitted by a black body varies with temperature and demonstrated the rule that would become known as the law of displacement. It was for this research into thermal radiation that he was eventually awarded the 1911 Nobel Prize in Physics.

The prestige of this award soon allowed him to become a member of the science academies of Berlin, Göttingen, Vienna, Stockholm, Christiania and Washington and an honorary member of the Physical Society of Frankfurt. Wien also lectured in many cities, finally moving to Munich in 1920, where he stayed with his family until his death eight years later. Wien's autobiography was posthumously published in 1930 and entitled *Aus dem Leben und Wirken eines Physikers (The Life and Work of a Physicist)*, demonstrating how closely he identified himself with his occupation.

Marie Curie

In recognition of her services to the advancement of chemistry by the discovery of the elements radium and polonium, by the isolation of radium and the study of the nature and compounds of this remarkable element.

Marie Curie, the first woman to be awarded a Nobel Prize as well as the first person to win a second one, was born Maria Sklodowska in Warsaw, Poland. A healthy, intelligent child with a formidable memory, her first contact with the world of science came from her encouraging father. While still a youth, she became involved in a revolutionary student organization and decided to leave her native Poland for vibrant Paris, France.

Although it took successive proposals, in 1895 Marie finally accepted the scientist Pierre Curie's hand in marriage. The two rejected the traditional religious ceremony, however, as Pierre was agnostic and Marie, despite a catholic upbringing, was anticlerical at the time of their wedding. The couple settled in Paris, had two daughters and Marie, despite her dedication to research, showed herself to be a concerned and zealous mother.

Only nine years after completing her studies at the Sorbonne, Curie won her first Nobel Prize, which she shared with her husband and Henri Becquerel, for the couple's research into Becquerel's discovery of the phenomenon of spontaneous radioactivity. The Curies' research was arduously performed with primitive equipment as they had very little financial or logistical support available to them at the time.

In 1906 the couple's happiness unfortunately ended with the accidental death of Pierre. After this, Marie accepted an invitation to lecture at the Sorbonne, taking over from her husband and becoming the first woman to lecture at the prestigious institution. The 1911 Nobel Prize in Chemistry was given to Marie Curie in her own right, for her discovery of radium and polonium. Although in 1903, due to illness, neither Curie could travel to Stockholm to receive the Nobel Prize in Physics, on the occasion of her second award, Marie, accompanied by her daughter Irène and her sister, was proudly present at the ceremony.

After receiving the second Nobel Prize, Marie Curie focused her attentions on the medical uses of radium to treat cancer. In this task she was aided by her daughter Irène and son-in-law Frédéric Joliot both of whom would be laureates in 1935 for the Nobel Prize in Chemistry.

Marie Currie died in France, from cancer caused by prolonged exposure to radiation, a risk she understood during the research to perfect its beneficial use.

1903 Physics | **Chemistry 1911**

Allvar Gullstrand

For his work on the dioptrics of the eye.

Allvar Gullstrand, eldest son of Dr. Pehr and Sofia Gullstrand, was born in Landskrona, Sweden. He began his studies at an early age, first in his hometown and later in Jönköping, a city on the southern tip of Lake Vättern, about 100 miles (150 km) east of Gothenburg.

In 1880 he enrolled in the prestigious Uppsala University, founded in 1477 and the oldest in the country. Gullstrand remained at this institution until 1885, when he decided to spend a year in Vienna, which at the time was the capital of powerful Austria-Hungary. From here he went on to Stockholm, where he resumed his studies. In 1888 he graduated with his degree in medicine, presented his doctoral thesis in 1890 and in 1891 was appointed a lecturer in ophthalmology. Three years later, after working briefly with the Swedish health ministry, he had the honor of being the first professor of ophthalmology at Uppsala University.

Gullstrand was married in 1885 to Signe Christina Breitholtz, and the couple had a daughter who died in infancy. Despite this personal loss, his professional career was very successful. On various occasions his work in the field of ophthalmology was distinguished with important prizes, including from the Royal Swedish Academy of Sciences, the Swedish Medical Association and the Uppsala Faculty of Medicine.

Gullstrand's service to the academic world, and his recognition for it, did not stop after he was awarded the 1911 Nobel Prize in Physiology or Medicine for his research into the dioptrics of the eye. He was a member of the Nobel Physics Committee of the Royal Swedish Academy of Sciences from 1911 to 1929 and was its chairman from 1922 to 1929.

Throughout a life dedicated to understanding the structure and function of the cornea and research into astigmatism, Gullstrand made many significant contributions to the field. Among other achievements, he improved the corrective lenses used after cataract surgery, invented the slit lamp used to study the eye, to which he gave his name, and reformulated German physicist Hermann von Helmholtz's theory to develop a mechanism that allowed the eye to focus both near and far within certain limits. When he died in Stockholm on the July 28, 1930, Gullstrand left an important legacy that revolutionized the practice of ophthalmology.

Maurice Maeterlinck

In appreciation of his many-sided literary activities, and especially of his dramatic works, which are distinguished by a wealth of imagination and by a poetic fancy, which reveals, sometimes in the guise of a fairy tale, a deep inspiration, while in a mysterious way they appeal to the readers' own feelings and stimulate their imaginations.

Count Maurice Polidore Marie Bernhard Maeterlinck achieved worldwide recognition through his literary output. He was born in Ghent, Belgium, into a wealthy family. He attended the Jesuit College of Saint-Barbe and Ghent University, where he obtained a law degree in 1885. Maeterlinck's early life suggested that he would follow a career in law, however, after a short period of time working as a lawyer at a small firm, Maeterlinck decided he was not suited to this profession.

Deciding to follow his love of literature, he moved to Paris. While there, he socialized with the literati, especially Villiers de L'Isle Adam, who ended up having a great influence on him. These experiences were so enriching that Maeterlinck decided to move permanently to Paris in 1896. Some time later, however, perhaps in search of peace and quiet, he moved to Saint-Wandrille and restored an old abbey for his retreat.

Maeterlinck's debut as a well-known writer in the French language had occurred some years earlier, in 1889, with the publication of a collection of poems entitled *Serres chaudes (Hothouses)*. That same year Octave Mirbeau, at the time the literary critic for *Le Figaro* newspaper, greatly praised Maeterlinck's first work for the theater, *La Princesse Maleine*, which made him an overnight success.

In the following years he continued to produce books full of mystery and adventure. The romantic drama *Pelléas et Mélisande* (1892), which was adapted to the stage, is considered a masterpiece of symbolist drama. *La Vie des abeilles (The Life of the Bee)*, published in 1900, is one of his most meditative works and shows his more transcendent side. *L'Intruse (The Intruder*, 1890), *Alladine et Palomides* (1894), *Aglavaine et Sélysette* (1896), and the pieces *Joyzelle* (1903) and *L'Oiseau bleu* (1909) — one of his most popular creations — also confirm the richness of his imagination and his poetic realm. These characteristics were the basis for his being awarded the 1911 Nobel Prize in Literature.

Maeterlinck was also awarded the Triennial Prize for Dramatic Literature in 1903, although he refused it, was made Grand Officer of the Order of Léopold in 1920, given the title of the Count of Belgium in 1932 and, in Portugal, the distinction of the Ordem de Santiago da Espada in 1939.

Maeterlinck married Renée Dahon in 1911, with whom he spent the rest of his days until his death in Nice, France.

Elihu Root

A man of engaging personality who has tried, with determination and independence, to put his ideals into practice.

Elihu Root, one of the most brilliant administrators in American history and distinguished with the Nobel Peace Prize in 1912, was born in Clinton, New York, on February 15, 1845. He studied at Hamilton College, where his father was a mathematics professor, and completed his secondary education in 1864 at the top of his class. In 1867 he completed his degree in law at New York University and, at the age of 30, was already a respected lawyer specializing in commercial law.

His great capacity to understand legal principles, his excellent analytical powers, disciplined attention to detail and ease of expression, both written and oral, gave Root an almost unequalled reputation. He became an advisor to banks and railroad and oil companies, quickly acquiring a fortune as he did so. In 1878 he married Clara Frances Wales, and the couple had three children together.

During this time Root also made tentative entries into politics, becoming involved in the local branch of the Republican Party. In 1899 President William McKinley, wanting a lawyer rather than a military figure to serve as his secretary of war, invited him to fill this position. Root accepted the call of what he termed "the greatest of all our clients, the government of the country," and served as the 41st United States secretary of war between August 1, 1899 and January 31, 1904.

While in office he reorganized the administrative system of the Defense Department, established new rules for promotion, created the general staff and imposed administrative discipline on the armed forces. During the Spanish-American War Root drew up a strategy to return control of Cuba to the Cuban people, designed a democratic plan for the government of the Philippines and eliminated tariffs imposed on goods imported from Puerto Rico.

In 1904 he returned to law, but he turned back to politics once more after being nominated as secretary of state by President Theodore Roosevelt. He left a notable body of work and solved many foreign policy problems that the country had been struggling with for years. Some of his actions include placing the Consular Service under the Civil Service, maintaining an "open door" policy with the Far East and working with Great Britain to resolve Alaskan territorial disputes between Canada and the United States.

As a senator between 1909 and 1915 he played an active role in resolving the conflict over fishing rights in the North Atlantic and campaigned for an end to American privileges in the Panama Canal. In 1915 he resigned as a senator and declined the Republican nomination as candidate for the presidency of the country. He continued, however, to be an active statesman. He opposed the neutrality adopted by President Woodrow Wilson during the early months of World War I but supported him after America declared war on Germany. He accepted Wilson's invitation in 1917 to head a special diplomatic mission to Russia, and he was later involved in both the signing of the Treaty of Versailles and the creation of the League of Nations.

Root, who was the first president of the Carnegie Endowment for International Peace, dedicated a significant part of his career to questions of international negotiation. Besides work on the creation of the Central American Court of Justice in 1907, he was heavily involved in establishing the Permanent Court for International Justice in 1921. In 1929, at the age of 84, he undertook intense diplomatic work in Geneva to establish a revised protocol for the Permanent Court.

In 1912 Root received the Nobel Peace Prize for his mediating efforts toward international peace. Known as one of the greatest diplomats of the 20th century, he acknowledged the need for an international perspective in this global age: "Gradually, everything that happens in the world is coming to be of interest everywhere in the world, and, gradually, thoughtful men and women everywhere are sitting in judgment upon the conduct of all nations." Some of Root's best known works are *Citizen's Part in Government* (1911), *Experiments in Government and the Essentials of the Constitution* (1913) and *Military and Colonial Policy in the United States* (1916).

This quest for peace and justice was the life's cause of an extraordinary statesman. Elihu Root died in New York City on February 7, 1937, and was buried at the Hamilton College Cemetery. The home that he purchased in 1893 is now a National Historic Landmark.

Alexis Carrel

In recognition of his work on vascular suture and the transplantation of blood vessels and organs.

Alexis Carrel was first educated at home and later attended Saint Joseph College in Sainte-Foy-lès-Lyon, his hometown. His father, a businessman, died prematurely while Carrel was still young.

In 1889 he received his Bachelor of Letters at the University of Lyon and a year later another degree in the sciences. In 1900 he took his doctorate, at which time he dedicated himself to medical work, including experimental surgery, at the Lyon Hospital and to teaching at the local university.

Carrel left for the United States in 1904 and took a position in the Department of Physiology at the University of Chicago. Eight years later he became a full member of the Rockefeller Institute for Medical Research in New York. Here he carried out the majority of the research that would earn him the 1912 Nobel Prize in Physiology or Medicine in recognition of his work on the vascular suture and transplanting blood vessels and organs. Other achievements of his included developing new methods of preventing postoperative hemorrhages and thromboses.

A year later, in 1913, Carrel married Anne-Marie-Laure Gourlez de La Motte. A devout Catholic, he complemented his work in medicine by working as a philosopher, writer and biologist throughout his life. During World War I he served as a major in the French Army Medical Corps and developed new treatments for the war wounded. When World War II broke out, Carrel returned to France as a member of a special mission for the French Ministry of Health. He held this position for a year and then served as director of the Carrel Foundation for the Study of Human Problems established by the Vichy Government.

Carrel received various distinctions from countries around the world, including Spain, Russia, Sweden, Holland, Vatican City, France and the United States. It was from America, his adopted country, that many say he developed his ingenuity, energy and determination. He died in Paris in 1944.

Safer transplants

At the beginning of the 20th century, Alexis Carrel was a pioneer in his work on vascular suturing and transplanting blood vessels and organs. Much has evolved since then. More recent discoveries, for example, have allowed the transplant of bone marrow cells.

Treatments such as chemotherapy and radiotherapy eliminated both cancerous and healthy cells. Cancer patients receive about 75% of all bone marrow transplants. However, such transplants are also appropriate in the fight against other diseases, such as aplastic anemia and falciform cell anemia, in which the bone marrow produces a small quantity or poorly formed blood cells.

Finding a Donor
About 70% of patients who need a bone marrow transplant cannot find a donor with compatible bone marrow.

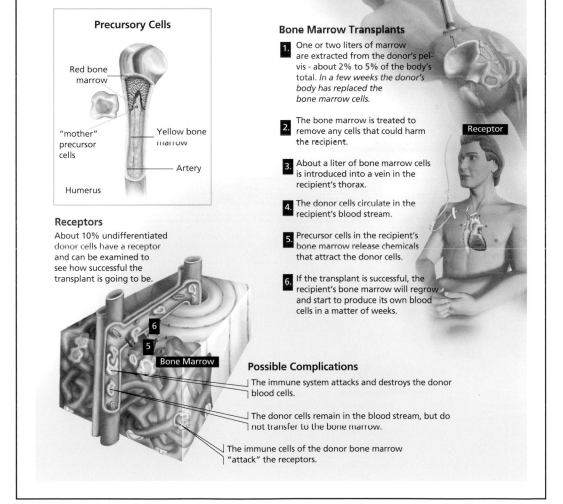

Donor

Receptor

Precursory Cells

Red bone marrow

"mother" precursor cells

Yellow bone marrow

Artery

Humerus

Receptors
About 10% undifferentiated donor cells have a receptor and can be examined to see how successful the transplant is going to be.

6

5

Bone Marrow

Bone Marrow Transplants

1. One or two liters of marrow are extracted from the donor's pelvis - about 2% to 5% of the body's total. *In a few weeks the donor's body has replaced the bone marrow cells.*

2. The bone marrow is treated to remove any cells that could harm the recipient.

3. About a liter of bone marrow cells is introduced into a vein in the recipient's thorax.

4. The donor cells circulate in the recipient's blood stream.

5. Precursor cells in the recipient's bone marrow release chemicals that attract the donor cells.

6. If the transplant is successful, the recipient's bone marrow will regrow and start to produce its own blood cells in a matter of weeks.

Possible Complications

The immune system attacks and destroys the donor blood cells.

The donor cells remain in the blood stream, but do not transfer to the bone marrow.

The immune cells of the donor bone marrow "attack" the receptors.

Rabindranath Tagore

Because of his profoundly sensitive, fresh and beautiful verse, by which, with consummate skill, he has made his poetic thought, expressed in his own English words, a part of the literature of the West.

Ravindranatha Thakur, under the pseudonym of Rabindranath Tagore, became for the world, but particularly India, a leading spiritual voice — even his physical appearance and demeanor seemed reminiscent of a prophet. Tagore was born into a large, distinguished family. He was the son of Maharishi Debendranath Tagore, leader of the Brahmo Samaj, a new religious sect. He was the youngest of 12 brothers who would have an important role in his development, particularly the older ones, due to the frequent absences of his father. Tagore showed a strong inclination toward writing from a very young age. He was educated at home in Bengali and later took English lessons. In the breaks between lessons he read Bengali poets and wrote poetry himself.

At the age of 17 Tagore's father gave his son the rare opportunity of studying in England and, although he returned to India without finishing his studies, he published several books of poetry, including *Manasi (The Ideal One)*. In the following year, 1891, he went to Shilaidah and Shazadpur to run the family estate. This experience, which lasted 10 years, proved very enriching for his literary activity, since he had close contact with the poverty and inequality that inspired many of his writings. During this period he published more pieces of poetry, including *Sonar Tari (The Golden Boat)* in 1894, and various pieces for the stage, such as *Chitrangada* in 1892.

In 1901 Tagore founded an experimental school in Shantiniketan, where the best traditions of India and the West were combined. This project began on a very small scale but proved successful and, in 1921, was enlarged into a university. As well as these literary and educational activities, Tagore was also a nonprofessional politician. He participated in the Indian nationalist movement and had a firm friendship with Mahatma Gandhi.

Tagore wrote novels, tales, essays, autobiographies, dramas and theater pieces, but, above all, he was a poet with a harmonious, rhythmic style and a rare gift as a wordsmith. He wrote sensitive, beautiful poetry with technical perfection, such as the well-known *Gitanjali: Song Offerings*, in 1912. He was awarded the 1913 Nobel Prize in Literature.

The translation of some of Tagore's works made it possible for his fame to spread beyond his own country. He participated in conferences, traveled and became a spokesperson for the independence of his country. He was also made a Knight of the British Empire in 1915, an honor that he denounced a few years later as a protest against English politics in India.

Henri Marie La Fontaine

For his efforts to establish and follow the principles of international understanding and cooperation among men.

Henri Marie La Fontaine was a lawyer, teacher, parliamentarian, diplomat, writer and bibliographer. He was, however, above all a pacifist and an internationalist. La Fontaine received his doctorate in law from the Free University of Brussels and was, for many years, one of Belgium's leading lawyers, writing a technical work on the rights and duties of contractors of public works in 1885 and collaborating on another concerning counterfeiting in 1888.

His involvement in liberal reform pushed him into politics. A socialist, he wrote papers for the Socialist Party, spoke at meetings and helped establish the newspaper *La Justice*. He was elected to the Belgian Senate and represented Hainaut between 1895 and 1898, Liège between 1900 and 1932 and Brabant between 1935 and 1936. He was secretary of the Senate for 13 years (1907–1919) and a vice-president for 14 years (1919–1932).

As a senator he devoted most of his time to issues concerning education, labor and foreign affairs. He took part in the reform of primary education and defended the funding of public schools. He also investigated the working conditions of miners and supported the reduction of the working week to 40 hours. In 1901 he asked the Belgian government if it would arbitrate in the Boer War and proposed various legislative measures that contributed to international cooperation and peace.

No sooner had he entered the Senate than La Fontaine, founder of the Belgian Society for Arbitration and Peace, joined the Interparliamentarian Union, the first permanent forum for multilateral political negotiations, which was established in 1889. The union, which included eight members who were or would go on to receive the Nobel Peace Prize, was seen by La Fontaine as the beginning of an international parliament and, eventually, a world government. La Fontaine also participated in the founding of the International Peace Bureau and became its president in 1907. This organization received the Nobel Peace Prize in 1910.

La Fontaine kept writing during this period and produced important works for the cause of peace. Particularly interested in creating bibliographies and methods of referencing, La Fontaine founded the International Bibliography Institute in 1895.

After receiving the Nobel Peace Prize in 1913, La Fontaine continued working as a writer and bibliographer but also as a politician and diplomat. He was a member of the Belgian delegation present at the Paris Peace Conference and a delegate at the first assembly of the League of Nations (1920–1921). He died in 1943.

Theodore Richards

In recognition of his accurate determinations of the atomic weight of a large number of chemical elements.

Outside of the work that made him famous, Theodore William Richards had diverse interests and a special appreciation for outdoor activities. Besides golf and sailing, drawing occupied a significant part of his free time. His artistic skills were likely inherited from his father, William T. Richards, who was a well-known landscape painter. His mother, Anna Matlack, was a respected poet and made sure the arts were a part of her son's upbringing.

Richards spent a large part of his childhood in Germantown, Pennsylvania, but traveled to France and England with his family. He was educated by his mother until the age of 15, when he entered Haverford College. In 1885 he graduated in the sciences and in the same year entered Harvard University, where he received a Bachelor of Arts degree in 1886 and a Master of Arts and Doctorate in 1888.

Richards spent the following year in Germany, where he studied under some of the greatest chemists of his day. On his return to Harvard, he served as a chemistry assistant until 1901, when he became a full professor. The discoveries he made during the next years of his life were of great importance to the understanding of atoms. Besides many other advances, he developed techniques that allowed him to determine the exact atomic weights of more than 30 elements, including oxygen, silver, chlorine, iodine, potassium, sodium and nitrogen.

This work was recognized with the 1914 Nobel Prize in Chemistry. However, due to traveling restrictions during World War I, Richards was unable to attend the ceremony in Stockholm. Besides this acknowledgment, he also received various honorary doctorates in science, medicine, philosophy, law and chemistry awarded by such universities as Yale, Harvard, Cambridge, Oxford, Manchester, Princeton and Prague. Over the years he was president of the American Chemical Society, the American Association for the Advancement of Science and the American Academy of Arts and Sciences.

Richards married Miriam Stuart Thayer in 1896, and they had two sons and a daughter. This notable chemist died in Cambridge, Massachusetts, on April 2, 1928.

Robert Bárány

For his work on the physiology and pathology of the vestibular apparatus.

Robert Bárány was born in Vienna, Austria, and was the eldest of six children. His father managed an estate and his mother, the daughter of a well-known Prague scientist, led the intellectual life of the family. While still young, Bárány contracted tuberculosis of the bones, which led him to have difficulty moving a knee. He did not let this physical disability prevent him from enjoying an active and healthy lifestyle: two of his favorite activities were playing tennis and hiking in the Alps.

It may be that Bárány's early illness inspired him to find cures for diseases, but, regardless, he finished his medical degree at the University of Vienna in 1900. He then studied at the psychiatric-neurological clinic of Professor Kraepelin in Germany. It was there that his attention was first drawn to neurological problems. Over the years he worked with various doctors and, following different theories, was finally able to clarify the physiology and pathology of the vestibular apparatus. It was for this important investigation that he was awarded the 1914 Nobel Prize in Physiology or Medicine.

The news surprised Bárány, who was in a Russian prisoner-of-war camp at the time. He had been captured while serving in the Austrian army as a civilian surgeon treating wounded soldiers. While a prisoner of war, he was deprived of any type of literature, laboratory facilities or other scientific assistance.

Through the intervention of Prince Carl of Sweden and in the name of the Red Cross he was liberated in 1916. That same year he went to Stockholm to receive the Nobel Prize. After this, Bárány returned to Vienna but was disappointed with the attitude of his Austrian colleagues, who accused him of giving incomplete references to other scientists' discoveries that had aided in his own. This tension in the scientific community finally led Bárány to accept an invitation to give lessons at the Otological Institute in Uppsala, where he remained until the end of his life.

Bárány married Ida Felicitas Berger in 1909, and the couple had two sons and a daughter. The eldest son became a professor of pharmacology at Uppsala University, the other an assistant professor of medicine at the Caroline Institute in Stockholm, while the daughter married a physician. In the last years of his life Bárány studied the causes of rheumatism and continued to work on a book about the subject even after he had suffered a stroke that left him nearly paralyzed. He died in 1936.

International Committee of the Red Cross

The only Nobel Peace Prize to be attributed during World War I, for the help given to prisoners of war, by serving as an intermediary between them and the countries that captured them and for sending delegates to inspect the camps.

The Red Cross began when Henri Dunant, a Swiss citizen, noted that there existed no organized medical services to help the wounded during the bloody Battle of Solferino. In 1862 his *Memory of Solferino* was published and just one year later Dunant managed to attract enough support to establish the International Committee for Aid to the Wounded in Geneva.

In 1864, with the help of the Swiss government, a diplomatic conference was held. Representatives signed a convention with legally binding articles declaring that the medical corps, its assistants and the wounded themselves could not be considered as the enemy on the battlefield. So that they could be identified, an emblem was created that could be universally recognized as a sign of neutrality: a red cross on a white background.

The International Committee's actions in times of war and peace have been recognized three times with a Nobel Peace Prize, more than any other organization. In 1917 and 1944 the award was given due to the work done during World War I and World War II. On the last occasion, in 1963, the prize was shared with the League of Red Cross Societies, now known as the International Federation of Red Cross and Red Crescent Societies (IFRC), which was founded in 1919.

The ICRC faced its first dramatic challenge during World War I. Immediately after the start of the conflict it established its Prisoners-of-War Agency, which was mostly staffed by international volunteers. By the end of the war the intervention of the agency was credited with the exchange of more than 200,000 prisoners between the warring parties, and by 1923 it had established a record system of more than 7 million prisoners or missing persons. This system aided in the identification of some 2 million prisoners of war and allowed communication to be established with their families. The International Committee of the Red Cross also distributed 20 million letters and messages, 1.9 million parcels and approximately 18 million Swiss francs in donations.

During World War II the ICRC carried out similar activities, although on a broader scale. The Central Information Agency on Prisoners of War contained information on 45 million prisoners and missing persons, delivered 120 million messages and organized relief efforts for civilian populations. After the world wars the ICRC continued to revise and expand its conventions, and in 1990 the United Nations General Assembly granted it observer status at its sessions.

The League of Red Cross Societies also received half of the 1963 prize.

1917, 1944, 1963 Peace

60

Red Cross Aid

More than 100 years after its foundation, the Red Cross movement - called the Red Crescent in Islamic countries - is still of great importance in aid activities all over the world. At the end of the 20th century, the Red Cross Federation and the Societies of the Red Crescent launched its 1999 Emergency Appeal to raise 207.5 million Swiss Francs to help 23 million people in 60 countries.

BIGGEST AID PROGRAMS:

Country or region	People affected	Aid (in Swiss Francs)
Ivory Coast, Guinea, Liberia, Sierra Leone	1.8 million	13.2 million
North Korea	5.8 million	12.3 million
Caucasus	500 thousand	13.0 million
Bangladesh	13.4 million	5.5 million
Afghanistan	2.24 million	7.9 million

TOTAL AID NECESSARY:

(In millions of Swiss Francs per region)

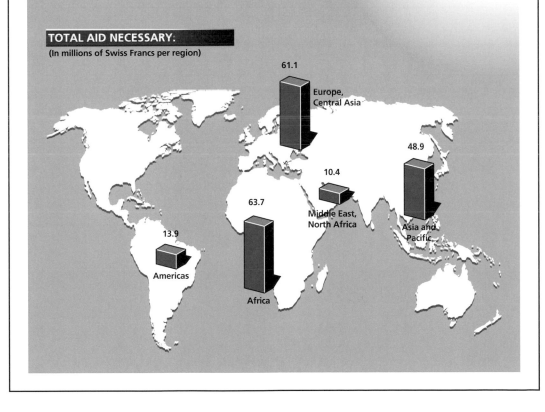

61.1 Europe, Central Asia

10.4 Middle East, North Africa

48.9 Asia and Pacific

63.7 Africa

13.9 Americas

Max Planck

In recognition of the services he rendered to the advancement of physics by his discovery of energy quanta.

Max Karl Ernst Ludwig Planck was one of the most important physicists of the 20th century, and his work in quantum and atomic physics made him one of the founding fathers of these fields. Born in Kiel, Germany, the son of Julius Wilhelm, a professor of constitutional law, Planck studied at the University of Munich and completed his doctorate there in 1879. In 1880 he began the first of five years of teaching at the University of Munich, after which he returned to the University of Kiel and taught theoretical physics until 1889. In that same year he was made associate professor at the University of Berlin, where he remained until his retirement in 1926.

Planck's first investigative work focused on questions of thermodynamics. But, on arriving in Berlin, he decided to study the distribution of energy in the spectrum of radiation of a black body, a phenomenon not explained by classical statistical mechanics. In 1900 Planck revealed that radiated energy was emitted or absorbed in a discontinuous manner and only in certain well-defined quantities, equal to a minimum value or a multiple of that value. Planck called this minimum quantity of energy, proportional to the frequency of the radiation emitted or absorbed, a "quantum" of energy or photon.

Although revolutionary, other physicists initially received these discoveries poorly. Nevertheless, soon the scientific community came to appreciate Planck's achievements, and he was awarded the 1918 Nobel Prize in Physics. In 1926 he was elected as a foreign member to the Royal Society, he received the Copley Society medal in 1928 and was president of the Kaiser Wilhelm Society (later renamed the Max Planck Institute) between 1930 and 1937.

Planck, unfortunately, had a private life marked by numerous tragedies. In 1909 his first wife Marie Merck, whom he had married in 1885, died, and he later lost two daughters. He remarried in 1911, to Marga von Hosslin. During World War II his eldest son was sent to the frontline, while the other was shot by the Gestapo for being involved in the attempt on Adolf Hitler's life on July 20, 1944. Vehemently opposed to the Nazi party, Planck was forced to leave Berlin in 1944, when the house he lived in was ruined. He escaped to Göttingen but never fully recovered from the accumulated sufferings he experienced during the war. He died in 1947.

Fritz Haber

For the synthesis of ammonia from its elements.

The German chemist Fritz Haber had broad interests in politics, history, economics and industry, but he is best remembered for his scientific work. Born in Breslau, Germany, now Wroclaw, Poland, Haber's family was one of the oldest and most respected in the community. He obtained a classical education in his hometown then went on to study chemistry at universities in Berlin, Heidelberg and Zurich before volunteering to return to Breslau and help in his father's business.

Haber's enterprising spirit led him to change his plans again, however, and he determined to follow an academic career. He first worked at the University of Jena with Ludwig Knorr but was, even at this time, uncertain whether to pursue his studies in physics or chemistry. In 1894 he finally accepted an invitation to be an assistant to Hans Bunte, professor of chemical technology at Technische Hochschule, in Karlsruhe. It was also in Karlsruhe that he met Carl Engler. These two men would have an enormous influence on Haber's professional life.

In 1911 he was appointed director of the Institute of Physical Chemistry and Electrochemistry, where he stayed for more than 20 years. He became a model leader of this vast institution, giving freedom to his colleagues while at the same time maintaining control over the school's diverse activities. Those who came into contact with him recognized his strong personality, management skills and work ethic.

When World War I broke out, Haber was appointed a consultant to the German War Office and had a decisive role in developing poison gas as a weapon of war. After the end of the conflict, the chemist once again showed his patriotism by trying to help Germany overcome its enormous war debt. To do so he began an unsuccessful attempt to extract gold from seawater.

At the height of his career, Haber was awarded the 1918 Nobel Prize in Chemistry "for the synthesis of ammonia from its elements." He left an important legacy of perfecting the Haber process, which combines nitrogen and hydrogen under pressure using iron as a catalyst to produce ammonia. This process can be used to produce fertilizers or explosives. Haber's most productive period coincided with the peak of the Institute for Physical Chemistry and Electrochemistry after World War I. Unfortunately Hitler's rise to power put an end to this growth, since Haber, as well as some of his colleagues, was Jewish. For the German authorities, the devotion that he had given to his country now meant little.

After leaving the Institute in 1933, he went to Cambridge in England but did not stay long, fearing the wet weather's effect on his heart condition. Haber died on January 29, 1934, in Basel, Switzerland.

Erik Axel Karlfeldt

He turned down the prize to dedicate himself to academy matters as a member and secretary from 1904 till the date of his death.

Erik Axel Eriksson came from old Swiss mining families on both his father's and mother's sides. He attended schools in his hometown of Folkarna as well as in Västerås. In 1889 Erik Axel adopted the name Karlfeldt, by which he would be known from then on. It was not a family name but was derived from the title of his father's property. Rural culture had an influence on him throughout his life, and it became a favorite subject of his future literary work.

Karlfeldt started to write poems while still a student and the first collection, *Vildmarks-och kärleksvisor (Songs of the Wilderness and of Love)*, was published in the autumn of 1895, three years after he had graduated from the University of Uppsala. His professional activity, however, had already begun when, between 1893 and 1896, he taught in a private elementary school in Djursholm and gave lessons to adults in Molkom. Besides this, he was also a journalist for a Stockholm periodical for a short period of time.

After concluding his studies, he worked in the Royal Library in Stockholm, Sweden, for five years and then was appointed librarian at the Agricultural Academy. Meanwhile his poetic talents had begun to be noticed and, in 1904, he was elected to the Swedish Academy, becoming a member of the Nobel Institute of the Academy as well as a member of the Nobel Committee. In 1912 he was appointed permanent secretary of the academy and dedicated himself entirely to the position and to poetry.

In 1916 he married Gerda Holmberg and the couple had four children. In 1918 he was awarded the Nobel Prize in Literature, which, for ethical reasons, Karlfeldt turned down due to his very strong links with the academy. The rejection was so firm that there were practically no records of the distinction; according to the official lists the prize was not attributed.

In 1931, however, Karlfeldt was once again recognized with the Nobel Prize in Literature, this time posthumously. It was the only way the academy found to thank Karlfeldt without giving him the opportunity to turn down the prize.

A Lutheran who did not like to expose his private life and more inner reflections — it was for this reason that he sought an alter ego to represent his feelings — Karlfeldt left a body of poetry replete with characters based on Swedish traditions. His works reflect his own position toward the world, with a sense of humor, integrity and beauty of benefit to the collective and the individual.

1918 Literature *Prize was refused.*
1931 Literature *Prize awarded posthumously.*

Johannes Stark

For his discovery of the Doppler effect in canal rays and the splitting of spectral lines in electric fields.

The German Johannes Stark was one of the scientists who supported Hitler, declaring his allegiance in 1924 and joining the Nazi party in 1930. A confirmed anti-Semite, he defended the idea of a "German science" as opposed to a "Jewish science" and opposed Jewish scientists like Einstein.

In 1933 he was elected president of the Reich Physical-Technical Institute and remained in this position until his retirement in 1939. During this period he also assumed the presidency of the German Research Association. Despite defending the need for Germany to carry out an applied investigation into the production of technological methods and industries of war, Stark's influence among his contemporaries was declining, even before the fall of the Third Reich. After World War II, he was sentenced to four years hard labor for his Nazi ties, a sentence that was later suspended.

In spite of his racial and political views, Stark's career was important to science and was distinguished in various ways. In 1910 he won the Baumgartner Prize of the Vienna Academy of Sciences and the Vahlbruch Prize of the Göttingen Science Academy in 1914. Stark was also a member of academies in Göttingen, Rome, Vienna and Calcutta. The Nobel Prize in Physics was awarded to him in 1919 for the "discovery of the Doppler effect in canal rays and the splitting of spectral lines in electric fields," an effect that was named after him. The prize enabled him to set up a private laboratory.

Stark was born in Schickenhof on one of his father's estates. Initially he studied in Bayreuth and Regensberg then went to the University of Munich in 1894. In 1900 he became an unpaid staff member at the University of Göttingen.

A prolific writer, Stark published more than 300 scientific papers. In 1902 his book, *Die Elektrizität in Gasen (Electricity in Gases)*, was published. He also founded the *Jahrbuch der Radioaktivität und Elektronik (The Yearbook of Radioactivity and Electronics)*, a publication he edited between 1904 and 1913.

He died on the June 21, 1957, in Traunstein, Germany. In his later years he continued his research in his private laboratory. Besides his scientific life and political convictions, Stark married Luise Uepler and had five children. His hobbies included forestry and the cultivation of fruit trees.

Jules Bordet

For his discoveries relating to immunity.

Jules Jean Baptiste Vincent Bordet, a Belgian doctor and microbiologist, achieved international respect as an authority in many areas of bacteriology and immunology, providing the medical sciences with invaluable discoveries in these fields. He was awarded the Grand Cordon de l'Ordre de la Couronne de Belgique in 1930, the Grand Cordon de l'Ordre de Léopold in 1937 and the Grand Croix de la Légion d'Honneur in 1938 besides many others honors. He was a permanent member of the Administrative Council of the University of Brussels, a professor of bacteriology, president of the first International Congress on Microbiology held in Paris in 1930, and he held important positions at the Scientific Council of the Pasteur Institute of Paris and the Royal Academy of Medicine of Belgium.

Jules Bordet was born in Soignies, Belgium, at the beginning of the summer of 1870. He studied at the University of Brussels, where he was made a doctor of medicine in 1892. Two years later he left for Paris to begin his work at the Pasteur Institute. With the experience he gained at this well-respected scientific establishment, Bordet returned to his homeland in 1901 to found a branch of the institute in the Belgian capital.

It was in these two establishments that he worked on developing the diagnosis and treatment of various contagious diseases. He contributed to the foundation of serology, the study of immunized reactions on bodily fluids, and, in partnership with Octave Gengou, he established the basis of serological tests for the propagative organisms of various diseases, including typhoid, tuberculosis and syphilis. He also discovered the bacteria related to whooping cough. Bordet, besides his work in the laboratories, dedicated time to recording and preserving his knowledge. The *Traité de l'immunité dans les maladies infectieuses (Treatise on Immunity in Infectious Diseases)* was one of his main works.

In 1919 he received the highest distinction for his work on immunology, the Nobel Prize in Physiology or Medicine. On the day of the award ceremony, Bordet's medal and diploma were presented to a high-ranking official of the Belgian state since the laureate was giving a speech in the United States at the time.

 He was married to Marthe Levoz in 1899 and was a father of three. His son Paul decided to follow in his footsteps, also becoming a professor of bacteriology, and succeeded him as head of the Pasteur Institute in Brussels. When he died in the Belgian capital, Jules Bordet had a worthy scientific successor in his son.

Woodrow Wilson

(1856–1924)

[For his] attempts to negotiate peace, with special reference to his speech "Fourteen Points," aimed at achieving a lasting Peace after World War I, and which would be fundamental in establishing the League of Nations.

The son of a Presbyterian minister, the young Wilson grew up in a home governed by religious values and education. He attended Princeton University then finished his law degree at the University of Virginia.

In 1886 he received his doctorate from Johns Hopkins University). He was president of Princeton between 1902 and 1910, and he became known for his passionate ideas on the reformation of the educational system.

Politics began to attract the young professor, and the Democrats persuaded him to run for governor of New Jersey in 1910. He won the election and continued to bolster his national image as an independent, personal representative of the people. He made his views clear in his speeches and publications over the coming years, affirming in 1912 that "the business of government is to organize the common interest against the special interest."

In 1912 Wilson was elected the 28th president of the United States in an election that split the Republican vote between William Howard Taft and Theodore Roosevelt. Wilson had run on a program called the New Freedom, which emphasized individualism and the rights of states.

In 1916, touting his legislation successes and the motto "he kept us out of the war," Wilson was narrowly reelected, but World War I would nevertheless constitute the biggest test of Wilson's presidency. American efforts slowly turned the tide in favor of the Allies, allowing them to achieve victory in Europe in 1918.

Wilson's role on the international scene grew after the end of the war, and in January he went before Congress and the Paris Peace Conference with his Fourteen Points, the last of which would establish "a general association of nations... affording mutual guarantees of political independence and territorial integrity to great and small states alike." Many of President Wilson's ideas were implemented in the Versailles Treaty and the League of Nations, which earned him the Nobel Peace Prize in 1919. However, when the U.S. Senate refused to give its approval to the U.S. joining the League, Wilson, against the advice of his doctors, made an exhausting national tour in an attempt to stir up support for the Versailles Treaty. He nearly died from a stroke while campaigning in Pueblo, Colorado, and had to be nursed by his second wife, Edith Bolling Galt, until his death in 1924.

Although unable to attend the Nobel ceremony because of his failing health, President Woodrow Wilson had a telegram read by the American minister in which he praised the legacy of Alfred Nobel, where the "cause of peace and the cause of truth are of one family."

Nobel Laureates

1910-1919

1910

Nobel Prize in Physics
Johannes Diderik van der Waals
Born November 23, 1837, in Leiden, Netherlands, and
died March 8, 1923, in Amsterdam.
For his work on the equation of state for gases and
liquids.

Nobel Prize in Chemistry
Otto Wallach
Born March 27, 1847, in Königsberg, Germany, and died
February 26, 1931, in Göttingen.
In recognition of his services to organic chemistry and
the chemical industry by his pioneer work in the field of
alicyclic compounds.

Nobel Prize in Physiology or Medicine
Albrecht Kossel
Born September 16, 1853, in Rostock, Germany, and
died July 5, 1927, in Heidelberg.
In recognition of the contribution to our knowledge of
cell chemistry made through his work on proteins,
including the nucleic substances.

Nobel Prize in Literature
Paul Johann Ludwig Heyse
Born March 5, 1830, in Berlin, Germany, and died April
2, 1914, in Munich.
As a tribute to the consummate artistry, permeated with
idealism, which he has demonstrated during his long
productive career as a lyric poet, dramatist, novelist and
writer of world-renowned short stories.

Nobel Peace Prize
Permanent International Peace Bureau
Founded in 1891, in Bern, Switzerland.
For facilitating communication between societies and
peoples, collecting information on the peace movement
and helping to prepare the Annual Peace Congress.

1911

Nobel Prize in Physics
Wilhelm Wien
Born January 13, 1864, in Gaffken, Germany, and died
August 30, 1928, in Munich.
For his discoveries regarding the laws governing the
radiation of heat.

Nobel Prize in Chemistry
Marie Curie, née Maria Sklodowska
Born November 7, 1867, in Warsaw, Poland, and died
July 4, 1934, in Savoy, France.
In recognition of her services to the advancement of
chemistry by the discovery of the elements radium and
polonium, by the isolation of radium and the study of the
nature and compounds of this remarkable element.

Nobel Prize in Physiology or Medicine
Allvar Gullstrand
Born June 5, 1862, in Landskrona, Sweden, and died
July 28, 1930, in Stockholm.
For his work on the dioptrics of the eye.

Nobel Prize in Literature
**Maurice Maeterlinck, pseudonym of
Maurice Polidore Marie Bernhard
Maeterlinck**
Born August 29, 1862, in Ghent, Belgium, and died May
6, 1949, in Nice, France.
In appreciation of his many-sided literary activities,
and especially of his dramatic works, which are
distinguished by a wealth of imagination and by a
poetic fancy, which reveals, sometimes in the guise
of a fairy tale, a deep inspiration, while in a mysterious
way they appeal to the readers' own feelings and
stimulate their imaginations.

Nobel Peace Prize
Tobias Michael Carel Asser
Born April 28, 1838, in Amsterdam, Netherlands, and
died July 29, 1913, in The Hague.
Practical statesman and a pioneer of the legal

regulation in international relations.
&
Alfred Hermann Fried
Born November 11, 1864, in Vienna, Austria, and died
May 5, 1921, in Vienna.
Author of literary works, which have eventually made
him the greatest pacifist of the last 20 years.

1912

Nobel Prize in Physics
Nils Gustaf Dalén
Born November 30, 1869, in Stenstorp, Sweden, and
died December 9, 1937, in Lidingö.
For his invention of automatic regulators for use in
conjunction with gas accumulators for illuminating
lighthouses and buoys.

Nobel Prize in Chemistry
Victor Grignard
Born May 6, 1871, in Cherbourg, France, and died
December 13, 1935, in Lyon.
For the discovery of the so-called Grignard reagent,
which in recent years has greatly advanced the progress
of organic chemistry.
&
Paul Sabatier
Born November 5, 1854, in Carcassonne, France, and
died August 14, 1941, in Toulouse.
For his method of hydrogenating organic compounds
in the presence of finely disintegrated metals whereby
the progress of organic chemistry has been greatly
advanced in recent years.

Nobel Prize in Physiology or Medicine
Alexis Carrel
Born June 28, 1873, in Sainte-Foy-lès-Lyon, France,
and died November 5, 1944, in Paris.
In recognition of his work on vascular suture and the
transplantation of blood vessels and organs.

Nobel Prize in Literature
Gerhart Johann Robert Hauptmann
Born November 15, 1862, in Bad Obersalzbrunn,
Germany, and died June 6, 1946, in Agnetendorf.
Primarily in recognition of his fruitful, varied and
outstanding production in the realm of dramatic art.

Nobel Peace Prize
Elihu Root
Born February 15, 1845, in Clinton, New York, United
States, and died February 7, 1937, in New York.
A man of engaging personality who has tried, with
determination and independence, to put his ideals into
practice.

1913

Nobel Prize in Physics
Heike Kamerlingh Onnes
Born September 21, 1853, in Groningen,
Netherlands, and died February 21, 1926, in Leiden,
Germany.
For his investigations on the properties of matter at low
temperatures which led, inter alia, to the production of
liquid helium.

Nobel Prize in Chemistry
Alfred Werner
Born December 12, 1866, in Mülhausen, Germany
(now France), and died November 15, 1919, in Zurich,
Switzerland.
In recognition of his work on the linkage of atoms in
molecules by which he has thrown new light on earlier
investigations and opened up new fields of research
especially in inorganic chemistry.

Nobel Prize in Physiology or Medicine
Charles Richet
Born August 25, 1850, in Paris, France, and died
December 4, 1835, in Paris.
In recognition of his work on anaphylaxis.

Nobel Prize in Literature
**Ravindranatha Thakur, pseudonym of
Rabindranath Tagore**
Born May 7, 1861, in Calcutta, India, and died August 7,
1941, in Calcutta.
Because of his profoundly sensitive, fresh and beautiful
verse, by which, with consummate skill, he has made
his poetic thought, expressed in his own English words,
a part of the literature of the West.

Nobel Peace Prize
Henri La Fontaine
Born April 22, 1854, in Brussels, Belgium, and died May

14, 1943, in Brussels.
For his efforts to establish and follow the principles of international understanding and cooperation among men.

1914

Nobel Prize in Physics
Max von Laue
Born October 9, 1879, in Pfaffendorf, Germany, and died April 24, 1960, in Berlin.
For his discovery of the diffraction of X-rays by crystals.

Nobel Prize in Chemistry
Theodore William Richards
Born January 31, 1868, in Germantown, Pennsylvania, United States, and died April 2, 1928, in Cambridge, Massachusetts.
In recognition of his accurate determinations of the atomic weight of a large number of chemical elements.

Nobel Prize in Physiology or Medicine
Robert Bárány
Born April 22, 1876, in Vienna, Austria, and died April 8, 1936, in Uppsala, Sweden.
For his work on the physiology and pathology of the vestibular apparatus.

Nobel Prize in Literature
Not awarded.

Nobel Peace Prize
Not awarded.

1915

Nobel Prize in Physics
Sir William Henry Bragg
Born July 2, 1862, in Westward, England, and died March 10, 1942, in London.
&
Sir William Lawrence Bragg
Born March 31, 1890, in Adelaide, Australia, and died July 1, 1971, in Ipswich, England.
For their services in the analysis of crystal structure by means of X-rays.

Nobel Prize in Chemistry
Richard Martin Willstätter
Born August 13, 1872, in Karlsruhe, Germany, and died August 3, 1942, in Locarno, Switzerland.
For his researches on plant pigments, especially chlorophyll.

Nobel Prize in Physiology or Medicine
Not awarded.

Nobel Prize in Literature
Romain Rolland
Born January 29, 1866, in Clamecy, France, and died December 30, 1944, in Vézelay.
As a tribute to the lofty idealism of his literary production and to the sympathy and love of truth with which he has described different types of human beings.

Nobel Peace Prize
Not awarded.

1916

Nobel Prize in Physics
Not awarded.

Nobel Prize in Chemistry
Not awarded.

Nobel Prize in Physiology or Medicine
Not awarded.

Nobel Prize in Literature
Carl Gustaf Verner von Heidenstam
Born July 6, 1859, in Olshammar, Sweden, and died May 20, 1940, in Övralid.
In recognition of his significance as the leading representative of a new era in our literature.

Nobel Peace Prize
Not awarded.

1917

Nobel Prize in Physics
Charles Glover Barkla
Born June 7, 1877, in Widnes, England, and died

October 23, 1944, in Braidwood, Scotland.
For his discovery of the characteristic Röntgen radiation of the elements.

Nobel Prize in Chemistry
Not awarded.

Nobel Prize in Physiology or Medicine
Not awarded.

Nobel Prize in Literature
Karl Adolph Gjellerup
Born June 2, 1857, in Praestö, Denmark, and died October 11, 1919, in Klotzsche, Germany.
For his varied and rich poetry, which is inspired by lofty ideals.
&
Henrik Pontoppidan
Born July 24, 1857, in Fredericia, Demark, and died August 21, 1943, in Charlottenlund.
For his authentic descriptions of present-day life in Denmark.

Nobel Peace Prize
International Committee of the Red Cross
Founded in 1863, in Geneva, Switzerland.
The only Nobel Peace Prize to be attributed during World War I, for the help given to prisoners of war, by serving as an intermediary between them and the countries that captured them, and for sending delegates to inspect the camps.

1918

Nobel Prize in Physics
Max Planck
Born April 23, 1858, in Kiel, Germany, and died October 3, 1947, in Göttingen.
In recognition of the services he rendered to the advancement of physics by his discovery of energy quanta.

Nobel Prize in Chemistry
Fritz Haber
Born December 9, 1868, in Breslau, Germany, and died January 29, 1934, in Basel, Switzerland.
For the synthesis of ammonia from its elements.

Nobel Prize in Physiology or Medicine
Not awarded.

Nobel Prize in Literature
Awarded to Erik Axel Karlfeldt who refused it.
Born July 20, 1864, in Folkarna, Sweden, and died April 8, 1931, in Stockholm.
He turned down the prize to dedicate himself to academy matters as a member and secretary from 1904 until the date of his death.

Nobel Peace Prize
Not awarded.

1919

Nobel Prize in Physics
Johannes Stark
Born April 15, 1874, in Schickenhof, Germany, and died June 21, 1957, in Traunstein.
For his discovery of the Doppler effect in canal rays and the splitting of spectral lines in electric fields.

Nobel Prize in Chemistry
Not awarded.

Nobel Prize in Physiology or Medicine
Jules Bordet
Born June 13, 1870, in Soignies, Belgium, and died April 6, 1961, in Brussels.
For his discoveries relating to immunity.

Nobel Prize in Literature
Carl Friedrich Georg Spitteler
Born April 24, 1845, in Liestal, Switzerland, and died December 29, 1924, in Lucerne, Switzerland.
In special appreciation of his epic *Olympian Spring*.

Nobel Peace Prize
Thomas Woodrow Wilson
Born December 28, 1856, in Staunton, Virginia, United States, and died February 3, 1924, in Washington, DC.
Attempts to negotiate peace, with special reference to his speech "Fourteen Points" aimed at achieving a lasting peace after World War I, and which would be fundamental in establishing the League of Nations.

Selected Profiles of Nobel Laureates

1920–1929

Anatole France

*In recognition of his brilliant literary achievements, characterized
as they are by a nobility of style, a profound human sympathy,
grace and true Gallic temperament.*

Anatole France, the pseudonym of Jacques-Anatole Thibault, created
remarkably clear works full of skepticism, irony and social criticism,
qualities that made him heir to the tradition of Voltaire.

The son of a bookseller, Thibault always lived surrounded by literary
works. Since he was devoted to reading from his youth, and throughout
his life he would maintain a passion for knowledge and storytelling. When
he was 7 years old, Thibault told his parents he wanted to be famous.
Although his mother was unhappy with what she considered to be her son's vanity, Thibault's
father believed that, with a bit of experience in the world, the young Jacques would soon grow
tired of fame. Time proved his prediction right.

Thibault received a classical education at Stanislas College, an all-boys school in his native
Paris, before a brief attendance at the Chartes School. Over the next years he worked at various
jobs, all of them involving writing. He was a freelance journalist from 1862 to 1877, a librarian at
the Senate from 1876 to 1890 and a literary critic for the newspaper *Le Temps* from 1888 to 1892.
Despite demanding occupations, Thibault, under the pseudonym Anatole France, dedicated
time to his personal writing. He explored almost all genres, but was a novelist and storyteller
at heart. He wrote in classical French, which lent itself wonderfully to his style and subject
matter.

France's first major success was *Le Crime de Sylvestre Bonnard (Sylvestre Bonnard's Crime)*,
published in 1881, and the novel received a prize from the prestigious French Academy.
Balthazar (1889) and *Thaïs* (1890) followed, but his most celebrated novel, *La Rôtisserie de
la Reine Pédauque (At the Sign of the Reine Pédauque)*, was published in 1893. A year later he
wrote *Histoire Contemporaine (Contemporary Stories)*, which marked a change in direction.
This collection protested against the Dreyfus case, a political scandal involving anti-Semitism
that divided the country for a decade, and showed his concern with other current events. In
later years France was increasingly concerned with social questions, and they filled the pages
of most of his last works.

His private life had three distinct periods. His first marriage, to Marie-Valérie Guérin de
Sauville, was celebrated in 1877 but ended in divorce 16 years later. He met Leontine Arman
de Caillavet, the inspiration for his *Thaïs*, in 1888 and had a relationship with her until 1910,
and then he married Emma Laprévotte in 1920.

Albert Einstein

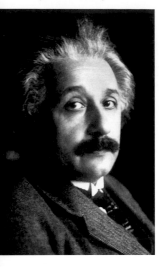

For his services to theoretical physics, and especially for his discovery of the law of the photoelectric effect.

Few men today are more closely associated with genius than Albert Einstein. Born in Ulm, Germany, on March 14, 1879, his family moved to Munich. His high school years were spent in Aarau, Switzerland, when his family moved once more, this time to Italy.

Einstein entered the Swiss Federal Polytechnic School at 18 with the intention of becoming a mathematics and physics teacher and, upon completion of his studies, was made a naturalized Swiss citizen in 1901.

Unable to get a job as a teacher, he went to work as a technical assistant at the Swiss Patent Office. In his free time, however, besides preparing for his doctorate degree — which he obtained in 1905 — Einstein was developing some of his most notable work, which was soon to shock the academic world.

In 1908 he was nominated to be an assistant in Berne, Switzerland, but the following year he was made an associate professor at the University of Zurich. In 1911 he took up the chair of theoretical physics at the University of Prague, and then he moved to Switzerland in 1912 to take up a similar position. Einstein returned to Germany in 1914, reacquired his citizenship, took up a chair at the University of Berlin and became head of the Kaiser Wilhelm Institute of Physics.

Einstein won the 1921 Nobel Prize in Physics for his extensive work in theoretical physics, particularly for discovering the law of photoelectric effect. He stayed in Berlin until 1933, the year in which he renounced his German citizenship for political reasons and immigrated to the United States, where he became a professor of theoretical physics at Princeton University. In 1940 he became a naturalized American citizen and retired five years later.

He abhorred all nationalism and in the postwar period became a prominent figure in the world government movement. He was invited to be president of the State of Israel, an offer he turned town, but he did collaborate with Chaim Weizmann in creating the Hebrew University of Jerusalem.

His work brought him numerous prizes besides the Nobel, including the Copley Medal of the Royal Society of London in 1925 and the Franklin Medal of the Franklin Institute a decade later. Einstein left the world a rich store of publications and manuscripts, the most significant of the scientific works being *Special Theory of Relativity* (1905), *General Theory of Relativity* (1916) and *The Evolution of Physics* (1938). His nonscientific works include *Why War?* (1933), *My Philosophy* (1934) and *Out of My Later Years* (1950).

He married twice, first in 1901 to Mileva Maritc, with whom he had a daughter and two sons, and after their divorce to his cousin Elsa Löwenthal in 1917. He was made a widower in 1936 and died 19 years later in Princeton, New Jersey.

The Earth's rotation disturbs the space-time structure

Researchers have discovered the first direct evidence of a bizarre effect first suggested more than 80 years ago by Einstein in his Theory of Relativity. Following the orbits of two satellites, the researchers discovered that the Earth resists the advance of time and space, while it is rotating.

"SpaceTime" The three dimensions of space and the dimension of time are called space-time. Einstein demonstrated that gravity is a distortion of space-time caused by the mass of an object.

Detecting the resistance:

1 Imagine the Earth in a grid representing space-time. The mass of the earth distorts the grid like a 10-pin bowling ball on a trampoline.

LAGEOS satellites

- Launched in 1976 and 1992
- Used in a study of the Earth's gravity and the movement of the crust.
- Its position in space can be measured very precisely

Reflector Prisms

The design:
- 60 cm in diameter
- 400 kg

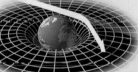

2 When an object passes Earth, the distortion alters its conduct.

4 The rotation of the Earth alters space-time in the direction of the rotation, in accordance with the Theory of "Structure Dragging." The effect is represented as a big revolving ball in syrup pulling the liquid around it.

5 According to the classic pre-Einstein theories, a satellite should maintain a stable orbit around the Earth.

6 Einstein's Theory predicts that the rotation of the Earth would alter the orbit.

Einstein's legacy

Some decades passed before experiments were carried out to test certain aspects of the Theory of Relativity. For example:

3 The Earth doesn't only have mass, it also has movement in the way it moves on its axis.

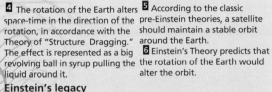

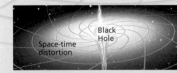

Black Hole

Space-time distortion

Material converted into energy:
Verified in atomic explosions and the creation of stars.

Gravity lensing: An object's gravity distorts space, in such a way that an object, like a galaxy, bends the light that crosses it.
The diagram and the Hubble space telescope demonstrate this phenomenon.

On a large scale

In 1997, astronomers observed distortion in hot x-ray gas emissions close to a dense black hole, a dead star. Structure dragging was the apparent cause.

Combination of lights

Luminous object

Earth

Galaxy

Dilating time: Objects that are moving very fast seem to be standing still.

Frederick Soddy

For his contributions to our knowledge of the chemistry of radioactive substances, and his investigations into the origin and nature of isotopes.

The son of a London merchant, Frederick Soddy was born on the September 2, 1877, in Eastbourne, Sussex, England. A man of strong principles and fixed ideas, he was always friendly with his students but showed a strict character with his colleagues. A notable scientist, he carried out research in the field of radioactive substances and developed the theory of isotopes, which earned him the 1921 Nobel Prize in Chemistry.

Soddy began his studies in his hometown before attending University College of Wales. He received a scholarship to Oxford in 1895 and graduated with honors at the age of 21. He then carried out research there for two years before moving to Canada. Between 1900 and 1902, he was an assistant in the department of chemistry at McGill University, Montreal, Canada. Along with the physicist Ernest Rutherford, winner of the 1908 Nobel Prize in Chemistry, he published a series of studies on radioactivity.

On his return to the United Kingdom, Soddy worked with the chemist William Ramsay at University College, London. He then lectured on physical chemistry, and radioactivity at the University of Glasgow between 1904 and 1914, continuing his experiments with radioactive material during this time.

Frederick Soddy reached the peak of his scientific career in 1913, when he became the first person to demonstrate the existence of isotopes. The following year, he was made professor of chemistry at the University of Aberdeen. The outbreak of World War I, however, prevented him from further major research. After the war ended, in 1919, Soddy began lecturing in chemistry at Oxford University. He remained at Oxford until 1937, the year his wife, Winifred Beilby, whom he had married in 1908, died.

The success he achieved as a chemist did not prevent Soddy from turning his attention to social, political and economic affairs. He was extremely critical of the failure of economic systems to take advantage of technological and scientific advances, but his theories in this area did not win much support. Nevertheless, he was recognized for his academic work and received an honorary doctorate from Oxford, was made a member of the Royal Society in 1910 and awarded the Albert Medal in 1951.

Frederick Soddy died in Brighton, Sussex, England. He left behind a number of significant scientific works, including *Radioactivity* (1904), *The Interpretation of Radium* (1909), *The Chemistry of the Radioactive Elements* (1912–1914), *The Interpretation of the Atom* (1932), *The Story of Atomic Energy* (1949) and *Atomic Transmutation* (1953).

Isotopes

In 1903 the British chemist Frederick Soddy discovered
the phenomenon of isotopes.

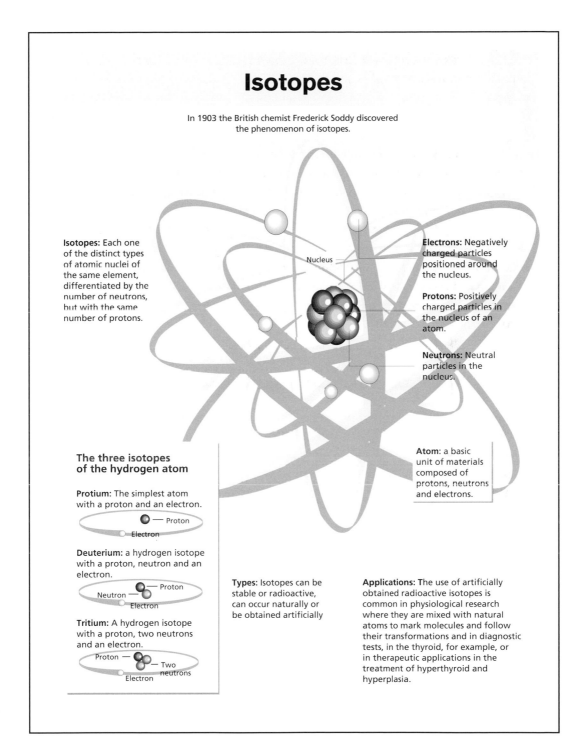

Isotopes: Each one
of the distinct types
of atomic nuclei of
the same element,
differentiated by the
number of neutrons,
but with the same
number of protons.

Nucleus

Electrons: Negatively
charged particles
positioned around
the nucleus.

Protons: Positively
charged particles in
the nucleus of an
atom.

Neutrons: Neutral
particles in the
nucleus.

Atom: a basic
unit of materials
composed of
protons, neutrons
and electrons.

The three isotopes of the hydrogen atom

Protium: The simplest atom
with a proton and an electron.

Proton
Electron

Deuterium: a hydrogen isotope
with a proton, neutron and an
electron.

Proton
Neutron
Electron

Tritium: A hydrogen isotope
with a proton, two neutrons
and an electron.

Proton
Two
neutrons
Electron

Types: Isotopes can be
stable or radioactive,
can occur naturally or
be obtained artificially

Applications: The use of artificially
obtained radioactive isotopes is
common in physiological research
where they are mixed with natural
atoms to mark molecules and follow
their transformations and in diagnostic
tests, in the thyroid, for example, or
in therapeutic applications in the
treatment of hyperthyroid and
hyperplasia.

Niels Bohr

For his services in the investigation of the structure of atoms and of the radiation emanating from them.

Niels Henrik David Bohr's father was an eminent physiologist, and his mother was born into a family long connected to higher education. With his younger brother, Harald, who would later become a professor in mathematics, Niels grew up in an atmosphere that allowed him to develop his genius, thanks mostly to his parents' efforts and influence.

He studied at the University of Copenhagen and was a student of the well-known physicist Christien Christiansen, receiving his doctorate degree in 1911. The first steps in his career were taken while he was still a student. Knowing that the Academy of Sciences in Copenhagen had announced a prize for whoever solved a specific scientific problem, Bohr started experimental research into superficial tension using oscillating fluid jets. He worked in his father's laboratory and won the Academy's gold medal prize for his work.

After a stay in Cambridge, England, Bohr started working in Professor Ernest Rutherford's laboratory in Manchester, where he studied radioactive phenomena. While there, he wrote a theoretical work on the absorption of alpha rays and started studying the structure of atoms as presented in Rutherford's model. Bohr introduced concepts to quantum theory, formulated by Max Planck, and managed to create a model of atomic structure that, with later adjustments, still serves to interpret the physical and chemical properties of elements.

Between 1913 and 1914, Bohr was a lecturer in physics at the University of Copenhagen, a position he also held at Victoria University in Manchester between 1914 and 1916. Following this, he worked as a professor of theoretical physics at the University of Copenhagen and from 1920 onward he was head of the Institute for Theoretical Physics at the same institution. Bohr wrote numerous scientific essays between 1933 and 1962, and he balanced his work with the presidency of the Royal Danish Academy of Sciences and other institutions.

He received honorary doctorates throughout his life from more than 30 universities. The 1922 Nobel Prize in Physics was awarded to Bohr in recognition of his work on atomic structure and contributions to solving problems in the field of quantum physics, particularly in the development of the concept of complimentarily.

During the Nazi occupation of Denmark, Bohr escaped to Sweden then spent the last two years of World War II in England and the United States, where he was associated with the Atomic Energy Project. The last years of his life were dedicated to the peaceful application of atomic physics and problems emerging from the development of atomic weapons.

Niels Bohr was married in 1912 to Margrethe Nørlund, and the couple had six sons.

Fridjtof Nansen

*For activities in favor of peace and his role in the cause
of refugees from war.*

Although it was as a peace worker that Fridjtof Nansen earned his place
in history, he was also a prominent naturalist and well known for his
adventurous lifestyle. The son of a prosperous lawyer, he was born in the
suburbs of Christiania (later renamed Oslo), in present-day Norway. He
inherited strong moral principles from his father, but it was his mother,
a strong-minded, athletic woman, who instilled in him a love of outdoor
living and sports. As an adult, he was capable of impressive feats, including
skiing more than 50 miles (80 km) in a day.

While he was a student, Nansen distinguished himself in the natural sciences and art. In
1881 he entered the University of Oslo to study zoology, hoping to prepare for a future that
united all his interests. For the next 15 years he would, indeed, combine his athletic prowess,
scientific interests, taste for adventure and drawing skills into a series of achievements that
would bring him international fame.

In 1882 he boarded the ship *Viking* and sailed to the east coast of Greenland. Years later, his
notes from the voyage were made into a book. But what stayed with him from that journey was
a passion for the world of ice and sea. Among other feats and scientific studies, he crossed
Greenland from end to end and was, at the time, the man to get closest to the North Pole.

In 1905 he interrupted his work to apply himself to the cause of separating Norway from
Sweden. He returned to his scientific work, but with the outbreak of World War I he fully
committed himself to international politics. Between 1917 and 1918, he headed a Norwegian
mission to Washington and negotiated a relaxation of the blockade, which made maritime
transport of essential food to his country possible. In 1919, he represented Norwegian
interests in the constitution of the League of Nations and played an important role in the
preparation of the Treaty of Versailles, contributing mostly to the recognition of smaller
countries' rights. He was the Norwegian delegate to the League until his death.

In the spring of 1920 Nansen led the process to repatriate prisoners of war, mostly being
held in Russia. Despite a lack of funds and other difficulties, he managed to repatriate a
pproximately 450,000 men in a year and a half. In 1921 he was nominated to direct the
League of Nation's High Commission for Refugees, and he created standards of procedure
that are still followed to this day. That same year he led a food relief program for the millions
of starving poor. It is estimated that Nasen's program contributed to saving millions of
people from starvation. His work with Greek and Armenian refugees was also important.

Fridjtof Nansen died on May 13, 1930. The funeral was delayed for four days so that he
could be buried on the 17th, the day commemorating Norwegian independence.

Frederick Banting
John Macleod

For the discovery of insulin.

The discovery of how to isolate insulin, the hormone that allows diabetic patients to combat excessive glucose in their blood, brought the Canadian Frederick Grant Banting and John James Richard Macleod the 1923 Nobel Prize in Physiology or Medicine.

It was Banting, along with his assistant Charles H. Best, who was the first person to successfully extract insulin from the pancreas. The Karolinska Institute in Stockholm, Sweden, which is responsible for attributing the Nobel Prize, decided, at Banting's suggestion, to also recognize Macleod, who had been receptive to the idea and offered his facilities for research.

Born in Alliston, Ontario, Canada, Frederick Banting was the youngest of five children. He completed his high school studies in his hometown then moved to Toronto. Although he initially enrolled in theology, Banting soon transferred to medicine. He graduated in 1916 and immediately enlisted in the Canadian Army Medical Corps and was sent to France. He was wounded during the battle of Cambrai, and later received the Military Cross for heroism under fire.

After the war he served as a doctor in several communities until he completed his MD in 1922. By this time he had already taken an interest in diabetes and related his ideas to a receptive John Macleod, then a professor of physiology at the University of Toronto. Born in Scotland, Macleod had traveled the world since obtaining his honors degree in medicine in 1898. He had worked in Leipzig, London, Cleveland and Montreal before he met Banting.

Besides the Nobel Prize, both received various awards and honorary titles. Macleod left a vast body of published work for posterity. Both Banting and Macleod loved to paint, and Banting even participated in a government-sponsored painting expedition above the Arctic Circle.

Macleod lived with his wife, Mary McWalter, and Banting married twice, first to Marion Robertson, with whom he had a son before their divorce, and then to Henrietta Ball. When World War II began, Banting served as a liaison officer between the English and American medical services. He was killed in a plane crash in Newfoundland while on active service.

Banting and Macleod each received half of the prize.

Insulin

Frederick Banting and John Macleod's discovery of a way of isolating insulin raised hopes amongst diabetics that the excess of sugar in the blood could be combated.

Around 135 million people in the world suffer from diabetes. Approximately 10% of these are Type I patients, who are insulin dependent and the remaining are Type II, non-insulin dependent patients.

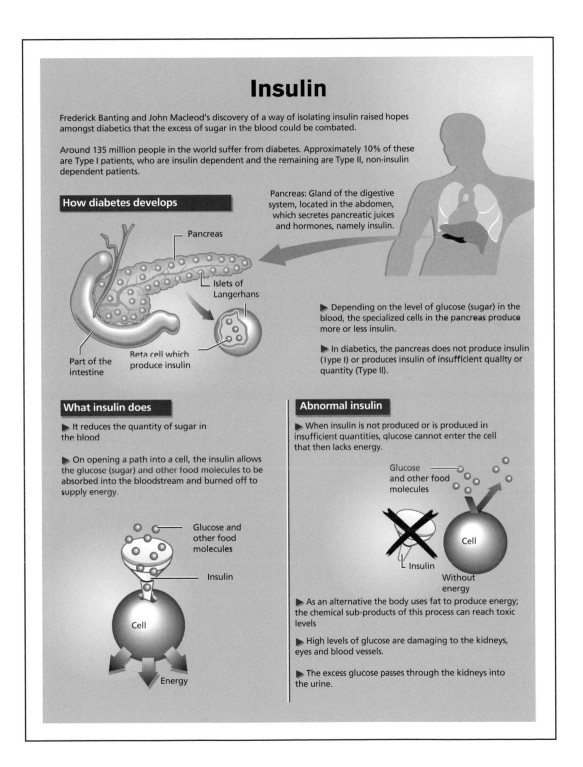

How diabetes develops

Pancreas: Gland of the digestive system, located in the abdomen, which secretes pancreatic juices and hormones, namely insulin.

Pancreas

Islets of Langerhans

Part of the intestine

Beta cell which produce insulin

► Depending on the level of glucose (sugar) in the blood, the specialized cells in the pancreas produce more or less insulin.

► In diabetics, the pancreas does not produce insulin (Type I) or produces insulin of insufficient quality or quantity (Type II).

What insulin does

► It reduces the quantity of sugar in the blood

► On opening a path into a cell, the insulin allows the glucose (sugar) and other food molecules to be absorbed into the bloodstream and burned off to supply energy.

Glucose and other food molecules

Insulin

Cell

Energy

Abnormal insulin

► When insulin is not produced or is produced in insufficient quantities, glucose cannot enter the cell that then lacks energy.

Glucose and other food molecules

Cell

Insulin

Without energy

► As an alternative the body uses fat to produce energy; the chemical sub-products of this process can reach toxic levels

► High levels of glucose are damaging to the kidneys, eyes and blood vessels.

► The excess glucose passes through the kidneys into the urine.

Gustav Hertz

For their discovery of the laws governing the impact of an electron upon an atom.

Gustav Ludwig Hertz was not the first member of his family to distinguish himself in the field of physics. In the year he was born, his uncle Heinrich discovered the photoelectric effect and in 1888 demonstrated the existence of electromagnetic waves. Conducting experiments of great importance to radio technology, Heinrich Hertz gave his name to a unit of frequency.

The son of a lawyer, Gustav was born in Hamburg on the July 22, 1887. He began his academic studies at the University of Göttingen at the age of 19 and continued them at the universities of Berlin and Munich. He graduated in 1911, and two years later he was a research assistant at the Physics Institute of the University of Berlin.

In 1914 Hertz was mobilized and served in the trenches of World War I, where he was seriously wounded the following year. He returned to Berlin in 1917 as a teacher, and between 1920 and 1925 he worked in the physics laboratory of the Phillips incandescent lamp factory in Eindhoven.

In 1935 he was made head of the research laboratory at Siemens after resigning from his position as director of the Physics Institute of the Charlottenburg Technological University. He had held the position since 1928 and resigned for political reasons. However, he developed a method to separate neon isotopes, among other discoveries, while at the institute.

Gustav Hertz's first professional experiments, conducted in 1913, were on the impact of accelerated electrons against the atoms of rarefied gases. Before being mobilized for the war, he dedicated much time and patience to the study of the ionization potential of various gases. The results of his research corresponded with Niels Bohr's theory on atomic structure, which, in turn, applied the quantum theory drawn up by Max Planck — these three Nobel recipients provided the foundation for modern physics.

After World War II Hertz led a research laboratory in the Soviet Union. Then in 1954 he was invited to serve as the director of the Physics Institute of Karl Marx University in Leipzig, East Germany. In 1961 he retired and moved back to Berlin. Throughout his life, he published numerous studies on the quantitative exchange of energy between electrons and atoms, the measurement of ionization potential and the separation of isotopes.

Besides receiving the 1925 Nobel Prize in Physics, Gustav Hertz was recognized with honorary doctorates from universities and was a recipient of the Max Planck Medal of the German Physical Society. From his marriage to Ellen Dihlmann came two sons, both physicists, to carry on his scientific legacy.

James Franck also received half of the prize.

George Bernard Shaw

For his work which is marked by both idealism and humanity, its stimulating satire often being infused with a singular poetic beauty.

George Bernard Shaw was born in Dublin. His father was an alcoholic. Shaw, influenced by his father's debauchery, was a vegetarian and shunned both alcohol and tobacco.

He went to live with an uncle who was a priest but refused to go to school, instead beginning to work as a junior clerk at the age of 15. In 1876 he determined to pursue a career as a writer and moved to London.

His first years in the British capital, however, were frustrating, since publishers kept rejecting his novels. After having some work printed in newspapers, Shaw's career expanded between 1895 and 1898, when Frank Harris recruited him to the *Saturday Review*, where he wrote theater reviews.

He was known for his strong attacks on the hypocrisy of the Victorian era, seen in such works as *Widower's Houses* and *Mrs. Warren's Profession*. Shaw's rationalism, allied with his complete rejection of the conventional, changed the stage into a forum for ideas.

Caesar and Cleopatra (1901), a story full of allusion to modern living, and *Androcles and the Lion* (1912), in which Shaw makes inferences about the Christian era, are two of his most significant plays. The comedy *Pygmalion*, performed in 1913, was his most popular and humorous work. In what is considered his masterpiece, *Saint Joan* (1923), the Irish playwright rewrote the story of the French heroine Joan of Arc who had been made a saint just four years before the play's publication. In it, he did not portray Joan as a gallant martyr but as a stubborn young woman whose flaws bring about her downfall.

Away from the stage Shaw supported socialism and became a member of the Fabian Society, for which he wrote many pamphlets and used his fame to further its causes. Many of his plays conveyed his philosophical and social ideas, particularly the freedom of spirit he wanted his audience to have in the face of the conformism demanded by conservative society. Shaw also defended the rights of women, the abolition of private property, income equality, reform of the voting system and simplified spelling.

Bernard Shaw was awarded the Nobel Prize for Literature in 1925, and although he accepted the honor, he refused the money accompanying the prize. His complete works include over 50 plays, which he continued to write into his 90s. Shaw saw several of these transformed into movies during his life, and others were produced after his death, including *My Fair Lady* (1964), based on *Pygmalion*. The popularity of his dramatic works remains strong to this day, and dozens of festivals and societies completely dedicated to performing his works exist.

On November 2, 1950, George Bernard Shaw died in Ayot St. Lawrence, Hertfordshire, England, at the age of 94.

Austen Chamberlain

For his participation in the development of Locarno Pact of 1925.

Austen Chamberlain came from one of the most eminent families in Great Britain; his father, Joseph Chamberlain, was the great statesman known as "the empire builder," and his half-brother, Neville Chamberlain, would go on to become the British prime minister between 1937 and 1940. Austen Chamberlain has gone down in history as one of the architects of the Locarno Pact (1925), in which Germany, France, Belgium, Great Britain and Italy agreed to go to war only as a means of defense.

After completing his university studies at Cambridge, Chamberlain spent nine months in Paris, where he attended the School of Political Sciences, followed by a year in Berlin, Germany. When he returned to his native Birmingham, England, in 1887, he became his father's personal secretary. At the age of 29 he was elected to the House of Commons as the Member of Parliament for East Worcestershire and, when his father died in 1914, he became the Member of Parliament for West Birmingham and held this seat until his own death.

Chamberlain's long political career can be divided into two stages. Between 1892 and 1922 he concentrated on home affairs, and he had a distinguished record on home affairs as Chancellor of the Exchequer in the postwar years (1919–1921). From 1922 on his main concern was international issues, for which he became better known.

In 1921, after Andrew Bonar Law retired, Chamberlain led the Conservative Party for 18 months. He lost this position when he sided with Lloyd George, then the leader of a coalition government, and his party overruled him. Bonar Law became Prime Minister in 1922, who was succeeded by Stanley Baldwin, who made Chamberlain Secretary of State for Foreign Affairs. He immediately rose to prominence when, speaking at the League of Nations, he rejected a protocol that gave the league authority over other states in times of crisis.

This rejection paved the way for Locarno. Supported by his French and German counterparts, Aristide Briand and Gustav Stresemann, Chamberlain meticulously prepared all eight Locarno Accords. As well as the Locarno Pact, individual treaties were signed between Germany and its wartime enemies, guaranteeing truces with France, Poland and Czechoslovakia; a collective document recommending Germany's entry into the League of Nations was also created.

The triumph of Locarno, for which he had worked so diligently, earned Chamberlain the title of Knight of the Garter in 1924, and a year later he was awarded the Nobel Peace Prize. Sir Austen Chamberlain died of apoplexy on March 17, 1937.

Charles Gates Dawes also received half of the prize.

1925 Peace

Aristide Briand

(1862–1932)

[For] actions which led to the Locarno Treaties of 1925.

Aristide Briand, born in Brittany, was a great diplomat who lived his life striving to put an end to all types of war. The son of a prosperous innkeeper, he first attended school in Nantes, France. There he was befriended by Jules Verne, who was then taking the initial steps in his brilliant career as a novelist. In one of his works, Verne writes of a 13-year-old boy named Briant who was audacious, a good companion and somewhat untidy: "Intelligent but so unwilling to waste good time studying that he was usually in the last quarter of his form. Occasionally he would spurt into a period of concentrated work, and then his quick understanding and remarkable memory helped him outstrip the rest." Throughout his life, Briand always read little and listened a lot. He never prepared a speech but was hailed as the best French orator of his generation.

Despite establishing a law practice, journalism was his great passion, and he preferred to write for newspapers like *La Peuple*, *La Lanterne* and *La Petite République*. He also collaborated with Jean Jaurès in founding *L'Humanité*. In 1894 Briand became leader of the French Socialist Party, but it was only in 1902, when he was elected a deputy, that politics became the center of his life. At the beginning of his public career he became the most visible member of the commission to promote the separation of church and state. He became premier of France for the first time in 1909, and his popularity was enormous.

Although opposed to armed conflicts, he nevertheless ended up leading his country for 18 months during World War I, when he managed, despite stiff opposition, to draw up a plan to attack Turkey, Bulgaria and Austria through Greece. He strengthened France's position and helped find a new ally in Italy. Briand returned to politics in 1925, when Painlevé made him Minister of Foreign Affairs. Five and a half years of diplomatic success followed, which started with the Locarno Pact, the result of collaboration with his German and British counterparts, Gustav Stresemann and Austen Chamberlain.

Using the Locarno model, Briand turned to the United States, proposing that this country and France renounce war as an instrument of national politics. Frank Kellogg, the American Secretary of State, preferred the treaty to be signed multilaterally, rather than bilaterally and, as a result, 15 countries signed the Paris Pact (or Kellogg-Briand Pact), renouncing war in 1928.

In 1932 Briand died unexpectedly and was buried in Cocherel.

Gustav Stresemann also received half of the prize.

Arthur Compton

For his discovery of the effect named after him.

Although he was the son of a philosophy professor, Arthur Holly Compton followed in the steps of his older brother and concentrated on physics. In his long career he would be recognized for his work on the behavior of X-rays and atomic energy.

Compton was born in Ohio on September 10, 1892. He obtained a bachelor's degree in sciences at Wooster University, where his father was dean, before earning his doctorate from Princeton in 1916. Four years later he headed the department of physics at Washington University, Saint Louis, and later lectured at the University of Chicago.

In 1941 Compton was appointed chairman of the National Academy of Sciences, which studied the military potential of atomic weapons. His research in this field contributed to the decision to build the first uranium reactors, which were responsible for producing the plutonium used in the nuclear bomb dropped over Nagasaki, Japan, on August 9, 1945. Compton outlined his role in convincing the American administration to use nuclear weapons in his book *Atomic Quest — A Personal Narrative* published in 1956.

Compton also presided over the American Physical Society in 1934, the American Association of Scientific Workers from 1939 to 1940 and the American Association for the Advancement of Science in 1942. For the next three years he was the director of the Metallurgy Laboratory of the University of Chicago, which developed the first self-sustainable atomic chain reaction and paved the way for the controlled release of nuclear energy.

He received the 1927 Nobel Prize in Physics for his discovery of what was named the Compton Effect, as well as many other honors and distinctions throughout his life, including the Rumford Gold Medal from the American Academy of Arts and Sciences in 1926, the Gold Medal from the Radiological Society of North America in 1928, and the Hughes Medal from the Royal Society and the Franklin Medal from the Franklin Institute in 1940.

Arthur Compton was married to Betty Charity McCloskey, and the couple had two sons. Compton died in Berkeley, California, on March 15, 1962.

Charles Thomson Rees Wilson also received half of the prize.

Charles Thomson Rees Wilson

For his method of making the paths of electrically charged particles visible by condensation of vapor.

The man known as Scot, or C.T.R., Wilson was once credited as inventing "the most important and original instrument in scientific history." This device, dating from 1912 and named after its creator, verified the ionization produced by charged particles, which in a supersaturated gas caused the formation of reappearing visible drops.

The proof of the value of this cloud chamber was seen in the following years as, around the world, physicists and scientists in other fields continued to credit the invention as aiding in their own discoveries. The Nobel Foundation awarded Wilson the 1927 Nobel Prize in Physics jointly with Arthur Holly Compton. Although Wilson had to wait 15 years to be acknowledged, he recognized the need for a deeper understanding of atomic structure before his creation could be truly appreciated.

Wilson was born in Glencorse, near Edinburgh, Scotland. Upon his father's death the family moved to Manchester; Wilson was just four years old at the time. In this new city, Scot attended a private school before later transferring to Owen College (now the University of Manchester). There he developed a love of medicine and determined to become a doctor, dedicating himself to biology. He was granted a scholarship in 1888 to Sidney Sussex College, Cambridge, but it was a physics degree that he obtained in 1892.

Wilson stayed for many years at the Cavendish Laboratory, where he was responsible for advanced teaching of experimental physics. At the same time he undertook studies of atmospheric electricity and continued his observations at the Solar Physics Observatory, where he started working in 1913. He also contributed to the revolutionary work of Compton's recoil electron, Anderson's positron, Blackett and Occhialini's visual demonstration of pair creation and annihilation of electrons and positrons, and Cockcroft and Walton's transmutation of atomic nuclei.

After retiring Wilson moved to Edinburgh and later, at 80 years old, to the town of Carlops. Even in this more secluded location, he maintained an active social life with his friends and colleagues. In these later years he also dedicated himself to finishing a long-promised manuscript on the theory of lightening electricity, which was published in 1956. "C.T.R.," as he was intimately known, died in Carlops in 1959, next to his wife, Jessie Fraser, whom he married in 1908.

Arthur Holly Compton also received half of the prize.

Henri Bergson

In recognition of his rich and vitalizing ideas and the brilliant skill with which they have been presented.

A French philosopher who in his youth was influenced by the theories of Spencer, Mill and Darwin (although he later came to criticize their rationalist systems), Henri Bergson was the founder of the so-called Philosophy of Life, based on intuition. He showed himself to be equally capable in the field of literature.

Henri Bergson's father, a talented musician, was from a Polish Jewish family on his father's side, and his mother, also Jewish, was Anglo-Irish.

His upbringing and the values instilled in him were, however, typically French, and the majority of his life was spent in and around Paris.

After attending the Lycée Condorcet, where he demonstrated a talent for both the sciences and humanities, Bergson studied philosophy at the École Normale Supérieure between 1878 and 1881, an institution dedicated to training university professors. He taught in various schools outside of Paris, first in Angers from 1881 to 1883 and then in Clermont-Ferrand during the next five years. He was also a teacher at the École Normale Supérieure and, between 1900 and 1921, held the chair of philosophy at the Collège de France.

In his book *Essai sur les donnés immédiates de la conscience (Time and Free Will)*, published in 1889, Henri Bergson interprets the existence of the consciousness on two levels: the first to be reached through deep introspection and the second an outward projection of the first. The method of intuitive introspection was later developed in 1903 with his work *Introduction à la métaphysique (Introduction to Metaphysics)*.

Matière et mémoire (Matter and Memory), published in 1896, was the result of five years of studying anything that had been published on memory and the psychological phenomena called aphasia. In this work Bergson returns to the theme of consciousness and concentrates on the relationship between mind and body. He concluded that the one was independent of the other. This work made him one of the most popular and influential writers of the period. *L'Évolution créatrice (Creative Evolution)*, published in 1907, is considered one of his most notable works and showed the influence of biology on his thought.

In 1891 Bergson married Louise Neuburger, cousin of the French novelist Marcel Proust, and the couple had a daughter. Despite his incredible intellectual energy, Bergson lived the quiet life of a French professor. He died in 1941.

Adolf Windaus

For the services rendered through his research into the constitution of sterols and their connection with vitamins.

Born on Christmas Day into a family of Berlin artisans involved in the drapery business, as a student Adolf Otto Reinhold Windaus was initially passionate about literature but was destined to make his name in chemistry. He was fortunate enough to study at the famous Französisches Gymnasium in Berlin, Germany, but upon entering university his attraction to the written word gave way to medicine and the sciences.

While still a medical student he was fascinated by a series of conferences given by Emil Fischer, who won the 1902 Nobel Prize in Chemistry, and decided to expand his studies to that field while continuing to pursue his plan of becoming a doctor. He graduated in 1900 from the University of Freiburg and successfully defended his thesis on cardiac poisons extracted from digitalis.

On his return to Berlin, Windaus started working with Fischer, who had first inspired him. It was not long, however, before he returned to Freiburg and, following a suggestion by his chemistry professor, started research into cholesterol because very little was known about the structure of cholesterol at the time. Windaus correctly believed that sterols, which are found in all cells, were the original substance of other groups of natural substances and, with this perspective, he developed his research.

In 1919, Windaus managed to transform cholesterol into a matter that had previously been isolated in the bile acids by Heinrich Wieland, a friend of his who won the 1927 Nobel Prize in Chemistry. This allowed him to demonstrate that the bile acids are closely related to sterols. In research carried out in conjunction with Knoop, he was able to synthesize histamine, a hormone of great physiological and pharmaceutical importance.

Windaus's work took him to the United States and, on an invitation from Alfred Hess, he joined a team studying the antirachitic vitamin D. His interests also allowed him to demonstrate the structure of vitamin B1. Among other studies, he investigated the possibility of using chemotherapy in the treatment of cancer.

Besides the 1928 Nobel Prize in Chemistry, which was awarded to Windaus in recognition of his work on the constitution of sterols and their relation to vitamins, he received many other prizes and honors. He was also a highly respected academic, helping students who would also make their mark on history, including Adolf Butenandt, who won the 1939 Nobel Prize in Chemistry. Windaus died at the age of 82 in Göttingen, Germany.

Thomas Mann

Principally for his great novel, Buddenbrooks, which has won steadily increased recognition as one of the classic works of contemporary literature.

A German forced to write in exile, Thomas Mann was a fervent opponent of the Nazi regime. He received American citizenship and only visited his homeland after World War II, preferring to base himself in Switzerland until the end of his days. He was born in Lübeck and was the second son of a respected merchant and senator of the city, Johann Heirich Mann. His mother, Julia da Silva Bruhns, was born in Rio de Janeiro and was taken to Germany when she was seven years old.

Mann described himself as a young man with an innate resistance to orders of any kind. As a result of this temperament he hated school. He said that his "official" instruction only gave him rudimentary knowledge, little more than a few grammatical rules that were later useful in learning foreign languages.

Thomas was 15 when his father died, a victim of septicemia, but the family grain firm provided a period of prosperous living for the Mann. His mother then went to live in Munich with the younger children. Mann followed her after finishing school poorly and beginning to work at an insurance company. He then prepared himself for a career in journalism by studying history, economics, art and literature. He lived in Rome for a year with his older brother Heinrich and shortly afterward, in 1898, he published his first collection of short stories, *Der Kleine Herr Friedmann (Little Herr Friedmann)* and started writing the novel *Buddenbrooks* (1901). In 1913 he published *Der Tod in Venedig (Death in Venice)*.

Mann moved to Switzerland in 1933, shortly after the Nazis had come to power in Germany and started a campaign against him. He was formally expatriated in 1936, and a year later the University of Bonn withdrew his honorary doctorate (later restored in 1946), an event that led him to launch a counteroffensive, describing his condition as a writer in exile.

Mann, who received the 1929 Nobel Prize in Literature, had warned of the rise of fascism during the Weimar Republic and continued to fight against it in pamphlets and speeches throughout the Nazi regime and World War II.

He became an American citizen in 1940 and lived in Santa Monica, California, from 1941 to 1953, frequently traveling to Europe after the war. In 1949 Mann was decorated with the Goethe Prizes of Weimar (East Germany) and Frankfurt (West Germany). When he left America for good, however, he chose to live near Zurich in Switzerland, where he died in 1955.

Frank Kellogg

*For his efforts in concluding the Pact of Paris
(Kellogg-Briand Pact) in 1928.*

Frank Billings Kellogg played a central role in the preparation of the Pact of
Paris (or Kellogg-Briand Pact), in which 15 nations agreed to banish war
for good, and was appropriately recognized for his work toward this most
important of all goals.

Kellogg was born in Potsdam, New York, but his family was caught
up in the great pioneering spirit that swept the western United States at
the end of the Civil War, and they established a wheat farm in Minnesota.
Frank did not have a regular education during these early years and, after
brief periods at schools in New York and Minnesota, he obtained a position at a lawyers'
office in Rochester, Minnesota. He was mainly self-taught, not just in matters of law, but also
in history, Latin and German — even the books he used were often lent to him by others.

He became an attorney first in Rochester and then Olmsted County. Frank Kellogg joined
a law firm where he stayed for the next 20 years. He amassed a considerable fortune in this
time, serving clients that included owners of Minnesota railroad companies, iron mines
and foundries.

Kellogg made friends with figures of high finance, including Andrew Carnegie, John D.
Rockefeller and James Hill. He managed to maintain these friendships without compromis-
ing his strong principles, which won him fame prosecuted monopolies as a special attorney
of the United States government at the request of President Theodore Roosevelt. One of these
antitrust campaigns saw him up against Rockefeller and the Standard Oil Company. It was
one of the most dramatic legal battles before World War I and in the following year, 1912,
Kellogg was nominated president of the American Bar Association.

A Republican, he was elected a senator in 1916. His difficulty in capturing the attention
of the electorate, however, meant that he lost his second election in 1922. It was then, after
an invitation from President Harding, that his diplomatic life began, when he participated
in the fifth Pan-American Conference in Chile. In 1923 President Coolidge nominated Kellogg
as ambassador to London, England. Two years later, he succeeded Charles Evans Hughes as
the American secretary of state.

Kellogg's most important achievement, which earned him the 1929 Nobel Peace Prize,
was to broker a unilateral pact in which the signators renounced war as an instrument of
national policy, thus improving the proposal of his French counterpart, Aristide Briand, who
merely wanted an accord of perpetual friendship between France and the United States. Until
his death on the eve of his 81st birthday, Kellogg never lost faith in the accord signed in Paris.

Nobel Laureates

1920-1929

1920

Nobel Prize in Physics

Charles Édouard Guillaume
Born February 15, 1861, in Fleurier, Switzerland, and died June 13, 1938, in Sèvres, France.
In recognition of the service he has rendered to precision measurements in Physics by his discovery of anomalies in nickel steel alloys.

Nobel Prize in Chemistry

Walther Hermann Nernst
Born June 25, 1864, in Briesen, Germany, and died November 18, 1941, in Muskau.
In recognition of his work in thermochemistry.

Nobel Prize in Physiology or Medicine

Schack August Steenberg Krogh
Born November 15, 1874, in Grenaa, Denmark, and died September 13, 1949, in Copenhagen.
For his discovery of the capillary motor regulating mechanism.

Nobel Prize in Literature

Knut Hamsun, pseudonym of Knut Pederson
Born August 4, 1859, in Gundrandsdalen, Norway, and died February 19, 1952, in Grimstad.
For his monumental work, Growth of the Soil.

Nobel Peace Prize

Léon Victor Auguste Bourgeois
Born May 21, 1851, in Paris, France, and died September 29, 1925, in Château d'Orger.
Mentor of the League of Nations, he drew up the original document which described the organization.

1921

Nobel Prize in Physics

Albert Einstein
Born March 14, 1879, in Ulm, Germany, and died April 18, 1955, in Princeton, New Jersey.
For his services to Theoretical Physics, and especially for his discovery of the law of the photoelectric effect.

Nobel Prize in Chemistry

Frederick Soddy
Born September 2, 1877, in Eastbourne, England, and died September 22, 1956, in Brighton.
For his contributions to our knowledge of the chemistry of radioactive substances, and his investigations into the origin and nature of isotopes.

Nobel Prize in Physiology or Medicine

Not awarded.

Nobel Prize in Literature

Anatole France, pseudonym of Jacques Anatole Thibault
Born April 16, 1844, in Paris, France, and died October 12, 1924, in Saint-Cyr-sur-Loire.
In recognition of his brilliant literary achievements, characterized as they are by a nobility of style, a profound human sympathy, grace, and true Gallic temperament.

Nobel Peace Prize

Karl Hjalmar Branting
Born November 23, 1860, in Stockholm, Sweden, and died February 24, 1925, in Stockholm.
For his role in constitutional pacifism and the activities he was involved in.
&
Christian Lous Lange
Born September 17, 1869, in Stavanger, Norway, and died December 11, 1938, in Oslo.
Dedication to international affairs and peace.

1922

Nobel Prize in Physics
Niels Henrik David Bohr
Born October 7, 1885, in Copenhagen, Denmark, and died November 18, 1962, in Copenhagen.
For his services in the investigation of the structure of atoms and of the radiation emanating from them.

Nobel Prize in Chemistry
Francis William Aston
Born September 1, 1877, in Harborne, England, and died November 20, 1945, in Cambridge.
For his discovery, by means of his mass spectrograph, of isotopes, in a large number of non-radioactive elements, and for his enunciation of the whole-number rule.

Nobel Prize in Physiology or Medicine
Archibald Vivian Hill
Born September 26, 1886, in Bristol, England, and died June 3, 1977, in Cambridge.
For his discovery relating to the production of heat in the muscle.
&
Otto Fritz Meyerhof
Born April 12, 1884, in Hanover, Germany, and died October 6, 1951, in Philadelphia, Pennsylvania.
For his discovery of the fixed relationship between the consumption of oxygen and the metabolism of lactic acid in the muscle.

Nobel Prize in Literature
Jacinto Benavente
Born August 12, 1866, in Madrid, Spain, and died July 14, 1954, in Madrid.
For the happy manner in which he has continued the illustrious traditions of the Spanish drama.

Nobel Peace Prize
Fridtjof Nansen
Born October 10, 1861, in Store Froen, Norway, and died May 13, 1930, in Lysaker.
For activities in favor of peace and his role in the cause of refugees from war.

1923

Nobel Prize in Physics
Robert Andrews Millikan
Born March 22, 1868, in Morrison, Illinois, United States, and died December 19, 1953, in San Marino, California.
For his work on the elementary charge of electricity and on the photoelectric effect.

Nobel Prize in Chemistry
Fritz Pregl
Born September 3, 1869, in Laibach, Austria, and died December 13, 1930, in Graz.
For his invention of the method of micro-analysis of organic substances.

Nobel Prize in Physiology or Medicine
Frederick Grant Banting
Born November 4, 1891, in Alliston, Ontario, Canada, and died February 21, 1941, in a plane crash over Newfoundland.
&
John James Richard Macleod
Born September 6, 1876, in Cluny, Scotland, and died March 16, 1935, in Aberdeen.
For the discovery of insulin.

Nobel Prize in Literature
William Butler Yeats
Born June 13, 1865, in Dublin, Ireland, and died January 28, 1939, in Roquebrune-Cap-Martin, France.
For his always inspired poetry, which in a highly artistic form gives expression to the spirit of a whole nation.

Nobel Peace Prize
Not awarded.

1924

Nobel Prize in Physics
Karl Manne Georg Siegbahn
Born December 3, 1886, in Örebro, Sweden, and died September 26, 1978, in Stockholm.
For his discoveries and research in the field of X-ray spectroscopy.

Nobel Prize in Chemistry
Not awarded.

Nobel Prize in Physiology or Medicine
Willem Einthoven
Born May 21, 1860, in Semarang, Dutch East Indies
(now Indonesia), and died September 28, 1927,
in Leiden.
For his discovery of the mechanism of the
electrocardiogram.

Nobel Prize in Literature
Wladyslaw Stanislaw Reymont
Born May 7, 1867, in Kobielo Wielkie, Poland, and died
December 5, 1925, in Warsaw.
For his great national epic, The Peasants.

Nobel Peace Prize
Not awarded.

1925

Nobel Prize in Physics
James Franck
Born August 26, 1882, in Hamburg, Germany, and died
May 21, 1964, in Göttingen.
&
Gustav Ludvig Hertz
Born July 22, 1887, in Hamburg, Germany, and died
October 30, 1975, in Berlin.
For their discovery of the laws governing the impact of
an electron upon an atom.

Nobel Prize in Chemistry
Richard Adolf Zsigmondy
Born April 1, 1865, in Vienna, Austria, and died
September 24, 1929, in Göttingen, Germany.
For his demonstration of the heterogeneous nature of
colloid solutions and for the methods he used, which
have since become fundamental in modern colloid
chemistry.

Nobel Prize in Physiology or Medicine
Not awarded.

Nobel Prize in Literature
George Bernard Shaw
Born July 26, 1856, in Dublin, Ireland, and died

November 2, 1950, in Ayot St. Lawrence, England.
For his work which is marked by both idealism and
humanity, its stimulating satire often being infused with
a singular poetic beauty.

Nobel Peace Prize
Joseph Austen Chamberlain
Born October 16, 1863, in Birmingham, England, and
died March 17, 1937, in London.
For his participation in the development of Locarno Trea-
ties of 1925.
&
Charles Gates Dawes
Born August 27, 1865, in Marietta, Ohio, United States,
and died April 23, 1951, in Evanston, Illinois.
He drew up the Dawes Plan.

1926

Nobel Prize in Physics
Jean Baptiste Perrin
Born September 30, 1870, in Lille, France, and died
April 17, 1942, in New York, New York, United States.
For his work on the discontinuous structure of matter,
and especially for his discovery of sedimentation
equilibrium.

Nobel Prize in Chemistry
Theodor Svedberg
Born August 30, 1884, in Fleräng, Sweden, and died
February 25, 1971, in Örebro.
For his work on disperse systems.

Nobel Prize in Physiology or Medicine
Johannes Andreas Fibiger
Born April 23, 1867, in Silkeborg, Denmark, and died
January 30, 1928, in Copenhagen.
For his discovery of the Spiroptera carcinoma.

Nobel Prize in Literature
Grazia Deledda
Born September 27, 1871, in Nuoro, Italy, and died
August 15, 1936, in Rome.
For her idealistically inspired writings which with plastic
clarity picture the life on her native island and with depth
and sympathy deal with human problems in general.

Aristide Briand
Born March 28, 1862, in Nantes, France, and died
March 7, 1932, in Paris.
[For] actions which led to the Locarno Treaties of 1925.
&
Gustav Stresemann
Born May 10, 1878, in Berlin, Germany, and died
October 3, 1929, in Berlin.
Successful efforts in the name of peace, through his
involvement in post-war German politics.

1927

Nobel Prize in Physics
Arthur Holly Compton
Born September 10, 1892, in Wooster, Ohio, United
States, and died March 15, 1962, in Berkeley, California.
For his discovery of the effect named after him.
&
Charles Thomson Rees Wilson
Born February 14, 1869, in Glencorse, Scotland, and
died November 15, 1959, in Carlops.
For his method of making the paths of electrically
charged particles visible by condensation of vapor.

Nobel Prize in Chemistry
Heinrich Wieland
Born June 4, 1877, in Pforzheim, Germany, and died
August 5, 1957, in Starnberg.
For his investigations of the constitution of the bile acids
and related substances.

Nobel Prize in Physiology or Medicine
Julius Wagner-Jauregg
Born March 7, 1857, in Wels, Austria, and died
September 27, 1940, in Vienna.
For his discovery of the therapeutic value of malaria
inoculation in the treatment of dementia paralytica.

Nobel Prize in Literature
Henri Bergson
Born October 18, 1859, in Paris, France, and died
January 4, 1941, in Paris.
In recognition of his rich and vitalizing ideas and the bril-
liant skill with which they have been presented.

Nobel Peace Prize
Ferdinand Buisson
Born December 20, 1841, in Paris, France, and died
February 16, 1932, in Thieuloy-Saint-Antoine.
For his defense of the principle that education of the
people should be the basis for work organized for peace.
Arduous work for the reconciliation of France and
Germany.
&
Ludwig Quidde
Born March 23, 1858, in Bremen, Germany, and died
March 4, 1941, in Geneva, Switzerland.
Significant services in the course of peace and his
involvement in pacifist movements.

1928

Nobel Prize in Physics
Owen Willans Richardson
Born April 26, 1879, in Dewsbury, England, and died
February 15, 1959, in Alton.
For his work on the thermionic phenomenon and
especially for the discovery of the law named after him.

Nobel Prize in Chemistry
Adolf Otto Reinhold Windaus
Born December 25, 1876, in Berlin, Germany, and died
June 9, 1959, in Göttingen.
For the services rendered through his research into the
constitution of the sterols and their connection with the
vitamins.

Nobel Prize in Physiology or Medicine
Charles Jules Henri Nicolle
Born September 21, 1866, in Rouen, France, and died
February 28, 1936, in Tunis, Tunisia.
For his work on typhus.

Nobel Prize in Literature
Sigrid Undset
Born May 20, 1882, in Kalundborg, Denmark, and died
June 10, 1949, in Lillehammer, Norway.
Principally for her powerful descriptions of Northern life
during the Middle Ages.

Nobel Peace Prize
Not awarded.

1929

Nobel Prize in Physics
Prince Louis-Victor Pierre Raymond de Broglie
Born August 15, 1892, in Dieppe, France, and died March 19, 1987, in Paris.
For his discovery of the wave nature of electrons.

Nobel Prize in Chemistry
Arthur Harden
Born October 12, 1865, in Manchester, England, and died June 17, 1940, in Bourne End.
&
Hans Karl August Simon von Euler-Chelpin
Born February 15, 1873, in Augsburg, Germany, and died November 6, 1964, in Stockholm, Sweden.
For their investigations on the fermentation of sugar and fermentative enzymes.

Nobel Prize in Physiology or Medicine
Christiaan Eijkman
Born August 11, 1858, in Nijkerk, Netherlands, and died November 5, 1930, in Utrecht.
For his discovery of the antineuritic vitamin.
&
Frederick Gowland Hopkins
Born June 20, 1861, in Eastbourne, England, and died May 16, 1947, in Cambridge.
For the discovery of the growth-stimulating vitamins.

Nobel Prize in Literature
Thomas Mann
Born June 6, 1875, in Lübeck, Germany, and died August 12, 1955, in Zurich, Switzerland.
Principally for his great novel, Buddenbrooks, which has won steadily increased recognition as one of the classic works of contemporary literature.

Nobel Peace Prize
Frank Billings Kellogg
Born December 22, 1856, in Potsdam, New York, and died December 21, 1937, in Saint Paul, Minnesota.
For his efforts in concluding the Paris Pact (Kellogg-Briand Pact), in 1928.

Selected Profiles of Nobel Laureates

1930–1939

(1866–1945)

Thomas Morgan

For his discoveries concerning the role played by the chromosome in heredity.

Born in Kentucky, the young Thomas Hunt Morgan was fascinated by natural history and began, at 10 years of age, to assemble bird, bird-egg and fossil collections. He graduated from the University of Kentucky in 1886 with a bachelor of science degree in zoology. He then undertook his postgraduate studies at Johns Hopkins University, where he studied morphology and physiology. Between 1888 and 1889 and from 1902 onward, he was a researcher for the United States Fish Commission in Woods Hole, Massachusetts.

He also made a journey to Europe in 1890 and worked at the Zoological Station in Naples, Italy, among other locations. There he met Hans Driesch, a German biologist and philosopher who described the creation of sea urchin larvae through the development of the embryo. Driesch, with whom he would later collaborate, had an enormous influence on Morgan and his decision to dedicate himself to experimental embryology.

For 24 years Thomas Morgan was a professor of experimental zoology at Columbia University, New York, and then he lectured in biology while he was the head of the G. Kerckhoff Laboratories at the California Institute of Technology, Pasadena. He remained connected with this institution until 1945, after which he had a private laboratory in Corona del Mar, California. His name has always been connected to research with fruit flies, and biology students around the world continue to replicate his experiments.

As a student himself Morgan was a critical and independent thinker. His first published works contested the heredity laws of the Austrian botanist Gregor Johann Mendel, known as the father of genetics, and he was equally skeptical of the concept of natural selection. In tandem with his work in the field of genetics, Thomas Morgan contributed to experimental embryology and regeneration, areas to which he dedicated the last years of his career.

Morgan was married to Lilian Vaughan Sampson in 1904, and she later became his research assistant. Among his collaborators at Columbia University was Hermann Joseph Muller, the North American geneticist who showed that X-rays greatly accelerated the mutation process; this discovery that earned him the Nobel Prize in Physiology or Medicine in 1946.

Thomas Morgan wrote *Heredity and Sex* (1913), *Embryology and Genetics* (1934), *The Theory of the Gene* (1926) and various other books, which are all considered fundamental works in the field of genetics. He went on to win the Nobel Prize in Physiology or Medicine in 1933 and was honored by many other institutions. He died in 1945.

Harold Urey

For his discovery of heavy hydrogen.

The grandson of Indiana pioneers and the son of Samuel Clayton Urey, a protestant minister, Harold Clayton Urey began his career as a teacher in rural schools. After three years he entered the University of Montana, from which he graduated in 1917 with a bachelor's degree in zoology. For two years he worked as an industrial chemist, then he returned to Montana as a chemistry instructor. He later went to the University of California, where he worked under the guidance of Professor Gilbert Lewis and received his doctorate degree in chemistry in 1923.

After spending a year in Copenhagen, Denmark, at Niels Bohr's Institute for Theoretical Physics, Urey returned to the United States and began his academic career. He first taught at Johns Hopkins University then transferred to Columbia University, where he worked as an associate professor. In 1934, the year he won the Nobel Prize, he was made a full professor.

Urey's first research focused on the entropy of diatomic gases, absorption spectra and the structure of molecules. In 1931 he developed a method to concentrate the isotopes of heavy hydrogen through the fractional distillation of liquid hydrogen, which led to the discovery of deuterium. Later, in collaboration with Dr. E.W. Washburn, he developed the electrolytic method to separate hydrogen isotopes and meticulously investigated their properties. This discovery was followed by work on the separation of isotopes and, at the end of his career, he dedicated himself to chemical investigations into the origin of the planets.

Between 1940 and 1945 Urey was Director of War Research in the atomic bomb project at Columbia University, New York. At the end of World War II he transferred to the Institute for Nuclear Studies, Chicago and, in 1958, was appointed professor-at-large at the University of California.

Throughout his career Urey wrote numerous articles and books on his several scientific interests, including *Atoms, Molecules and Quanta* (1930) and *The Planets* (1952). He was internationally recognized and awarded the Willard Gibbs Medal from the American Chemical Society in 1934, the Davy Medal from the Royal Society in 1940, the Franklin Medal from the Franklin Institute in 1943 and the Medal for Merit in 1946, among many others.

Harold Urey married Frieda Daum in 1926, and the couple had three daughters and a son together. Away from his work, he was very concerned with international politics and made great efforts to find posts for refugee scientists during the war. He died at the age of 88.

Luigi Pirandello

For his bold and ingenious revival of dramatic and scenic art.

Contrary to the wishes of his father, who made his fortune in a sulfur mine in Sicily, Luigi Pirandello did not want to enter into business, preferring to spend his time in the academic and literary worlds. He went on to write novels, tales and plays, seen by many as precursors for the theater of the absurd. *Sei personaggi in cerca d'autore (Six Characters in Search of an Author)*, published in 1921, is one of his most acclaimed works, its title illustrating the innovation that Pirandello brought to modern drama.

Luigi Pirandello was born in Agrigento and began his studies in Palermo, the Sicilian capital. In 1887 he began his university studies in Rome but only stayed for a year because of a bitter quarrel with a professor of Latin. He then determined to move to Bonn, Germany, where he obtained his doctorate degree in philology after defending a thesis on his native dialect. In 1894 his father managed to convince him to marry his partner's daughter, Antonietta Portulano.

Pirandello's first significant works were short stories published in magazines with little financial return. In 1903, however, a landslide forced his father to close the mine in which he had invested his fortune, and Pirandello found himself suddenly impoverished. Around this time, and partly as a result of their disastrous financial situation, his wife began to have serious mental problems and was admitted to a mental institution in 1919.

This bitter experience definitively determined the theme of Pirandello's work, which was already making itself apparent in his short stories — the exploration of the enigma of the human personality and the ambiguity of truth and reality. The dramatist transferred to the stage the idea that a person has more than one personality, which depends on the way others see that person. Pirandello closely studied psychology and the works of the then-revolutionary Sigmund Freud, the founder of psychoanalysis.

With *Sei personaggi in cerca d'autore*, about six characters who appear on stage without their characters having being completed, and *Enrico IV (Henry IV)*, finished in 1922, he became one of the most influential dramatists of the 20th century, on a level with the Scandinavians Henrik Ibsen and August Strindberg. These plays were staged between 1925 and 1928 by the Teatro d'Arte di Roma, which Pirandello founded with the support of Benito Mussolini, but they were stopped and the company went bankrupt and dissolved in 1928. His relationship with the dictator is still hotly debated.

Pirandello won the 1934 Nobel Prize in Literature and was honored by other institutions, but he stipulated in his will that there should be no public ceremony after his death and that he only wanted "a cart, a horse and a driver." He died in Rome on December 10, 1936.

James Chadwick

For the discovery of the neutron.

Born in Cheshire, England, James Chadwick went on to revolutionize physics and influence the entire world with the application of his findings. Besides discovering the neutron, he worked with Ernest Rutherford, the father of nuclear physics and winner of the 1908 Nobel Prize in Chemistry, and he later participated in the building of the first atomic bomb.

Chadwick studied at Manchester University and Cambridge as well as at the Technische Hochschule in Berlin, under the guidance of Hans Geiger, the physicist who invented the Geiger-Müller counter used to demonstrate the presence and quantity of highly energized ionized particles. Chadwick then returned to Manchester to work with Rutherford on the chemistry of radioactive substances and the nucleus of the atom. By 1919 Rutherford had created the first artificial nuclear reaction and had been recognized by institutions around the world for his scientific efforts.

Although he collaborated with Rutherford at Manchester between 1911 and 1913, Chadwick's most important research was at the University of Cambridge's Cavendish Laboratory, from 1923 onward, where he eventually became assistant director of research. At this time Chadwick and Rutherford studied the transmutation of elements by bombarding them with alpha particles and researched the nature of atomic nuclei.

Chadwick stayed at Cambridge until 1935, when he won the Nobel Prize in Physics for the discovery of the neutron, and was nominated for the Lyon Jones Chair of Physics at the University of Liverpool. Between 1943 and 1946 he worked in the United States, serving as head of the British Mission attached to the Manhattan Project to develop the atomic bomb. Back in England, he left research in 1948, three years after being knighted. Sir James Chadwick was also a member of the United Kingdom Atomic Energy Authority between 1957 and 1962.

Throughout his life he received numerous awards and honorary doctorates, associating himself with various academies and institutions, both in Europe and the United States. Elected a member of the Royal Society in 1927, Chadwick published works on radioactivity and its related problems. Along with Rutherford and C.D. Ellis, he was the author of *Radiations from Radioactive Substances.*

In 1925 James Chadwick married Aileen Stewart-Brown from Liverpool, and the couple had twin daughters. They lived in Denbigh in the north of Wales, where Chadwick enjoyed his favorite hobbies of gardening and fishing.

Irène Joliot-Curie & Jean Frédéric Joliot

In recognition of their synthesis of new radioactive elements.

Irène Joliot-Curie, daughter of Marie and Pierre Curie, and her husband, Jean Frédéric Joliot, had remarkable scientific careers of their own. The two managed to synthesize new radioactive elements and, in 1934, produced a thesis summarizing their findings entitled *Artificial Production of Radioactive Elements*. This publication was followed by *Chemical Proof of the Transmutation of Elements*, a work that earned the couple the Nobel Prize in Chemistry a year later.

While Joliot-Curie was born into a world of science — her parents jointly won the 1903 Nobel Prize in Physics, and her mother won the 1911 prize for Chemistry — Joliot was the son of a merchant and maintained an attachment to the arts throughout his life. Nevertheless, he demonstrated his brilliance in the sciences and in 1925 became Marie Curie's assistant at the Radium Institute; it was here he met Marie's daughter, and the two were married a year later. The couple, both individually and in partnership, carried out important work in the field of natural and artificial radioactivity, transmutation of elements and nuclear physics.

After studying at the Faculty of Science in Paris, Irène served as a nurse radiographer during World War I. She was appointed a lecturer at her alma mater in Paris in 1932 and became a professor five years later. She was soon performing important research into the action of neutrons on heavy elements, which was a step toward the discovery of the fission of uranium. In 1946 she was made director of the Radium Institute, and two years later she participated in the building of the first French nuclear reactor. Irène's last efforts were devoted to planning a large nuclear physics center in Orsay. After her death, her husband saw the project through to completion.

Frédéric and Irène had very parallel careers. Nominated a professor at the Collège de France in 1937, Joliot left the Radium Institute and set up the first cyclotron in Western Europe at his new laboratory. Along with Hans von Halban, Lew Kowarski and Francis Perrin, he worked on successfully building a nuclear reactor using uranium and heavy water. They registered five patents for their revolutionary work. With the German advance on France in 1940, Joliot managed to send all the documentation and material related to his work to England, thus preventing it from falling into enemy hands. During the occupation he played an active role in the Resistance, was President of the National Front and founded the French Communist Party.

Before the war Frédéric Joliot had divided his attention between science and social problems, and he was active in institutions such as the League for the Rights of Man. Irène Joliot-Curie was also especially dedicated to the social and intellectual concerns, as well as the advance of women's rights, and she was involved in various aid organizations.

Nuclear fission

On observing the spontaneous disintegration of elements obtained by bombarding other elements with particles, the French couple Frederic Joliot-Curie and Irene Joliot-Curie developed new radioactive elements. These were experiments that led to artificial radiation.

Radioactivity proceeds directly after the disintegration of a stage, or indirectly through a series of disintegrations in which they transmute into another element. This process is named chain disintegration (nuclear fission). When this produces more neutrons, which in turn are absorbed by other nuclei that split, this leads to more neutrons and can cause a chain reaction.

CHAIN REACTION

1 A slow or thermal neutron combines with a U-235 nucleus, one of the first fission isotopes used in nuclear weapons and nuclear reactors.

2 In the combination unstable U-236 is formed. This disintegrates immediately to form two smaller atoms (like barium and krypton) with the release of three neutrons.

3 These neutrons disintegrate three more U-235 nuclei.

4 Nine more neutrons are released and so, successively, the chain reaction accelerates.

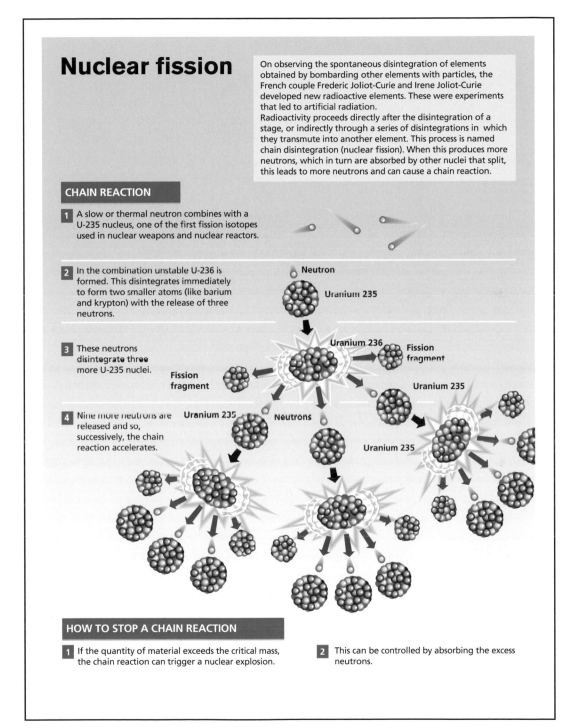

Neutron

Uranium 235

Uranium 236

Fission fragment

Fission fragment

Uranium 235

Uranium 235

Neutrons

Uranium 235

HOW TO STOP A CHAIN REACTION

1 If the quantity of material exceeds the critical mass, the chain reaction can trigger a nuclear explosion.

2 This can be controlled by absorbing the excess neutrons.

Peter Debye

For his contributions to our knowledge of molecular structure through his investigations on dipole moments and on the diffraction of X-rays and electrons in gases.

Petrus Josephus Wilhelmus Debije was born in Maastricht, Netherlands. His first degree, obtained in 1905, was in electrical technology and earned him a place as an assistant in technical mechanics at the RWTH Aachen University, in Aachen, Germany, where he stayed for two years. He then obtained a similar position in the department of theoretical physics at the University of Munich and received his doctorate degree in 1908.

In 1911 Debye moved to Switzerland, where he was offered the post of professor of theoretical physics at the University of Zurich. However he returned to the Netherlands the following year to head the department of theoretical physics at Utrecht University. This roving academic lifestyle was slowed the following year, when Debye was invited to run the theoretical department of the Physics Institute at the University of Göttingen, Germany. It did not take long before he became the director of the entire institute, and he gained fame with his conferences on experimental physics. In 1915 he had become the editor of the *Physikalische Zeitschrift*, a magazine devoted to physics, a position he held until 1940.

Debye returned to the University of Zurich in 1920 where, as well as being a professor of physics. In 1927 he once again moved to Germany, first to Leipzig and later, between 1934 and 1939, to Berlin, where he ran the Max Planck Institute while simultaneously working as a professor of physics at the University of Berlin. It was during this period, which marked the end of his European career, that Peter Debye was awarded the 1936 Nobel Prize in Chemistry for his research into dipole moments and the diffraction of X-rays and electrons in gases.

When World War II began he immigrated to the United States; awaiting him was the leadership of the department of chemistry at Cornell University. In 1946 he became an American citizen. He resigned from his position in 1952 and, already a distinguished professor, continued working as a much sought-after speaker at the great universities of the world.

Although extremely dedicated to physics and chemistry, and internationally recognized for his work, Peter Debye found time to share his life with Mathilde Alberer, with whom he had two children. He died in 1966.

The power of microscopes

A simple law limits the smallest object a microscope can detect - the length of the energy wave that passes through the microscope. Ordinary optical microscopes use visible light.

The electron microscope was a step forward in amplification power. Then came x-ray microscopes. One of the people that has contributed greatly to the advancement of this science was Peter Debye, who determined by x-ray diffraction the size of gas molecules.

Optical Microscope
- Developed in the 17th century:
- It uses lenses to diffract light onto an object.
- The image is magnified about a thousand times without losing clarity.

Wavelength of visible light:
Approximately a millionth of an inch.

Electron Microscope
- It was developed in Germany in the 1930s.
- Images are magnified by about a million times.
- It uses a beam of electrons in a vacuum.

Electron Microscope Exploration

1 Magnetic lenses and electron beams.

2 Electrons hit the sample, which is coated with vaporized metal.

3 Electronic detector captures 3-D images.

Wavelength of electrons:
Approximately 10 millionths of an inch.

X-ray Diffraction Microscope
- They were developed in the 1960s. Research into x-rays and light diffraction through gases carried out by Peter Debye contributed to this advance.
- It uses an x-ray beam diffracted by a crystal.
- Images are magnified by about 100 million times

Wavelength of x-rays:
Approximately a billionth of an inch.

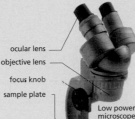

ocular lens
objective lens
focus knob
sample plate
Low power microscope

What can be observed by different microscopes:

Optical Microscope
- Bacteria
- Chromosomes
- Plant and animal cells

Electron Microscope
- Virus
- Cell components (nuclei, etc.)
- Position of genes on a chromosome

X-ray Microscope
- Position of atoms on large molecules such as DNA

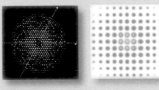

Head of domestic fly under magnification.

The image reveals the orientation of the atoms in the crystal.

Eugene O'Neill

For the power, honesty and deep-felt emotions of his dramatic works, which embody an original concept of tragedy.

The only playwright from the United States to be awarded the Nobel Prize in Literature, Eugene Gladstone O'Neill was a great force in the American theater of the 1920s, transforming it into a cultural movement on a par with the best literature, painting and music of the time. When his *Beyond the Horizon* was first performed, Broadway shows consisted mostly of weak melodramas and farces, with the exception of musicals and some quality plays imported from Europe. However, when O'Neill passed away in 1953, American theater had been transformed into a progressive, booming art form.

He was the son of James O'Neill, the romantic actor best known for his performance in *The Count of Monte Cristo*. He first went to Catholic schools then entered Princeton University in 1906. He was expelled the following year, however, and began wandering the world, seeking an education through life experience.

During this time O'Neill held various jobs, including gold prospecting in the rugged Honduras countryside. After a brief period on the stage, he was hospitalized for six months with tuberculosis, which was diagnosed at the end of 1912. Shortly before his illness he had visited the ports of Buenos Aires, Liverpool and New York, drowning himself in alcohol and suicidal thoughts. His illness made him rethink his lifestyle and so, in 1913, he determined to begin playwriting.

Although he criticized his father for the wandering life he had submitted his family to — which led his mother to drug addiction — O'Neill had the theater in his blood. He always had an intensely personal vision for his plays, which required constant rewrites until he was satisfied that the text expressed exactly what he wanted to say. This dedication and the powerful conveyance of his emotions earned him the 1936 Nobel Prize in Literature.

In 1956, the posthumous performance of *Long Day's Journey into Night*, written between 1939 and 1941, showed the world an agonizing autobiography, and it is considered one of O'Neill's most brilliant works. The action centers on four characters: a drug-addict mother, a father who is weak as both an actor and a husband, an older son who is a bitter alcoholic and a younger son who is suffering from tuberculosis, is disillusioned with his youth and has little chance of surviving physically or psychologically.

This tragic outlook on life was felt equally by his children. O'Neill's oldest son committed suicide at the age of 40, and the youngest became severely emotionally unstable. He severed relations with his 18-year-old daughter, Oona, who infuriated him by marrying Charlie Chaplin, who was the same age as O'Neill at the time.

Carlos Lamas

For his support of the South American Antiwar Pact, established in Latin America and submitted to the League of Nations.

Carlos Saavedra Lamas studied law at the University of Buenos Aires, receiving his doctorate in 1903, but it was in diplomacy that he left his mark. Born into Argentina's aristocracy, he married the daughter of a former head of state, which opened certain doors for him. When Agustin Justo became president in 1932, he called Lamas to be a part of his government. He held the position of minister of justice and education in 1915, then of foreign affairs between 1932 and 1938. The fruits of his appointment were soon apparent. Lamas insisted that his country rejoin the League of Nations after a 13-year absence, and from then on he represented Argentina at all meetings of the organization. His most important work was still to come, however.

He led the international mediation committee that arranged the 1935 armistice in the Chaco War. For three years this region shared by Argentina, Bolivia and Paraguay had been the scene of a bloody conflict — which arose over oil exploration and resulted in the loss of more than 80,000 lives. Lamas's efforts earned him the 1936 Nobel Peace Prize and two years later he once more played an important role in negotiations that resulted in an accord for permanent peace between the nations. He was also responsible for a nonaggression treaty signed by six South American countries in October 1933, which two months later was signed by all the nations at the Seventh Pan-American Conference held in Montevideo, Uruguay. The following year he presented the League of Nations with the South American Antiwar Pact, a document that had been signed by 11 countries. All of these efforts led to his election as president of the assembly of this international organization in 1936.

Carlos Lamas also dedicated many years of his life to teaching, and pioneered labor law legislation in Argentina. He founded the International Labor Organization (ILO) in 1919, and he was president of a conference held by the organization in Geneva in 1928. For many years he wrote the outlines of international laws in areas of political asylum, colonization, emigration and peace.

Carlos Lamas diligently worked to bring international prestige to Argentina and was widely recognized for his dedication to the task. He died in 1959 and will be remembered as a man who was demanding in his work, logical at the conference table, charming as a host and elegant in his wardrobe. He appreciated the arts, ran his own art gallery, was revered as a professor and was recognized by a dozen nations for his work toward peace.

Norman Haworth

For his investigations on carbohydrates and vitamin C.

It was after joining his father to learn the linoleum business and working with dyes that Walter Norman Haworth developed an interest in chemistry. He left school when he was 14, but this new world awoke in him an enormous thirst for knowledge. He found private tutors in Preston, England, to prepare him for university. The success of these private lessons allowed him to pass the entrance exam of University of Manchester, where he enrolled in chemistry under the guidance of W.H. Perkin II. He graduated with honors in 1906.

After working for three years in research, Haworth left Manchester with a scholarship for a place in the laboratory of Otto Wallach, the winner of the 1910 Nobel Prize in Chemistry. Here, in Göttingen, Germany, he obtained his doctorate degree in chemistry then returned to Manchester to finish another doctorate in the sciences the following year. He gained these qualifications in an incredibly short period of time, and he was praised for his swift comprehension and enthusiasm.

From there, Haworth's academic career moved to Imperial College, London, and the University of St. Andrews, Scotland, until he was invited, in 1920, to lecture in chemistry at Durham University. He became director of the department the following year. After five years the University of Birmingham invited him to be a professor of chemistry there, where he stayed until his retirement in 1948, serving as dean of the faculty of science for his last two years. During this time he had also helped manage important institutions, including the British Chemical Society and the Royal Society.

At the time chemists believed there was little left to discover about carbohydrates after the work of Emil Fischer, the 1902 Nobel laureate in chemistry. Haworth was one of those who showed there was still more to discover. In fact, at the University of Birmingham he developed areas of research that determined the structure of various elements, including maltose, cellobiose, lactose, melibiose and raffinose. As testament to this research, he wrote a series of scientific essays, which were collected in the book *Constitution of Sugars*, published in 1929. He then turned his attention to studying vitamin C and carbohydrates, research which brought him together with Paul Karrer, and earned them the 1937 Nobel Prize in Chemistry.

Once removed from his busy professional life, Haworth had more time for his wife and two sons. His death in 1950 was entirely unexpected. He left behind a life full of scientific success, which was recognized with a knighthood in 1947, among numerous other honors.

Paul Karrer also received half of the prize.

Paul Karrer

*For his investigations on carotenoids, flavins and vitamins
A and B2.*

The son of Swiss parents, Paul Karrer was born in Moscow and lived the first three years of his life there. His studies took place, however, in his parents' native country, firstly in Wildegg and later in Lenzburg, Aarau. When he was ready to enter the University of Zurich, he enrolled in chemistry under the guidance of Professor Alfred Werner. Upon his graduation in 1911, Karrer stayed on as a chemistry assistant for a further year. In 1913 his mentor was awarded the Nobel Prize in Chemistry for work on the linkage of atoms in molecules.

When he left Zurich Paul Karrer went to work as a chemist in Frankfurt, Germany, but he returned to his alma mater six years later to be a lecturer. In 1919 he became a full professor and was made the director of the Chemistry Institute there.

His early years of research were dedicated to examining complex metal compounds, but his most important work was related to plant pigments, the yellow carotenoids in particular. It was Karrer who discovered the chemical structure of carotenoids and, simultaneously, showed that some of these substances transformed into vitamin A in animal bodies. In 1930 his work in this field allowed him to determine the formula of beta-carotene — one of the substances that can be transformed into vitamin A. It was the first time that the structure of a provitamin had been established, which consequently paved the way for research into the structure of vitamin A itself. Later on he confirmed Albert von Szent-Györgyi's idealized structure of ascorbic acid (vitamin C) and extended his research to vitamins B2 and E.

Karrer's studies in the field of organic chemistry resulted in the publication of more than a thousand scientific works throughout his career, focusing particularly on vitamins A, B2, C, E and K, coenzymes, carotenoids and other vegetable pigments, curare and other alkaloids, amino acids and carbohydrates. His book *Textbook of Organic Chemisty* was published in 1930 and has since been translated into several languages, including English.

The 1937 Nobel Prize in Chemistry, jointly awarded to Norman Haworth, was the result of a successful and brilliant career. After this he was president of the 14th Congress of Pure and Applied Chemistry in Zurich, received honorary doctorates at various European and American universities, was awarded the Marcel Benoist and Cannizzaro prizes and became a member of the most important scientific academies in the world. He died in 1971 at the age of 82.

Walter Norman Haworth also received half of the prize

Robert Cecil

One of the architects of the League of Nations.

Lawyer, parliamentarian and minister Edgar Algernon Robert Gascoyne-Cecil was internationally recognized for the role he played in the foundation of the League of Nations, an institution he tirelessly defended until its dissolution in 1946. Through a long life dedicated nearly exclusively to law and politics, both domestic and international, he came to be known as one of the leading proponents of peace during the last century.

Son of the 3rd Marquess of Salisbury, who was Benjamin Disraeli's minister of foreign affairs, Cecil received a private education. This he considered more worthwhile than years spent in school, as he explained in his 1949 autobiography, *All the Way*, yet he also admitted that, when he arrived at the University of Oxford, he changed his way of thinking about education and became an exemplary student.

Robert Cecil entered court as a lawyer for the first time when he was 23, but his eloquence had already shone at university. Between 1887 and 1906 his life was dedicated to law, although during this period his interest in politics was gaining ground. He represented Marylebone East constituents as a Conservative in the House of Commons between 1906 and 1910 before losing his seat, and then he returned to the British Parliament in 1911 as an Independent Conservative for the Hitchin Division of Hertfordshire.

He was 50 years old at the outbreak of World War I and went to work for the Red Cross. The formation of a coalition government, however, forced him to relinquish his humanitarian work in 1915 to become undersecretary for foreign affairs. He then held the position of minister of blockade between 1916 and 1918. At the beginning of 1918, with the war still raging, he became assistant secretary of state for foreign affairs.

Distraught by the effects of World War I, both in terms of the destruction of human life and human values, Robert Cecil was convinced that civilization could only survive with the creation of an international system to guarantee peace. Therefore, in 1916 he circulated a memorandum with proposals to prevent any new major conflicts. This document, in his own words, was the first British diplomatic step leading to the creation of the League of Nations.

The League was created with the signing of the Treaty of Versailles on the June 28, 1919, and was based in Geneva. Although it signified a nonaggression pact between the signatory countries, the League of Nations failed in its proposals of cooperation and development of peace; a second world war, even more destructive than the first, was soon on Europe's doorstep.

Robert Cecil was finally awarded the Nobel Peace Prize in 1937 in recognition of his tremendous efforts and his devotion to the organization, which continued even after he resigned from government in 1927. He died in 1958.

Pearl Buck

For her rich and truly epic descriptions of peasant life in China and for her biographical masterpieces.

Pearl Comfort Sydenstricker, better known by her pen name, Pearl Buck, was born in Hillsboro, West Virginia, in the summer of 1892. Her parents, Caroline and Absalom Sydenstricker, were Presbyterian missionaries in China, and their daughter spent a great deal of time in this country, whose culture would have such a profound influence on her.

In these early years Pearl's mother and a Chinese tutor, a Confucian scholar, laid all the foundations necessary for her official student career. At 15 Pearl was sent to a boarding school in Shanghai for the next three years. The family then left for Lynchburg, Virginia, and enrolled the young Pearl in the Randolph-Macon Woman's College. After obtaining a degree in psychology in 1914, she returned to China and, later, became a university professor in Nanking.

Her first novel, *East Wind: West Wind* was published in 1930 and contrasts Eastern and Western civilizations. A year later she achieved fame with the book *The Good Earth*, a story of the misery, conflicts, disappointments and joy in the life of a Chinese peasant family. *The Good Earth* was the turning point in Pearl Buck's literary career, earning her the 1932 Pulitzer Prize and remaining a bestseller for months after its publication. Over the years this book has been translated into more than 30 languages, adapted for Broadway and served as a screenplay.

After *The Good Earth* Pearl Buck continued writing about China in books such as *Sons* and *A House Divided*. Meanwhile, her parents' strong personalities led her to write their biographies, entitled *The Exile* and *Fighting Angel*. In 1938 she received the Nobel Prize in Literature for her biographies as well as her depiction of Chinese life. She was the first North American woman to receive the award.

Pearl Buck was married in 1917 to the missionary John L. Buck, and they had a daughter named Carol, who was handicapped. Their marriage ended in 1935, but, despite the divorce, she kept the surname Buck. The same year she married a New York editor, Richard J. Walsh, and moved permanently to the United States. Over the years she adopted nine children of different nationalities, opened an adoption agency for Asian-American children and, in 1964, created a foundation in her name also aiming to help orphaned Asian children. By the time of her death in 1973 in Danby, Vermont, Pearl Buck had written more than 100 books as well as innumerable speeches, articles and scripts.

Enrico Fermi

For his demonstrations of the existence of new radioactive elements produced by neutron irradiation, and for his related discovery of nuclear reactions brought about by slow neutrons.

To escape Benito Mussolini's dictatorship, Enrico Fermi immigrated to the United States in 1938, immediately after being awarded the Nobel Prize in Physics. He died in Chicago at the age of 53, after having dedicated many years to the field of nuclear energy. Along with other great names in science, he was one of the leaders of a team who developed the first atomic bomb.

He was born in Rome on September 29, 1901, the son of Ida de Gattis and Alberto Fermi, chief inspector of the ministry of communications. From an early age he demonstrated an aptitude for mathematics and physics, which was encouraged by his father's colleagues. He graduated in 1922 after four years at the University of Pisa. The following year the Italian Government granted him a scholarship that allowed him to continue his studies in Göttingen, Germany. He also studied in Leiden before returning to his home country in 1924 to take up the position of lecturer of mathematical physics and mechanics at the University of Florence. In 1927 he was appointed professor of theoretical physics at the University of Rome, a post he held until he received the Nobel Prize.

At the time of his Nobel win, Fermi was the world's greatest specialist in neutrons and continued his research upon his arrival in the United States. He was made professor of physics at Columbia University in 1939 and worked there until 1942. His involvement in the Manhattan Project enabled him to solve many problems in the field of physics.

He became a naturalized American citizen in 1944 and, at the end of World War II, accepted an invitation to become professor of physics at the University of Chicago. He stayed there until his unexpected death in 1954. In the final days of his life, Enrico Fermi concerned himself with the origin of cosmic rays.

At only 28 years old, near the beginning of his career as a researcher, Fermi was one of the original 30 members of the Royal Academy of Italy. His prestige continued to grow and, after dedicating himself to teaching, many Italian and foreign academies wanted him as a lecturer at their institutions. In the United States he was the first scientist to receive a special prize of $50,000 from the U.S. government for his work on atoms, a prize which today bears his name (the Enrico Fermi Award).

Enrico Fermi married Laura Capon in 1928, and the couple had two children together. He enjoyed spending his free time hiking, mountaineering and competing in winter sports.

The nuclear age

The first nuclear battery was tested on the 2nd of December, 1942 at the University of Chicago by the Italian physicist Enrico Fermi. Using graphite as an unrefrigerated moderator and supplied by uranium and uranium oxide, the battery generated 200 Watts. The experiment was a success and marked the world's entry into the nuclear age.

A-bomb

At the end of the Second World War on the 6th of August, 1945 the American bomber *Enola Gay* released "Little Boy," the first atomic bomb, over Hiroshima. The bomb, which weighed 4.5 tones with 20 kilos of uranium 235 exploded 600 meters above the ground. In two minutes, the mushroom cloud generated by the explosion went up to 10 kilometers high. The result was simply devastating: 175,000 Japanese killed. "Little Boy" was a product of the Manhattan Project, led by the physicist Robert Oppenheimer.

■ Equivalent to 13 thousand tons of TNT.

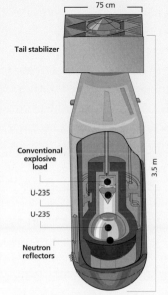

75 cm

Tail stabilizer

Conventional explosive load

U-235

U-235

Neutron reflectors

3.5 m

Medical sub-products

Nuclear applications in the field of medicine are vast. This is the case of radiation therapy, used to destroy cancerous cells, computerized axial tomography (known as the CAT scan and developed in the United Kingdom in 1972 by converting x-rays into a video signal, thus allowing for detailed images of the inside of the body) and magnetic resonance imaging (a diagnostic tool which allows the doctor to identify abnormal tissues without recourse to surgery).

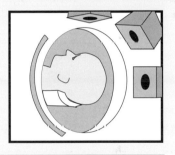

Energy

The first nuclear reactor - the name by which the batteries became known - designed for producing electricity was built in the Soviet Union at Obninsk, 100 kilometers from Moscow. It started working in the middle of 1954 and generated a modest five Megawatts of power.

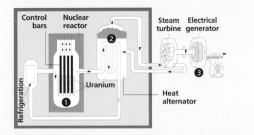

Control bars · Nuclear reactor · Steam turbine · Electrical generator · Refrigeration · Uranium · Heat alternator

In a reactor to produce electricity, a controlled nuclear chain reaction heats water (1), which is transformed into steam (2) that then turns the turbines (3).

In the fission method, under the impulse of the neutron, a heavy atomic nucleus (uranium 235, for example) is split into two parts of comparable mass. This process results in new neutrons, which are essential in a self-sustaining reaction, and large quantities of energy.

In the fusion process, which does not produce the so-called nuclear residues, the nuclei - instead of being split as in fission - are fused, releasing large quantities of energy in a reaction that is also self-sustaining. Until now, it has only been possible to achieve a fusion for a few seconds, enough time for it to be used in military applications (H-bomb) but not long enough to make it profitable in the production of electrical energy.

Ernest Lawrence

For the invention and development of the cyclotron and for results obtained with it, especially with regard to artificial radioactive elements.

Ernest Orlando Lawrence's research centered on nuclear physics, and it was for the invention of the cyclotron in 1929 that he received the Nobel Prize in Physics 10 years later. Besides being a physicist, he was also a respected author. From 1924 to 1940 his name appeared on more than 50 articles, the majority of which were published in the *Physical Review* and the *Proceedings of the National Academy of Sciences*.

Ernest was born in Canton, South Dakota, to Carl Gustavus and Gunda Lawrence, descendants of Norwegian immigrants. Here he began his studies at Canton High School before attending St. Olaf College. In 1919 he left his hometown to study at the University of South Dakota, where he graduated in chemistry three years later. He decided to continue his studies and obtained his MA from the University of Minnesota the following year and his PhD from Yale University in 1925. Lawrence stayed on as a researcher and assistant professor at Yale for three more years, before accepting an invitation in 1928 to lecture in physics at the University of California, Berkeley, where he was the youngest professor at the institution. In 1936 he took on the functions of director of the Radiation Laboratory there, a position he held until his death.

Ernest Lawrence made fundamental contributions to the development of the atomic bomb during World War II. He was part of the Manhattan Project, as head of the program responsible for developing an electromagnetic process to separate uranium 235. After the war he participated in an attempt to obtain an international accord to suspend atomic bomb tests and was a member of the American delegation at the Geneva Conference held in 1958.

As a physicist of international renown, Lawrence received many prizes from various countries and honorary doctorates from 14 universities. He was also a member of many scientific societies, both at home and abroad. Despite his hectic professional life, he was not dedicated exclusively to physics and spent time on hobbies, including sailing, tennis and skating. His large family was another of his priorities; he had six children with Mary Kimberly Blumer, whom he married in 1932. Lawrence died on August 27, 1958, in Palo Alto, California.

Gerhard Domagk

For the discovery of the antibacterial effects of prontosil.

It was desperation that led Gerhard Domagk to give a human being what up until then had only been used in experiments on mice and rabbits. The person receiving the experimental drug was his daughter, who was suffering from a bacterial infection, and she completely recovered with the dose of prontosil that Domagk administered. Thus, the antibiotic effect of the first sulphanilamide was proven, and the German pathologist would go on to win the 1939 Nobel Prize in Physiology or Medicine. Owing to the war, however, he only received his medal and diploma in 1947.

While working in field hospitals during World War I, Gerhard Domagk noted the doctors' incapacity to deal with cholera, typhoid or diarrhea-related infections. At the time, the young serviceman from Brandenburg, Germany, was already a medical student, and he was strongly affected by the lack of sterile conditions in the surgery. As a result, amputations and other radical treatments were almost always the rule for the severe bacterial infections that would often result.

At the end of the war Domagk returned to his medical studies in Kiel and graduated in 1921. He was a lecturer in pathological anatomy at the universities of Greifswald and Münster, and later became a full professor at the latter. During his time at Münster he took a leave of absence to dedicate himself to research in the I.G. Farbenindustrie, a pharmaceutical company, laboratories in Wuppertal.

In 1929 the same company created a new institution to perform research in the fields of pathological anatomy and bacteriology. Three years later he was director of the laboratory and made the dramatic discovery of prontosil; it was not until 1935, however, after more testing had been done, that he revealed using the drug on his daughter.

Domagk's contribution to medicine was not limited to the effect of sulphanilamides. He also carried out research and made important discoveries concerning tuberculosis and cancer. When laboratory work became impossible for the tireless pathologist, Gerhard Domagk returned to the University of Münster and dedicated himself to sharing his experiences and new knowledge in the field of oncology.

Nobel Laureates

1930-1939

1930

Nobel Prize in Physics
Chandrasekhara Venkata Raman
Born November 7, 1888, in Trichinopoly, India, and died November 21, 1970, in Bangalore.
For his work on the scattering of light and for the discovery of the effect named after him.

Nobel Prize in Chemistry
Hans Fischer
Born July 27, 1881, in Hoechst, Germany, and died March 31, 1945, in Munich.
For his researches into the constitution of haemin and chlorophyll and especially for his synthesis of haemin.

Nobel Prize in Physiology or Medicine
Karl Landsteiner
Born June 14, 1868, in Vienna, Austria, and died June 26, 1943, in New York, New York, United States.
For his discovery of human blood groups.

Nobel Prize in Literature
Sinclair Lewis
Born February 7, 1885, in Sauk Centre, Minnesota, United States, and died January 10, 1951, in Rome, Italy.
For his vigorous and graphic art of description and his ability to create, with wit and humor, new types of characters.

Nobel Peace Prize
Lars Olof Jonathan (Nathan) Söderblom
Born January 15, 1866, in Trönö, Sweden, and died July 12, 1931, in Uppsala.
For promoting international understanding.

1931

Nobel Prize in Physics
Not awarded.

Nobel Prize in Chemistry
Carl Bosch
Born August 27, 1874, in Cologne, Germany, and died April 26, 1940, in Heidelberg.
&
Friedrich Bergius
Born October 11, 1884, in Goldschmieden, Germany (now Wroclaw, Poland), and died March 30, 1949, in Buenos Aires, Argentina.
In recognition of their contributions to the invention and development of chemical high-pressure methods.

Nobel Prize in Physiology or Medicine
Otto Heinrich Warburg
Born October 8, 1883, in Freiburg, Germany, and died August 1, 1970, in Berlin.
For his discovery of the nature and mode of action of the respiratory enzyme.

Nobel Prize in Literature
Erik Axel Karlfeldt
Born July 20, 1864, in Folkärna, Sweden, and died April 8, 1931, in Stockholm.
The poetry of Erik Axel Karlfeldt.

Nobel Peace Prize
Jane Addams
Born September 6, 1860, in Cedarville, Illinois, United States, and died May 21, 1935, in Chicago.
&

Nicholas Murray Butler
Born April 2, 1862, in Elizabeth, New Jersey, United States, and died December 7, 1947, in New York, New York.
Lives dedicated to trying to instill the idea of peace in the North American people and the entire world.

1932

Nobel Prize in Physics
Werner Karl Heisenberg
Born December 5, 1901, in Würzburg, Germany, and died February 1, 1976, in Munich.
For the creation of quantum mechanics, the application of which has, inter alia, led to the discovery of the allotropic forms of hydrogen.

Nobel Prize in Chemistry
Irving Langmuir
Born January 31, 1881, in Brooklyn, New York, United States, and died August 16, 1957, in Falmouth, Massachusetts.
For his discoveries and investigations in surface chemistry.

Nobel Prize in Physiology or Medicine
Edgar Douglas Adrian
Born November 30, 1889, in London, England, and died August 4, 1977, in London.
&
Charles Scott Sherrington
Born November 27, 1857, in London, England, and died March 4, 1952, in Eastbourne.
For their discoveries regarding the functions of neurons.

Nobel Prize in Literature
John Galsworthy
Born August 14, 1867, in Kingston Hill, England, and died January 31, 1933, in Grove Lodge.
For his distinguished art of narration which takes its highest form in The Forsyte Saga.

Nobel Peace Prize
Not awarded.

1933

Nobel Prize in Physics
Paul Adrien Maurice Dirac
Born August 8, 1902, in Bristol, England, and died October 20, 1984, in Tallahassee, Florida, United States.
&
Erwin Schrödinger
Born August 12, 1887, in Vienna, Austria, and died January 4, 1961, in Vienna.
For the discovery of new productive forms of atomic theory.

Nobel Prize in Chemistry
Not awarded.

Nobel Prize in Physiology or Medicine
Thomas Hunt Morgan
Born September 25, 1866, in Lexington, Kentucky, United States, and died December 4, 1945, in Pasadena, California.
For his discoveries concerning the role played by the chromosome in heredity.

Nobel Prize in Literature
Ivan Alekseyevich Bunin
Born October 22, 1870, in Voronezh, Russia, and died November 8, 1953, in Paris, France.
For the strict artistry with which he has carried on the classical Russian traditions in prose writing.

Nobel Peace Prize
Ralph Norman Angell Lane
Born December 26, 1872, in Holbeach, England, and died October 7, 1967, in Croydon.
[For] various writings defending the peace cause.

1934

Nobel Prize in Physics
Not awarded.

Nobel Prize in Chemistry
Harold Clayton Urey
Born April 29, 1893, in Walkerton, Indiana, United States, and died January 5, 1981, in La Jolla, California.
For his discovery of heavy hydrogen.

Nobel Prize in Physiology or Medicine
George Richards Minot
Born December 2, 1885, in Boston, Massachusetts, United States, and died February 25, 1950, in Brookline.
&
William Parry Murphy
Born February 6, 1892, in Stoughton, Wisconsin, United States, and died October 9, 1987, in Brookline, Massachusetts.
&
George Hoyt Whipple
Born August 28, 1878, in Ashland, New Hampshire, United States, and died February 1, 1976, in Rochester, New York.
For their discoveries concerning liver therapy in cases of anemia.

Nobel Prize in Literature
Luigi Pirandello
Born June 28, 1867, in Agrigento, Italy, and died December 10, 1936, in Rome.
For his bold and ingenious revival of dramatic and scenic art.

Nobel Peace Prize
Arthur Henderson
Born September 13, 1863, in Glasgow, Scotland, and died October 20, 1935, in London, England.
For the role he played as president of the World Conference for the Disarmament of the League of Nations.

1935

Nobel Prize in Physics
James Chadwick
Born October 20, 1891, in Cheshire, England, and died July 24, 1974, in Cambridge.
For the discovery of the neutron.

Nobel Prize in Chemistry
Frédéric Joliot
Born March 19, 1900, in Paris, France, and died August 14, 1958, in Paris.
&
Irène Joliot-Curie
Born September 12, 1897, in Paris, France, and died March 17, 1956, in Paris.
In recognition of their synthesis of new radioactive elements.

Nobel Prize in Physiology or Medicine
Hans Spemann
Born June 27, 1869, in Stuttgart, Germany, and died September 9, 1941, in Freiburg.
For his discovery of the organizer effect in embryonic development.

Nobel Prize in Literature
Not awarded.

Nobel Peace Prize
Carl von Ossietzky
Born October 3, 1889, in Hamburg, Germany, and died May 4, 1938, in Berlin.
Symbol of the fight for peace.

1936

Nobel Prize in Physics
Carl David Anderson
Born September 3, 1905, in New York, New York, United States, and died January 11, 1991, in San Marino, California.
For his discovery of the positron.
&
Victor Franz Hess
Born June 24, 1883, in Waldstein Castle, Austria, and died December 17, 1964, in Mount Vernon, New York, United States.
For his discovery of cosmic radiation.

Nobel Prize in Chemistry
Peter Debye
Born March 24, 1884, in Maastricht, Netherlands, and died November 2, 1966, in Ithaca, New York, United States.
For his contributions to our knowledge of molecular structure through his investigations on dipole moments and on the diffraction of X-rays and electrons in gases.

Nobel Prize in Physiology or Medicine
Henry Hallett Dale
Born June 9, 1875, in London, England, and died July 23, 1968, in Cambridge.
&
Otto Loewi
Born June 3, 1873, in Frankfurt am Main, Germany, and died December 25, 1961, in New York, New York, United States.
For their discoveries relating to chemical transmission of nerve impulses.

Nobel Prize in Literature
Eugene Gladstone O'Neill
Born October 16, 1888, in New York, New York, United States, and died November 27, 1953, in Boston, Massachusetts.
For the power, honesty and deep-felt emotions of his dramatic works, which embody an original concept of tragedy.

Nobel Peace Prize
Carlos Saavedra Lamas
Born November 1, 1878, in Buenos Aires, Argentina, and died May 5, 1959, in Buenos Aires.
For his support of the South American Antiwar Pact , established in Latin America and submitted to the League of Nations, where he also worked.

1937

Nobel Prize in Physics
Clinton Joseph Davisson
Born October 22, 1881, in Bloomington, Illinois, United States, and died February 1, 1958, in Charlottesville, Virginia.
&
George Paget Thomson
Born May 3, 1892, in Cambridge, England, and died September 10, 1975, Cambridge.
For their experimental discovery of the diffraction of electrons by crystals.

Nobel Prize in Chemistry
Walter Norman Haworth
Born March 19, 1883, in Chorley, England, and died March 19, 1950, in Birmingham.
For his investigations on carbohydrates and vitamin C.
&
Paul Karrer
Born April 21, 1889, in Moscow, Russia, and died June 18, 1971, in Zurich, Switzerland.
For his investigations on carotenoids, flavins and vitamins A and B2.

Nobel Prize in Physiology or Medicine
Albert von Szent-Györgyi
Born September 16, 1893, in Budapest, Hungary, and died October 22, 1986, in Woods Hole, Massachusetts, United States.
For his discoveries in connection with the biological combustion processes, with special reference to vitamin C and the catalysis of fumaric acid.

Roger Martin du Gard
Born March 23, 1881, in Neuilly-sur-Seine, France, and died August 22, 1958, in Bellême.
For the artistic power and truth with which he has depicted human conflict as well as some fundamental aspects of contemporary life in his novel-cycle Les Thibault.

Nobel Peace Prize
Robert Gascoyne-Cecil
Born September 14, 1864, in London, England, and died November 24, 1958, in Tunbridge Wells.
"One of the architects of the League of Nations."

1938

Nobel Prize in Physics
Enrico Fermi
Born September 29, 1901, in Rome, Italy, and died November 28, 1954, in Chicago, Illinois, United States.
For his demonstrations of the existence of new radioactive elements produced by neutron irradiation, and for his related discovery of nuclear reactions brought about by slow neutrons.

Nobel Prize in Chemistry
Richard Kuhn
Born December 3, 1900, in Vienna, Austria, and died August 1, 1967, in Heidelberg, Germany.
For his work on carotenoids and vitamins.

Nobel Prize in Physiology or Medicine
Corneille Jean François Heymans
Born March 28, 1892, in Ghent, Belgium, and died July 18, 1968, in Knokke.
For the discovery of the role played by the sinus and aortic mechanisms in the regulation of respiration.

Nobel Prize in Literature
Pearl Buck, pseudonym of Pearl Comfort Walsh, née Sydenstricker
Born June 26, 1892, in Hillsboro, West Virginia, United States, and died March 6, 1973, in Danby, Vermont.
For her rich and truly epic descriptions of peasant life in China and for her biographical masterpieces.

Nobel Peace Prize
Nasen International Office for Refugees
Founded in 1921, in Geneva, Switzerland, and authorized by the League of Nations in 1930. Its activity was ended on December 31, 1938.
For its humanitarian work in the support of refugees.

1939

Nobel Prize in Physics
Ernest Orlando Lawrence
Born August 8, 1901, in Canton, South Dakota, United States, and died August 27, 1958, in Palo Alto, California.
For the invention and development of the cyclotron and for results obtained with it, especially with regard to artificial radioactive elements.

Nobel Prize in Chemistry
Adolf Friedrich Johann Butenandt
Born March 24, 1903, in Bremerhaven-Wesermünde, Germany, and died January 18, 1995, in Munich.
For his work on sex hormones.
&
Leopold Ruzicka
Born September 3, 1887, in Vukovar, Crotia, and died September 26, 1976, in Zurich, Switzerland.
For his work on polymethylenes and higher terpenes.

Nobel Prize in Physiology or Medicine
Gerhard Domagk
Born October 30, 1895, in Lagow, Germany, and died April 24, 1964, in Burgberg.
For the discovery of the antibacterial effects of prontosil.

Nobel Prize in Literature
Frans Eemil Sillanpää
Born September 16, 1888, in Ylä-Satakunta, Finland, and died June 3, 1964, in Helsinki.
For his deep understanding of his country's peasantry and the exquisite art with which he has portrayed their way of life and their relationship with nature.

Nobel Peace Prize
Not awarded.

Selected Profiles of Nobel Laureates

1940–1949

Wolfgang Pauli

For the discovery of the exclusion principle, also called the Pauli principle.

Wolfgang Pauli was born in Vienna, Austria, and grew up in an academic family. He was influenced by his father, Wolfgang Joseph Pauli, a respected physician and chemistry professor who was descended from a Jewish family but had converted to Catholicism. His son was also baptized as a Catholic.

Pauli's later studies took place at the University of Munich under the guidance of his mentor, Arnold Sommerfeld. At just 21 years old, and with little experience, he wrote an encyclopedic 200-page article on the theory of relativity. Albert Einstein himself considered the work quite accurate and expressed that he was extremely impressed with the young student's work. Pauli obtained his doctorate degree in 1921 and then spent a year at the University of Göttingen, as Max Born's assistant. He occupied a similar position with Niels Bohr in Copenhagen, Denmark, before being appointed a lecturer at the University of Hamburg.

Pauli was part of a group of the most brilliant physicists of the mid-20th century. He rose quickly to fame and, in 1928, was made a professor of theoretical physics at the Federal Institute of Technology in Zurich, Switzerland. It was because of his academic supervision during this time that the institute became a respected center for research in physics in the years following World War II.

Pauli was respected by his students, who were loyal to him, and he continued to garner recognition from the international community, particularly in the United States. In 1945 he was awarded the Nobel Prize in Physics in recognition of his formulation of the exclusion principle, also known as the Pauli principle, and its relation to quantum theory. He was a member of the Royal Society of London, the Swiss Physical Society and the American Association for the Advancement of Science, among other organizations. Pauli was presented with various awards over his life in addition to the Nobel, including the Lorentz Medal in 1931, the Franklin Medal in 1952 and the Max Planck Medal in 1958.

Despite his brilliant academic life, Pauli was prone to bouts of depression. On the advice of his father he consulted the famous psychologist Carl Gustav Jung and maintained a relationship with him for many years. He was briefly married to the Berlin dancer Kate Deppner, but this marriage ended in divorce in 1930. Three years earlier, in 1927, his mother had committed suicide. In 1934 he remarried, this time to Franciska Bertram, but the couple remained childless.

Pauli and his wife fled from advancing Nazi forces, and he took up a position at Princeton University in 1940. He continued his research, and it was there that he received the news that he had won a Nobel Prize in 1945. He died in Zurich, Switzerland, on December 15, 1958.

Exclusion principle

In 1925 the physicist Wolfgang Pauli formulated the exclusion principle, which is also known as the Pauli principle. Despite this principle initially only being valid for electrons, it has been shown to be important for hydrogen nuclei - protons - and neutrons as well. Pauli also played an important role in the creation of the Quantum Theory.

$$\Psi^{Fermion}_{I=\{i,i\}}(\vec{r_1},\vec{r_2}) = \frac{1}{\sqrt{2}}\{\varphi_i(\vec{r_1})\varphi_i(\vec{r_2}) - \varphi_i(\vec{r_2})\varphi_i(\vec{r_1})\} = 0$$

$$\Psi^{Fermion}_{I=\{i,j\}}(\vec{r_1},\vec{r_1}) = \frac{1}{\sqrt{2}}\{\varphi_i(\vec{r_1})\varphi_j(\vec{r_1}) - \varphi_i(\vec{r_1})\varphi_j(\vec{r_1})\} = 0$$

According to the exclusion principle, two electrons with the same set of quantum numbers cannot be present in an atom. As a result, at most, there can only be two electrons (elemental sub-atomic particles) in the same spin around the nucleus of an atom, where the electron-cloud can be situated.

A quantum number only characterizes the state of an electron and its position in the atom. There are four quantum numbers: the principal; the angular quantum number; the magnetic number and the spin number. Normally all four quantum numbers are needed to define the energy of an electron.

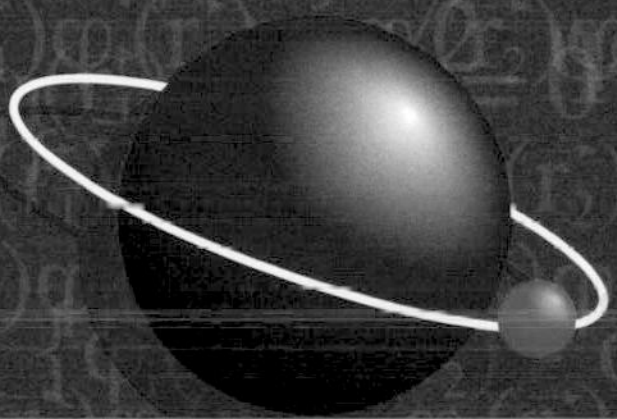

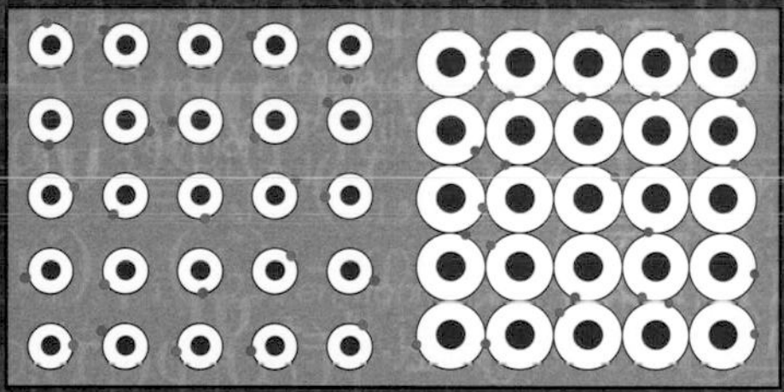

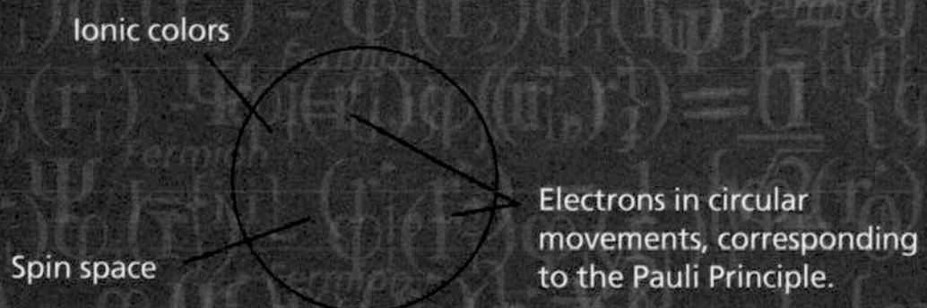

Ionic colors

Spin space

Electrons in circular movements, corresponding to the Pauli Principle.

Artturi Virtanen

For his research and inventions in agricultural and nutrition chemistry, especially for his fodder preservation method.

Artturi Ilmari Virtanen, son of Kaarlo Virtanen and Serafiina Isotalo, was born and died in Helsinki, Finland. From a young age Virtanen took his studies very seriously, studies that would one day lead him to a career as an internationally recognized biochemist. He is best remembered today for his work's applications to agriculture and the dairy industry.

At university he concentrated on chemistry, biology and physics, graduated with a general science degree in 1916 and received his doctorate three years later. He studied physical chemistry in Zurich, Switzerland, and bacteriology and enzymology in Stockholm, Sweden. During this time Virtanen associated with some of the most famous scientists, including H. von Euler-Chelpin, who won the 1929 Nobel Prize in Chemistry and would oversee his studies in enzymology between 1923 and 1924.

Virtanen married Lilja Moisio in 1920, and the couple had two children, the first was named Kaarlo, after his grandfather, and the second was called Olavi. With a stable personal life and a promising professional career in biochemistry, Virtanen confronted his objectives with dedication and enthusiasm.

He was the first assistant at the Central Laboratory of Industries in Helsinki, Finland, between 1916 and 1917. Two years later Virtanen took up the position of chemist at the Valio laboratory of the Finnish Cooperative Dairies' Association, becoming its director in 1921. A decade later he became the director of the Biochemical Research Institute in Helsinki. Virtanen was also a professor of biochemistry at the Finland Institute of Technology and at the University of Helsinki.

From 1948 on he was a member and president of the State Academy of Science and Arts in Finland, a position that earned him wide recognition and respect. Virtanen's honors are not limited to his native country, however. He was a member of the science academies of Norway, Sweden and Flanders and the engineering sciences academies of Sweden and Denmark. He received numerous awards and distinctions from private, national and international organizations, culminating in the 1945 Nobel Prize in Chemistry for his work in agricultural and nutrition chemistry.

The banquet speech given in Artturi Virtanen's honor when he received the Nobel Prize captured his patriotic spirit and utter dedication to his work throughout his life: "through his work he has confirmed that a person who puts his sincerity and zeal at the service of his people and country, without thinking of himself or personal gain, also serves the interests of humanity." He died 28 years later, in 1973.

Gabriela Mistral

For her lyric poetry which, inspired by powerful emotions, has made her name a symbol of the idealistic aspirations of the entire Latin American world.

Lucila Godoy y Alcayaga became famous for her poetry, which she wrote under the pseudonym Gabriela Mistral. The first name comes from the Archangel Gabriel, and *mistral* is the name given to the warm, strong wind that blows across the south of France. At the award ceremony Mistral attended to receive the 1945 Nobel Prize in Literature, she was admirably described by Hjalmar Gullberg as having made a most "notable pilgrimage from the seat of teacher to the throne of poetry."

Lucila Alcayaga was born in Vicuña, a small village in the Andes Valley of Chile. Her father was a primary school teacher with poetical ambitions but an irresponsible lifestyle; he abandoned his family while Lucila was still young. Professionally, she always wanted to offer children what she had had to teach herself through reading books, and so she spent 15 years as a primary school teacher and also taught in various secondary schools.

Her desire to write came through personal tragedy. In 1907, while working as an assistant in a school in La Cantera, she fell in love with Romelio Ureta, a young railway employee. They separated because of constant disagreements, but, two years later, Ureta committed suicide after being convicted of embezzlement, leaving Gabriela distraught. She expressed her feelings in *Sonetos de la Muerte*, which made her a well-known poet in Latin America and, some years later, brought her an award by the Writers Society of Santiago.

In addition to *Desolación (Desolation)*, Mistral's first collection of poems, published in 1922, she was the author of *Ternura (Tenderness)*, published in 1924, a volume of poetry whose dominant theme is childhood, and *Tala (Destruction)* published in 1938, in which maternity plays an important role. Her complete works were published in New York a year after her death.

Writing became a way for Gabriela Mistral to articulate her innermost thoughts, but she was also a woman of the world. Besides playing an important role in the educational systems of Mexico and Chile, she was an active presence in the cultural committees of the League of Nations and was consul in Naples, Madrid and Lisbon. As well as receiving several honorary doctorates, she taught Spanish literature at three universities in the United States and at the University of Puerto Rico.

Although she longed to have children, Gabriela Mistral never married; she did adopt a child later in life, who later died. Her work has been her legacy, and she continues to be admired by many.

Alexander Fleming

For the discovery of penicillin and its curative effect in various infectious diseases.

Alexander Fleming's discovery of the antibacterial properties of penicillin advanced the fight against infectious diseases and has protected the health of hundreds of millions of people. For his work he was knighted in 1944 and spent the next 10 years of his fame traveling the world. Born in Lochfield, Scotland, Fleming moved to London in 1895, where he studied at the Regent Street Polytechnic before working four years in a shipping office. He then entered St. Mary's Medical School at the University of London. He distinguished himself as a brilliant student and passed the various academic examinations with little difficulty. After finishing his degrees in 1908, Fleming stayed on at the university in the famous inoculation laboratory of Almroth Wright.

In 1914 he joined the Army Medical Corps, and he served for the duration of the war in a military hospital in Boulogne, France. While there he carried out research on the two great scourges of the trenches: gangrene and tetanus. At the end of World War I he returned to St. Mary's to become a lecturer and, in 1928, a professor of bacteriology.

Although Fleming's early research was carried out while he was still a student under the guidance of Professor Almroth Wright, a pioneer of vaccination, it was after the war that he made his greatest scientific discoveries. They began when Fleming had a cold and, curious, placed his nasal mucus in a petri dish; he observed that the bacteria near the mucus were destroyed. It was thus that he discovered lysozyme, a naturally occurring antibacterial enzyme found in mucus, tears and eggwhite.

He continued to study bacterial cultures in mold and, in 1928, deduced that penicillin was an antibiotic substance that was effective against a wide range of pathogenic bacteria. It took a further 15 years before Fleming saw penicillin produced industrially. Since then, it has become the most widely used antibiotic in the world.

Fleming was elected a member of various scientific institutions, including the Royal College of Surgeons (in 1909), the Royal Society (in 1943) and the Royal College of Physicians (in 1944). He also received numerous prizes in addition to the 1945 Nobel Prize in Physiology or Medicine, including the United States Medal for Merit, in 1947, and the Grand Cross of Alphonse X the Wise from Spain, in 1948. Over his lifetime he received honorary doctorate degrees from more than 30 European and American universities.

In 1915 Fleming married Sarah Marion McElroy, who died in 1949, and, in 1953, he married Dr. Amalia Koutsouri-Voureka, a Greek colleague from St Mary's. He died in 1955, and his ashes are interred in St. Paul's Cathedral.

Ernst Boris Chain and Howard Walter Florey also each received a third of the prize.

Penicillin

Alexander Fleming studied bacteria inhibition in moulds and in 1928 he deduced that this secreted an antibiotic substance - penicillin.

Dedicated to finding antibiotic substances, Fleming observed that colonies of bacteria did not grow in an area of a culture that had been accidentally contaminated by a green mould.

He isolated this mould and grew it in a liquid and reached the conclusion that he had produced a substance - penicillin - capable of eliminating most of the common bacteria that infected man.

Nine years after Alexander Fleming had discovered penicillin, Ernst Chain and Sir Howard Florey joined forces with Fleming to develop the antibiotic substance. Their joint work led to the industrial production of penicillin.
For their work the three scientists received the Nobel Prize for Physiology or Medicine in 1945. Ernst Boris Chain was born in Berlin in 1906. In 1933 he immigrated to England and two years later was invited to lecture at Oxford University. Sir Howard Walter Florey, a British doctor of Australian origin, was appointed professor of Pathology in Great Britain.

131

Cordell Hull

[For] tireless work for good understanding between nations.

Cordell Hull was born in a log cabin in rural Pickett County, Tennessee, the third of the five sons of William and Elizabeth Hull. He distinguished himself from his brothers by being the only one who was interested in getting an education, and he had his first lessons in a one-room schoolhouse built by his father.

Hull wanted to be a lawyer from his early youth. He graduated with a law degree in 1891 after completing his studies at Cumberland University, Tennessee. Not yet 20, he decided to set up a law practice in Celina, and thus achieved his childhood dream. While still a student, however, he had taken part in a political campaign, and this experience made him decide to concentrate on politics.

Hull immediately joined the Democrat Party and, from 1893 to 1897, was a member of the Tennessee House of Representatives. He left politics in 1898 to serve in the Spanish-American War and, upon returning, took up law once again. In 1903 he was made a judge. "Judge" would be a nickname that he would keep throughout the rest of his life; even his wife, Rose Frances Whitney, whom he married in 1917, called him Judge.

He was elected a senator for the 1931–1937 term, yet he chose to resign from the Senate in 1933 to become secretary of state under President Franklin D. Roosevelt. It was only in 1944, due to ill health, that he stepped down from this position; he served nearly 12 years, the longest term of office in American history.

During his time as secretary of state, Hull dealt with many of the problems affecting the world during these tumultuous years. He advocated rearmament before World War II and warned the military to be prepared for surprise attacks before the bombing of Pearl Harbor. He supported giving aid to struggling democracies and warned against the threat of dictatorships. After the war he played a major role in establishing the United Nations, which was dedicated to international peace and development.

Hull's tireless work for better understanding between nations was recognized with the Nobel Peace Prize in 1945. As he could not be present at the award ceremony, Lithgow Osborne, the American ambassador to Norway, received it in his name.

In contrast to many other politicians, Hull was not a gifted speaker. Tall, thin and somewhat shy, he was nevertheless determined and sincere in his thoughts and actions. Disdaining the social scene in Washington, D.C., Cordell Hull preferred the simplicity of his private life and maintained a quiet interest in golf and croquet. In his will, he left numerous artifacts and documents to form a small museum in Pickett County, Tennessee.

Hermann Hesse

For his inspired writings which, while growing in boldness and penetration, exemplify the classical humanitarian ideals and high qualities of style.

Herman Hesse was born in Calw in the Black Forest — a mountainous region in southwest Germany. His father and grandfather had been missionaries in India, and this perhaps explains the fascination with eastern cultures that would later manifest itself in his work. On his father's orders he attended German boarding schools in Wuerttemberg and the Maulbronn Seminary. His strong personality, however, came into conflict with the strict, religious education he received. As a result, and despite being a good student, Hesse left the Maulbronn seminary and apprenticed to a mechanic at a clock factory in his hometown.

At the age of 19 he began working in a bookstore in Tübingen. Hesse, who had dreamed of being a writer since he was 12, remained at the bookstore until 1904, when he launched his literary career and published his first novel, *Peter Camenzind*. This story of a failed writer became a great success.

Hesse wrote *Gertrud* (1910) and *Rosshalde* (1914), both with central themes of man finding his essential spirit through breaking the rules imposed by traditional society. Depression, however, soon caused him to seek the help of the well-known Swiss psychiatrist Carl Gustav Jung, whose influence can be seen in Hesse's work *Demian* (1919).

A visit to India allowed him to see firsthand the culture that had been described to him in the tales of his father and grandfather. In 1922 he published *Siddharta*, a lyrical novella based on Buddha's youth.

During World War I Hesse lived in Switzerland, a neutral country. In his writings he denounced militarism and nationalism, and he edited a newspaper for German prisoners. In 1923 he became a Swiss citizen and settled in Montagnola, where remained until his death. In 1946 he received news of being awarded the Nobel Prize in Literature. He was greatly excited by the news, despite not being able to go to Sweden to receive the award in person, due to health problems. He received the Goethe Prize of Frankfurt that same year and, in 1955, the Peace Prize of the German Book Trade.

In 1904 he married Maria Bernoulli, with whom he lived for almost two decades. From this marriage came the novelist's three children, Bruno, Heiner and Martin. They divorced in 1923, and Hesse married on two more occasions, first to Ruth Wenger and then to Ninon Ausländer Dolbin.

(1867–1961)

Emily Balch

For leading the women's international peace movement.

Emily Greene Balch was born into a large Boston family and grew up with four sisters and a brother. Her father was a distinguished lawyer, yet it was her mother who was the center of her life growing up and the greatest influence on her.

Balch first attended private schools and was always considered a talented student. She began to concentrate on literature, then economics, but she was always more affected by the written word than by human interaction. Emily Balch met Jane Addams, who won the 1931 Nobel Peace Prize, a figure who would have an important influence on her career as a peace activist. She also participated in movements for women's right to vote, racial justice and regulating child labor.

Balch was a member of the first graduating class from Bryn Mawr College in 1889, and she then spent a year independently studying sociology. From 1890 to 1891 she used a European Fellowship to study economics in Paris and write *Public Assistance of the Poor in France*, which was published in 1893. Her formal studies were completed at Harvard and the University of Chicago.

In 1915 she began her duties as a delegate at the International Congress of Women. She later established and operated the Women's International Committee for Permanent Peace, afterward called the Women's International League for Peace and Freedom.

As a teacher and lecturer, Balch impressed her students with her clear thinking and insistence that they could make their own value judgments. After more than two decades of teaching at Wellesley College in Massachusetts, she decided to concentrate on implementing her ideas for peace in the period between the world wars. Shocked by the Nazis, in the 1940s she put her talents at the disposal of governments, international organizations and various committees.

At the age of 79 Emily Balch was awarded the 1946 Nobel Peace Prize, which was awarded in recognition of her important contributions to peace while she was a leader of international women's movements. After this she continued to promote conferences and movements in the search for peace.

When she reached the age of 92, Balch recognized that life had gone well and had been lived on her own terms, without great physical or psychological suffering. She lamented experiencing "only a small part of life," having never married or had children. She was hailed as a citizen of the world when she died in Cambridge, Massachusetts, in 1961.

John Raleigh Mott also received half of the prize.

John R. Mott

(1865–1955)

For his role as a church leader in missionary movements. He demonstrated respect for individual differences and humanitarian efforts in a time of war.

The American John Raleigh Mott decided on the course of his life on January 14, 1886, after attending a conference held by J. Kynaston Studd. He reflected on three sentences in particular: "Seekest thou great things for thyself? Seek them not. Seek ye first the Kingdom of God." Until this moment, Mott, despite distinguishing himself in history, literature and public speaking while a student, had not made a decision about his future. On that day, however, he determined that he wanted to spend the rest of his life talking to young people about Christ. In so doing, he gave up opportunities in law and at his father's lumber business.

While attending Cornell University, Mott was the local representative for the Young Men's Christian Association (YMCA) at the first international meeting of young Christian students. From then on he spent much of his time traveling across North America, spreading the good news of the gospel and following the path he felt he had been called to.

These, however, were merely the first of many journeys for Mott. Later secretary-general and then president of the YMCA's World Committee, some have calculated that he traveled the circumference of the world 70 times on his mission. Additionally, he never visited a country without first studying its culture, customs, religion and politics; he could arrive anywhere in the world and demonstrate that he knew the place, the people and their ways of life.

Known as a man with an open mind, he was receptive to new influences and ways of thinking and looking at the world. He liked to have contact with people from all walks of life, including political leaders and scientists, but principally young people. For more than three decades Mott organized and led young Christians. Although a Methodist, he tried to be an impartial apostle of what has been handed down through the Bible.

In 1913 President Wilson invited him to be the U.S. ambassador to China, a position that he turned down in favor of continuing his work with international social and religious organizations. President Wilson's response was, "I don't remember being so disappointed." During World War I Mott helped support soldiers and their respective families by leading the YMCA's National War Work Council, efforts for which he was awarded the Distinguished Service Medal.

In 1946 he was awarded the Nobel Peace Prize in recognition of his dynamic role in Christian youth movements around the world and his humanitarian efforts in times of war. He died at home in Orlando, Florida on January 31, 1955.

Emily Balch also received half of the prize.

Edward Appleton

For his investigations of the physics of the upper atmosphere, especially for the discovery of the so-called Appleton layer.

Edward Victor Appleton was born in Bradford, England, to a working class family. His father, Peter Appleton, was a warehouse worker and a talented musician. He also had two sisters, one of whom died early, in 1911, and the second was born two years later, making an age difference of more than 20 years between her and Edward.

At school Appleton showed an aptitude for music, which led his father to think he might become a professional musician, but the boy also enjoyed sports and wanted to be a professional cricket player. When he was 11, however, he went to Hanson Grammar School, where he stayed for the next six years. He was the only pupil to have the key to the physics laboratory, so he could work at this newfound passion at night. One of his habits was to carry around a small notebook in which he wrote down important events and sayings. He also spent many Saturday mornings in the local library.

Appleton's studies continued at St. John's College, Cambridge, where he obtained a degree in natural science in 1913. Some temporary positions allowed him to gain more practical experience and establish contact with some notable figures, including Sir J.J. Thomson and Ernest Rutherford. He then served in the Royal Engineers during World War I, and on his return he dedicated himself to radio technology.

He worked at the Cavendish laboratory from 1920 onward, until he was invited to lecture on physics at London University. In 1932, after 12 years at this institution he returned to Cambridge to lecture in natural philosophy. Three years later he was made secretary of Cambridge's Department of Scientific and Industrial Research. He moved to the University of Edinburgh in 1949 and became principal and vice-chancellor.

Appleton was knighted in 1941 for the various contributions he made to science, and he received the 1947 Nobel Prize in Physics for his research into the upper atmosphere and the discovery of the Appleton layer, an atmospheric layer that reflects shortwaves around the earth. In 1947 he received the Congressional Medal of Merit from the United States and was made an Officer of the French Legion of Honour. He was later appointed by the Pope to the Pontifical Academy of Science.

Accompanying this successful career was his 1915 marriage to Jessie Longson, with whom he had two daughters. He was widowed in 1964 and was remarried a year later to Helen F. Allison. A month after the wedding, Appleton died in Edinburgh.

The Appleton layer

Edward Appleton broke new ground in Physics with his research into the upper atmosphere and, especially, with the discovery of the Appleton layer. His methods, which allowed research into the Earth's atmosphere by means of radio waves, were extremely important in solving problems in other scientific areas, such as astronomy, geophysics, and meteorology and were crucial in communications technology.

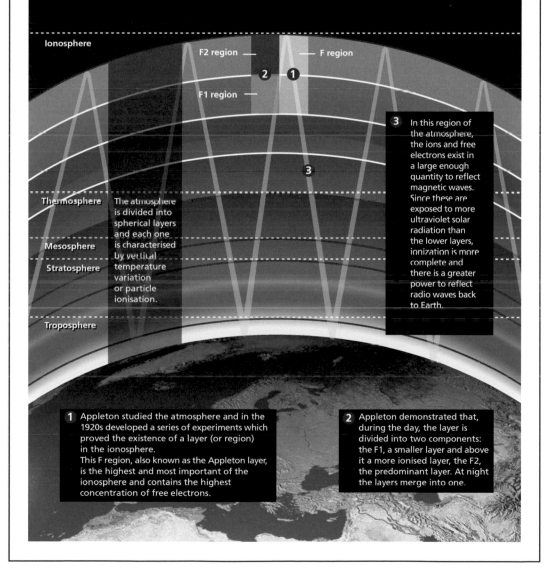

Ionosphere

F2 region — — F region

2 **1**

F1 region —

3 In this region of the atmosphere, the ions and free electrons exist in a large enough quantity to reflect magnetic waves. Since these are exposed to more ultraviolet solar radiation than the lower layers, ionization is more complete and there is a greater power to reflect radio waves back to Earth.

Thermosphere The atmosphere is divided into spherical layers and each one is characterised by vertical temperature variation or particle ionisation.

3

Mesosphere

Stratosphere

Troposphere

1 Appleton studied the atmosphere and in the 1920s developed a series of experiments which proved the existence of a layer (or region) in the ionosphere.
This F region, also known as the Appleton layer, is the highest and most important of the ionosphere and contains the highest concentration of free electrons.

2 Appleton demonstrated that, during the day, the layer is divided into two components: the F1, a smaller layer and above it a more ionised layer, the F2, the predominant layer. At night the layers merge into one.

Carl Cori & Gerty Cori

For their discovery of the course of the catalytic conversion of glycogen.

Carl Ferdinand Cori and Gerty Theresa Radnitz first met during an anatomy class in the fall of 1914 at the German University of Prague; from this moment the two shared most of their personal and academic lives. Both were born in the Czech capital in 1896 and both became doctors of medicine in 1920 from the University of Prague. They married the same year and had a son named Thomas. In 1922 they immigrated to America.

The Coris worked together for many years but also distinguished themselves in independent research. They received various prizes, but the most significant was the 1947 Nobel Prize in Physiology or Medicine, which was awarded for their discovery of the catalytic conversion of glycogen. The prize was additionally shared with Bernardo Alberto Houssay: "for his discovery of the part played by the hormone of the anterior pituitary lobe in the metabolism of sugar." The couple focused their research on hormones and glands for most of their lives, and they offered inspiration for other biochemists in their many articles for The Journal of Biological Chemistry and other scientific periodicals.

Gerty proved an excellent hostess and, thanks to her dedication, the Coris' home was full of flowers, art, books and music. The couple's favorite hobby was gardening, once again performed as a team; Gerty looked after the flowers while Carl busied himself with the vegetables. Gerty, whose sister was a painter, loved the impressionist artists, read voraciously and enjoyed her favorite composers, Mozart, Beethoven and Bach.

Despite her hectic life, Gerty Cori still had time for friends and to exchange letters. At the age of 15 she decided to study medicine and was particularly encouraged in this by her uncle Robert, a professor in pediatrics.

Medicine became the cornerstone of her life, and she worked with her husband for many years, but fate cut her time short. She died of an incurable disease in Saint Louis after a 10-year illness. Numerous world-famous scientists attended her funeral.

After Gerty's death Carl Cori continued with his research and was remarried in 1960 to Anne FitzGerald Jones. This shy and gracious man spent part of his childhood in Trieste, in present-day Italy, where his father, a zoologist, was director of the Marine Biological Station. It was his father who first aroused his interest in science, but Carl was also stimulated by visits he made in the summer to his grandfather, a professor of theoretical physics in Prague. After immigrating to America he accepted a position at the Institute for the Study of Malignant Diseases in Buffalo, New York, in 1922. He then served as a professor of pharmacology and biochemistry at the Washington University School of Medicine in Saint Louis, beginning in 1931. Carl Cori died in 1984 in Cambridge, Massachusetts.

Bernardo Alberto Houssay also received half of the prize.

André Gide

*For his comprehensive and artistically significant writings, in
which human problems and conditions have been presented with a
fearless love of truth and keen psychological insight.*

André Paul Guillaume Gide was born on November 22, 1869, in Paris,
France, to a father descended from Huguenots — the name given to
Calvinists during the religious wars — and a Catholic mother. True to
his father's heritage, he was seen as a revolutionary against conventional
morals for much of his life, particularly for his defense of the freedom of
expression.

At the age of 8 Gide was sent to École Alsacienne College in Paris.
His education was interrupted on a number of occasions, however, due to serious health
problems. When his father, a professor of law at the University of Paris, died unexpectedly in
1880, little André's health became the center of his mother's attention. She was a devoted and
austere woman who rarely allowed her son to leave the house during this time, having him
educated by various tutors and a governess instead. Gide obtained his bachelor's degree in
1889 and dedicated himself entirely to writing, music and traveling.

In 1891 his first work, of an autobiographical nature and written in the first person, *Les
Cahiers d'André Walter (The Notebooks of André Walter)*, appeared. A trip to Algeria at the end
of the 19th century proved a decisive event in the young writer's life. In this North African
country, he fell gravely ill and was near death, an event that helped spark, upon his recovery,
the revolt against his puritanical past. From then on, his writing took on a completely different character.

A passion for freedom dominates *Les Nourritures terrestres (Fruits of the Earth)*, published
in 1897, while sincerity pervades *L'Immoraliste (The Immoralist)*, which appeared in 1902.
One of the results of his revolt was the unprecedented freedom with which he wrote about
controversial sexual material, including homosexuality; it is said that Gide assumed a
homosexual lifestyle after meeting Oscar Wilde in North Africa in 1894. Corydon and the
autobiography *Si le grain ne meurt (If It Die...)*, both published in 1924, illustrate his attempts
to be liberated from the conservative ideas of the day.

André Gide's interests were vast and extended beyond French literature. He translated
works by foreign writers, including Shakespeare and Walt Whitman, into French. Besides
literary works, he was also noted for his strong opinions on social and political questions.

In 1895 he married his cousin, Madeleine Rondeaux, but in 1923 he had a daughter,
named Catherine, with a Miss Maria van Rysselberghe. Some time before he died in his native Paris, Gide gratefully received the news that he had been awarded the 1947 Nobel Prize
for Literature. For health reason he was unable to accept in person. He died in 1951.

Patrick Blackett

For his development of the Wilson cloud chamber method, and his discoveries therewith in the fields of nuclear physics and cosmic radiation.

Patrick Maynard Stuart Blackett, a renowned English physicist, both lived and died in London. He attended the Osborne Naval College and Dartmouth College with the intention of following a career in the Royal Navy. He began his military career as a cadet and participated in the battles of the Falkland Islands and Jutland during World War I. At the end of the war he retired as a lieutenant and chose to concentrate on the sciences.

Physics, in particular, fascinated him, and Blackett entered Cambridge University, where he worked with Lord Rutherford, the winner of the 1908 Nobel Prize in Chemistry. Rutherford opened his student's eyes to new avenues of knowledge and further influenced him to dedicate his life to science. Blackett obtained his BA from Cambridge in 1921.

In Cambridge's Cavendish Laboratory the young scientist began his research with cloud chambers. In 1924 Blackett's work produced the first photographs of the transmutation of nitrogen into an oxygen isotope. That same year he married Constanza Bayon, with whom he had a daughter and a son.

After a brief period working in Göttingen, Germany, Blackett returned to Cambridge to continue his research. In conjunction with the Italian scientist, Guiseppe Occhialini, he created a new cloud chamber in 1932, in which photographs of cosmic rays were taken automatically. As a result they managed to confirm the existence of the positron, a particle with a mass equal to the electron but with a positive charge. That same year Blackett became a professor of physics at Birkbeck College, London, but still continued with his studies of cosmic rays. He accepted an invitation to lecture at the University of Manchester in 1937.

Meanwhile, he founded a group to study cosmic rays and stimulate development in other new areas. This initiative led to the formal creation of the field of radio astronomy at the University of Manchester and the construction of the Jodrell Bank Experimental Station for Radio Astronomy.

In consequence of his research in the area of cosmic rays, Blackett became interested in the origin of the earth's magnetic field and concentrated on studying magnetism in rocks. At this time he also published one of his most celebrated books, *Military and Political Consequences of Atomic Energy* (1948).

Besides winning the 1948 Nobel Prize in Physics for his perfection of Wilson's cloud chamber and his discoveries in the area of nuclear physics and cosmic radiation, he was also elected president of the Royal Society in 1965 and was made a life peer in Britain in 1969.

Cosmic radiation

Research related to cosmic radiation has attracted many researchers who have tried to understand the particles that reach the earth from space. Patrick Blackett, a physicist who specialized in cosmic radiation, made many important discoveries in this area. He developed Wilson's automatic apparatus, in which cosmic rays could be photographed.

The study of the quantity and type of these particles helps understand the Sun's process of acceleration and the study of its composition, as well as other celestial bodies in the distant galaxy. Cosmic rays include galacticos, which come from outside the solar system, anomalos, which come from inter-stellar space and particles of solar energy, associated with the Sun.

Cosmic Radiation
As the name suggests cosmic radiation comes from space. It has a high energy level and strong penetrative power and is made up of protons and other particles that reach the Earth

Ozone layer

Cosmic rays

Cosmic Rays
They are made up of very short wave radiation, coming from outer space. There is a large quantity of low-energy cosmic rays, although some also have high-energy. The majority of cosmic radiation particles are made up of atomic nuclei or electrons. Some cosmic particles are the most energetic in nature.

141

Arne Tiselius

For his research on electrophoresis and adsorption analysis, especially for his discoveries concerning the complex nature of serum proteins.

Arne Wilhelm Kaurin Tiselius attended school in Gothenburg, Sweden, and graduated from the Realgymnasium in 1921. At the University of Uppsala he specialized in chemistry and became an assistant to Theodor Svedberg, a famous physicist and chemist who went on to win the 1926 Nobel Prize in Chemistry. At the time he could not imagine that he would one day win the same award. Tiselius was one of Svedberg's favorite students and, under his guidance, launched his scientific career.

He first found work at an ultracentrifuge — built by Svedberg to research the behavior of large molecules, such as proteins, carbohydrates and polymers, in solution — but later his professor encouraged him to dedicate his studies to the movement of electrically charged particles in solution subjected to a force field (electrophoresis). Tiselius presented his doctoral thesis based on this work in 1930.

That same year he was invited to become an assistant professor of chemistry at the University of Uppsala, Sweden, and, between 1931 and 1935, he published a series of papers on research related to adsorption. He continued these studies when he visited H.S. Taylor's laboratory at Princeton. Tiselius's American colleagues influenced him to concentrate his studies on proteins and the application of physical methods to biochemical problems, which he did when he returned to Uppsala in 1937.

In 1946 his department at the University of Uppsala became known as the Institute of Biochemistry. Tiselius's laboratory became a world center for research into electrophoresis techniques, and it received young biochemists who showed special potential. Among these was Florence Seibert, the American known for her work on tuberculosis and recipient of the Garvan Medal from the American Chemical Society in 1942.

Arne Tiselius accepted the 1948 Nobel Prize in Chemistry in recognition of his work on two biochemical methods of studying proteins and other macromolecules, electrophoresis and adsorption analysis. At the time he was a member of the Nobel Committee for Chemistry and vice president of the Nobel Foundation — he would later be president of the foundation, between 1960 and 1964. However, his colleagues believed that his role in the organization should not bar his being recognized for his work outside of it.

Tiselius married Ingrid Margareta Dalén in 1930, and they had two children. His son became a doctor at the Academic Hospital in Uppsala, while his daughter married a respected physician. In 1971 Tiselius died of a heart attack in Uppsala.

T.S. Eliot

For his outstanding, pioneer contribution to present-day poetry.

Thomas Stearns Eliot was born in Saint Louis, Missouri, into an old, well-established New England family. The son of a successful businessman and a poetess, he had a broad and distinctive education. Considered brilliant even as a youth, he entered Harvard in 1906 and completed his bachelor's degree in three years, instead of the usual four. He obtained his PhD from Harvard, having carefully studied Asian philology and philosophy. T.S. Eliot, as he was widely known, then completed his education at Oxford and the Sorbonne, Paris.

In 1914 he met, Ezra Pound, one of the greatest figures of 20th century literature, who became a close friend, and he decided to remain permanently in Europe. He married Vivian Haigh-Wood in 1915, but the marriage was an unhappy one. It ultimately provided inspiration for *The Waste Land* (1922), a highly influential poem that represented the disillusionment of the postwar generation.

His first years in London were spent working as a teacher, bank clerk and literary consultant. However, his fame as a poet, critic and dramatist came quickly after the publication of *The Sacred Wood* in 1920. *The Waste Land* followed, which earned him a place at the forefront of modern English poetry. Between 1922 and 1939 he founded and worked as the editor of the *Criterion*, the most important international literary journal of the time. In 1927 Eliot gave up his American citizenship to become a British subject and joined the Anglican Church.

When Harvard University offered him the Charles Eliot Norton professorship for 1932 to 1933, Eliot accepted, leaving his wife in England. In 1933 they officially separated but remained married. Vivian was committed to a mental institution in 1938 and died there in 1947, having never been visited by Eliot. He was remarried in 1957 to Valerie Fletcher, and this experience proved much happier than the first. The couple lived contentedly until the poet's death in London on January 4, 1965.

In 1943 *Four Quartets*, which Eliot considered his masterpiece, was published; in it, he expresses his spiritual experiences, drawing heavily from mysticism, philosophy and Christian thought. "The Love Song of J. Alfred Prufrock" and its famous opening lines comparing the evening sky to "a patient etherised upon the table," is another well-known poem that has maintained its popularity.

T.S. Eliot also wrote critical essays and plays. *Murder in the Cathedral* was based on the death of Thomas Becket and opened at the Canterbury Festival in 1935. It is his best-known dramatic work, partially due to the film version, which was released in 1952. Four years earlier T.S. Eliot had received the Nobel Prize in Literature for his original contributions to contemporary poetry. In 1948 he received the Order of Merit from King George VI and received the Presidential Medal of Freedom in 1964, a year before his death.

Egas Moniz

For his discovery of the therapeutic value of leucotomy in certain psychoses.

Antonio Caetano de Abreu Freire Egas Moniz was born in Avanca, Portugal, on November 29, 1874 and received a grammar school education at the Colégio de San Fiel, of the Jesuit Order, and the Liceu de Viseu.

He enrolled in the Coimbra Faculty of Medicine in 1894, and in 1901 he obtained his doctorate degree. Between 1902 and 1911 he was a member of the teaching staff at Coimbra University, where he served as a substitute lecturer in anatomy, histology and general pathology. In 1911 he transferred to the Lisbon Faculty of Medicine and was made professor of neurology, a subject that was officially created only a short time before. He became director of the institution in 1929.

Before this time Moniz had obtained fame in other fields, including politics. He was a deputy in the Portuguese parliament between 1903 and 1917, was made minister of foreign affairs in 1917, and was the Portuguese ambassador to Spain between 1918 and 1919. He was also a writer who focused not just on medicine but teaching, politics, history and social questions.

In 1944, when he reached retirement age, he was given his pension, but only stopped teaching in 1949. That same year he was awarded the Nobel Prize in Physiology or Medicine, for his development of the leucotomy procedure (he shared the prize with the Swiss Walter Hess, who won for his discovery of the correlation between the interbrain and the activities of the internal organs). Moniz led a medical team that carried out the first surgical intervention of this type on the brain in 1935. He believed that the prefrontal leucotomy could be used as a surgical treatment for psychoses. The procedure involved sectioning some of the connections of the white matter on the prefrontal lobes of the brain's hemispheres. The prefrontal leucotomy was not, however, the Portuguese neurosurgeon's only contribution to medicine. The cerebral angiograph, which he created in 1927, and his description and systemization of the encephalitic veins and arteries and the patterns of various tumors were even more important efforts.

Besides his Nobel Prize, Egas Moniz was widely recognized for his contributions to science, being awarded the Oslo Prize in 1945, made a Commander of the Legion of Honor in France and awarded honorary doctorates from the universities of Lyon and Bordeaux. Moniz was shot in 1939 by a psychiatric patient, but he recovered fully from the attack. He died in Lisbon in 1955.

Walter Rudolf Hess also received half of the prize.

Leucotomy and angiography

LEUCOTOMIA

A leucotomy was conceived and carried out for the first time on the 27th of December, 1935 by a team of doctors led by Egas Moniz. The first surgical method for the treatment of certain mental conditions consisted of making an incision in the white substance of the brain's frontal lobes.

BASIS

Egas Moniz started from the principle that, in certain mental conditions due to the lack of change in certain symptoms, there must be a greater degree of inflexible connections between groups of nerve cells in different areas of the brain. Therefore, if certain nerve fibers were selected, the functioning of the whole of the various regions of the brain would be altered and psychotic symptoms could disappear. The front region was chosen for being associated with the psychic life.

Frontal lobe

TECHNIQUE

After making an incision in the outer surfaces two holes were made three centimeters either side of the central line. Into these holes an instrument (leucotome) was introduced which made cuts in the cerebral tissue.

APPLICATIONS

The leucotomy was used in various neurosurgical and psychiatric situations as a therapy for certain mental conditions. This operation, which was the basis for developing other psychosurgical procedures, resulted in a better understanding of the anatomy and physiology of the brain, amongst other things.

CEREBRAL ANGIOGRAPHY

The cerebra angiograph is an X-ray of the encephalitic blood vessels, both veins and arteries. The first X-ray, which led to the discovery of brain circulation, was obtained in 1927 by a team of doctors led by Egas Moniz.

BASIS

The encephalitic veins and arteries cannot be seen using ordinary X-rays. Egas Moniz found a contrast liquid: the first used was sodium iodite, which was later replaced by thorotrast, considered to be safer to the organism.

TECHNIQUE

After 12 ccs of contrast product have been injected into the carotid artery, a first X-ray is taken, which produces images of the arteries (arterial encephalography).

Four seconds later, when 16 ccs of contrast liquid have been introduced, (the injection of the product is only stopped after the second X-ray is taken), a second X-ray is taken, this time of the veins.

Superimposing the two X-ray images allows for a complete study of cerebral circulation.

APPLICATIONS

The cerebral angiograph is an important diagnostic tool and in locating brain tumors.

Nobel Laureates

1940-1949

1940

Nobel Prize in Physics
Not awarded.

Nobel Prize in Chemistry
Not awarded.

Nobel Prize in Physiology or Medicine
Not awarded.

Nobel Prize in Literature
Not awarded.

Nobel Peace Prize
Not awarded.

1941

Nobel Prize in Physics
Not awarded.

Nobel Prize in Chemistry
Not awarded.

Nobel Prize in Physiology or Medicine
Not awarded.

Nobel Prize in Literature
Not awarded.

Nobel Peace Prize
Not awarded.

1942

Nobel Prize in Physics
Not awarded.

Nobel Prize in Chemistry
Not awarded.

Nobel Prize in Physiology or Medicine
Not awarded.

Nobel Prize in Literature
Not awarded.

Nobel Peace Prize
Not awarded.

1943

Nobel Prize in Physics
Otto Stern
Born February 17, 1888, in Sorau, Germany (now
ary, Poland), and died August 17, 1969, in Berkeley,
California, United States.
For his contribution to the development of the molecular
ray method and his discovery of the magnetic moment
of the proton.

Nobel Prize in Chemistry
George de Hevesy
Born August 1, 1885, in Budapest, Hungary, and died
July 5, 1966, in Freiburg, Germany.
For his work on the use of isotopes as tracers in the
study of chemical processes.

Nobel Prize in Physiology or Medicine
Henrik Carl Peter Dam
Born February 21, 1895, in Copenhagen, Denmark,
and died April 17, 1976, in Copenhagen.
For his discovery of vitamin K.
&
Edward Adelbert Doisy
Born November 3, 1893, in Hume, Illinois, United States,
and died October 23, 1986, in Saint Louis, Missouri.
For his discovery of the chemical nature of vitamin K.

Nobel Prize in Literature
Not awarded.

Nobel Peace Prize
Not awarded.

1944

Nobel Prize in Physics
Isidor Isaac Rabi
Born July 29, 1898, in Rymanów, Austria (now Poland), and died January 11, 1988, in New York, New York, United States.
For his resonance method for recording the magnetic properties of atomic nuclei.

Nobel Prize in Chemistry
Otto Hahn
Born March 8, 1879, in Frankfurt am Main, Germany, and died July 28, 1968, in Göttingen.
For his discovery of the fission of heavy nuclei.

Nobel Prize in Physiology or Medicine
Joseph Erlanger
Born January 5, 1874, in San Francisco, California, United States, and died December 5, 1965, in Saint Louis, Missouri.
&
Herbert Spencer Gasser
Born July 5, 1888, in Platteville, Wisconsin, United States, and died May 11, 1963, in New York, New York.
For their discoveries relating to the highly differentiated functions of single nerve fibers.

Nobel Prize in Literature
Johannes Vilhelm Jensen
Born January 20, 1873, in Farso, Denmark, and died November 25, 1950, in Copenhagen.
For the rare strength and fertility of his poetic imagination with which is combined an intellectual curiosity of wide scope and a bold, freshly creative style.

Nobel Peace Prize
International Committee of the Red Cross
Founded in 1863 in Geneva, Switzerland.
For humanitarian activities during World War Two.

1945

Nobel Prize in Physics
Wolfgang Pauli
Born April 25, 1900, in Vienna, Austria, and died December 15, 1958, in Zurich, Switzerland.
For the discovery of the exclusion principle, also called the Pauli principle.

Nobel Prize in Chemistry
Artturi Ilmari Virtanen
Born January 15, 1895, in Helsinki, Finland, and died November 11, 1973, Helsinki.
For his research and inventions in agricultural and nutrition chemistry, especially for his fodder preservation method.

Nobel Prize in Physiology or Medicine
Ernst Boris Chain
Born June 19, 1906, in Berlin, Germany, and died August 12, 1979, in Mulranny, Ireland.
&
Alexander Fleming
Born August 6, 1881, in Lochfield, Scotland, and died March 11, 1955, in London, England.
&
Howard Walter Florey
Born September 24, 1898, in Adelaide, Australia, and died February 21, 1968, in Oxford, England.
For the discovery of penicillin and its curative effect in various infectious diseases.

Nobel Prize in Literature
Gabriela Mistral, pseudonym of Lucila Godoy y Alcayaga
Born April 7, 1889, in Vicuña, Chile, and died January 10, 1957, in New York, New York, United States.
For her lyric poetry which, inspired by powerful emotions, has made her name a symbol of the idealistic aspirations of the entire Latin American world.

Nobel Peace Prize
Cordell Hull
Born October 2, 1871, in Overton County (now Pickett County), Tennessee, United States, and died July 23, 1955, in Bethesda, Maryland.
[For] tireless work for good understanding between nations.

1946

Nobel Prize in Physics
Percy Williams Bridgman
Born April 21, 1882, in Cambridge, Massachusetts, United States, and died August 20, 1961, in Randolph, New Hampshire.
For the invention of an apparatus to produce extremely high pressures, and for the discoveries he made therewith in the field of high pressure physics.

Nobel Prize in Chemistry
John Howard Northrop
Born July 5, 1891, in Yonkers, New York, United States, and died May 27, 1987, in Wickenberg, Arizona.
&
Wendell Meredith Stanley
Born August 16, 1904, in Ridgeville, Indiana, United States, and died June 15, 1971, in Salamanca, Spain.
For their preparation of enzymes and virus proteins in a pure form.
&
James Batcheller Sumner
Born November 19, 1887, in Canton, Massachusetts, United States, and died August 12, 1955, in Buffalo, New York.
For his discovery that enzymes can be crystallized.

Nobel Prize in Physiology or Medicine
Hermann Joseph Muller
Born December 21, 1890, in New York, New York, United States, and died April 5, 1967, in Indianapolis, Indiana.
For the discovery of the production of mutations by means of X-ray irradiation.

Nobel Prize in Literature
Hermann Hesse
Born July 2, 1877, in Calw, Germany, and died August 9, 1962, in Montagnola, Switzerland.
For his inspired writings which, while growing in boldness and penetration, exemplify the classical humanitarian ideals and high qualities of style.

Nobel Peace Prize
Emily Greene Balch
Born January 8, 1867, in Boston, Massachusetts, United States, and died January 9, 1961, in Cambridge.
For leading the women's international peace movement.
&
John Raleigh Mott
Born May 25, 1865, in Livingston Manor, New York, United States, and died January 31, 1955, in Orlando, Florida.
For his role as a church leader in missionary movements. He demonstrated respect for individual differences and humanitarian efforts in a time of war.

1947

Nobel Prize in Physics
Edward Victor Appleton
Born September 6, 1892, in Bradford, England, and died April 21, 1965, in Edinburgh, Scotland.
For his investigations of the physics of the upper atmosphere, especially for the discovery of the so-called Appleton layer.

Nobel Prize in Chemistry
Robert Robinson
Born September 13, 1886, in Rufford, England, and died February 8, 1975, in Great Missenden.
For his investigations on plant products of biological importance, especially the alkaloids.

Nobel Prize in Physiology or Medicine
Carl Ferdinand Cori
Born December 5, 1896, in Prague, Czechoslovakia (now Czech Republic), and died October 20, 1984, in Cambridge, Massachusetts, United States.
&
Gerty Theresa Cori, née Radnitz
Born August 15, 1896, in Prague (now Czech Republic), and died October 26, 1957, in Saint Louis, Missouri, United States.
For their discovery of the course of the catalytic conversion of glycogen.
&
Bernardo Alberto Houssay
Born April 10, 1887, in Buenos Aires, Argentina, and died September 21, 1971, Buenos Aires.
For his discovery of the part played by the hormone of the anterior pituitary lobe in the metabolism of sugar.

Nobel Prize in Literature
André Paul Guillaume Gide
Born November 22, 1869, in Paris, France, and died February 19, 1951, Paris.
For his comprehensive and artistically significant writings, in which human problems and conditions have been presented with a fearless love of truth and keen psychological insight.

Nobel Peace Prize
American Friends Service Committee (The Quakers)
Founded in 1672, with its headquarters in Washington, D.C.
&
Friends Service Council
Founded in 1647, with its headquarters in London, England.
For activities in humanitarian assistance during and after World War Two.

1948

Nobel Prize in Physics
Patrick Maynard Stuart Blackett
Born November 18, 1897, in London, England, and died July 13, 1974, in London.
For his development of the Wilson cloud chamber method, and his discoveries therewith in the fields of nuclear physics and cosmic radiation.

Nobel Prize in Chemistry
Arne Wilhelm Kaurin Tiselius
Born August 10, 1902, in Stockholm, Sweden, and died October 29, 1971, in Uppsala.
For his research on electrophoresis and adsorption analysis, especially for his discoveries concerning the complex nature of serum proteins.

Nobel Prize in Physiology or Medicine
Paul Hermann Müller
Born January 12, 1899, in Olten, Switzerland, and died October 12, 1965, in Basel.
For his discovery of the high efficiency of DDT as a contact poison against several arthropods.

Nobel Prize in Literature
Thomas Stearns Eliot
Born September 26, 1888, in Saint Louis, Missouri, United States, and died January 4, 1965, in London, England.
For his outstanding, pioneer contribution to present-day poetry.

Nobel Peace Prize
Not awarded.

1949

Nobel Prize in Physics
Hideki Yukawa
Born January 23, 1907, in Tokyo, Japan, and died September 8, 1981, in Kyoto.
For his prediction of the existence of mesons on the basis of theoretical work on nuclear forces.

Nobel Prize in Chemistry
William Francis Giauque
Born May 12, 1895, in Niagara Falls, Ontario, Canada, and died March 28, 1982, in Berkeley, California, United States.
For his contribution in the field of chemical thermodynamics, particularly concerning the behavior of substances at extremely low temperatures.

Nobel Prize in Physiology or Medicine
Antonio Caetano de Abreu Freire Egas Moniz
Born November 29, 1874, in Avanca, Portugal, and died December 13, 1955, in Lisbon.
For his discovery of the therapeutic value of leucotomy in certain psychoses.
&
Walter Rudolf Hess
Born March 17, 1881, in Frauenfeld, Switzerland, and died August 12, 1973, in Locarno.
For his discovery of the functional organization of the interbrain as the coordinator of the activities of the internal organs.

Nobel Prize in Literature
William Faulkner
Born September 25, 1897, in New Albany, Mississippi, United States, and died July 6, 1962, in Byhalia.
For his powerful and artistically unique contribution to the modern American novel.

Nobel Peace Prize
John Boyd Orr
Born September 23, 1880, in Kilmaurs, Scotland, and died June 25, 1971, in Edzell.
For efforts to end hunger and for promoting unity and world peace.

Selected Profiles of Nobel Laureates

1950–1959

Bertrand Russell

In recognition of his varied and significant writings in which he champions humanitarian ideals and freedom of thought.

Bertrand Arthur William Russell, philosopher, mathematician and pacifist, was born in Trelleck, Wales, to Viscount Amberley and Katherine, daughter of the 2nd Baron Stanley of Alderley. His parents died when he was just three years old, and he was raised by his paternal grandparents, Lord John Russell, who had twice been prime minister, and his wife, Lady John.

A solitary and thoughtful child, Russell had a private education with governesses and tutors that involved little contact with other children. At the age of 11 his first religious doubts appeared, and by 14 he no longer believed in God, free will or immortality.

He entered Trinity College, Cambridge, in 1890 and distinguished himself in mathematics and philosophy. While at Cambridge Russell began to read widely, particularly works by modern writers, including George Bernard Shaw, Walt Whitman and Friedrich Nietzsche. After completing his studies he traveled to Paris, and for some months he worked at the British Embassy. He then returned to Cambridge in 1895 and became a Fellow at Trinity College. After time in Berlin he returned to Paris, in 1900, to visit the Mathematical Congress. Impressed with the work of Peano, an Italian mathematician, he was inspired to write *The Principles of Mathematics*, published in 1903, which outlined his belief that the foundations of mathematics could be deduced from only a few logical ideas.

Russell was appointed a lecturer at his alma mater in 1910, but with the outbreak of World War I he became heavily involved in pacifist activities. In 1918 he was imprisoned for six months after having a pacifist article published in the *Tribunal*.

In 1920 Russell traveled to Russia to observe the rise of bolshevism firsthand; that same year he went to China and lectured on philosophy at Peking University. Russell abandoned pacifism during World War II, but in his final years he was a leading voice against the use of nuclear weapons. In 1964 he established the Bertrand Russell Peace Foundation.

In 1908 he had been elected a fellow of the Royal Societ. He was also awarded the Sylvester Medal by the Royal Society and the De Morgan Medal by the London Mathematical Society in 1934. For extensive work expressing his highly developed humanitarian ideas and philosophies of knowledge, Bertrand Russell was awarded the 1950 Nobel Prize in Literature.

On February 2, 1970, Bertrand Russell died of influenza at the age of 98. When he was asked what he would say if he found himself before God, Russell replied, "I should reproach him for not giving us enough evidence." He remains today one of the most widely read philosophers of the 20th century.

Ralph Bunche

For his mediation in the war between Israel, Egypt, Jordan, Lebanon and Syria, which followed the United Nations plan of 1947 to partition Palestine.

Ralph Johnson Bunche was born to a poor African-American couple in Detroit on August 7, 1904. His father was a barber in an establishment that only served white customers. He graduated from Jefferson High School in Los Angeles in 1922 as valedictorian and was awarded a scholarship to UCLA, from which he graduated summa cum laude in 1927. A year later Bunche earned his master's degree from Harvard University.

Professionally Bunche was concerned with social issues and international relations. He was asked to organize a political science department at Howard University in Washington, D.C., but he left the institution to work on his doctorate at Harvard.

Conscious of the existing discrimination and racism in America at the time, Bunche always raised his voice to defend what he considered just. In 1936 he published his first book, *World View of Race*. In 1965 he helped in leading the marches organized by Martin Luther King, Jr., in Montgomery, Alabama.

It was at the service of the UN that, between June 1947 and August 1949, he undertook the most important mission of his life, which would bring him the Nobel Peace Prize in 1950. The United Nations had appointed Count Folke Bernedotte as a mediator for the Middle Eastern nations during the Arab-Israeli conflict, and Bunche was his principal aide. They had the mission of achieving a peaceful resolution between the Arabs and the Israelis, who were at war in Palestine. Four months later Count Bernedotte was assassinated, and Bunch was forced to take over the mission. After 11 months of negotiation he managed to obtain a ceasefire between the Arab states and Israel.

In later years Bunche worked with the UN to resolve the Suez Crisis in Egypt and attempted to stabilize the former Belgian Congo. In addition to the Nobel Prize, he was awarded the Theodore Roosevelt Association Medal of Honor in 1954, the Presidential Medal of Honor in 1963 and, in 1991, was inducted into the African American Hall of Fame.

After 25 years of service to the United Nations he resigned due to failing health; both his family life and fitness had suffered because of his dedication to international causes. He died on December 9, 1971, in New York.

John Cockcroft

For their pioneer work on the transmutation of atomic nuclei by artificially accelerated atomic particles.

John Douglas Cockcroft was born in Todmorden, England, and attended the University of Manchester, where he studied mathematics under the guidance of Horace Lamb from 1914 to 1915. He served with the Royal Field Artillery during World War I, and in 1918 he returned to Manchester and studied electrical engineering at the College of Technology.

Cockcroft next went to St. John's College, Cambridge, where he worked at the famed Cavendish Laboratory, a common experience for many physics and chemistry Nobel laureates. He worked with Lord Rutherford and then collaborated with Pyotr Kapitsa, who went on to win the 1978 Nobel Prize in Physics, in the production of intense magnetic fields and low temperatures.

In 1928 he concentrated on the acceleration of protons by high voltages and was soon joined by Ernest Walton in this work. Four years later the pair presented the Cockcroft-Walton accelerator, which they used to transmute lithium atoms by bombarding them with high-energy protons. They went on to perform more work in the splitting of other atoms, and they established the importance of accelerators as a tool in nuclear research.

In parallel with his scientific career, Cockcroft also had time to lecture. In 1929 he obtained a fellowship to St. John's College, Cambridge, and, a decade later, became a professor of natural philosophy there. During World War II he was appointed Assistant Director of Scientific Research in the Ministry of Supply. Before the war ended he was released from these duties and went to Canada to head an atomic energy project, later becoming director of the Chalk River and Montreal Laboratories. He held this position until 1946, when he returned to England as the director of the Atomic Energy Research Establishment. He was awarded honorary doctorates from more than 20 universities around the world and became a member of many of the most prominent scientific societies. He was knighted in 1948 and, in 1951, shared the Nobel Prize in Physics with Ernest Walton for their pioneering work on the transmutation of atomic nuclei by artificially accelerated atomic particles.

He married Eunice Elizabeth Crabtree in 1925, with whom he had four daughters and a son. Cockcroft died in Cambridge in 1967.

Ernest Thomas Sinton Walton also received half of the prize.

Ernest Walton

For their pioneer work on the transmutation of atomic nuclei by artificially accelerated atomic particles.

Ernest Thomas Sinton Walton was born in Dungarvan, Waterford, on the south coast of Ireland. The son of a Methodist minister from County Tipperary, he received a religious education, which stayed with him all his life. Because of his father's position Walton moved frequently, and he had an interrupted early education until 1915, when he became a boarder at Methodist College, Belfast.

There, mathematics and the sciences became his favorite subjects. He won a scholarship and, in 1922, continued his studies at Trinity College, Dublin, where he shone as a scholar. He graduated in 1926 with honors in mathematics and experimental sciences. One year later he obtained a master's degree. He then went to Cambridge University to work at the Cavendish Laboratory under the guidance of Lord Rutherford.

It was at Cambridge that Walton met John Cockcroft, who became his principal scientific partner and with whom he shared the 1951 Nobel Prize in Physics. Both scientists were dedicated to developing the first nuclear particle accelerator, later known as the Cockcroft-Walton accelerator, which was the result of pioneering work in the transmutation of atomic nuclei by artificially accelerated atomic particles. It was for these developments and discoveries that the pair was awarded the Nobel Prize.

In 1934, and after having taken his doctorate degree, Walton returned to Trinity College, where he continued to lecture for the next 40 years. He married Winifred Isabel Wilson who, like Walton, came from a Methodist family and was a former student at the Methodist College, Belfast. They had two sons and two daughters together.

Even though Walton had a career very much connected to teaching, this Irish physicist was involved in many other fields. He was a member of numerous commissions, including the School of Cosmic Physics, the Institute of Advanced Studies in Dublin, the Royal Hospital of Dublin, the Royal Irish Academy and the Royal Dublin Society. He also participated in various governmental and religious committees.

Another of Walton's favorite activities was writing. He published a series of essays in the journals of esteemed societies, especially on the themes of hydrodynamics, nuclear physics and microwaves. Besides the Nobel Prize, he was jointly recognized with John Cockcroft with the Hughes Medal in 1938 and received an honorary doctorate from Queen's University, Belfast, in 1959.

He died in Belfast, Ireland, in 1995.

John Douglas Cockcroft also received half of the prize.

Glenn Seaborg

For their discoveries in the chemistry of the transuranium elements.

Glenn Theodore Seaborg received many honors throughout his career, but the most long lasting was that a chemical element, element 106 in the periodic table, was named seaborgium in his honor. In addition to his career in chemistry he was recognized as one of the most prominent nuclear physicists in the world. For many decades his tall, thin figure was a constant presence at the world's principal scientific meetings, and he proved always ready to passionately, but unpretentiously, explain nuclear science to anyone who was interested — one of the characteristics that endeared him to his students.

Seaborg was born in Ishpeming, a mining town in Michigan, but, at the age of 10, his family moved to California. Since his parents were first- and second-generation Swedish immigrants, it is not surprising that Seaborg learnt Swedish before he could speak a word of English. Nevertheless, he quickly acquired the language and soon began to distinguish himself academically.

In 1929 he concluded his secondary studies at David Starr Jordan High School and was the class valedictorian. Seaborg's science teacher at this small institution had a great influence on him, and he went out of his way to study both chemistry and physics while he was there. That the same year he entered UCLA and, he finished his chemistry studies at their campus in Berkeley in 1937.

Between 1942 and 1946 Seaborg carried out research in chemistry and nuclear physics as part of the Manhattan Project, the American initiative to create the first atomic bombs during World War II. He was later asked many times about his view of the bombings of Hiroshima and Nagasaki, but Seaborg always maintained his belief that they were actions necessary to end the war, despite the massive loss of life.

In 1951 Seaborg, who had a decisive role in isolating plutonium, shared the Nobel Prize in Chemistry with Edwin McMillan in recognition of their discoveries in the chemistry of the transuranium elements. Throughout his career he also occupied positions of importance in governmental and at scientific institutions, and he was a fellow at many of the leading academic societies. His honors include the 1947 American Chemical Society's Award in Pure Chemistry, the 1957 Perkin Medal from the Society of the Chemical Industry and the 1959 Atomic Energy Commission's Enrico Fermi Award. He also received more than a dozen honorary degrees.

In 1942 he married Helen Griggs and they went on to have six children. He died on February 25, 1999, at his home in Lafayette, California.

Edwin Mattison McMillan also received half of the prize.

Edwin McMillan

For their discoveries in the chemistry of the transuranium elements.

Edwin Mattison McMillan was born at Redondo Beach, California, but a year later moved with his parents to Pasadena, where he spent the rest of his childhood. The son of Edwin Harbaugh McMillan, a doctor, and his wife, Anne Marie, his early interests in science and mechanics were both encouraged and nurtured.

He obtained his bachelor's degree from the California Institute of Technology in 1928 and his master's degree a year later. He then transferred to Princeton University and completed his doctorate there in 1932.

That same year McMillan entered the University of California, Berkeley, as a National Research Fellow. After two years he became a staff member at Berkeley's Radiation Laboratory, working under the guidance of Ernest Lawrence, studying nuclear reactions and their products. He was appointed a full professor at the Department of Physics at Berkeley in 1946.

McMillan married Elsie Walford Blumer, who came from a family long connected to the medical profession, in 1941, and they had three children. This harmonious and genial family was the stability in McMillan's life, and he reveled in the responsibilities of a father. He also enjoyed natural history and spent much time outdoors, exploring and gardening.

With the arrival of World War II, he contributed his knowledge to developing the first atomic bombs and worked in the Radiation Laboratory at the Massachusetts Institute of Technology and in the U. S. Navy Radio and Sound Laboratory, San Diego. Following the war, however, he became critical about the use of nuclear weapons.

Having discovered a uranium isotope, which was given the name neptunium, he was honored with many prizes. The Nobel Prize in Chemistry was awarded to him in 1951 for "discoveries in the chemistry of the transuranium elements," and he shared it with Glenn Seaborg. Other distinctions he received include the Atoms for Peace Award in 1963 and honorary doctorates from the Rensselaer Polytechnic Institute and Gustavus Adolphus College.

Edwin McMillan, who appreciated science, nature, friends and family, died on September 7, 1991, in El Cerrito, California. He left behind a body of work that has led to many more discoveries and developments.

Glenn Theodore Seaborg also received half the prize.

Max Theiler

For his discoveries concerning yellow fever and how to combat it.

Max Theiler was born in Pretoria, South Africa, and was the son of a well-known researcher in veterinary medicine, Sir Arnold Theiler. He studied in local schools and then attended Rhodes University College and the University of Cape Town Medical School.

In 1918 he left for England to study at St. Thomas' Hospital and the London School of Tropical Medicine, where he obtained his medical degree in 1922. That same year he moved to the United States and became an assistant at the Department of Tropical Medicine at Harvard Medical School, where he later became an instructor.

By the age of 20 Theiler was already a specialist in tropical diseases. He focused on the study of yellow fever, which, at the time, was a very prevalent, dangerous disease that had already infected and killed a number of researchers. Theiler was certain that yellow fever was caused by a virus, but at the time microscopes were incapable of showing viruses. This deficiency wasn't the only difficulty, however. Everything pointed to the fact that monkeys were the only animals that could be useful in studying diseases that affected humans, but this limitation made research impractical, since no laboratory could support the financial costs of the hundreds of primates necessary for an effective study. The solution was to use mice, which had already been tried unsuccessfully by other researchers. Theiler, however, got them to contract yellow fever with a solution of the liver of an infected monkey, which was then injected into the mouse's brain cells. As a result, laboratory research into yellow fever was now possible.

During his research Theiler noted that by passing the virus from mouse to mouse the disease weakened to such an extent that, after this long process, the mice were able to survive the disease. After the 176th mouse, the disease was no longer contracted. Eventually, this weakened virus was injected into a monkey, which did not show signs of the disease. The creation of an antivirus was now possible and, some time later, the vaccine against yellow fever, known as 17D, was produced.

Theiler was recognized for this important work with the 1951 Nobel Prize in Physiology or Medicine. Theiler also researched other diseases and occupied high-ranking positions, including the director of the Medicine and Public Health laboratories of the Rockefeller Foundation in New York.

Max Theiler married Lillian Graham in 1928, and the couple had a daughter together. He died in New Haven, Connecticut, on August 11, 1972.

Winston Churchill

For his mastery of historical and biographical description as well as for brilliant oratory in defending exalted human values.

Winning a Nobel Prize is, for most people, the pinnacle of their professional life and the way they will be remembered by later generations. This, however, is certainly not the case with the Right Honourable Sir Winston Leonard Spencer Churchill, who many people, in fact, are unaware won the 1953 Nobel Prize in Literature.

Born into an aristocratic family, he was the son of Lord Randolph Churchill, a respected conservative politician, and an American mother. Winston Churchill's early studies were at Harrow, a famous boys' boarding school, and the Royal Military Academy Sandhurst. He then briefly served as Second Lieutenant in the 4th Queen's Own Hussars after his father's death in 1895, but he obtained leave and worked for the *London Daily Graphic* as a reporter. From 1896 to 1897 he again served in the military, this time in India, but continued to be involved in journalism. While in India he wrote the basis of what would be published in 1898 as *The Story of the Malakand Field Force*. In this work he wrote, "It is better to be making the news than taking it; to be an actor rather than a critic." He would soon make the transition himself, and to an unprecedented degree.

For a further two years he served in Africa, finally resigning his commission in 1899 and becoming a correspondent for the *London Morning Post* during the Boer War. *The River War: An Account of the Reconquest of the Sudan* (1899) and *My African Journey* (1908) are two of Churchill's books about this period of his life. Both were popular and related his daring adventures during the Boer War.

In 1900 he was elected a member of Parliament as a Conservative. However, he joined the Liberal Party four years later, and for the next half-decade he filled several government posts, including Minister of Commerce in 1908, Home Secretary in 1910 and First Lord of the Admiralty in 1911. With the outbreak of World War I Churchill worked in the War Office, taking on diplomatic work. He worked to strengthen the British Navy and supported the development of the tank, but he received heavy blame for his part in the failed Gallipoli landings. In 1915 he resigned from government, feeling his efforts were no longer appreciated. He then rejoined the army and rose to the rank of colonel.

He returned to government in 1917, in 1924 he left the Liberal Party to rejoin the Conservatives. During this period he served as the Chancellor of the Exchequer from 1924 to 1929, and he is remembered for his work in defeating the General Strike of 1926. His economic policies, however, were strongly criticized. After the defeat of the Conservatives in 1929, Churchill remained out of politics for a decade. Between 1933 and 1939 he wrote *Marlborough: His Life and Times*, a four-volume biography of one of his ancestors.

When World War II broke out Churchill was made First Lord of the Admiralty, a position he had held between 1910 and 1915. In 1940 he was called to take on the positions of prime minister and minister of defense. He was known as a clever strategist, a great statesman and the face of British opposition to the Nazi regime. He emerged from the war as a national and international hero, despite controversy over various actions and policies. His passionate radio speeches were given much credit for bolstering the national spirit during the dark years of the war, and they are frequently quoted today. President George W. Bush used an adaptation of Churchill's: "We shall not flag nor fail. We shall go on to the end... We shall fight on the beaches... we shall fight in the fields and in the streets... we shall never surrender" after the terrorist attacks on September 11, 2001.

Despite his enormous prestige, Churchill was beaten by the Labour Party in the general election after the war. He returned to power in 1951, but he retired from political life four years later for health reasons. He was one of the forces behind the creation of NATO, and the first person to use the phrase "iron curtain" in 1946, warning of what would develop into the Cold War.

Despite being a less well known aspect of his life, Churchill was a talented and diligent writer. Besides his early works, he published his only novel, *Savrola*, in 1900 and six years later a biography of his father, simply entitled *Lord Randolph Churchill*. He also published a six-volume history of World War I, entitled *The World Crisis*. His most famous work, however, is his history *The Second World War*, compiled in six volumes between 1948 and 1954. After retiring he wrote the four-volume *History of the English-Speaking Peoples*, which appeared between 1956 and 1958. Churchill was also a talented painter and, above all, a great orator. His speeches were collected in 12 volumes, among which were the famous "The Unrelenting Struggle" (1942), "The Dawn of Liberation" (1945) and "Victory" (1946).

Churchill married Clementine Ogilvy Hozier in 1908, and the couple had four children, one son and three daughters. His marriage and family provided him with much-needed stability as he steered his nation and events all over the world. On his 75th birthday Churchill said, "I am ready to meet my Maker, whether my Maker is prepared for the ordeal of meeting me is another matter." He died on January 24, 1965.

George Marshall

For his promotion of peace in the aftermath of the Second World War.

During World War II George Catlett Marshall was chief of staff for the most powerful army in the world, but, despite being a great general, he earned his place in history for his role, while he was secretary of state, in devising the celebrated "Marshall Plan," which helped the economic recovery of European nations in the aftermath of the war. For this work he won the 1953 Nobel Peace Prize.

Marshall was born on New Year's Eve, 1880. His father ran a prosperous coal company in Pennsylvania, but the junior Marshall was determined to pursue a career in the military. He entered the Virginia Military Institute and graduated in 1901 as the senior first captain of the Corps of Cadets. After serving in the Philippines and the United States, he graduated with honors in 1907 from the Infantry-Cavalry School in Fort Leavenworth. In 1908 he graduated equally successfully from the Army Staff College.

During the following nine years, the young officer distinguished himself in various posts, which led him to be called to the General Staff in World War I and embark for Europe with the troops of the First Division. His work as a strategist was decisive in the battles of Cantigny, Aisne-Marne, St. Michel, Meuse-Argonne and other battles on the western front.

After the war ended, Marshall worked in military academies; was aide-de-camp to General John J. Pershing, the army chief of staff, between 1920 and 1924; and served in China for three years. He was promoted to brigadier general in October 1936 and was in command of Vancouver Barracks in Washington until 1938. That same year he was once again called to the General Staff.

In 1939 he was promoted to full general and nominated by President Franklin D. Roosevelt to be army chief of staff. Until the United States entered World War II, after the attack on Pearl Harbor, he urged an increase in military spending. After Pearl Harbor he was responsible for transforming the poorly equipped force of 200,000 he had inherited into the battle-ready eight million soldiers the U.S. Army deployed during the conflict. He was also instrumental in composing and coordinating Allied operations, including Operation Overlord and the invasion of Normandy, and he selected Dwight D. Eisenhower as supreme commander in Europe. He was named *Time* magazine's Man of the Year in 1944 and on December 16 was promoted to the five-star rank — the newly created rank General of the Army.

With the end of the war in 1945, Marshall finished his military career but still continued serving his country. He participated in various peace conferences and was a mediator in China between the Communists under Mao Zedong and the Nationalists allied to the United States under Chiang Kai-shek; these negotiations ultimately failed, however, and he returned to the U.S. in 1947.

As secretary of state between 1947 and 1949 he devised the celebrated Marshall Plan, eventually adopted by 17 European countries. He outlined the program in a speech given at Harvard University: "It is logical that the United States should do whatever it is able to do to assist in the return of normal economic health to the world, without which there can be no political stability and no assured peace. Our policy is not directed against any country, but against hunger, poverty, desperation and chaos." In exchange for its economic aid, America wanted to establish democratic governments in Western Europe and put a stop to the spread of Soviet influence. To such an end, and to coordinate the implementation of the program, the Organization for European Economic Co-operation was created with the signing of the Marshall Plan by President Truman on April 3, 1948. Congress would approve more than $12 billion in aid over the following four years.

The American Defense Department stumbled under the leadership of Secretary Louis A. Johnson during the first months of the Korean War, and a frustrated President Truman replaced him with George Catlett Marshall on September 21, 1950. He served as defense secretary until September 12, 1951.

Besides the Nobel Prize, Marshall received dozens of U.S. and foreign military honors, including the Distinguished Service Medal, the Silver Star and the National Defense Service Medal, as well as civilian honors such as the Distinguished Achievement Award in 1948 and the establishment of the Marshall Scholarship by the British Parliament in recognition of his contributions to Anglo-American relations. Even after resigning from his final post of secretary of defense at the age of 70, Marshall was still a much sought-after public speaker. He died on October 16, 1959, in Washington, D.C., and is buried in Arlington National Cemetery.

Linus Pauling

For his research into the nature of the chemical bond and its application to the elucidation of the structure of complex substances.

When he reached the end of his life, Linus Carl Pauling was the only man in history to have accepted two Nobel Prizes in two different countries. In 1963, nine years after going to Stockholm to receive the 1954 Nobel Prize in Chemistry, he went to Oslo to receive the Nobel Peace Prize.

Of German and English ancestry, Linus Pauling was born on February 28, 1901, in Portland, Oregon. He was the son of Herman Henry William Pauling, a pharmacist, and grew up immersed in the world of chemistry and medicine. Pauling attended public schools near his native city then entered Oregon State College in 1917; he received his bachelor's degree in chemical engineering five years later. From 1919 to 1920 he taught quantitative analysis full time at the college. He was then made a teaching fellow in chemistry at the California Institute of Technology, while he completed his graduate studies. In 1925 he received his doctorate degree, summa cum laude, in chemistry, with minors in physics and mathematics.

It was Linus Pauling who introduced the concept of electronegativity to the scientific world. He applied quantum mechanics to the study of molecular structures and discovered the helix structure in proteins. He was also the author of more than a thousand publications, including articles for scientific journals, prefaces and reviews.

Pauling was as equally passionate an antinuclear activist as he was a chemist. He was behind multiple campaigns against nuclear tests and wrote the book *No More War!* in 1958. Immediately after World War II, at Albert Einstein's behest, Pauling and seven other scientists formed the Emergency Committee of Atomic Scientists, of which Einstein was the president, which alerted the world to the dangers of the new era of nuclear weapons.

At the end of the 1950s Linus Pauling and his wife, Ava Helen Pauling, managed to collect the signatures of 11,021 scientists appealing to the United Nations to ban nuclear testing. When, in August 1961, the USSR announced that it would resume its test program after a period during which the superpowers had voluntarily abstained from testing, Pauling doubled his efforts to convince the Soviet Union, the United States and Great Britain to sign a prohibition treaty. The Nuclear Test Ban Treaty was eventually signed in July 1963, and it came into force on October 10 of the same year. On the same day the Norwegian Nobel Committee announced the 1963 Nobel Peace Prize winners and also awarded the 1962 prize to Linus Pauling for his work toward universal disarmament. He is the only person in history to receive two undivided Nobel prizes.

Linus Pauling died on August 19, 1994, at the age of 93.

Ernest Hemingway

For his mastery of the art of narrative, most recently demonstrated in The Old Man and the Sea, and for the influence that he has exerted on contemporary style.

"Man is not made to be defeated. A man can be destroyed but not beaten," wrote Hemingway in *The Old Man and the Sea*. Whatever the final fate of humanity, however, Ernest Miller Hemingway chose to end his own life with the squeeze of a trigger. He had been for many years obsessed with the idea of death and felt incapable of submitting to infirmity and old age. The highly influential American writer left numerous works and many friends on both sides of the Atlantic.

Ernest Hemingway was born in Oak Park, in the suburbs of Chicago, Illinois. His father, a doctor, instilled in him a love of sports. While he was still young Hemingway started to write articles for student magazines, and at the age of 18 he was already working for the *Kansas City Star* newspaper. In April 1918 he left for Italy and served as a volunteer in an ambulance unit for the Red Cross during World War I. He was wounded and spent a considerable amount of time in a military hospital in Milan and was decorated by the Italian government.

On his return to North America in 1919, Hemingway resumed writing for American and Canadian newspapers. Later he worked as a correspondent in Europe and was in France when the Nazi invasion took place during World War II. Before this, however, he lived in Paris, where he socialized in literary circles and with American expats. Hemingway wrote about this time in the book *The Sun Also Rises* (1926), one of his most significant works, which describes the life of an American journalist who had been wounded during World War I.

The theme of war returned in *A Farewell to Arms* (1929), and it would return once more when he was a correspondent covering the Spanish Civil War. *For Whom the Bell Tolls* (1940), one of his best-known books, was inspired by the civil war in Spain.

Hemingway loved traveling, and it inspired many of his other works. Visits to Spain, Africa and Cuba encouraged him to explore other themes, including bullfighting and hunting. In *Death in the Afternoon*, published in 1932, Hemingway talks of bullfighting, meditating on its rituals and, in particular, on death. In *Green Hills of Africa* (1935) he describes a visit to the continent as well as the adventures of a safari. *The Old Man and the Sea* (1952) tells the story of a fisherman from Havana who captures a giant fish. It is seen by many as a tale of victorious struggle, despite the fact that sharks devour the protagonist's catch as he struggles to bring it out of the Gulf Stream.

On July 2, 1961, Hemingway shot himself with his favorite rifle. He had been awarded the Nobel Prize in Literature in 1954.

Office of the United Nations High Commissioner for Refugees

For its work in favor of and with refugees.

The Office of the United Nations High Commissioner for Refugees (UNHCR) was created in 1951 by the UN General Assembly as a temporary organization that should last no more than three years. It has periodically been resurrected, however, because conflicts, persecution and fear do not stop, and people, unable to stand these conditions, flee.

The UNHCR replaced the International Refugee Organisation which was in operation between 1947 and 1952. This latter organization had itself taken on the work carried out between 1943 and 1947 by the United Nations Relief and Rehabilitation Administration.

According UNHCR's definition, a refugee is generally a person who, because of persecutory acts motivated by his race, creed or political convictions, is living outside his country or does not want the protection of his country. UNHCR assures refugees international protection in accordance with the stipulations of the Convention Relating to the Status of Refugees, which has been ratified by more than 60 countries. In 1967 an act expanded the stipulations of the convention and introduced new groups of refugees. The United Nations Declaration on Territorial Asylum further increased the range of international protection, focusing on promoting international legal instruments that are aimed at benefiting refugees in matters such as the right to work and social security.

With its headquarters in Geneva, UNHCR has 30 offices around the world in strategic locations as well as special representatives and correspondents. The high commissioner is nominated by the secretary-general and elected by the General Assembly. Its action is fundamentally centered on coordinating international action and establishing links between governments, UN special agencies, intergovernmental organizations and nongovernmental organizations.

The United Nations covers UNHCR's administrative expenses but permits the high commissioner to receive financing from the governments involved and to accept private donations from individuals and organizations. Today a staff of more than 6,300 works in 110 countries to alleviate the plight of refugees, most recently in Kenya, Ethiopia and Darfur. One of the organization's most visible goodwill ambassadors is Angelina Jolie, who accepted the position of August 27, 2001. UNHCR has received the Nobel Peace Prize in 1954 and again in 1981.

Lester Pearson

Because of his personal qualities – the powerful initiative, strength and perseverance he has displayed in attempting to prevent or limit war operations and to restore peace.

Lester Bowles, or "Mike" as he was known to his friends, Pearson was a man in whom intelligence and compassion were combined with a strong practical streak and a genuine desire to serve others. He made friends and earned respect wherever he went and succeeded in his desire to leave the world a better place than he had found it. Born in Newtonbrook, Ontario, in 1897 both Pearson's father and grandfather had been Methodist ministers. He entered the University of Toronto in 1913 but left in 1914 to serve with a hospital unit during the First World War. Two years later he was commissioned into the army and posted to the Royal Flying Corps. After being injured in an accident Pearson was invalided home and served as a training instructor for the duration of the war. He received his degree from the University of Toronto in 1919 and attended Oxford University on a scholarship, receiving his Master's degree.

From 1924 to 1928 he taught history at the University of Toronto before joining the Department of External Affairs in 1928. He participated in the Geneva World Disarmament Conference and in sessions of the League of Nations.

After serving in the office of the High Commissioner for Canada in London from 1935 to 1941, he was then posted to Washington D.C. and was named Ambassador to the United States in 1945. He was deeply involved in the work to establish the United Nations and participated in the United Nations Relief and Rehabilitation Administration.

Returning to Canada, Pearson won a seat in the House of Commons and served as Minister of External Affairs from 1948 to 1957. During this time he was involved in the formation of the North Atlantic Treaty Organization (NATO) and was elected president of the Seventh Session of the General Assembly of the United Nations (1952 – 53). As Chairman of the UN's Special Committee on Palestine, he helped construct the groundwork for the creation of the state of Israel in 1947. During the Suez Crisis of 1956 he proposed the UN Emergency Force to police the area and reestablish the peace.

In 1963 the Liberal Party of Canada won the election and Pearson became Prime Minister of Canada. He was a strong supporter of Canada's role as a peacemaker and continued his work for disarmament and peaceful resolution of international questions. As well as his contributions to peace and world affairs, during his time as Prime Minister some of Canada's most significant domestic legislation was implemented including the establishment of the Canada Pension Plan and universal Medicare as well as the adoption of the country's new flag in 1965.

Pearson retired from the leadership of his party in 1968 and died in Ottawa in 1972.

Peace 1957

John Bardeen

For their researches on semiconductors and their discovery of the transistor effect.

John Bardeen was twice awarded the Nobel Prize in Physics. The first time was in 1956, with his colleagues William Shockley and Walter Brattain, for their research into semiconductors that resulted in the development of transistors, which proved fundamental to developing the microprocessor. The second time was in 1972, along with two other Americans, Leon Cooper and Robert Schrieffer, for the development of the theory of superconductivity.

Born on May 23, 1908, in Madison, Wisconsin, Bardeen's father was dean of the Medical School of the University of Wisconsin. His mother died when he was just 12 years old. Bardeen completed his high school studies at Madison Central High School, and then he enrolled in an electrical engineering course at the University of Wisconsin, where he demonstrated his abilities in both mathematics and physics.

After completing this course he began working for the Engineering Department of the Western Electric Company in Chicago. He returned to his studies the next term and graduated in 1928. Bardeen stayed in Wisconsin as a graduate research assistant for the next six years, working on mathematical problems in applied geophysics as well as radiation from antennas. It was during this period that he first became acquainted with quantum theory.

John Bardeen followed Professor Leo J. Peters, with whom he had carried out research in the field of geophysics in Wisconsin, to the Gulf Research Laboratories in Pittsburgh, Pennsylvania. Between 1930 and 1933 he developed methods to interpret magnetic and gravitational surveys.

Desiring to focus more on pure than applied science, however, Bardeen left the laboratories to carry out research in the fields of mathematics and physics at Princeton University. Before he concluded his doctorate thesis on the theory of the work function of metals, he was offered a position at the Society of Fellows of Harvard University, where he stayed between 1935 and 1938. After World War II Bardeen focused on electrical conduction in semiconductors and metals, the superficial properties of semiconductors and the diffusion of atoms in solids.

Between 1959 and 1962 Bardeen was a member of the United States President's Science Advisory Committee. He was elected to the National Academy of Sciences in 1954 and received decorations from various institutions connected to teaching and the sciences.

He was married to Jane Maxwell in 1938, and the couple had three children together. John Bardeen died in 1991.

William Bradford Shockley and Walter Houser Brattain each received one-third of the 1956 prize. Leon Neil Cooper and John Robert Schrieffer each received one-third of the 1972 prize.

A small invention that changed history

The 1956 Physics laureates, John Bardeen, Walter H. Brattain and William Shockley, revolutionized electronics and the world by inventing a semiconductor that amplified electrical currents and tensions, creating electrical oscillations and carrying out modulation and detection functions. This electrical component is known as a transistor.

John Bardeen,
Walter H. Brattain and
William Shockley (from left to right)

spring

germanium (semiconductor element)

gold foil

crystal

1947

First transistor: can amplify a weak signal while still providing nuances in volume.

Vacuum tube

1920 – 1948

Before transistors, vacuum tubes, which were large, fallible and expensive, were used to amplify sound.

How a transistor works

The transistor is made of semi-conductive material and normally consists of minute layers of germanium or silicon. A semiconductor has less electrical resistance than an isolator and more than a conductor.

1950s

Transistors can be made ever smaller, but they still work in the same way.

Actual Size

current flow

An **electrical current** only flows from type n silicon rich in electrons to a type p silicon poor in electrons.
This is the principle of how a transistor works.

Type P   Type N

Transistor

A transistor can regulate the current passing through it and function as an amplifier, oscillator, photoelectric cell or commuter, while working from a low power source.

Battery

Transistor

Microphone

Amplification

1 When no sound enters the microphone, the electrons circulate in the microphone and fill the type p conductor.

2 When sound enters the microphone, it releases the semiconductor's electrons. The battery forces the entry of the electrons into the transistor and for the loudspeaker, creating sound.

Actual Size

1959

Integrated circuits combine many transistors

Actual Size

1960s

Microchips are integrated circuits containing millions of transistors

Modern Transistors: hundreds are placed in a silicon tablet

Aluminum conductors carry current to a poly-silicon conductor

Semiconductors allow or impede the passage of current depending on how the conductors are charged

1998

The most recent development has been in miniaturization and increasing complexity. A tiny microchip is placed in a plastic base and connected to pins that conduct electrical signals.

Albert Camus

For his important literary production, which with clear-sighted earnestness illuminates the problems of the human conscience in our times.

Twenty four years after his death, Albert Camus's name appeared once again in the bookstores of the world with the publication of Le Premier Homme (The First Man) in 1995. In this uncompleted autobiographical novel, found in the mud after his fatal car crash, the author brings a new forceful, intimate style to his work, unlike anything he had ever done before.

Born in Algeria into a poor family, he never knew his father, who was killed early in the Battle of the Marne in 1914. Growing up in impoverished circumstances, the young Albert nevertheless soon started to frequent intellectual circles and developed a special love of philosophy. He married Simone Hié in 1934, yet when he left for France at the age of 25, just before the outbreak of World War II, they had already separated. In the meantime he had met Francine Faure, who would stay with him until the end of his life.

While in Algeria Camus had worked for the press, and after the liberation of France he spent a year as a columnist for *Paris-Soir*. During the war he had joined the Resistance and, between 1943 and 1944, was a journalist for *Combat*, the official newspaper of the movement; he then assumed the editorship and remained in the position until 1947, when he became famous for his novel *La Peste (The Plague)*.

Novels, philosophical essays, chronicles and plays make up Camus's vast body of work, which he himself planned in three cycles: "First I wanted to express negation... in three forms. The novel... *L'Étranger* [*The Outsider*, 1942]. Drama... *Caligula* [1944] and *Le Malentendu* [*The Misunderstanding*, 1944]. Ideology... *Le Mythe de Sysyphe* [*The Myth of Sisyphus*, 1942]... I knew that one can't live in negation and said so in the preface to *The Myth of Sisyphus*; I have also dealt with the positive in three forms. The novel... The Plague. Drama... *L'État de Siège* [*The State of Siege*, 1948] and *Les Justes* [*The Just Assassins*, 1950]. Ideology... *L'Homme Révolté* [*The Rebel*, 1951]. I have started a third cycle on the theme of love."

Le Premier Homme (The First Man) was the beginning of this love cycle. He had found a place to escape the bustle of Paris, the Provençal village of Lourmarin, and it was there that he began the work. He spent Christmas of 1959 and New Year's Eve there with his family and his friend and editor, Michel Gallimard. On January 2 Francine returned to Paris with the couple's twins. Camus decided to go back the following day with Gallimard. Near Villeblevin he lost control of the car and hit a tree head on. Michel Gallimard was thrown from the car and died a few days later; Camus was in the driver's seat and, with a fractured skull and broken back, was killed upon impact. He had won the 1957 Nobel Prize in Literature as well as several other awards during his lifetime.

Boris Pasternak

For his important achievement both in contemporary lyrical poetry and in the field of the great Russian epic tradition.

When the manuscript of the novel *Doctor Zhivago* was smuggled out of the Soviet Union to Italy, where it was published in 1957, the world gained access to what many consider the triumph of Boris Leonidovich Pasternak's career. The novel, finished shortly before his death, is a sensitive and poetic tragedy set against the background of the Russian Revolution of 1917. The book was immortalized in popular culture through David Lean's 1965 film, with Omar Sharif as Yuri Zhivago and Julie Christie as Lara.

Pasternak was born in Moscow into a family of talented artists. His mother was a well-known concert pianist, while his father, a painter, illustrated some of Leo Tolstoy's works. Pasternak considered other fields before he concentrated on literature. At the age of 14, and under the influence of the pianist and composer Alexander Scriabin, he studied musical composition. In 1912, however, he concluded that music was not his vocation, and he entered the University of Marburg, in Germany, to study philosophy. After just four months of study and a visit to Italy, he was once more dissatisfied and decided to return to Russia and become a writer.

The first books of poetry Boris Pasternak published were practically unnoticed. He would only gain a place of respect among his contemporary Russian poets with *Sestra moya zhizn (My Sister's Life)*, published in 1922, and *Temy i variatsii (Themes and Variations)*, published in 1923, the latter of which was marked by a particularly strong, sober style. In 1924 he published *Vysokaya bolezn (Sublime Malady)*, in which he gives a very personal view of the failed Russian Revolution of 1905. The same theme would be addressed in two more works.

His autobiography, *Okhrannaya gramota (Safe Conduct)*, appeared in 1931, and the following year Pasternak published a collection of lyrical poems entitled *Vtoroye rozhdenie (Second Birth)*. These works were followed by the publication of his translations of some Georgian poets as well as most of the works of William Shakespeare, Goethe, Schiller, Kleist and Ben Jonson, among others.

Doctor Zhivago, Boris Pasternak's only novel, first appeared in the West translated into Italian. It was immediately acclaimed by many critics as a successful attempt to combine a lyrical-descriptive style with an epic drama. Another autobiographical sketch appeared in 1959 under the title *Biografichesky ocherk (An Essay in Autobiography)*; again, it was first published in Italian then translated into English.

Boris Pasternak was prevented by the Soviet authorities from receiving the 1958 Nobel Prize in Literature. This situation was only rectified in 1989, when his son, Evgeny B. Pasternak, received the award in Stockholm in his name. Boris Pasternak died on May 30, 1960, in Peredelkino, in the suburbs of the Russian capital.

Arthur Kornberg

For their discovery of the mechanisms in the biological synthesis of ribonucleic acid and deoxyribonucleic acid.

Arthur Kornberg, American doctor, biochemist and physicist, received the 1959 Nobel Prize in Physiology or Medicine, in conjunction with his associate Severo Ochoa, for their discovery of the mechanisms in the biological synthesis of RNA (ribonucleic acid) and DNA. (deoxyribonucleic acid).

Born in Brooklyn, New York, Kornberg completed his university studies in the city of his birth. He attended City College of New York and obtained his bachelor's degree in science before transferring to the University of Rochester, where he completed his medical training. He later returned to these institutions to receive honorary doctorates in law and sciences.

Between 1941 and 1942 Kornberg was an intern at the Strong Memorial Hospital of the University of Rochester. He then left his position to work for the U.S. Public Health Service. He was first assigned as a ship's doctor for the U.S. Navy and then as a research scientist at the National Institute of Health in Bethesda, Maryland, between 1947 and 1953. Over these years he also had training in enzymology at New York University School of Medicine and Washington University School of Medicine.

Between 1953 and 1959 Kornberg was the head of the Department of Microbiology of the University of Washington in Saint Louis, Missouri, from where he moved to head the Department of Biochemistry at the Stanford University School of Medicine.

Throughout his career Arthur Kornberg focused his research on biochemistry, enzyme chemistry and, of course, the synthesis of DNA by exhaustively studying the nucleic acids that control heredity in animals, plants, bacteria and viruses. He also spent a considerable time teaching graduate, medical and postdoctoral students and recording his scientific finding. Some of his most significant publications are *DNA Synthesis* (1974), *DNA Replication* (1980) and his autobiography, *For the Love of Enzymes: The Odyssey of a Biochemist* (1989).

Kornberg was a member of the National Academy of Sciences, the American Philosophical Society and the Royal Society, London. Besides the Nobel, he also received the Paul-Lewis Laboratories Prize from the American Chemical Society in 1951, the National Medal of Science in 1979 and the Cosmo Club Award in 1995.

While he was working in the public sector in 1943, Arthur Kornberg married, Sylvy Ruth Levy another New Yorker, who was also a researcher in biochemistry. The couple had three sons, two of whom followed their father's example and entered the sciences. Sylvy passed away in 1986; her husband outlived her by nearly 20 years and remarried on two other occasions.

Severo Ochoa also received half of the prize.

How proteins are made

Arthur Kornberg and Severo Ochoa were awarded the Nobel Prize for Physiology and Medicine in 1959 for "their discovery of the mechanisms in the biological synthesis of ribonucleic acid and deoxyribonucleic acid." Contributions that have extended the frontiers of Science.

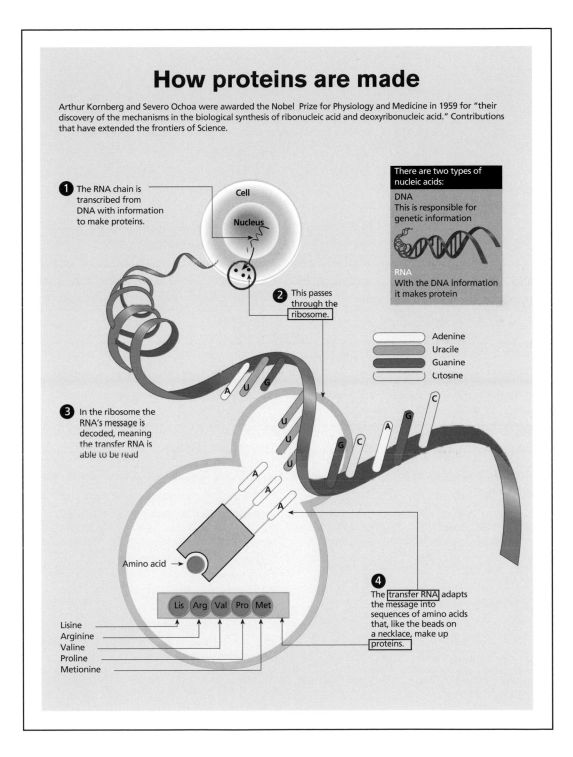

1 The RNA chain is transcribed from DNA with information to make proteins.

Cell

Nucleus

There are two types of nucleic acids:

DNA
This is responsible for genetic information

RNA
With the DNA information it makes protein

2 This passes through the ribosome.

Adenine
Uracile
Guanine
Citosine

3 In the ribosome the RNA's message is decoded, meaning the transfer RNA is able to be read

Amino acid →

Lis Arg Val Pro Met

Lisine
Arginine
Valine
Proline
Metionine

4 The transfer RNA adapts the message into sequences of amino acids that, like the beads on a necklace, make up proteins.

Nobel Laureates

1950-1959

1950

Nobel Prize in Physics
Cecil Frank Powell

Born December 5, 1903, in Tonbridge, England, and died August 9, 1969, near Milan, Italy.

For his development of the photographic method of studying nuclear processes and his discoveries regarding mesons made with this method.

Nobel Prize in Chemistry
Kurt Alder

Born July 10, 1902, in Königshütte, Prussia (now Chorzów, Poland), and died June 20, 1958, in Cologne, Germany.

&

Otto Paul Hermann Diels

Born January 23, 1876, in Hamburg, Germany, and died March 7, 1954, in Kiel.

For their discovery and development of the diene synthesis.

Nobel Prize in Physiology or Medicine
Philip Showalter Hench

Born February 28, 1896, in Pittsburg, Pennsylvania, United States, and died March 30, 1965, in Ocho Rios, Jamaica.

&

Edward Calvin Kendall

Born March 8, 1886, in South Norwalk, Connecticut, United States, and died May 4, 1972, in Princeton, New Jersey.

&

Tadeus Reichstein

Born July 20, 1897, in Wloclawek, Poland, and died August 1, 1996, in Basel, Switzerland.

For their discoveries relating to the hormones of the adrenal cortex, their structure and biological effects.

Nobel Prize in Literature
Bertrand Arthur William Russell

Born May 18, 1872, in Trelleck, Wales, and died February 2, 1970, in Penrhyndeudraeth.

In recognition of his varied and significant writings in which he champions humanitarian ideals and freedom of thought.

Nobel Peace Prize
Ralph Johnson Bunche

Born August 7, 1904, in Detroit, Michigan, United States, and died December 9, 1971, in New York, New York.

For his mediation in the war between Israel, Egypt, Jordan, Lebanon and Syria, which followed the United Nations plan of 1947 to partition Palestine.

1951

Nobel Prize in Physics
John Douglas Cockcroft

Born May 27, 1897, in Todmorden, England, and died September 18, 1967, in Cambridge.

&

Ernest Thomas Sinton Walton

Born October 6, 1903, in Dungarvan, Ireland, and died June 25, 1995, in Belfast, Northern Ireland.

For their pioneer work on the transmutation of atomic nuclei by artificially accelerated atomic particles.

Nobel Prize in Chemistry
Edwin Mattison McMillan

Born September 18, 1907, in Redondo Beach, California, United States, and died September 7, 1991, in El Cerrito.

&

Glenn Theodore Seaborg

Born April 19, 1912, in Ishpeming, Michigan, United States, and died February 25, 1999, in Lafayette, California.

For their discoveries in the chemistry of the transuranium elements.

Nobel Prize in Physiology or Medicine
Max Theiler
Born January 30, 1899, in Pretoria, South Africa, and died August 11, 1972, in New Haven, Connecticut, United States.
For his discoveries concerning yellow fever and how to combat it.

Nobel Prize in Literature
Pär Fabian Lagerkvist
Born May 23, 1891, in Växjö, Sweden, and died July 11, 1974, in Stockholm.
For the artistic vigor and true independence of mind with which he endeavors in his poetry to find answers to the eternal questions confronting mankind.

Nobel Peace Prize
Léon Jouhaux
Born July 1, 1879, in Paris, France, and died April 28, 1954, in Paris.
For his work to improve the conditions of the working classes and his fight against war.

1952

Nobel Prize in Physics
Felix Bloch
Born October 23, 1905, in Zurich, Switzerland, and died September 10, 1983, in Zurich.
&
Edward Mills Purcell
Born August 30, 1912, in Taylorville, Illinois, United States, and died March 7, 1997, in Cambridge, Massachusetts.
For their development of new methods for nuclear magnetic precision measurements and discoveries in connection therewith.

Nobel Prize in Chemistry
Archer John Porter Martin
Born March 1, 1910, in London, England, and died July 28, 2002, in Llangarron.
&
Richard Laurence Millington Synge
Born October 28, 1914, in Liverpool, England, and died August 18, 1994, in Norwich.

For their invention of partition chromatography.

Nobel Prize in Physiology or Medicine
Selman Abraham Waksman
Born July 22, 1888, in Priluka, Russia (now Pryluky, Ukraine), and died August 16, 1973, in Hyannis, Massachusetts, United States.
For his discovery of streptomycin, the first antibiotic effective against tuberculosis.

Nobel Prize in Literature
François Mauriac
Born October 11, 1885, in Bordeaux, France, and died September 1, 1970, in Paris.
For the deep spiritual insight and the artistic intensity with which he has in his novels penetrated the drama of human life.

Nobel Peace Prize
Albert Schweitzer
Born January 14, 1875, in Kaysersberg, Germany (now France), and died September 4, 1965, in Lambaréné, Gabon.
"For his efforts in the name of the Brotherhood of Nations."

1953

Nobel Prize in Physics
Frits Zernike
Born July 16, 1888, in Amsterdam, Netherlands, and died March 10, 1966, in Naarden.
For his demonstration of the phase contrast method, especially for his invention of the phase contrast microscope.

Nobel Prize in Chemistry
Hermann Staudinger
Born March 23, 1881, in Worms, Germany, and died September 8, 1965, in Freiburg.
For his discoveries in the field of macromolecular chemistry.

Nobel Prize in Physiology or Medicine
Hans Adolf Krebs
Born August 25, 1900, in Hildesheim, Germany, and died November 22, 1981, in Oxford, England.

For his discovery of the citric acid cycle.

&

Fritz Albert Lipmann

Born June 12, 1899, in Königsberg, Germany (now Kaliningrad, Russia), and died July 24, 1986, in Poughkeepsie, New York, United States.

For his discovery of co-enzyme A and its importance for intermediary metabolism.

Nobel Prize in Literature

Winston Leonard Spencer Churchill

Born November 30, 1874, in Blenheim Palace, England, and died January 24, 1965, in London.

For his mastery of historical and biographical description as well as for brilliant oratory in defending exalted human values.

Nobel Peace Prize

George Catlett Marshall

Born December 31, 1880, in Uniontown, Pennsylvania, United States, and died October 16, 1959, in Washington, D.C.

For his promotion of peace in the aftermath of the Second World War.

1954

Nobel Prize in Physics

Max Born

Born December 11, 1882, in Breslau, Germany (now Wroclaw, Poland), and died January 5, 1970, in Göttingen, Germany.

For his fundamental research in quantum mechanics, especially for his statistical interpretation of the wave function.

&

Walther Bothe

Born January 8, 1891, in Oranienburg, Germany, and died February 8, 1957, in Heidelberg.

For the coincidence method and his discoveries made therewith.

Nobel Prize in Chemistry

Linus Carl Pauling

Born February 28, 1901, in Portland, Oregon, United States, and died August 19, 1994, in Big Sur, California.

For his research into the nature of the chemical bond and its application to the elucidation of the structure of complex substances.

Nobel Prize in Physiology or Medicine

John Franklin Enders

Born February 10, 1897, in West Hartford, Connecticut, United States, and died September 8, 1985, in Waterford.

&

Frederick Chapman Robbins

Born August 25, 1916, in Auburn, Alabama, United States, and died August 4, 2003, in Cleveland, Ohio.

&

Thomas Huckle Weller

Born June 15, 1915, in Ann Arbor, Michigan.

For their discovery of the ability of the poliomyelitis viruses to grow in cultures of various types of tissue.

Nobel Prize in Literature

Ernest Miller Hemingway

Born July 21, 1899, in Cicero (now Oak Park), Illinois, United States, and died July 2, 1961, in Ketchum, Idaho.

For his mastery of the art of narrative, most recently demonstrated in *The Old Man and the Sea*, and for the influence that he has exerted on contemporary style.

Nobel Peace Prize

Office of the United Nations High Commissioner for Refugees

Founded by the United Nations in 1951, with its headquarters in Geneva, Switzerland.

For its work in favor of and with refugees.

1955

Nobel Prize in Physics

Polykarp Kusch

Born January 26, 1911, in Blankenburg, Germany, and died March 20, 1993, in Dallas, Texas, United States.

For his precision determination of the magnetic moment of the electron.

&

Willis Eugene Lamb, Jr.

Born July 12, 1913, in Los Angeles, California.

For his discoveries concerning the fine structure of the hydrogen spectrum.

Nobel Prize in Chemistry
Vincent du Vigneaud
Born May 18, 1901, in Chicago, Illinois, United States, and died December 11, 1978, in White Plains, New York. For his work on biochemically important sulfur compounds, especially for the first synthesis of a polypeptide hormone.

Nobel Prize in Physiology or Medicine
Axel Hugo Theodore Theorell
Born July 6, 1903, in Linköping, Sweden, and died August 15, 1982, in Stockholm.
For his discoveries concerning the nature and mode of action of oxidation enzymes.

Nobel Prize in Literature
Halldór Kiljan Laxness, pseudonym of Halldór Kiljan Gudjónsson
Born April 23, 1902, in Reykjavik, Iceland, and died February 8, 1998, in Mosfellsbær
For his vivid epic power which has renewed the great narrative art of Iceland.

Nobel Peace Prize
Not awarded.

1956

Nobel Prize in Physics
John Bardeen
Born May 23, 1908, in Madison, Wisconsin, United States, and died January 30, 1991, in Boston, Massachusetts.
&
Walter Houser Brattain
Born February 10, 1902, in Amoy, China, and died October 13, 1987, in Seattle, Washington, United States.
&
William Bradford Shockley
Born February 13, 1910, in London, England, and died August 12, 1989, in Palo Alto, California, United States.
For their researches on semiconductors and their discovery of the transistor effect.

Nobel Prize in Chemistry
Cyril Norman Hinshelwood
Born June 19, 1897, in London, England, and died October 9, 1967, in London.
&
Nikolay Nikolaevich Semenov
Born April 15, 1896, in Saratov, Russia, and died September 25, 1986, in Moscow, Union of Soviet Socialist Republics (now Russia).
For their researches into the mechanism of chemical reactions.

Nobel Prize in Physiology or Medicine
André Frédéric Cournand
Born September 24, 1895, in Paris, France, and died February 19, 1988, in Great Barrington, Massachusetts, United States.
&
Werner Forssmann
Born August 29, 1904, in Berlin, Germany, and died June 1, 1979, in Schopfheim.
&
Dickinson Woodruff Richards, Jr.
Born October 30, 1895, in Orange, New Jersey, United States, and died February 23, 1973, in Lakeville, Connecticut.
For their discoveries concerning heart catheterization and pathological changes in the circulatory system.

Nobel Prize in Literature
Juan Ramón Jiménez
Born December 24, 1881, in Moguer, Spain, and died May 29, 1958, in San Juan, Puerto Rico.
For his lyrical poetry, which in Spanish language constitutes an example of high spirit and artistical purity.

Nobel Peace Prize
Not awarded.

1957

Nobel Prize in Physics
Tsung-Dao Lee
Born November 24, 1926, in Shanghai, China.
&

Chen Ning Yang
Born September 22, 1922, in Hofei, China.
For their penetrating investigation of the so-called parity laws which has led to important discoveries regarding the elementary particles.

Nobel Prize in Chemistry
Alexander Robertus Todd
Born October 2, 1907, in Glasgow, Scotland, and died January 10, 1997, in Cambridge, England.
For his work on nucleotides and nucleotide coenzymes.

Nobel Prize in Physiology or Medicine
Daniel Bovet
Born March 23, 1907, in Neuchâtel, Switzerland, and died April 8, 1992, in Rome, Italy.
For his discoveries relating to synthetic compounds that inhibit the action of certain body substances, and especially their action on the vascular system and the skeletal muscles.

Nobel Prize in Literature
Albert Camus
Born November 7, 1913, in Mondovi, Algeria, and died January 4, 1960, in Villeblevin, France.
For his important literary production, which with clear-sighted earnestness illuminates the problems of the human conscience in our times.

Nobel Peace Prize
Lester Bowles Pearson
Born April 23, 1897, in Toronto, Ontario, Canada, and died December 27, 1972, in Ottawa.
For his efforts for peace which have contributed to the resolution of the 1956 Suez Canal crisis.

1958

Nobel Prize in Physics
Pavel Alekseyevich Cherenkov
Born July 15, 1904, in Novaya Chigla, Russia, and died January 6, 1990, in Moscow, Union of Soviet Socialist Republics (now Russia).
&

Ilya Mikhailovich Frank
Born October 10, 1908, in Saint Petersburg, Russia, and died June 22, 1990, in Moscow, Union of Soviet Socialist Republics (now Russia).
&
Igor Yevgenyevich Tamm
Born July 8, 1895, in Vladivostok, Russia, and died April 12, 1971, in Moscow, Union of Soviet Socialist Republics (now Russia).
For the discovery and the interpretation of the Cherenkov effect.

Nobel Prize in Chemistry
Frederick Sanger
Born August 13, 1918, in Rendcomb, England.
For his work on the structure of proteins, especially that of insulin.

Nobel Prize in Physiology or Medicine
George Wells Beadle
Born October 22, 1903, in Wahoo, Nebraska, United States, and died June 9, 1989, in Pomona, California.
&
Edward Lawrie Tatum
Born December 14, 1909, in Boulder, Colorado, United States, and died November 5, 1975, in New York, New York.
For their discovery that genes act by regulating definite chemical events.
&
Joshua Lederberg
Born May 23, 1925, in Montclair, New Jersey, United States, and died February 2, 2008, in New York, New York.
For his discoveries concerning genetic recombination and the organization of the genetic material of bacteria.

Nobel Prize in Literature
Boris Leonidovich Pasternak
Born February 10, 1890, in Moscow, Russia, and died May 30, 1960, Peredelkino, Union of Soviet Socialist Republics (now Russia).
For his important achievement both in contemporary lyrical poetry and in the field of the great Russian epic tradition.

Dominique Pire, né Georges Charles Clement Ghislain Pire
Born February 10, 1910, in Dinant, Belgium, and died January 30, 1969, in Louvain.
For his defense of European refugees and work in the humanitarian field.

1959

Nobel Prize in Physics
Owen Chamberlain
Born July 10, 1920, in San Francisco, California, United States, and died February 28, 2006 in Berkeley.
&
Emilio Gino Segrè
Born February 1, 1905, in Tivoli, Italy, and died April 22, 1989, in Lafayette, California, United States.
For their discovery of the antiproton.

Nobel Prize in Chemistry
Jaroslav Heyrovsky
Born December 20, 1890, in Prague, Czechoslovakia (now Czech Republic), and died March 27, 1967, in Prague.
For his discovery and development of the polarographic methods of analysis.

Nobel Prize in Physiology or Medicine
Arthur Kornberg
Born March 3, 1918, in Brooklyn, New York, United States, and died October 26, 2007, in Stanford, California.
&
Severo Ochoa
Born September 24, 1905, in Luarca, Spain, and died November 1, 1993, in Madrid.
For their discovery of the mechanisms in the biological synthesis of ribonucleic acid and deoxyribonucleic acid.

Nobel Prize in Literature
Salvatore Quasimodo
Born August 20, 1901, in Modica, Italy, and died June 14, 1968, in Naples.
For his lyrical poetry, which with classical fire expresses the tragic experience of life in our own times.

Nobel Peace Prize
Philip John Noel-Baker
Born November 1, 1889, in London, England, and died October 8, 1982, in London.
[He] is probably today the man who possesses the greatest store of knowledge on the subject of disarmament and who best knows the difficulties involved. In his latest book ... *The Arms Race*... he has pointed out the way we should go.

Selected Profiles of Nobel Laureates

1960–1969

Albert Lutuli

For his pacifist resistance to apartheid.

Thirty-three years before Nelson Mandela was recognized with the Nobel Peace Prize for his fight against racial discrimination, Albert John Lutuli had already been awarded the same prize for the same reasons. A Zulu chief, teacher, religious leader and president of the African National Congress, he led approximately 10 million black Africans in a nonviolent campaign in favor of equal civil rights in South Africa.

Persecuted for years by the South African government, Lutuli nevertheless maintained his noble and charitable character, serving as an alliance between the culture of his native Africa and Christian democracies abroad. The grandson of the chief of a small tribe in Groutville and the son of a Christian missionary who spent his last years in Rhodesia, Albert John Lutuli was probably born in 1898, although he was himself unsure. After his father's death he left for Groutville in 1906 with his mother.

Mtonya Gumede wanted to educate her son, so she sent him to the local Congregationalist mission school for his primary education. Lutuli then attended the Ohlange Institute and a Methodist institution in Edendale, where he completed a teaching course about 1917. For two years Albert Lutuli was principal of an intermediary school. However, so that he could support his mother, he turned down a scholarship that would have allowed him to continue his academic studies at University College, Fort Hare, and accepted a job at Adams College, where he had taken his teacher training.

In 1928 he became secretary of the African Teacher's Association and was made its president in 1933. At the same time he maintained a strong presence in the Christian church, being a lay preacher for many years and serving as chairman of the South African Board of the Congregationalist Church of America.

When he married Nokukhanya Bhengu, a fellow teacher, in 1927, he moved back to Groutville, where the first of their seven children was born. A few years later the Zulus elders asked him to be chief of the tribe, a position he accepted in 1936. He served the community of 5,000, acting as their magistrate, mediator and representative until 1952, when he was removed from office by the National Party of South Africa and their policy of apartheid.

The freedoms of Africans continued to be restricted in the coming years, and while Lutuli assumed leadership of the African National Congress between 1952 and 1967 he was jailed and prevented from participating in public meetings and from going farther than 20 miles (32 km) from his house. However, in 1961 he was given a special 10-day license to travel so that he could receive the 1960 Nobel Peace Prize in Oslo. Despite the efforts of the government of South Africa, Lutuli became internationally recognized and honored for his work.

Willard Libby

For his method to use carbon 14 for age determination in archaeology, geology, geophysics and other branches of science.

Willard Frank Libby developed the radioactive-carbon method of establishing the age of organic materials. Through analyses using carbon 14, it is now possible to date objects of historic and archaeological interest, although the method can also be used in other fields, including to study photosynthesis. It was for this discovery that he was awarded the 1960 Nobel Prize in Chemistry.

Born on the December 17, 1908, Willard Libby was raised by his parents in Grand Valley, Colorado, and entered the University of California, Berkeley, in 1927. He received his bachelor's degree in 1931 and his doctorate two years later. Libby was then appointed an instructor at his alma mater and remained there for nearly a decade, rising to the position of associate professor. In 1941 he was awarded a Guggenheim Memorial Foundation Fellowship to Princeton, but America's entry into World War II put a hold on his academic career.

Libby moved to Columbia University in New York to work on the Manhattan Project, and he remained there until the end of the war in 1945. He then served as a professor of chemistry at the Institute of Nuclear Studies (now the Enrico Fermi Institute) at the University of Chicago, until he was nominated by President Eisenhower to become a member of the U.S. Atomic Energy Commission in 1954.

Two years later this position was renewed for an additional five years, but Libby resigned in 1959 to become a professor of chemistry at UCLA, where he became director of the Institute of Geophysics and Planetary Physics. In parallel with teaching, Willard Libby was widely sought after for scientific advice and technical consultation by the industries associated with Chicago's Institute of Nuclear Studies. He also collaborated with the defense department, scientific organizations and other universities.

Libby was widely recognized for his work as a physical chemist and expert in radiochemistry. Besides the Nobel Prize, which he won for developing carbon-14 dating, he was awarded the Research Corporation Award in 1951, the Elliott Cresson Medal of the Franklin Institute in 1957, the Albert Einstein Medal in 1959 and the Day Medal of the Geological Society of America in 1961, among many other honors. In 1952 the University of Chicago published his book *Radiocarbon Dating*, and he was the author of numerous articles published in scientific journals. Libby was a member of the Editorial Board of Science, the Heidelberg Science Academy, the Bolivian Anthropology Society and a Foreign Member of the Swedish Royal Academy of Sciences.

Willard Libby died on September 8, 1980, in Los Angeles, California.

Carbon 14 dating

In 1960 Willard Frank Libby was awarded the Nobel Prize for Chemistry for developing the method of dating using carbon 14. This was an important advance in sciences such as archaeology, geology and geophysics.

Carbon 14 (14C) is produced in the atmosphere by cosmic radiation and is then absorbed by plants through photosynthesis and animals through feeding. It remains stable until the death of the living organism, when its radioactive breakdown begins. Libby was able to demonstrate that using the quantity of 14C in the dead organism compared with that in a living one, it was possible to date, for example, a skeleton or even a piece of fabric (in this case by the age of the plants which made up the material).

The half-life of 14C was calculated at approximately 5580 years, which means that comparing the quantity of 14C in a dead organism with a living example of the same species, means the date of death of the former can be calculated quite accurately when the time involved is similar to that of the half-life of carbon 14.

Even though this seems perfect, there are various technical problems in the method proposed by Libby. The level of 14C undergoes alterations quite easily. Sources of pollution, which don't contain 14C, have over the years diminished its proportion in the atmosphere. On the other hand, Hydrogen bomb tests have increased the level of 14C in the atmosphere.

Fossils are constantly contaminated by carbon. Materials collected in damp earth are invaded by carbonates that alter the composition of 14C. Chemical and/or biological changes can take place in the fossils, which implies alterations in its composition.

A source of controversy.

The most controversial case using C14 dating took place in 1988, when some scientists, using this method stated that the Turin Shroud - the cloth believed to cover Jesus Christ in the tomb - dated from the 13th or 14th century, while two scientists announced in 1999 that they had found 2000 year old pollen.

Critics stated that the scientist did not take into account that the Shroud had been boiled in oil in 1503 to prove its "saintliness" and that in 1532 it had been singed, which had left marks on it. 14C dating was used on panels both before and after they had been exposed to flame. The result was a correction of about 600 years.

The lack of precision of these tests could equally be caused by the presence of microscopic organisms on the materials being analyzed. A group of scientists from the University of Texas presented an example of the Carbon 14 dating carried out on Egyptian mummies showed a difference of a thousand years between the bones and the cloths surrounding them.

As a result of so much disagreement concerning the precision of C14 testing, other methods have been developed - such as potassium argon dating - at the same time as 14C dating can now use instruments which are far more advanced (like the mass spectroscopy accelerator) than those at Libby's disposal.

Dag Hammarskjöld

For his work in favor of peace in the Congo.

The Swedish economist and politician Dag Hammarskjöld was honored with the Nobel Peace Prize posthumously, although he was nominated before his death, and it was, in fact, during a diplomatic mission that he lost his life. In July 1960 the newly liberated Congo was experiencing serious unrest, with mutiny in its military and the secession of the province of Katanga. The United Nations sent a peacekeeping force under the direction of Hammarskjöld to assist in establishing peace. Between the night of the September 17, 1961, and the morning of the 18th, the plane that Hammarskjöld was taking to meet with President Tshombe, in response to a fresh outbreak of violence against UN troops, crashed near the border of Northern Rhodesia (now Zambia), killing all 16 people on board.

Dag Hammarskjöld was born on July 29, 1905, the youngest of the four sons of Agnes and Hjalmar Hammarskjöld, a future prime minister of Sweden, member of the Hague Tribunal and chairman of the Board of the Nobel Foundation. In 1953 Hammarskjöld gave a radio address in which he discussed the influence of his parents: "From generations of soldiers and government officials on my father's side, I inherited a belief that no life was more satisfactory than one of selfless service to your country — or humanity. This service required a sacrifice of all personal interests, but likewise the courage to stand up unflinchingly for your convictions. From scholars and clergymen on my mother's side, I inherited a belief that, in the very radical sense of the Gospels, all men were equals as children of God and should be met and treated by us as our masters in God."

A notable student in his youth, at the age of 20 Hammarskjöld completed his degree at the University of Uppsala, with linguistics, literature and history as areas of particular interest. In 1928 he completed a second degree from Uppsala, in economics, and then he earned a law degree two years later and his doctorate in economics in 1933.

He also mastered English, French and German, besides his own native language, and he could brilliantly discuss the complexities of poetry in all of them. The French impressionists were his favorite painters, and he enjoyed classical music, particularly the works of Beethoven. Later in life he distinguished himself in Christian theology. Always an active man, Hammarskjöld also enjoyed gymnastics, skiing and mountaineering.

Although international politics came to occupy most of his life, he first worked in economics, teaching at Stockholm University in 1933. Soon, however, he determined to employ his talents and honor his heritage by entering public service, where he would work for 31 years in Swedish financial affairs and international relations.

Hammarskjöld first distinguished himself as secretary to a government commission on unemployment between 1930 and 1934, and then he held a similar position at the Bank of Sweden during 1935. From 1936 to 1945 he was undersecretary in the Ministry of Finance and, midway through his service there, also became the head of the Bank of Sweden. After World War II he was widely praised for his financial negotiations with Great Britain concerning the economic reconstruction of Europe and, later, the execution of the Marshall Plan. His first links with the Swedish Ministry of Foreign Affairs came about in 1946, when he accepted the position of financial advisor. Five years later he became deputy foreign minister, although he remained distant from any political affiliation.

Hammarskjöld maintained his policy of international economic cooperation throughout his two five-year terms as secretary-general of the United Nations; he was first elected in 1953, when he received an incredible 57 votes out of 60. Hammarskjöld's first great victory as a diplomat was to personally negotiate for the release of American soldiers captured by the Chinese during the Korean War, but his efforts for peace also extended to the 1956 Suez Crisis. During this time he ordered the formation of the United Nations Emergency Force and deployed it to the region, basing the UN Observation Group in Lebanon and the UN Office in Jordan. Through such actions he brought about the withdrawal of American and British forces and stabilized the conflict peacefully.

His only book, Vägmärken (Markings), was posthumously published in 1963. These diary-like reflections cover 1925 to his death in 1961. The work became popular among American university students and has been studied by theological leaders for its Christian perceptive and mysticism; in his journals he describes his diplomatic work as an "inner journey."

Dag Hammarskjöld will be remembered by many generations to come for his work toward international peace. On July 22, 1997, the UN Security Counsel established the Dag Hammarskjöld Medal to recognize those who have given their lives in peacekeeping missions under the control of the United Nations.

James Watson

For their discoveries concerning the molecular structure of nucleic acids and its significance for information transfer in living material.

A native of Chicago, Illinois, James Dewey Watson was born on April 6, 1928, and was the only child of Jean Mitchell and James D. Watson. Watson's special interest from an early age was bird watching, and this hobby slowly developed into a love of genetics.

After obtaining his bachelor's degree in zoology at the University of Chicago in 1947, Watson earned his doctorate in the same field at the University of Indiana at the age of just 22. During this period he was influenced by well-known geneticists, especially the famed Hermann Joseph Müller, who demonstrated the influence of X-rays in the acceleration of mutation processes and was awarded the 1946 Nobel Prize in Physiology or Medicine. It was under the guidance of Salvador Luria, the Italian microbiologist, however, that Watson wrote his doctoral thesis on the effects of hard X-rays on bacteriophage multiplication. These viruses that infect bacteria were the basis of studies developed by Luria, who later won the 1969 Nobel Prize in Physiology or Medicine for this work.

Between 1950 and 1951 Watson was in Europe studying the DNA of virus particles that cause infections. He then traveled to Naples, Italy, where he met Maurice Wilkins. Together they saw, for the first time, the X-ray diffraction pattern of crystalline DNA. This discovery led Watson to concentrate his research on the structural chemistry of nucleic acids and proteins. With Luria's help he was able to join the team at Cambridge's Cavendish Laboratory for this purpose.

It was here that he met Francis Crick, and the pair soon discovered their shared interest in the structure of DNA. In 1953, and after some joint experiments, Watson and Crick established that the molecular model of DNA was a double helix. After a two-year study at the California Institute of Technology, where he collaborated with studies on RNA, Watson returned to Cavendish and renewed his partnership with Crick. The two published numerous studies on the general principles of virus construction.

Watson also worked in Harvard's Biology Department for many years, and he was a member of the American Academy of Arts and Sciences, among other institutions, and served as a consultant for the President's Scientific Advisory Committee. The 1962 Nobel Prize in Physiology or Medicine was awarded to him for his part in the discovery of the structure of nucleic acids, which are the chemical substances responsible for the transmission of hereditary characteristics from generation to generation.

Francis Harry Compton Crick and Maurice Hugh Frederick Wilkins also each received one-third of the prize.

John Steinbeck

*For his realistic and imaginative writings, combining as they do
sympathetic humor and keen social perception.*

John Steinbeck was born on February 27, 1902, in Salinas, California, into
a family of limited means. He studied at local schools in his early years and
during the summers worked on ranches, where he gained experience in
the subject matter that would bring him fame. He later attended Stanford
University but did not complete his studies and, in 1925, traveled to New
York to seek a career in literature. He soon returned to California and
managed to get some novels and short stories published, but these works
failed to attract attention. Success would only come in 1935, with the
publication of a series of humorous stories called *Tortilla Flat*, in which he portrays with
sympathy the lazy, carefree ways of a group of Mexican-Americans who are determined to
enjoy life in the days just before prohibition.

Moving from one extreme to another, Steinbeck exchanged humorous fiction for a more
serious and aggressive investigation of social issues, particularly the growing materialism in
America and the disruption of the traditional agricultural lifestyle. Above all other subjects,
Steinbeck is best remembered for his novels about rural life in California and, because of this,
is sometimes classified as a regional writer.

In 1936 he published *In Dubious Battle*, which depicts the strikes of California's migrant
fruit-pickers. Following this novel were *Of Mice and Men* (1937), a tragic tale of two displaced
ranch workers in California during the Depression, and a series of short stories collected in
the volume *The Long Valley* (1938).

For *The Grapes of Wrath*, published in 1939, Steinbeck was awarded the Pulitzer Prize.
In this book, considered his masterpiece, Steinbeck tells the saga of a family of Oklahoma
tenant farmers who leave for California, where they become migrant workers and experience
the corruption and cruelty of the major landowners.

Steinbeck also wrote, among other works, *Sea of Cortez* (1941), *The Pearl* (1947), *East of
Eden* (1952) and *The Winter of Our Discontent* (1961). *Travels with Charley*, published in 1962, is
a travelogue of the novelist's impressions during a three-month trip across 40 states. During
World War II he served as a correspondent for the New York Herald and wrote for the film
industry, including for Alfred Hitchcock's Lifeboat (1944). In 1967, during the Vietnam War,
he wrote for Newsday.

Besides the 1962 Nobel Prize in Literature, John Steinbeck was also awarded the United
States Medal of Freedom by President Lyndon B. Johnson. John Steinbeck died of heart
disease on December 20, 1968, in New York.

Martin Luther King, Jr.

For his fight for racial integration in the U.S.A., without recourse to violence.

On April 4, 1968, while standing on the balcony of his hotel room in Memphis, Tennessee, Martin Luther King, Jr., was assassinated. He had come to the city to lead a protest march of striking garbage workers. One year after the event, James Earl Ray confessed to the killing and was sentenced to 99 years in prison. King was assassinated because of the prominent role he played in the fight for equal rights in America and around the world, and it is for this very work that he was awarded the 1964 Nobel Peace Prize.

Born Michael Luther King, Jr., in Atlanta, Georgia, on January 15, 1929, his father later changed his own and his son's name to Martin Luther King to honor the German protestant leader. His father came from a family of distinguished Baptist preachers, and he would, despite his dedication to the fight for civil rights, go on to serve as co-pastor with his father at the Ebenezer Baptist Church in Atlanta, Georgia.

He first attended segregated public school in Georgia then, like his father and grandfather, entered Morehouse College, a distinguished African-American academic institution, graduating in 1948. King then earned his bachelor of divinity degree after theological studies at the Crozer Theological Seminary in Pennsylvania, and he was elected president of the predominately white class. In 1955 he received his doctorate from Boston University. It was in this city that he met Coretta Scott, a young woman blessed with intellectual and artistic skills; the couple married on June 18, 1953, and had four children.

King rose to prominence after the first major nonviolent demonstration for equal rights in America. It took place after Rosa Parks, an African American woman in Montgomery, Alabama, refused to comply with the laws that required her to give up her seat on a bus to a white person. To protest segregated buses, on December 1, 1955, activists organized in Montgomery under King's leadership — the celebrated "bus boycott," which lasted 381 days. As a result, on December 20, 1956, the Supreme Court declared the law of segregation on public transport unconstitutional, meaning that passengers would be treated the same regardless of their color. During the boycott King was arrested, saw his house bombed and was physically abused.

In 1957 he was elected president of the Southern Christian Leadership Conference; in this organization he successfully combined Christian ideals and Mahatma Gandhi's operational methods. In the following years and until his death, Martin Luther King, Jr., developed an active but nonviolent movement that attracted many supporters of all races from all over the nation and around the world. A demonstration for civil rights that took place on August 28, 1963, in Washington, D.C., involved a peace march of around 250,000 people. It was on this day that King made one of his most celebrated speeches from the steps of the Lincoln Memorial; the best-known section is:

> *I am not unmindful that some of you come here out of great trials and tribulations. Some of you have come fresh from narrow jail cells. Some of you have come from areas where your quest for freedom left you battered by the storms of persecution and staggered by the winds of police brutality... I say to you today, my friends, that in spite of the difficulties of today and tomorrow, I still have a dream. It is deeply rooted in the American dream. I have a dream that one day this nation will rise up and live out the true meaning of its creed: "We hold these truths to be self-evident: that all men are created equal." I have a dream that one day... the sons of former slaves and the sons of former slave owners will be able to sit down together at the table of brotherhood... With this faith we will be able to work together, to pray together, to struggle together, to go to jail together, to stand up for freedom together, knowing that we will be free one day.*

Most of these dreams were made into legal realities with the Civil Rights Act of 1964 and the Voting Rights Act of 1965, although the struggle over the hearts and minds of some is still ongoing.

King was arrested more than 20 times and physically attacked on at least four occasions during his life. At the age of 35 he was, at the time, the youngest recipient of the Nobel Peace Prize and, on hearing of the decision, announced the prize money would be donated to the movement for civil rights. He was also recognized with the Pacem in Terris Award and the American Liberties Medallion by the American Jewish Committee for his "exceptional advancement of the principles of human liberties" in 1965. Posthumously, he was awarded the Marcus Garvey Prize for Human Rights by the Jamaican government and the 1977 Presidential Medal of Freedom from President Jimmy Carter. On November 2, 1983, President Ronald Reagan signed a bill to create a federal holiday, celebrated on the third Monday of every January, to honor Martin Luther King, Jr. He is buried with his wife at the Martin Luther King Jr. National Historic Site in Atlanta, Georgia.

Jean-Paul Sartre

For his work which, rich in ideas and filled with the spirit of freedom and the quest for truth, has exerted a far-reaching influence on our age.

Jean-Paul Sartre turned down the 1964 Nobel Prize in Literature because he thought that accepting it would put his integrity as a writer in doubt. A highly intelligent man of firm convictions, this was how he was described by his lifelong partner, Simone de Beauvoir: "Sartre lived to write, he felt it his duty to witness everything and use this evidence as necessary."

A native of Paris, Jean-Paul Sartre was born on June 21, 1905, to Jean-Baptiste, a naval officer, and his wife, Anne-Marie Schweitzer, but his father died when he was only a year old, and he was subsequently raised by his mother and grandfather. He entered the École Normale Supérieure in 1924 and graduated in philosophy five years later. In 1931 he became a high school professor in Le Havre, France, and the next year studied the philosophical works of Edmund Husserl and Martin Heidegger in Berlin with a stipend from the Institut Français. He returned to France, and after another brief period working at Le Havre and then in Laon, he accepted a position at the Lycée Pasteur, in Paris, where he stayed until 1939.

Sartre's first novel, *La Nausée (Nausea)* was published in 1938. In it the central character, a provincial intellectual, is disturbed by the lack of meaning in nature or human life. A firm philosophical position was always at the center of all of Sartre's artistic creations.

Jean-Paul Sartre formulated a new existentialism, which emphasized consciousness and freedom. Beginning in the 1950s he became increasingly interested in politics and made a passionate attempt to reconcile Marxism with existentialism. For Sartre, the non-existence of God was an unquestioned fact, and people were condemned to freedom from all types of authority. He argued that this freedom had been denied throughout history, but that it had to be faced if one wanted to be a moral being. He believed the individual had to find his or her own meaning in order to fulfill the role he or she intends to assume in the world.

After Stalin's death, Sartre criticized the Soviet Union; in 1954 he visited the country and had a love affair with his interpreter, Lena Zonina. He actively supported the student rebellions of the 1960s and 1970s and opposed the Vietnam War. After 1973, however, his eyesight began failing him and by his death on April 15, 1980, he was blind. Arlette Elkaïm, his mistress since 1965, received the rights to his literary estate.

Charles Townes

For fundamental work in the field of quantum electronics, which has led to the construction of oscillators and amplifiers based on the maser-laser principle.

Charles Hard Townes was born in Greenville, South Carolina, on July 28, 1915. He was influenced by his father, an attorney, and also fascinated by natural history and modern languages. He entered Furman University in Greenville and obtained a bachelor's degree, summa cum laude, in modern languages in 1935; he was only 19 years old at the time. During his years at the university, he was the curator of the museum and spent his summer holidays collecting specimens for the biology camp. Townes was also active on the school newspaper and was a member of the swimming and football teams.

Despite all these other interests, however, physics would prove to be his constant partner in the coming years. He had been fascinated with the "beautiful logical structure" of the subject ever since his first course in it during his sophomore year. In 1936 Townes received his master's degree in physics from Duke University and then entered graduate school at the California Institute of Technology, from which he earned his doctorate degree in 1939 with a thesis on isotope separation and nuclear spins.

By this time he was already a part of the technical staff at the Bell Telephone Laboratories, where he stayed until 1947. During World War II he worked tirelessly on the development of microwave techniques for radar bombing systems. After the war he concentrated on applying his findings to the field of spectroscopy, realizing the potential to study atomic and molecular structure and control electromagnetic waves.

When he arrived at Columbia University in 1948 he continued research in microwave physics. A few years later, with the help of his colleagues, Townes devised the "maser," a devise that amplified microwaves by the stimulated emission of radiation. In 1958 — in conjunction with Dr. A.L. Schawlow, his brother-in-law and winner of the 1981 Nobel Prize in Physics — he theoretically demonstrated how the maser could work in the visual and infrared spectrum. Several publications followed.

Townes was the executive director of the Columbia Radiation Laboratory from 1950 to 1952, and he spent many more years teaching. Between 1959 and 1961 he served as vice president and director of research for the Institute of Defense Analyses in Washington, D.C. He then became provost and a professor of physics at the Massachusetts Institute of Technology (MIT) and has been involved with the Harvard Biology Department since 1956.

He as awarded the 1964 Nobel Prize in Physics for research in the field of quantum electronics. Prior to this, he had won the Eli Lilly Award in Biochemistry in 1959 and the Research Corporation Prize in 1962.

Nikolay Basov and Aleksandr Prokhorov also each received one quarter of the prize.

United Nations International Children's Emergency Fund

For its recognition that the well-being of today's children is inseparable from world peace tomorrow.

On December 11, 1946, the UN General Assembly approved the creation of an organization dedicated to helping children in need of basic food, clothes and medical attention, particularly in Europe. Although the United Nations International Children's Emergency Fund (UNICEF) was established by a unanimous decision, certain circles in New York believed that the UN was a political forum of such importance that it should not be dealing with "peripheral and minor" questions, such as helping children. History has proven them wrong: in 1965 UNICEF received the Nobel Peace Prize.

In the postwar period up to 1950, UNICEF concentrated on providing food and clothing and some limited, mostly preventative, medical assistance. As a result, $112 million was spent on distributing articles to five million children in 12 countries, on vaccinating eight million children against tuberculosis and on reconstructing facilities crucial to processing milk and distributing food. At the height of this campaign in Europe, the organization provided a meal for millions of children every day.

Between 1951 and 1960 it continued to answer to the most urgent needs and broadened its field of action, running campaigns to prevent diseases such as tuberculosis, leprosy and malaria and working to ensure sanitation and environmental safety. In parallel, UNICEF encouraged maternity and child health-care education for mothers and helped countries produce foods rich in protein at low costs. In the 1960s the efforts of the organization were extended to children in the world's poorest countries. Attentive to the physical, vocational, psychological and intellectual needs of children, UNICEF gave assistance in the areas of education, curricular reform and technology. All of these diverse programs, developed over decades, reflect the organization's foundational belief that children are the future agent of economic and social change, and that all children, regardless of their race, religion or native country, deserve respect and the basic necessities of life.

The organization's statistics for its first 25 years leave no room to doubt its enormous influence: 71 million children examined for trachoma — a once-prominent eye disease — with 43 million cured, 400 million vaccinated against tuberculosis and 415,000 cured of leprosy. UNICEF is also active in building schools and community centers and aiding the victims of natural disasters.

Peyton Rous

For his discovery of tumor-inducing viruses.

Peyton Rous was born on October 5, 1879, in Baltimore, Maryland. He obtained his bachelor's degree from Johns Hopkins University in 1900, but disaster struck during his second year at the medical school there. One day, while dissecting a tuberculous bone, he accidentally scratched his finger on it. This scratch caused an infection that eventually reached his axillary glands. After undergoing surgery to remove the infected glands, he was told that no more treatment could be done. Despite this potentially fatal event, he would live to the age of 91.

This episode did, however, lead him to Texas, where an uncle got him a job on a ranch to fill his time during his recovery. As a result, Peyton missed a year of medical school, and upon his return he decided he was unfit to become a practicing physician. Instead he continued his studies and, in 1905 received his master's degree from the Johns Hopkins Medical School. He then became an instructor in pathology at the University of Michigan — on a very insufficient salary. His laboratory work was little more than that of a technician, since the institution had limited funds for research. Rous unhappily labored there until 1907, when Alfred Warthin, the head of the Pathology Department, offered to teach his summer classes in his place and allow him to keep his salary if he promised to learn German and go to a hospital in Dresden to study pathological anatomy.

When Rous returned to the United States, he managed to get a job at the Rockefeller Institute for Medical Research, and after a few months there the director of the institute handed over responsibility for the cancer research laboratory to him. Rous finally had sufficient means to continue with his scientific work and soon began researching tumors. In 1911 he turned his attention to pathological problems, including cancer.

Richard Shope, a close friend and colleague at the Rockefeller Institute for Medical Research, asked Rous in 1934 if he would study a virus he had discovered that was responsible for giant warts that appeared frequently on wild rabbits. Rous could not resist such a challenge and proved that these warts were tumors that were initially benign but frequently degenerated into cancer. In his later years he also played a pioneering role in the field of blood transfusions, work that led to the creation of the world's first blood bank in Belgium.

Three years before Peyton Rous jointly won the 1966 Nobel Prize in Physiology or Medicine with Canadian-born surgeon Charles Huggins, the same award had gone to one of his son-in-laws, Alan Hodgkin.

He married Marion deKay in 1915, and the couple had three daughters. Peyton Rous died in 1970.

Charles Brenton Huggins also received half of the prize.

Luis Alvarez

For his decisive contributions to elementary particle physics, in particular the discovery of a large number of resonance states, made possible through his development of the technique of using hydrogen-bubble-chamber and data analysis.

Luis Walter Alvarez was born in San Francisco, California, on June 13, 1911, and enjoyed a quiet, normal childhood. He received his bachelor's degree from the University of Chicago in 1932, his master's two years later and his doctorate in 1936, at the age of 25.

Immediately upon completing his studies, Alvarez joined the Radiation Laboratory of the University of California as a researcher, and he went on to spend the majority of his scientific career there. However, between 1940 and 1943 he was on leave at the Massachusetts Institute of Technology (MIT), and he worked at the University of Chicago between 1943 and 1944 and at the Los Alamos Laboratory from 1944 to 1945.

At the beginning of his career, Alvarez studied optics and cosmic rays and codiscovered the "east-west effect" of the latter. Then for many years he focused on the field of nuclear physics and, in 1937, was the first person to experimentally demonstrate the existence of the phenomenon of the K electron captured by nuclei. Around this time he also developed a method to produce beams of very slow moving neutrons.

In research undertaken with Jacob Wiens, a colleague at the Radiation Laboratory, Luis Alvarez produced the first 198Hg lamp, which was later perfected by the National Bureau of Standards into its present form. Even before World War II Alvarez and Robert Cornog, another colleague, discovered the radioactivity of 3H (tritium) and showed that 3H was a stable constituent of ordinary helium. Tritium is best known as a source of thermonuclear energy, and 3H has become an important subject in low-temperature research.

While at MIT Alvarez was responsible for three important radar systems: the microwave early-warning system, the Eagle high-altitude bombing system and a blind-landing system of civilian, as well as military, value known as ground-controlled approach, or GCA. While at the Los Alamos Laboratory in 1944 and 1945 he developed plutonium bomb detonators and flew as a scientific observer during the Alamogordo and Hiroshima explosions. He is also responsible for devising and constructing the 40-foot linear proton accelerator known as "Berkeley."

Luis Alvarez won the 1968 Nobel Prize in Physics for his incredible contributions to the field of physics, but it was only the pinnacle of a lifetime of honors that includes winning the Medal for Merit in 1947, being named California Scientist of the Year in 1960 and receiving the Albert Einstein Medal in 1961. He died in 1988 at the age of 77.

René Cassin

For his defense of the rights of man, as established in the respective Universal Declaration.

René Samuel Cassin received the 1968 Nobel Peace Prize at the age of 81. A French jurist who was seriously wounded during World War I, he was well respected as a teacher, but it is for his work as a humanist that he has gone down in history. He was one of the founders of the United Nations Commission on Human Rights and drew up the Universal Declaration of Human Rights, adopted by the General Assembly of the United Nations on December 10, 1948.

René Cassin was born in Bayonne, France, on October 5, 1887. While he was at the Lycée of Nice he demonstrated a brilliant intellect, as he did at the University of Aix en Provence, where he took humanist studies and law. There, in 1914, he placed first in a competitive examination given by the Law Department and also obtained his doctorate in juridical, economic and political sciences. By that time he was already practicing law in Paris, but his career was interrupted by the start of World War I.

In 1916 he was seriously wounded by splinters from a German grenade. He only survived because his mother, who was a nurse in the hospital where he was taken, convinced the doctors to operate on him. Although he recovered, he would suffer severe discomfort for the rest of his life. This injury, however, did not stop him from marrying Simone Yzombard and returning to Aix-en-Provence in the same year to lecture in law.

At the end of the 1920s he took the chair in civil and fiscal law at the University of Paris, which he kept until he officially retired from teaching in 1960. His teaching career also took him to other academies in Europe, French Africa and the Middle and Far East. For many years he also presided over various organizations and occupied high judicial positions, both in France and other European countries. Between 1944 and 1960 he was the vice president of the French Council of State, the highest juridical organization in cases involving personal and legal administration, and between 1965 and 1968 he presided over the European Court of the Rights of Man in Strasbourg.

René Cassin actively participated in his country's political life but always as a moderate. It is said he was the first civilian to leave Bordeaux to join Charles De Gaulle, responding to the latter's appeal from London after the armistice was signed between Germany and the capitulated French government in 1940. He was also one of the founders of the UN Commission on Human Rights in 1946 and was the driving force behind the Universal Declaration of Human Rights. He also played an active part in the foundation of UNESCO, the organization founded by the UN to support education, science and culture.

Samuel Beckett

For his writing, which — in new forms for the novel and drama — in the destitution of modern man acquires its elevation.

Poet, novelist and playwright Samuel Beckett waited almost half a century for his work to be recognized at an international level. It was from Paris, the city in which he lived from the 1930s onward, that the Irish writer became known as the "father of the theater of the absurd," with the publication of *Waiting for Godot* in 1952. Although awarded the 1969 Nobel Prize in Literature, he did not attend the award ceremony.

Beckett was born in Foxrock, in the outskirts of Dublin, in 1906 and attended protestant schools in Northern Ireland and Dublin before entering Trinity College in Dublin. Between 1928 and 1929 he was an English reader at École Normale Supérieure in Paris, but he returned to Trinity College the following year to act as a French reader. Before he rejected both Ireland and an academic career, Beckett traveled to England, France and Germany before finally settling in Paris, where he lived until his death at the age of 83.

In 1929 he had his first work published, which was an essay on his compatriot James Joyce. This essay was followed by another entitled *Proust* (1931). Samuel Beckett nearly lost his life in 1938 when he was knifed by a stranger while out walking with some friends. He later went to visit the assailant in prison and asked why he had done it, but the man was unable to explain. While recovering from his injuries he met his life-long partner, Suzanne Deschevaux-Dumesnil, with whom he joined the French resistance during World War II. To escape the Germans they fled to the south of France in 1942. From there, Beckett sent messages for the resistance and worked in farming.

Beckett did not achieve fame until, in the space of three years, he had five pieces published in Paris: the novel *Molloy* and its sequel *Malone Meurt (Malone Dies)* both published in 1951, the play *Waiting for Godot* (1952) and the novels *The Unnamable* (which completed the trilogy begun with *Molloy*) and *Watt*, both published in 1953.

In *Waiting for Godot*, an austere tragicomedy in two acts that most critics consider his masterpiece, Beckett escapes convention in terms of characters and dialogue. Just as in his other works, the author's bitter irony results from the contrast between the hope people have for their existence and the often-brutal reality. Beckett thoroughly explored themes such as solitude, suffering and the absurdity of the human condition, and he presented new means of expression in fiction and drama.

Beckett married Suzanne Deschevaux-Dumesnil in 1961. Both died in 1989 in Paris, France.

Murray Gell-Mann

For his contributions and discoveries concerning the classification of elementary particles and their interactions.

The American physicist Murray Gell-Mann was particularly noted for his work in developing the field of classifying subatomic particles. It was he who suggested the possibility of the existence of quarks, and his research was the subject of international recognition in 1969, when he went to Stockholm to receive the Nobel Prize in Physics.

Gell-Mann was born in New York and began his higher education at Yale University, where, in 1948, he obtained his bachelor's degree in physics. Three years later he received his doctorate from the Massachusetts Institute of Technology (MIT), after which he became a member of the Institute for Advanced Study.

Between 1952 and 1955 he taught at the University of Chicago, which he left to become an associate professor at the California Institute of Technology. He began the research that would lead to his Nobel Prize while he was still in Chicago, and he concluded it in California.

The questions that motivated him were related to the interactivity of protons and neutrons. Gell-Mann was able to group related particles in multiples or families based on a property, which he called the "strangeness number," that he attributed to particles in strong electromagnetic interaction. It was from these notions that he was able to put forward the quark theory in 1963, which was also put forward by his colleague George Zweig around this time, although the two had not worked together. What Gell-Mann concluded was that quarks — particles with fractional electric charges — are the smallest particles of existing material. This idea has since been used as a starting point in particle physics research, and researchers in this branch of physics have discovered evidence to support the theory. (The name "quark" comes from *Finnegans Wake*, the 1939 novel written by the Irish writer James Joyce.)

Ten years before receiving the Nobel Prize, Murray Gell-Mann was awarded the Dannie Heinemann Prize of the American Physical Society. He became a fellow of this society and was also made a member of the National Academy of Sciences, which acted as a type of scientific conscience for American political power.

He married J. Margaret Dow in 1955, and the couple had two children. Gell-Mann was widowed in 1981 and married his second wife, Marcia Southwick, in 1992.

International Labour Organization (ILO)

Underneath the foundation stone laid in the International Labour Organization's headquarters in Geneva, Switzerland, a message was placed that read, "Si vis pacem, cole justitiam" ("If you desire peace, cultivate justice"). It was to this organization that the Nobel Committee of the Norwegian Parliament awarded the 1969 Nobel Peace Prize.

The ILO is a specialized organization that focuses its efforts on improving the working conditions of people all over the world, promoting productive employment and social progress and increasing the general quality of life for workers. Created in 1919, the ILO started as an autonomous department of the League of Nations and, in 1946, became part of the United Nations.

A total of 178 member states make up this organization. Contrary to other UN agencies, the ILO includes government representatives as well as representatives for workers and employers: each member-state has two delegates nominated by their respective government, an employer delegate and a worker delegate. The member states of the ILO meet at the International Labour Conference, which is held annually in Geneva. Its objective is to create international standards for the working world. Conventions are drawn up, which are later ratified voluntarily by each member country. At the same time recommendations are made to each government to guide future legislation.

The plague of unregulated child labor is one of the fundamental concerns of the organization, but it also dedicates special attention to questions related to employment for people with special needs, cases of discrimination, human rights abuses, protecting mothers and forced labor. It falls to the organization to supervise the application of ratified conventions, and it is also the organization to which workers, employers or governments may present complaints.

The ILO offers technical assistance to member states to help them implement established standards. The organization's staff works in diverse areas, including the promotion of employment, professional training, hygiene and safety in the workplace and social security. Although based in Geneva, the ILO has permanent offices in 40 countries.

When the Nobel Prize was awarded to it, the then-Chairman of the Nobel Committee, Aase Lionaes, stated "in the course of its 50 years of existence, the ILO has adopted a total of 128 conventions and 132 recommendations." Today the ILO has hundreds of experts working in countries around the world.

Ragnar Frisch

For having developed and applied dynamic models for the analysis of economic processes.

Born into a family that had been goldsmiths since the 17th century, the Norwegian Ragnar Frisch graduated in economics because, when it came to enrolling at university, he chose the course that lasted for the shortest amount of time. This, however, did not prevent him from becoming a brilliant economist and being awarded the 1969 Nobel Prize in Economics for his pioneering work in econometrics. The prize, initiated the year before and with the full title of "The Sveriges Riksbank Prize in Economic Sciences in Memory of Alfred Nobel," was shared between Frisch and Jan Tinbergen. Frisch was one of the first people to implement the new science of econometrics, which consists of using mathematical and statistical formulas to solve economic problems.

Ragnar Frisch, who was born in Oslo on March 3, 1895, was expected by his father to enter the family business. It was his mother, Ragna Fredrikke Kittilsen, who understood that he would never be at home in the world of gold and silver and encouraged him to further his education. Ragnar studied economics and mathematics in other countries, particularly France, which he considered his second home, Germany, Great Britain, the United States and Italy.

He obtained his doctorate in 1926 from the University of Oslo with a thesis on statistics, and it was in his hometown that he forged a notable academic career. He was a member of scientific academies all over the world and received various honorary doctorates. During a short stay at Yale University he helped found the Econometrics Society there, in 1930. He was also the editor of the highly influential journal *Econometrica* until 1955 and was director of researach of the Economic Institute of the University of Oslo.

Frisch was married for the first time in 1920 to Marie Smedal, with whom he had his only daughter. He was widowed in 1952 and, a year later, married Astrid Johannessen, a childhood friend who stayed with him for the rest of his life. He said of her, "Ever since our marriage, Astrid has been my unfailing companion and has sustained me devotedly in all the ups and downs of life."

Ragnar Frisch loved the outdoor life. He was a mountaineer on a modest scale but his main hobby was beekeeping. He said that this activity was not exactly a pleasure for his free time, "it is more in the nature of an obsession which I shall never be able to get rid of." He died in 1973.

Jan Tinbergen also received half of the prize.

Sveriges Riksbank Prize in Economic Sciences in Memory of Alfred Nobel 1969

Jan Tinbergen

For having developed and applied dynamic models for the analysis of economic processes.

It was his role in the development of econometrics that brought the Dutch Jan Tinbergen the 1969 Nobel Prize in Economics, an award he shared with the Norwegian Ragnar Frisch, who also played a significant role in the same field.

Born in The Hague, Jan Tinbergen achieved international fame through his work in economics. His higher education took place at Leiden University, a well-known institution halfway between Rotterdam and Amsterdam. It was from here that he received his doctorate degree in 1929.

Early on in his career he focused on statistical work. Between 1929 and 1945 he worked for the Central Bureau of Statistics in the Netherlands, and in addition to that he was an expert on economic matters at the League of Nations Secretariat between 1936 and 1938. After World War II Tinbergen was director of the Central Planning Bureau of the Netherlands government for 10 years.

His solid reputation meant that he was sought after all over the world. He was an advisor to various developing countries, including the United Arab Republic — a political union between Egypt and Syria that existed between 1958 and 1971 — Venezuela, Suriname, Indonesia and Pakistan, among others. He also shared his knowledge with international organizations such as the European Coal and Steel Community — which was the forerunner of the European Economic Community and then the European Union — the International Bank for Reconstruction and Development, and the United Nations Secretariat.

It was in the 1930s that he concentrated on the new science of econometrics, which uses mathematical and statistical formulas to solve economic problems. He was a member of the Royal Netherlands Academy of Science as well as scientific academies in other countries. Tinbergen was awarded 15 honorary doctorates, mostly from European universities.

His body of published works emphasized the development and application of dynamic models in the analysis of economic processes. These publications include *Business Cycles in the United States, 1919–1932* (1939), *Business Cycles in the United Kingdom, 1870–1914* (1951), *Centralization and Decentralization in Economic Policy* (1954) and *The Element of Space in Development Planning* (1969), which he wrote together with L.B.M. Mennes and J.G. Waardenburg. Jan Tinbergen died in 1994 at the age of 91.

Ragnar Frisch also received half of the prize.

Nobel Laureates

1960-1969

1960

Nobel Prize in Physics
Donald Arthur Glaser
Born September 21, 1926, in Cleveland, Ohio, United States.
For the invention of the bubble chamber.

Nobel Prize in Chemistry
Willard Frank Libby
Born December 17, 1908, in Grand Valley, Colorado, United States, and died September 8, 1980, in Los Angeles, Callfornla.
For his method to use carbon 14 for age determination in archaeology, geology, geophysics and other branches of science.

Nobel Prize in Physiology or Medicine
Frank Macfarlane Burnet
Born September 3, 1899, in Traralgon, Australia, and died August 31, 1985, in Melbourne.
&
Peter Brian Medawar
Born February 28, 1915, in Rio de Janeiro, Brazil, and died October 2, 1987, in London, England.
For the discovery of acquired immunological tolerance.

Nobel Prize in Literature
Saint-John Perse, pseudonym of Alexis Saint-Léger Léger
Born May 31, 1887, in Saint-Léger-les-Feuilles, Lesser Antilles, and died September 20, 1975, in Presqu'île de Giens, France.
For the soaring flight and the evocative imagery of his poetry which in a visionary fashion reflects the conditions of our time.

Nobel Peace Prize
Albert John Lutuli
Born approximately July 21, 1898, in Southern Rhodesia (now Zimbabwe), and died July 21, 1967, in Groutville, South Africa.
For his pacifist resistance to apartheid.

1961

Nobel Prize in Physics
Robert Hofstadter
Born February 5, 1915, in New York, New York, United States, and died November 17, 1990, in Stanford, California.
For his pioncering studics of clcctron scattcring in atomic nuclei and for his thereby achieved discoveries concerning the structure of the nucleons.
&
Rudolf Ludwig Mössbauer
Born January 31, 1929, in Munich, Germany.
For his researches concerning the resonance absorption of gamma radiation and his discovery in this connection of the effect which bears his name.

Nobel Prize in Chemistry
Melvin Calvin
Born April 8, 1911, in Saint Paul, Minnesota, United States, and died January 8, 1997, in Berkeley, California.
For his research on the carbon dioxide assimilation in plants.

Nobel Prize in Physiology or Medicine
Georg von Békésy
Born June 3, 1899, in Budapest, Hungary, and died June 13, 1972, in Honolulu, Hawaii, United States.
For his discoveries of the physical mechanism of stimulation within the cochlea.

Nobel Prize in Literature
Ivo Andric
Born October 10, 1892, in Dolac, Bosnia and
Herzegovina, and died March 13, 1975, in Belgrade,
Yugoslavia (now Serbia).
For the epic force with which he has traced themes and
depicted human destinies drawn from the history of his
country.

Nobel Peace Prize
Dag Hjalmar Agne Carl Hammarskjöld
Born July 29, 1905, in Jönköping, Sweden, and died
September 18, 1961, near Ndola, Northern Rhodesia
(now Zambia).
For his work in favor of Peace in the Congo.

1962

Nobel Prize in Physics
Lev Davidovich Landau
Born January 22, 1908, in Baku, Russia
(now Azerbaijan), and died April 1, 1968, in Moscow,
Union of Soviet Socialist Republics (now Russia).
For his pioneering theories for condensed matter,
especially liquid helium.

Nobel Prize in Chemistry
John Cowdery Kendrew
Born March 24, 1917, in Oxford, England, and died
August 23, 1997, in Cambridge.
&
Max Ferdinand Perutz
Born May 19, 1914, in Vienna, Austria, and died Febru-
ary 6, 2002, in Cambridge, England.
For their studies of the structure of globular proteins.

Nobel Prize in Physiology or Medicine
James Dewey Watson
Born April 6, 1928, in Chicago, Illinois, United States.
&
Maurice Hugh Frederick Wilkins
Born December 15, 1916, in Pongaroa, New Zealand,
and died October 5, 2004, in London, England.
&

Francis Harry Compton Crick
Born June 8, 1916, in Northampton, England, and died
July 28, 2004, in La Jolla, California, United States.
For their discoveries concerning the molecular structure
of nucleic acids and its significance for information
transfer in living material.

Nobel Prize in Literature
John Steinbeck
Born February 27, 1902, in Salinas, California, United
States, and died December 20, 1968, in New York, New
York.
For his realistic and imaginative writings, combining as
they do sympathetic humor and keen social perception.

Nobel Peace Prize
Linus Carl Pauling
Born February 28, 1901, in Portland, Oregon, United
States, and died August 19, 1994, in Big Sur, California.
For his role in peace and disarmament campaigns.

1963

Nobel Prize in Physics
Johannes Hans Daniel Jensen
Born June 25, 1907, in Hamburg, Germany, and died
February 11, 1973, in Heidelberg.
&
Maria Goeppert-Mayer
Born June 28, 1906, in Kattowitz, Germany
(now Kattowice, Poland), and died February 20, 1972,
in San Diego, California, United States.
For their discoveries concerning nuclear shell structure.
&
Eugene Paul Wigner
Born November 17, 1902, in Budapest, Hungary, and
died January 1, 1995, in Princeton, New Jersey, United
States.
For his contributions to the theory of the atomic nucleus
and the elementary particles, particularly through the
discovery and application of fundamental symmetry
principles.

Nobel Prize in Chemistry
Giulio Natta
Born February 26, 1903, in Imperia, Italy, and died May 2, 1979, in Bergamo.
&
Karl Ziegler
Born November 26, 1898, in Helsa, Germany, and died August 12, 1973, in Mülheim.
For their discoveries in the field of the chemistry and technology of high polymers.

Nobel Prize in Physiology or Medicine
John Carew Eccles
Born January 27, 1903, in Melbourne, Australia, and died May 2, 1997, in Contra, Switzerland.
&
Alan Lloyd Hodgkin
Born February 5, 1914, in Banbury, England, and died December 20, 1998, in Cambridge.
&
Andrew Fielding Huxley
Born November 22, 1917, in London, England.
For their discoveries concerning the ionic mechanisms involved in excitation and inhibition in the peripheral and central portions of the nerve cell membrane.

Nobel Prize in Literature
Giorgos Seferis, pseudonym of Giorgos Sefcriadis
Born March 13, 1900, in Smyrna, Ottoman Empire (now Izmir, Turkey), and died September 20, 1971, in Athens, Greece.
For his eminent lyrical writing, inspired by a deep feeling for the Hellenic world of culture.

Nobel Peace Prize
International Committee of the Red Cross
Founded in 1863 in Geneva, Switzerland.
&
League of Red Cross Societies
Founded in 1919 in Geneva, Switzerland.
One of the great miracles in human history.

1964

Nobel Prize in Physics
Nikolay Gennadievich Basov
Born December 14, 1922, in Usman, Union of Soviet Socialist Republics (now Russia), and died July 1, 2001, in Moscow, Russia.
&
Aleksandr Mikhailovich Prokhorov
Born July 11, 1916, in Atherton, Australia, and died January 8, 2002, in Moscow, Russia.
&
Charles Hard Townes
Born July 28, 1915, in Greenville, South Carolina, United States.
For fundamental work in the field of quantum electronics, which has led to the construction of oscillators and amplifiers based on the maser-laser principle.

Nobel Prize in Chemistry
Dorothy Crowfoot Hodgkin
Born May 12, 1910, in Cairo, Egypt, and died July 29, 1994, in Shipston-on-Stour, England.
For her determinations by X-ray techniques of the structures of important biochemical substances.

Nobel Prize in Physiology or Medicine
Konrad Emil Bloch
Born January 21, 1912, in Neisse, Germany (now Nysa, Poland), and died October 15, 2000, in Burlington, Massachusetts.
&
Feodor Lynen
Born April 6, 1911, in Munich, Germany, and died August 6, 1979, in Munich.
For their discoveries concerning the mechanism and regulation of the cholesterol and fatty acid metabolism.

Nobel Prize in Literature
Jean-Paul Sartre
Born June 21, 1905, in Paris, France, and died April 15, 1980, in Paris.
For his work which, rich in ideas and filled with the spirit of freedom and the quest for truth, has exerted a far-reaching influence on our age.

Nobel Peace Prize

Martin Luther King, Jr., né Michael Luther King, Jr.

Born January 15, 1929, in Atlanta, Georgia, United States, and died April 4, 1968, in Memphis, Tennessee.

For his fight for racial integration in the U.S.A., without recourse to violence.

1965

Nobel Prize in Physics

Richard Phillips Feynman

Born May 11, 1918, in New York, New York, United States, and died February 15, 1988, in Los Angeles, California.

&

Julian Schwinger

Born February 12, 1918, in New York, New York, United States, and died July 16, 1994, in Los Angeles, California.

&

Sin-Itiro Tomonaga

Born March 31, 1906, in Tokyo, Japan, and died July 8, 1979, in Tokyo.

For their fundamental work in quantum electrodynamics, with deep-ploughing consequences for the physics of elementary particles.

Nobel Prize in Chemistry

Robert Burns Woodward

Born April 10, 1917, in Boston, Massachusetts, United States, and died July 8, 1979, in Cambridge.

For his outstanding achievements in the art of organic synthesis.

Nobel Prize in Physiology or Medicine

François Jacob

Born June 17, 1920, in Nancy, France.

&

Jacques Lucien Monod

Born February 9, 1910, in Paris, France, and died May 31, 1976, in Cannes.

&

André Lwoff

Born May 8, 1902, in Ainay-le-Château, France, and died September 30, 1994, in Paris.

For their discoveries concerning genetic control of enzyme and virus synthesis.

Nobel Prize in Literature

Mikhail Aleksandrovich Sholokhov

Born May 24, 1905, in Veshenskaya, Russia, and died February 21, 1984, in Veshenskaya, Union of Soviet Socialist Republics (now Russia).

For the artistic power and integrity with which, in his epic of the Don, he has given expression to a historic phase in the life of the Russian people.

Nobel Peace Prize

United Nations Children's Fund (Unicef)

For its recognition that the well-being of today's children is inseparable from world peace tomorrow.

1966

Nobel Prize in Physics

Alfred Kastler

Born May 3, 1902, in Guebwiller, Germany (now France), and died January 7, 1984, in Bandol, France.

For the discovery and development of optical methods for studying Hertzian resonances in atoms.

Nobel Prize in Chemistry

Robert Sanderson Mulliken

Born June 7, 1896, in Newburyport, Massachusetts, United States, and died October 31, 1986, in Arlington, Virginia.

For his fundamental work concerning chemical bonds and the electronic structure of molecules by the molecular orbital system.

Nobel Prize in Physiology or Medicine

Charles Brenton Huggins

Born September 22, 1901, in Halifax, Nova Scotia, Canada, and died January 12, 1997, in Chicago, Illinois, United States.

For his discoveries concerning hormonal treatment of prostate cancer.

&

Peyton Rous

Born October 5, 1879, in Baltimore, Maryland, United States, and died February 16, 1970, in New York, New York.

For his discovery of tumor-inducing viruses.

Nobel Prize in Literature
Shmuel Yosef Agnon
Born July 17, 1888, in Buczacz, Galicia, Austria-Hungary (now Buchach, Ukraine), and died February 17, 1970, in Rehovot, Israel.
For his profoundly characteristic narrative art with motifs from the life of the Jewish people.
&
Leonie Nelly Sachs
Born December 10, 1891, in Berlin, Germany, and died May 12, 1970, in Stockholm, Sweden.
For her outstanding lyrical and dramatic writing, which interprets Israel's destiny with touching strength.

Nobel Peace Prize
Not awarded.

1967

Nobel Prize in Physics
Hans Albrecht Bethe
Born July 2, 1906, in Strasbourg, Germany (now France), and died March 6, 2005, in Ithaca, New York, United States.
For his contributions to the theory of nuclear reactions, especially his discoveries concerning the energy production in stars.

Nobel Prize in Chemistry
Manfred Eigen
Born May 9, 1927, in Bochum, Germany.
&
Ronald George Wreyford Norrish
Born November 9, 1897, in Cambridge, England, and died June 7, 1978, in Cambridge.
&
George Porter
Born December 6, 1920, in Stainforth, England, and died August 31, 2002, in Canterbury.
For their studies of extremely fast chemical reactions, effected by disturbing the equilibrium by means of very short pulses of energy.

Nobel Prize in Physiology or Medicine
Ragnar Arthur Granit
Born October 30, 1900, in Helsinki, Finland, and died March 12, 1991, in Stockholm, Sweden.
&

Haldan Keffer Hartline
Born December 22, 1903, in Bloomsburg, Pennsylvania, United States, and died March 17, 1983, in Fallston, Maryland.
&
George Wald
Born November 18, 1906, in New York, New York, United States, and died April 12, 1997, in Cambridge, Massachusetts.
For their discoveries concerning the primary physiological and chemical visual processes in the eye.

Nobel Prize in Literature
Miguel Angel Asturias
Born October 19, 1899, in Guatemala City, Guatemala, and died June 9, 1974, in Madrid, Spain.
For his vivid literary achievement, deep-rooted in the national traits and traditions of Indian peoples of Latin America.

Nobel Peace Prize
Not awarded.

1968

Nobel Prize in Physics
Luis Walter Alvarez
Born June 13, 1911, in San Francisco, California, United States, and died September 1, 1988, in Berkeley.
For his decisive contributions to elementary particle physics, in particular the discovery of a large number of resonance states, made possible through his development of the technique of using hydrogen-bubble-chamber and data analysis.

Nobel Prize in Chemistry
Lars Onsager
Born November 27, 1903, in Oslo, Norway, and died October 5, 1976, in Coral Gables, Florida, United States.
For the discovery of the reciprocal relations bearing his name, which are fundamental for the thermodynamics of irreversible processes.

Nobel Prize in Physiology or Medicine
Robert William Holley
Born January 28, 1922, in Urbana, Illinois, United States, and died February 11, 1993, in Los Gatos, California.
&

Har Gobind Khorana
Born January 9, 1922, in Raipur, India (now Pakistan)
&
Marshall Warren Nirenberg
Born April 10, 1927, in New York, New York, United States.
For their interpretation of the genetic code and its function in protein synthesis.

Nobel Prize in Literature
Yasunari Kawabata
Born June 11, 1899, in Osaka, Japan, and died April 16, 1972, in Zushi.
For his narrative mastery, which with great sensibility expresses the essence of the Japanese mind.

Nobel Peace Prize
René Samuel Cassin
Born October 5, 1887, in Bayonne, France, and died February 20, 1976, Paris.
For his defense of the rights of man, as established in the respective Universal Declaration.

1969

Nobel Prize in Physics
Murray Gell-Mann
Born September 15, 1929, in New York, New York, United States.
For his contributions and discoveries concerning the classification of elementary particles and their interactions.

Nobel Prize in Chemistry
Derek Harold Richard Barton
Born September 8, 1918, in Gravesend, England, and died March 16, 1998, in College Station, Texas, United States.
&
Odd Hassel
Born May 17, 1897, in Oslo, Norway, and died May 11, 1981, in Oslo.
For their contributions to the development of the concept of conformation and its application in chemistry.

Nobel Prize in Physiology or Medicine
Max Delbrück
Born September 4, 1906, in Berlin, Germany, and died March 9, 1981, in Pasadena, California, United States.
&
Alfred Day Hershey
Born December 4, 1908, in Owosso, Michigan, United States, and died May 22, 1997, in Syosset, New York.
&
Salvador Edward Luria
Born August 13, 1912 in Turin, Italy, and died February 6, 1991, in Lexington, Massachusetts, United States.
For their discoveries concerning the replication mechanism and the genetic structure of viruses.

Nobel Prize in Literature
Samuel Barclay Beckett
Born April 13, 1906, in Dublin, Ireland, and died December 22, 1989, in Paris, France.
For his writing, which — in new forms for the novel and drama — in the destitution of modern man acquires its elevation.

Nobel Peace Prize
International Labour Organization (ILO)
Founded in 1919 in Geneva, Switzerland.
For its success in putting into practice the idea on which it is based, namely the field of social justice.

The Sveriges Riksbank Prize in Economic Sciences in Memory of Alfred Nobel
Ragnar Frisch
Born March 3, 1895, in Oslo, Norway, and died January 31, 1973, in Oslo.
&
Jan Tinbergen
Born April 12, 1903, in The Hague, Netherlands, and died June 9, 1994, in Amsterdam.
For having developed and applied dynamic models for the analysis of economic processes.

Selected Profiles of Nobel Laureates

1970–1979

Aleksandr Solzhenitsyn

For the ethical force with which he has pursued the indispensable traditions of Russian literature.

Aleksandr Isayevich Solzhenitsyn studied mathematics before he became a well-known writer — practical training that may well have saved his life. He was arrested in 1945 and sentenced to eight years in labor camps for anti-Stalinist sentiments he expressed in letters to a school friend. For the first four years of his imprisonment Solzhenitsyn was placed with a group of scientific researchers instead of the labor gangs. If his mathematical skills had not allowed him to escape the labor gangs, he later wrote, "I would probably not have survived." He was then sent to the Ekibastuz detention camp, where he worked as a miner, among other jobs. He developed a malignant tumor, which was removed, but he never fully recovered his health.

A month after he completed his sentence, Solzhenitsyn was still in the camp and, rather than be released, he was instead exiled to Kok-Terek in South Kazakhstan, where he remained from 1953 until 1956. His cancer spread during these years, and he admitted, "I was very near to death," but he persevered and saw freedom once again. He was eventually expelled from the Soviet Union, only having his citizenship restored in 1990.

Born on December 11, 1918, in Kislovodsk, Russia, Aleksandr Solzhenitsyn was brought up by his mother; his father, an artillery officer who had fought at the German front, had died in battle six months before he was born. He spent his childhood and youth in Rostov and hoped to study literature in Moscow. This dream, though, was not possible: his mother was ill and the two lived in impoverished circumstances.

With some manuscripts already written but no one interested in publishing them, Solzhenitsyn entered the Department of Mathematics of the Rostov University. Despite his great success in the subject, however, he was determined not to spend the rest of his life working in mathematics.

He concentrated on writing in the greatest of secrecy. His prison experiences inspired his first novel, *Odin den iz zhizni Ivana Denisovicha (One Day in the Life of Ivan Denisovich)*, which was published in 1962 when he was 44 years old. He won the 1970 Nobel Prize in Literature, but the Soviet authorities seized the published book. In 1974 the government also seized the manuscript for *Arkhipelag Gulag (The Gulag Archipelago)*. In this book he lays bare the prison system, state terrorism and the methods of the Soviet secret police. For such honesty he was deprived of Soviet citizenship and deported to West Germany; he then spent a brief period in Switzerland before moving to the United States. He returned to his native country in 1994 and on June 5, 2007, received a top state award from then President Vladimir Putin.

Paul Samuelson

For the scientific work through which he has developed static and dynamic economic theory and actively contributed to raising the level of analysis in economic science.

Born in Gary, Indiana, in 1915, Paul Anthony Samuelson is passionate about research and teaching. He once described himself by saying, "In an era of specialization, I sometimes think I am the last generalist in economics." A critic of classical economic terms, he insists that the basis of understanding economic analysis resides in mathematics.

Paul Samuelson studied at the University of Chicago and received his BA in 1935. He then transferred to Harvard University and earned his master's degree the next year; in 1941 he received his doctorate and had already begun his career as a professor at the Massachusetts Institute of Technology (MIT).

He was also a columnist for Newsweek, heavily involved in American wartime and post-war economic management, a consultant to research organizations like the Rand Corporation and the board of the Federal Reserve Bank, as well as an advisor to presidents John F. Kennedy and Lyndon Johnson.

In 1947 he published his first important work, *Foundations of Economic Analysis*. A year later he published *Economics: An Introductory Analysis*, which has been translated into at least 12 languages and sold more than four million copies. In it, Samuelson explores in quantitative and mathematical terms his philosophy, which is largely based on the theories of the famed English economist John Maynard Keynes.

Calling himself a generalist, Samuelson applies mathematics to practical problems in international trade, industrial production, marketing and defense plans. He is equally well known for his work on inflation, unemployment and American economic growth, and he has developed mathematical techniques and formulas to relate the gross national product (GNP) with levels of employment.

As a result of this broad and valuable work, Samuelson has received many awards, including the David A. Wells Prize in 1941 from Harvard University and the 1970 Nobel Prize in Economics. A professor at the MIT for many years, he was also a Guggenheim Fellow from 1948 to 1949 and is a member of the American Academy of Arts and Sciences and the American Economic Association. In 1947 he was awarded the John Bates Clark Medal for being the economist under 40 "who has made the most distinguished contribution to the main body of economic thought and knowledge."

Paul Samuelson married Marion Crawford in 1938, and the couple has six children. They currently reside in Belmont, Massachusetts.

Sveriges Riksbank Prize in Economic Sciences in Memory of Alfred Nobel 1970

Dennis Gabor

For his invention and development of the holographic method.

Dennis Gabor was born in Budapest, Hungary, at the turn of the last century, but it was at the University of London where he invented the hologram — a lens-less system of three-dimensional photography — which brought him the 1971 Nobel Prize in Physics.

His love of physics appeared as a sudden passion at the age of 15. He wrote, "I could not wait until I got to the university"; in the meantime he learnt calculus, devouring a book by O.D. Chwolson that was the most important then available on the subject. He was also fascinated by Ernst Abbe's theory of the microscope and by Gabriel Lippmann's method of color photography, which, 30 years later, would have a decisive influence on his own work. His enthusiasm for physics was enormous, and Gabor even built a laboratory with his brother, where they could repeat experiments by the most famous scientists of the day.

When the time finally came for Gabor to go to university, however, he chose to enter an engineering program instead. He justified this by explaining, "Physics was not yet a profession in Hungary." In 1924 he graduated in electrical engineering from the Technische Hochschule in Berlin, where three years later he received his doctorate. Whenever he could, though, he would visit the University of Berlin, where names like Einstein, Planck, Nernst and von Laue were ushering in the golden age of physics in Germany.

With Hitler's rise to power, however, Gabor decided to leave Germany and, after a short period in Hungary, moved to England in 1934. During World War II he worked for the British Thomson-Houston Company. The following years were his most fruitful: during this time he wrote his first pieces on the communication theory, developed a system of stereoscopic cinematography and, in 1948, carried out his first experiments related to holography. One year later he became a British citizen.

Gabor was also involved in the attempt to build an improved electron microscope capable of visualizing isolated electrons. The results were encouraging but ultimately unsuccessful, and it would take a further 20 years before techniques were developed that allowed the advance of electronic holography.

He retired in 1967 but maintained links with the Imperial College of Science and Technology. In his later years he began to be concerned about the future of industrialized civilization and was convinced that social inventions and research must be placed above technological progress. He tried to explain his ideas in books such as *Inventing the Future* (1963), *Innovations* (1970) and *The Mature Society* (1972).

Earl Sutherland, Jr.

For his discoveries concerning the mechanisms of the action of hormones.

On November 19, 1915, Earl Wilbur Sutherland, Jr., was born in Burlingame, Kansas. He obtained his bachelor's degree in science in 1937 from Washburn College. He then transferred to the School of Medicine at Washington University in Saint Louis, Missouri, where he received his doctorate in 1942. For the next 20 years this American biochemist would dedicate himself to research, notably in conjunction with Carl Cori, who was a laureate for the Nobel Prize in Physiology or Medicine in 1947. The high point of his work was the moment he isolated the cyclic adenosine monophosphate and demonstrated its involvement in many metabolic processes.

During World War II Sutherland served as a battalion surgeon with the U.S. Army. After his discharge in 1945 he went to lecture at Washington University, then in 1953 he moved to the School of Medicine at Western Reserve University in Cleveland, Ohio, where he remained for a decade. In 1963 he married his second wife, Claudia Sebeste Smith, and became a professor of physiology at Vanderbilt University in Nashville, Tennessee. A year before his death he took a position at the University of Miami in Florida.

Sutherland's research focused on the mechanisms by which adrenaline regulates the metabolism of glycogen into glucose in the liver. He discovered that this hormone is responsible for activating the enzyme phosphorylase, which controls the transformation. Later on it was understood that this activation took place because of an intermediary substance, which occurs during the process. The discovery and chemical characterization of this intermediary substance, which Sutherland called a second messenger (the first is the hormone), was of great importance in understanding the mechanism of the action of adrenaline and many other hormones. When he identified this substance he saw that he was dealing with a nucleotide, which he called cyclic adenosine monophosphate, or cyclic AMP.

In 1960 Sutherland suggested that these conclusions could explain the effects of many other hormones. He postulated that the various hormones do not penetrate the cells but are "captured" on the cell walls by adrenaline, which activates the process of forming the cyclic AMP, which, in turn, stimulates or inhibits various metabolic processes once inside the cell.

In 1971 Earl Wilbur Sutherland, Jr., was awarded the Nobel Prize in Physiology or Medicine; a year earlier he had received the Gairdner International Foundation Award and the Albert Lasker Basic Medical Research Award. He died a few years later, in 1974.

Pablo Neruda

For a poetry that, with the action of an elemental force, brings alive a continent's destiny and dreams.

Pablo Neruda, the world-famous Chilean poet, received the 1971 Nobel Prize in Literature and is considered one of the greatest poets of the 20th century, and this despite his belief that "all books should be anonymous." Born Neftalí Ricardo Reyes Basoalto in 1904, he started to use his pseudonym at the age of 16, when he began working for the literary journal *Selva Austral*, in homage to the Czech poet Jan Neruda (1834–1891).

The son of a railway worker in Parral, he published his first poem, "Entusiasmo y perseverancia" ("Enthusiasm and Perseverance"), at the age of 13 in the daily newspaper *La Mañana*. Others were collected in the anthology *Crepusculario*, which was published in 1923. Neruda achieved fame at an early age. The book *Veinte poemas de amor y una canción desesperada* (*Twenty Love Poems and a Song of Despair*, published in 1924) was an immense success, and the author was soon acclaimed as one of the most important young poets in Latin America. Meanwhile he studied French and pedagogy at the University of Chile in Santiago.

Between 1927 and 1935 he traveled the world as an honorary consul, spending time in Burma, Ceylon, Java, Singapore, Buenos Aires, Barcelona and Madrid. During this period he wrote, among other things, a collection of esoteric, surrealist poems entitled *Residencia en la Tierra* (*Residence on earth*, 1933), which is seen as a turning point in his literary career.

He favored the Republican side during the Spanish Civil War after the death of Federico García Lorca, whom he knew personally. It was at this time that he wrote *España en el Corazón* (*Spain in the Heart*, 1933), a book that had an enormous impact on the frontline. While living in Mexico Neruda rewrote *Canto general de Chile* (*General Song of Chile*, 1943), transforming it into an epic work on nature, people and the destiny of all South America; the work's new title was, simply, *Canto general* (1950). The book was published in Mexico and circulated underground in Chile, and it is considered by many to be his most important piece of poetry.

He returned to Chile in 1943 and, two years later, was elected a senator and joined the Communist Party. However, his protests against the repressive acts of President González Videla forced him into exile. After living in various European countries he returned to Chile in 1952. During this time he only wrote poems of a political nature, such as the verses collected in *Las uvas y el viento* (*The Grapes and the Wind*, 1954) and *Odas elementales* (*Elementary Odes*, 1954–1959).

Pablo Neruda died in 1973 at the age of 69.

Willy Brandt

For his efforts to help respect human rights and the total freedom of movement for the people of West Berlin, as well as his role in the creation of conditions for peace in Europe.

In 1971 Chancellor Willy Brandt became the fourth German citizen to receive the Nobel Peace Prize. For a number of years he had been a political refugee in Norway. He was also a refugee in Sweden and only returned to his native country after World War II, when he began his political career.

Born Herbert Ernst Karl Frahm on December 18, 1913, in the city of Lübeck. He was still a young man when the Nazis came to power. He quickly became active in politics, first joining the Socialist Party of Germany (SPD) in 1930 and more radical movements later; he assumed his new name in 1933 in an attempt to avoid arrest by the gestapo.

When he was 20 Willy Brandt left for Norway, where he studied history and journalism and helped the victims of Nazi persecution. While still a refugee Brandt played an important role in the process of awarding the 1935 Nobel Peace Prize to the German pacifist Carl von Ossietzky, a journalist who was arrested and spent five years in concentration camps for his writings. During this time Brandt was stripped of his German citizenship.

When Germany invaded Norway in 1940 Brandt was forced to flee the country and became a refugee in Sweden. At the end of World War II he moved to West Berlin and a year later he reacquired his German citizenship. As a Social Democrat Willy Brandt was elected a deputy in the first legislature of the Federal Republic of Germany in 1949. In 1957, he became the mayor of West Berlin.

In 1961 he assumed the leadership of the Social Democratic Party. He served as vice chancellor and foreign minister from 1966 to 1969. He finally achieved his goal in 1969, becoming chancellor, and he was also reelected in the 1972 general elections.

Willy Brandt won the 1971 Nobel Peace Prize for his work in diffusing the tension between Eastern and Western Europe. His policy, known as Ostopolitik, led Germany to sign nonaggression pacts with the USSR, Czechoslovakia and Poland. Ostopolitik was based on Brandt's acceptance of Germany's loss of more than 40,000 square miles (103 500 sq. km) of German land, which was awarded to Poland after World War II, and Germany's moral responsibility for atrocities carried out during the war. He was the first German leader to effectively resolve these lingering issues, and they helped to pave the way for his nation's new place in Europe. He was named *Time* magazine's Man of the Year in 1970 for his influence on world events during the delicate rebuilding of Europe after World War II. He died on October 8, 1992, at the age of 78.

Simon Kuznets

For his empirically founded interpretation of economic growth, which has led to new and deepened insight into the economic and social structure and process of development.

Simon Kuznets is best known for his development of the concept of gross national product (GNP), put forth in his book *National Income and Its Composition, 1919–1938*, published in 1941. Later he would help the U.S. Department of Commerce standardize the measurement of GNP, but his contributions to the field of economics were diverse. He also became a pioneer in the study of American business cycles and economic growth.

Simon Kuznets was born into a family of Russian Jews in 1901, but he left his native country at the age of 21 to join his father, who had immigrated to the United States before World War I. He took some academic material he had worked on with him and completed his studies at the Columbia University, where he received his doctorate in 1926. The following year he joined the National Bureau of Economic Research, where he worked for many years with Wesley C. Mitchell. It was to this economist that Kuznets confessed a deep intellectual debt, and he dedicated his study of economic cycles to him.

Kuznets remained associated with the National Bureau of Economic Research until the beginning of the 1960s, balancing his research with teaching. He also taught economics and statistics at the University of Pennsylvania between 1931 and 1954 and political economics at Johns Hopkins University from 1954 to 1960. In addition he lectured at Harvard University, where he was a professor for 11 years, until his retirement in 1971.

Simon Kuznets's interpretation of economic growth was considered as a new perspective to understand world economics and social structure. Many specialists came to see him as an empiricist. His most important published works are *Secular Movements in Production and Prices* (1930), *Long-Term Changes in the National Income of the United States of America since 1870* (1951) and *Modern Economic Growth* (1966).

He received the 1971 Nobel Prize in Economics and collaborated with several research institutions, including the American Economic Association, of which he was president in 1954, the American Statistical Association, the Economic History Association, the Econometric Society, the International Statistical Institute and the Royal Statistical Society of England.

Simon Kuznets lived in Cambridge, Massachusetts, with his wife, Edith. They had two children together, and one of them, Paul, followed in his father's footsteps and taught economics at Indiana University.

Heinrich Böll

For his writing, which through its combination of a broad perspective on his time and a sensitive skill in characterization, has contributed to a renewal of German literature.

Heinrich Theodor Böll played an important role in postwar German literature. Along with other writers in the early 1950s, he was a member of Group 47 — created by left-wing intellectuals interested in revitalizing German literature — which they considered deeply damaged by Nazi propaganda. Hans Werner Richter and Alfred Andersch, the founders of this forum for readings and discussions, were just two of the names that influenced Böll's career. Another was Günter Grass, who went on to win the 1999 Nobel Prize in Literature. The leaders of Group 47 advocated a new style in reaction to the classical, flowery language of the past; at the same time, they promoted the work of young revolutionary writers.

Born on December 21, 1917, to a sculptor and cabinet-maker, Viktor Böll, and his wife, Maria, Heinrich Böll's first incursion into literature took place when he was 21, during a brief experience as an apprentice bookseller. He was conscripted to fight in World War II and was captured by the Americans in 1945. Only months after the war he returned to his native Cologne, accompanied by his wife and family, and set himself up in a damaged house and, bit by bit, took up writing again.

He had short stories published between 1946 and 1949, as well as his first book, the novella *Der Zug war pünktlich (The Train Was on Time)*, in which he criticized the futility and horrors of World War II. With the novel *Wo Warst du, Adam? (And where were you, Adam?)*, published in 1951, Heinrich Böll shed light on the political and social forces that deceived the ordinary people during Nazi leadership. Other works told of the difficult conditions in postwar Germany and denounced what he called the dehumanized materialism of the Federal Republic of Germany. His criticism of social values is well expressed in the short narrative *Die verlorene Ehre der Katharina Blum (The Lost Honor of Katharina Blum)*, published in 1974; the work includes harsh attacks on judicial proceedings and journalism. Its success led to its adaptation into a film.

Heinrich Böll built a career that marked the rebirth of German literature, and he produced novels, short stories, plays and essays over his lifetime. In 1972 he received the Nobel Prize in Literature and two years later was made an honorary member of the American Academy of Arts and Letters.

In 1942 he married Annemarie Cech, who proved to be a tireless companion, equally affected by the Nazi regime and a conscientious critic of German literature. Heinrich Böll died at the age of 68 in 1985.

Henry Kissinger

For their negotiations to end the Vietnam War.

Henry Alfred Kissinger was the 56th United States Secretary of State, and the first to be born outside of the United States. In 1973 he received the Nobel Peace Prize along with the Vietnamese Le Duc Tho, who turned it down, for negotiating a ceasefire in the Vietnam War.

On May 27, 1923, Kissinger was born in Fuerth, Germany. He was 15 when his parents took him to the United States to escape the persecution of Jews in Europe, and on June 19, 1943, he became an American citizen. He received his BA, summa cum laude, from Harvard University in 1950, his master's degree two years later and his doctorate in 1954.

Upon completion of his PhD Kissinger became a member of the faculty at Harvard and remained with the institution until 1971. During these years he worked in the Department of Government and the Center for International Affairs, was study director of the Nuclear Weapons and Foreign Policy division of the Council of Foreign Relations and director of the Harvard International Seminar and of the Harvard Defense Studies Program. During World War II Kissinger worked in the U.S. Army Counterintelligence Corps from 1943 to 1946, when he was made a captain in the Military Intelligence Reserve, a position he held until 1949.

In the 1950s and 1960s he was occasionally an advisor in international politics to presidents Dwight D. Eisenhower, John F. Kennedy and Lyndon B. Johnson. It was with President Richard Nixon, however, that Kissinger's name was most closely connected, and he served as the 8th U.S. National Security Advisor from 1969 to 1975. International affairs were Nixon's principal focus, and Kissinger was always at his side. President Nixon began his term by saying that America was entering an "era of negotiation," and began the gradual withdrawal of troops involved in the Vietnam War.

There then followed the U.S. invasion of Cambodia, the bombing of Hanoi and the mining of the port of Haiphong. It was in these conditions that Kissinger, as National Security Advisor, began the negotiations with the North Vietnamese in 1972 that led to the Paris Peace Accords signed in January 1973. The agreement called for the withdrawal of American troops and the release of all prisoners of war by the North Vietnamese government; neither party, however, fully respected the agreement. The United States continued to support Saigon, and North Vietnam continued to attack South Vietnam with increasing intensity until the Americans were forced to hurriedly withdraw in 1975.

Before his work during the Vietnam War, Kissinger was a consultant to the Department of State, the United States Arms Control and Disarmament Agency, the National Security

Council, the Weapons Systems Evaluation Group of the Joint Chiefs of Staff and the director of the Psychological Strategy Board.

He was also at President Nixon's side on important diplomatic visits abroad, and he negotiated the Anti-Ballistic Missile Treaty with the USSR and formalized relations with China, ending decades of isolation and hostility between the nations. He was involved in numerous other interventions, including those in Chile and Argentina. In September 1973 he became head of American diplomacy as secretary of state under President Nixon. That same year he negotiated the end of the Yom Kippur War. Kissinger's reputation survived Nixon's resignation in August 1974 in the aftermath of the Watergate scandal, and he continued in his role as secretary of state when Vice President Gerald Ford became president.

After leaving his government positions he established Kissinger Associates, an international consulting firm. In 2002 President George W. Bush appointed Kissinger to a committee investigating the attacks of September 11th. Leading Democrats complained of conflicts of interest, however, and he stepped down the same year. In 2006 he met regularly with the president and Vice President Dick Cheney to give advice on the war in Iraq; a year earlier he wrote in his column in *The Washington Post* that "victory over the insurgency is the only meaningful exit strategy."

Some of Kissinger's many works on international affairs, foreign policy and diplomatic history are *Nuclear Weapons and Foreign Policy* (1957), *Years of Upheaval* (1982) and *Diplomacy* (1994). He received the Woodrow Wilson Prize in 1958, the American Institute for Public Service Award, the Veterans of Foreign Wars Dwight D. Eisenhower Distinguished Service Medal and the Hope Award for International Understanding in 1973, the Presidential Medal of Freedom in 1977 and the Medal of Liberty in 1986.

He married Ann Fleischer in 1949 and was divorced in 1964. In 1974 he married Nancy Maginnes, and they currently reside in Connecticut.

Le Duc Tho also received half of the prize.

Le Duc Tho

For their negotiations to end the Vietnam War.

When he was awarded the Nobel Peace Prize along with Henry Kissinger in 1973, Le Duc Tho refused the award because true peace had not yet been re-established in Vietnam. In fact, it was necessary to wait another three years for the country to stabilize after decades of war. The seeds of this peace were sown by Le Duc Tho, however, and their effects were already evident before the ceasefire agreement that stipulated the withdrawal of American troops from the former French colony.

Le Duc Tho, whose real name was Phan Dinh Khai, was born in the north of Vietnam, then known as French Indochina, on October 14, 1911. His political activities, including forming the Indochina Communist Party in 1930, led to his imprisonment twice by the French, first from 1930 to 1936 and then again from 1939 to 1944. One year after he was released for the second time he went to Hanoi, recently declared the capital of French Indochina (now the capital of Vietnam), and joined members of the Viet Minh. This organization sought independence from the occupying French and gained enormous popularity after the surrender of the Japanese, who had occupied the country during World War II.

The War of Independence began in 1946, when the French bombed Haiphong, and it only finished with the Geneva Accords of 1954, which resulted in the division of the country into two parts: the Democratic Republic of Vietnam, allied to communist nations, and the Republic of Vietnam, allied to the United States and other democratic countries. During this troubled period Le Duc Tho was a high-ranking member of the Viet Minh. From 1955 until 1986 he was a member of the Politburo of the Vietnamese Workers' Party, renamed the Communist Party in 1976.

War broke out once more in 1955 and lasted for 20 bloody years. At this time Le Duc Tho took on a new role, as leader of the Viet Cong (the North Vietnamese), against the government of South Vietnam. Le Duc Tho contributed to the 1973 Paris Peace Accords, which established a ceasefire. As the special advisor of the North Vietnamese delegation he had participated in the peace conferences with the Americans since 1968 and, thanks to his negotiation skills, he became his country's main spokesperson during the process. In 1975 he led the North Vietnamese offensive that resulted in the final defeat of South Vietnam. It was only then that lasting peace appeared to be possible in the newly named Socialist Republic of Vietnam.

Henry Alfred Kissinger also received half of the prize.

Gunnar Myrdal

For their pioneering work in the theory of money and economic fluctuations and for their penetrating analysis of the interdependence of economic, social and institutional phenomena.

Gunnar Myrdal was born in Gustafs, Sweden, on December 6, 1898. His early education was at the law school of Stockholm University, from which he graduated in 1923. Myrdal practiced law for a number of years, although he continued to study and, in 1927, received his doctorate in economics.

Between 1925 and 1929 he also studied at German and English universities, and then, with the aid of a grant from the Rockefeller Foundation, he spent a year in the United States. During this period he published his first books, among which was *The Political Element in the Development of Economic Theory*. He then returned to Europe to teach in Geneva and stayed there for a year; in 1933 he returned to his native country to take the Lars Hierta chair of political economy and public finance at Stockholm University.

Besides his academic career, Myrdal was also an active politician. As a member of the Social Democrat Party he was elected to the Swedish Senate in 1934. In 1938 the Carnegie Foundation in New York commissioned him to study the integration problems of African Americans. The result was the book *An American Dilemma: The Negro Problem and Modern Democracy* (1944).

Once more at home, Myrdal became part of the board of the Bank of Sweden and also presided over the Commission of Post-War Planning. Between 1945 and 1947 he was the minister of commerce, but he left the government to become the executive secretary of the United Nations Economics Commission for Europe. In 1961, on returning to Sweden, he was made a professor of international economics and established the Institute for International Economic Studies. Myrdal also ran the Research Institute for International Peace and the Stockholm Latin American Institute.

He was a member of many societies and was awarded 30 honorary degrees, the first of which was from Harvard University in 1938. He won the 1974 Nobel Prize in Economics as a result of 10 years of research into the social and economic conditions in Southeast Asia.

Myrdal died one year after his wife, whom he had married in 1924. Alva Reimer Myrdal worked for the United Nations in the area of social affairs; she was the director of UNESCO's Department of Social Sciences, a Swedish ambassador to India and the Swedish minister for disarmament between 1966 and 1973. Alva's work and the various books she published on disarmament earned her the Nobel Peace Prize in 1982.

Friedrich August von Hayek also received half of the prize.

Sveriges Riksbank Prize in Economic Sciences in Memory of Alfred Nobel 1974

Andrei Sakharov

For his defense of fundamental principles of peace between men.

The nuclear physicist and political dissident Andrei Dmitrievich Sakharov was an active voice in the defense of human rights and attempted to improve relations between the Soviet Union and non-Communist countries. From 1968 onward his career as a researcher gave way to his work as a spokesperson for freedom in his country, disarmament and controlling nuclear arms at an international level. It was this work that earned him the 1975 Nobel Peace Prize.

Sakharov was born on May 21, 1921, and had a happy childhood, living in a communal apartment in Moscow with his large, hardworking family. He was the son of a physics teacher and accomplished pianist, but Sakharov held special affection for his grandmother, Maria Petrovna, who brought up six children and, at the age of 50, taught herself English. In the evenings she delighted her grandchildren by reading stories aloud. In this comfortable environment it was not difficult for Andrei Sakharov to take his first lessons at home, but he would go on to have some difficulty in adapting to life in the classroom.

Nevertheless, he graduated from Moscow State University in 1942 and continued his studies during World War II, defending his doctoral thesis on nuclear physics in 1947 at the Lebedev Institute under the direction of the physicist Igor Evgenyevich Tamm. In 1948 he joined a group of scientists who were working on developing nuclear weapons. The head of this group was Tamm, with whom Sakharov made a proposal that led to the construction of the Soviet hydrogen bomb.

He worked for 20 years in the strictest security and under great pressure, first in Moscow and later in a secret research center. As the situation evolved, however, Andrei Sakharov became increasingly aware of the inherent moral problems of the research he was conducting. In 1961 he made a formal protest against atmospheric tests of the hydrogen bomb carried out by the Soviet Union. Seven years later he made his position public in articles and books and was removed from his top-secret work. He returned to the Lebedev Institute in 1969 and started researching elemental particles, gravitation and cosmology.

The Soviet government did not authorize his trip to Norway to receive the Nobel Peace Prize, and Andrei Sakharov was exiled to Gorky in 1980 because of his political activity. He was granted permission to return to Moscow six years later, however, and in 1989 was elected to the Congress of People's Deputies. He held the position of spokesperson on human rights and political and economic reform until his death a few months later.

Milton Friedman

For his achievements in the fields of consumption analysis, monetary history and theory and for his demonstration of the complexity of stabilization policy.

Famed American economist and champion of neoliberalism Milton Friedman received the 1976 Nobel Prize in Economics for his work related to consumption analysis, monetary history, monetary theory and for demonstrating the complexity of stabilization policy. His economic visions are expressed in books such as *Capitalism and Freedom* (1962), *A Monetary History of the United States, 1867–1960* (1963), *Dollars and Deficits* (1968), *A Theoretical Framework for Monetary Analysis* (1971) and *Free to Choose*, co-written with Rose Friedman (1980).

Born in Brooklyn, New York, on July 31, 1912, and the youngest of four children, he was the son of Sarah Ethel and Jeno Saul Friedman, who had immigrated to the United States in their teens. They were originally from Carpatho-Ruthenia, a region that, at the time they left, belonged to the Austro-Hungarian Empire, was then part of Czechoslovakia between the two world wars, then annexed as part of the Soviet Union and is now part of Russia. The family was poor, but, as Friedman himself said, there was always food on the table and the atmosphere was "warm and supportive."

His father died when he was in his last year of high school, but Friedman was still determined to attend university, even if it required hard work and long hours. He attended Rutgers University, which at the time was "a relatively small university and predominantly private," and the University of Chicago. "I had the good fortune to be exposed to two remarkable men," he said, referring to two professors, Arthur F. Burns and Homer Jones, who had an important influence on his career.

In 1950 he went to Paris to help administer the Marshall Plan. He also contributed a triweekly column to *Newsweek*, alternating with Paul Samuelson and Henry Wallich. He entered the world of politics as a member of the President's Economic Policy Advisory Board during the administration of Ronald Reagan, from whom he received the Presidential Medal of Freedom in 1988. That same year he was awarded the National Medal of Science.

Despite being known for winning the Nobel Prize, working with governments around the world and being a leading exponent of neoliberal politics at the end of the 20th century, Friedman never considered his public life as his priority; his "primary interest" he insisted, "continues to be my scientific work." In 1998 the University of Chicago published *Two Lucky People*, the couple's memoirs.

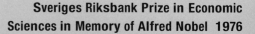

Sveriges Riksbank Prize in Economic Sciences in Memory of Alfred Nobel 1976

Vicente Aleixandre

For a creative poetic writing which illuminates man's condition in the cosmos and in present-day society, at the same time representing the great renewal of the traditions of Spanish poetry between the wars.

Vicente Aleixandre was born on April 26, 1898, in Seville, in the heart of Andalusia. He completed a degree in law from the University of Madrid in 1920, but he dedicated himself to literature. He received the Nobel Prize in Literature in 1977, which marked more than half a century of achievements in contemporary Spanish poetry.

The son of a civil engineer, Vicente Aleixandre spent his childhood in Malaga but moved to Madrid in 1909. His early experiences of the Mediterranean proved inspirational for his later masterpieces, including *Sombra del paraíso (The Shadow of Paradise)*, which was published in 1944. In the Spanish capital he also studied law and business management and seemed set on a career as a teacher. He taught commercial law between 1920 and 1922, but he developed renal tuberculosis and started writing poetry in 1925 to pass the time during his recovery.

His first book of poetry, *Ambito (Ambit)*, was published in 1928, and from that point on Vicente Aleixandre never stopped writing. This book showed a special interest in nature, but time, solitude, erotic love and death were other important motifs for the author, while his antifascist convictions were reflected in his later works. Aleixandre's work is divided into these two phases: the first begins with *Ambito* and ends with *Nacimiento ultimo (Last Birth*, published in 1953), and the second begins with *Historia del corazón (History of the Heart*, 1954) and continues to his last books, of which *Diálogos del conocimiento (Dialogues of Insight*, 1974) is an example. The poet acknowledged this division: "In the first phase of my work, I saw the poet as having his feet on the ground and an expression of the forces which grow within the plants... In the second part of my work, I saw the poet as an expression of the difficulties of human life."

Aleixandre was on the Republican side during the Spanish Civil War. His work was subsequently banned between 1936 and 1944, but in 1949 he was elected to the Royal Spanish Academy. The Nobel Prize in Literature was awarded for his lifetime's work, which was first compiled in *Complete Poems* (1960) and then in *Total Anthology* (1975), less than a decade before his death in Madrid on December 14, 1984. He had suffered from chronic kidney disease since his youth and had been a semi-invalid since his late 20s.

Mother Teresa

For her actions favoring children and refugees.

Agnes Gonxha Bojaxhiu dedicated her life to the poor, a vocation she felt called to when just 12 years old. The daughter of an Albanian farmer who was murdered when she was seven, Bojaxhiu was born in Skopje, today the capital of Macedonia, on August 26, 1910. She abandoned her homeland at the age of 18 to join the Sisters of Loreto in Ireland, a teaching order of nuns with missions across India. After some training in Dublin she left for Calcutta where, on May 24, 1931, she took her initial vows as a nun and the name Sister Mary Teresa. Between 1929 and 1948 she taught at St. Mary's High School in Calcutta and made her final profession of vows on May 24, 1937.

The poverty and suffering outside the convent walls left a great impression on her. After much introspection she asked her superiors if she could work with the poorest of the poor in the slums of Calcutta; permission was granted two years later. The order of the Missionaries of Charity was established on October 7, 1950. This Catholic order of nun's main priority is to give aid, both physical and spiritual, to those whom nobody else is prepared to help.

In 1952 she opened the first "home for the dying" outside Calcutta, with land provided by the government. Over the coming years she would establish many more institutions to take care of the victims of leprosy and other diseases.

Mother Teresa started more than 50 projects in India, and the order's work spread into others countries. She was awarded the 1979 Nobel Peace Prize, which she accepted "for the glory of God and in the name of the poor," but she refused the banquet and donated the prize money to charities in India. Mother Teresa was also awarded the Pope John XXIII Peace Prize in 1971, the Nehru Prize for supporting peace and international understanding in 1972 and the Presidential Medal of Freedom from the United States in 1985.

With her failing health, Mother Teresa of Calcutta was forced to reduce her workload in 1990, although she continued to travel. In March 1997 she blessed her newly elected successor, Nirmala Joshi, as superior general of the Missionaries of Charity. Shortly afterward she made her final visit to Pope John Paul II. She then returned to Calcutta, where she spent her final weeks, and died on September 5, 1997, at the age of 87. She was given a state funeral by the Indian government.

Much speculation has arisen over Mother Teresa's longtime inner struggle with feelings of separation from God, which she termed "the darkness." Despite these personal internal struggles, Mother Teresa remained faithful to her calling and to those whom no one else was prepared to help.

Amnesty International

For protecting prisoners against violations of human rights.

One of the most powerful humanitarian organizations in the world — and independent of political and economic powers — Amnesty International uses peaceful means to defend human rights and denounce injustice across the five continents, without regard to the creed or color of the victims. This vital work has gone on for more than 40 years, largely thanks to the efforts of volunteer groups working in 55 countries. Amnesty International was awarded the 1977 Nobel Peace Prize for defending human dignity against violence and subjugation.

The organization was founded in 1961 by the British lawyer Peter Benenson, who wrote in his article "The Forgotten Prisoners," "Open your newspapers any day of the week, and you will find a story from somewhere of someone being imprisoned, tortured or executed because his opinions are unacceptable to his government... The newspaper reader feels a sickening sense of impotence. Yet if these feelings of disgust could be united into common action, something effective could be done." Truly, Benenson's dream has been realized.

Amnesty International presently has well over two million members, some 4,000 working groups and can count on sympathizers and supporters in more than 150 nations. It is financed by donations and also by annual membership fees paid by its members. Some of Amnesty International's activities include public demonstrations, vigils, charity concerts, petitions, letter-writing campaigns, human-rights education and the publication of detailed reports based on original research collected by their experts. On the intergovernmental level, Amnesty International campaigned for the creation of a United Nations High Commissioner for Human Rights, which was established in 1993, and an International Criminal Court, which was founded in 2002. The group's foundation and philosophy is derived from the Universal Declaration of Human Rights, which was adopted by the UN General Assembly on December 10, 1948.

Over the years Amnesty International has worked on campaigns to free prisoners of conscience (those imprisoned for political or religious convictions), but also to help those held or discriminated against because of their ethnic origin, color, sex or language. Another important facet of their work is the denunciation of torture and other types of physical and psychological violence, which occur in prisons all over the world. Every year Amnesty International reports on shocking acts of cruelty and, because of their efforts, many have accepted that torture is still practiced in a number of countries, even in those with official policies forbidding the practice. Amnesty International has also brought the actions of security forces and paramilitary groups under scrutiny and has campaigned hard for the abolition of the death penalty. Since 1991 the violation of human rights based on sexual orientation have also been a part of the permanent concerns Amnesty International monitors and campaigns against.

Although Amnesty International receives wide support from many active members and sympathetic nations, it has also received considerable criticism. It was denounced by the USSR for espionage and by Morocco for the defense of lawbreakers, and its annual report in 1983 was banned in Argentina. Although White House officials often cite the organization's work, including Secretary Donald Rumsfeld, who spoke in 2003 about his "careful reading of Amnesty International" and their documentation of the repressive regime of Saddam Hussein, government relationships are not always so amiable. In 2005 the Bush administration voiced its opposition when Irene Khan, secretary general of Amnesty International, compared the U.S. government's detention facilities in Guantanamo Bay, Cuba, to a Soviet gulag. Other nations have also complained that the organization does not consider national security as a mitigating factor in the treatment of individuals.

Despite ongoing criticism, Amnesty International continues to garner growing support and international recognition. In their tireless fight the organization adheres to Mahatma Gandhi's belief that "Nonviolence is a more active and real fight against wickedness than retaliation whose very nature is to increase wickedness. It is not a weapon of the weak. It is a weapon of the strongest and bravest."

(1913–1992) (1918–1981)

Menachem Begin & Anwar Sadat

For their contribution to the peace agreements between Egypt and Israel, which were signed at Camp David, on the 17th of September, 1978.

Menachem Begin and Mohamed Anwar al-Sadat were at Camp David, under the mediation of President Jimmy Carter, when they signed one of the 20th century's most important peace treaties. The then prime minister of Israel and president of Egypt celebrated the first Israeli-Arab peace accord and earned the Nobel Peace Prize in 1978 for their efforts.

It should not be thought, however, that these two statesmen had a past dedicated to peace; quite the opposite is true. Both of them had a service record full of medals obtained in fighting their adversary.

Begin was born in Brest-Litovsk, now Brest in Belarus, on August 16, 1913; he was descended from a respected rabbinical family on his mother's side and his father was a community leader and dedicated Zionist. He received his law degree in 1935 from the University of Warsaw in Poland, and while he never practiced law, he did become well versed in classical literature. During this period he also became heavily involved in Zionist activities; he fled to eastern Poland with the outbreak of World War II but was captured by the Russians in 1940. He was sentenced to eight years in Soviet gulags but was released within a year under the Sikorski-Mayski Agreement. He then joined the Polish Army and was later sent to Palestine. Both of his parents perished during the Holocaust.

While in Palestine Begin joined the Irgun, an underground militant Zionist group, and criticized other Zionists for cooperating too closely with colonial British ideology. Between 1944 and 1948 he called for rebellion against the occupying British forces, and hundreds of attacks were launched; as a result, a £10,000 dead-or-alive bounty was placed on Begin. With the end of the Israeli War of Independence and the Declaration of the Establishment of the State of Israel on May 14, 1948, Irgun was disbanded.

In the coming years Menachem Begin helped establish the right-wing Herut (Liberty) Party, and in 1967 he was made a minister without portfolio in the National Unity Govern-ment in the aftermath of the Six-Day War. Then, in 1973, he agreed to an alliance of opposi-tion parties, known as Likud, devised by Ariel Sharon. In 1977 Likud dramatically won the national elections and Begin became Prime Minister of Israel.

Anwar al-Sadat had a comparable history. He came from a poor family, was one of 13 children and was trained at the Royal Military Academy in Cairo, where he met Gamal Abdel

Nasser, with whom he conspired to overthrow the monarchy and rid his country of British influence in the Egyptian Revolution of 1952. When Nasser, then president, died suddenly in 1970, Sadat, who was serving as vice president, became his successor. Conflicts with Israel were commonplace during this period. In 1967 the Egyptian forces had been destroyed in the Six-Day War, but Sadat rebuilt the country's military power and launched the Yom Kippur War in 1973. Even though the Israelis, who had been surprised during one of their most important religious festivals, managed to beat off the attack, Sadat recovered the Suez Canal area.

In 1977, however, Sadat accepted an invitation from Menachem Begin and visited Israel hoping to arrive at a permanent peace settlement. The next year they met once more, this time at Camp David, the country retreat of American presidents. At the end of 13 days of negotiations, Sadat, Begin and Jimmy Carter announced the conclusion of two accords, one concerning peace in the Middle East and another assuring the basis of a peace treaty between Egypt and Israel.

By taking such steps Sadat steered Egypt to a more strategic relationship with the United States and the international community, but he deeply angered fundamental Islamists who were set to eliminate Zionism and Israel. Egypt was expelled from the Arab League in 1979 and remained so for a decade. Sadat also came under corruption changes and many of his domestic policies were criticized.

During a military parade on October 6, 1961, fundamentalist militants, led by Khalid Islambouli, sprang from a truck and shot him; 11 others were killed and 28 were wounded. Anwar Sadat was survived by his second wife, Jehan Sadat, and their son; he had married once before, to Ehsan Madi, and the couple had three daughters before their divorce.

Menachem Begin remained prime minister until his retirement in 1983; during these years he was responsible for the successful bombing of Iraq's Tammuz nuclear reactor and the unpopular 1982 invasion of Lebanon. His wife, Aliza Begin, passed away in 1982, a decade before her husband. The political careers of Menachem Begin and Anwar Sadat are still considered controversial, but their influence has been undeniably enormous and their efforts to bring peace between their nations were recognized with the 1978 Nobel Peace Prize.

Menachem Begin and Mohamed Anwar Sadat each received half of the prize.

Allan Cormack

For the development of computer-assisted tomography.

The acronym CAT has become commonplace, and it stands for computerized axial tomography. It is an important method of diagnosis in modern medicine and was developed by two scientists working independently. One of them was Allan MacLeod Cormack, the nuclear physicist who was a co-laureate of the 1979 Nobel Prize in Physiology or Medicine.

Shortly before World War I, the Cormacks left the north of Scotland and moved to the South African city of Johannesburg, where their three children were born. Allan, the youngest, only lived for a short time in that city, since his father's job as an engineer for the post office required the family to move frequently. After his father's death in 1936, however, the family settled in Cape Town.

In high school he dedicated himself to astronomy and began to study mathematics and physics with enthusiasm. When he discovered that there were few opportunities to earn a living in astronomy, however, he followed in his father's footsteps and took a course in electrical engineering at Cape Town University. Two years later he left engineering and took up studying physics full time.

For his graduate work Cormack went to St. John's College, Cambridge, as a research student. He worked in the Cavendish Laboratory under the guidance of Professor Otto Frisch. A year and a half later he accepted an invitation to work in the Physics Department in the University of Cape Town and returned to South Africa.

Cormack then started to work in the field of nuclear physics, but there were very few scientists working in this area in South Africa. At this time his American wife wanted to return to the United States, and he willingly agreed to the move since there were much better research opportunities on the other side of the Atlantic. He worked at Harvard University, where he carried out experiments with the cyclotron (a particle accelerator) and at Tufts University.

In 1957 his family moved to Winchester, Massachusetts, where he died on May 7, 1998.

Godfrey Newbold Hounsfield also received half of the prize.

The human body in 3-D

Allan Cormack and Godfrey Hounsfield, laureates in Physiology or Medicine in 1979, developed a diagnostic technique named computerized axial tomography (CAT). This was one of the most revolutionary diagnostic techniques but has been superseded by even more sophisticated inventions that allow three-dimensional images inside the human body.

The Digital Holography system, developed by the North American company Voxel, can show an image captured by magnetic resonance or an image captured by computerized axial tomography with a three-dimensional hologram.

Holograms have been used in surgery, for example in the evaluation of brain tumors, and to observe various layers of tissue and bone at the same time

1 About 200 transversal section images are collected

2 The data is sent to a computerized system; the best images are selected and the contrast adjusted

3 On a single holographic film, various images captured by RM or CAT are combined

4 Copies are made of the original film

5 The Monitor is where the captured images are shown

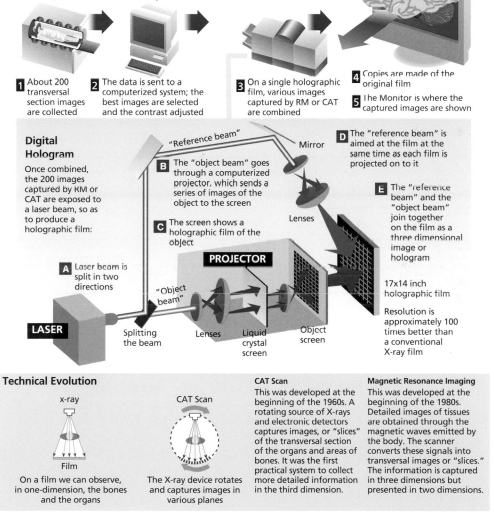

Digital Hologram

Once combined, the 200 images captured by RM or CAT are exposed to a laser beam, so as to produce a holographic film:

"Reference beam"

Mirror

B The "object beam" goes through a computerized projector, which sends a series of images of the object to the screen

C The screen shows a holographic film of the object

PROJECTOR

A Laser beam is split in two directions

LASER

"Object beam"

Splitting the beam

Lenses

Liquid crystal screen

Object screen

Lenses

D The "reference beam" is aimed at the film at the same time as each film is projected on to it

E The "reference beam" and the "object beam" join together on the film as a three dimensional image or hologram

17x14 inch holographic film

Resolution is approximately 100 times better than a conventional X-ray film

Technical Evolution

x-ray

Film

On a film we can observe, in one-dimension, the bones and the organs

CAT Scan

The X-ray device rotates and captures images in various planes

CAT Scan

This was developed at the beginning of the 1960s. A rotating source of X-rays and electronic detectors captures images, or "slices" of the transversal section of the organs and areas of bones. It was the first practical system to collect more detailed information in the third dimension.

Magnetic Resonance Imaging

This was developed at the beginning of the 1980s. Detailed images of tissues are obtained through the magnetic waves emitted by the body. The scanner converts these signals into transversal images or "slices." The information is captured in three dimensions but presented in two dimensions.

Nobel Laureates

1970-1979

1970

Nobel Prize in Physics
Hannes Olof Gösta Alfvén
Born May 30, 1908, in Norrköping, Sweden, and died April 2, 1995, in Djursholm.
For fundamental work and discoveries in magnetohydro-dynamics with fruitful applications in different parts of plasma physics.
&
Louis Eugène Félix Néel
Born November 22, 1904, in Lyon, France, and died November 17, 2000, in Brive.
For fundamental work and discoveries concerning antiferromagnetism and ferrimagnetism which have led to important applications in solid state physics.

Nobel Prize in Chemistry
Luis Federico Leloir
Born September 6, 1906, in Paris, France, and died December 2, 1987, in Buenos Aires, Argentina.
For his discovery of sugar nucleotides and their role in the biosynthesis of carbohydrates.

Nobel Prize in Physiology or Medicine
Julius Axelrod
Born May 30, 1912, in New York, New York, United States, and died on the December 29, 2004, in Rockville, Maryland.
&
Bernard Katz
Born March 26, 1911, in Leipzig, Germany, and died April 20, 2003, in London, England.
&
Ulf von Euler
Born February 7, 1905, in Stockholm, Sweden, and died March 9, 1983, in Stockholm.
For their discoveries concerning the humoral transmittors in the nerve terminals.

Nobel Prize in Literature
Alexandr Isayevich Solzhenitsyn
Born December 11, 1918, in Kislovodsk, Russia.
For the ethical force with which he has pursued the indispensable traditions of Russian literature.

Nobel Peace Prize
Norman Ernest Borlaug
Born March 25, 1914, in Cresco, Iowa, United States.
For his leadership of the 'Green Revolution' in developing countries and helping to reduce world hunger.

The Sveriges Riksbank Prize in Economic Sciences in Memory of Alfred Nobel
Paul Anthony Samuelson
Born May 15, 1915, in Gary, Indiana, United States.
For the scientific work through which he has developed static and dynamic economic theory and actively contributed to raising the level of analysis in economic science.

1971

Nobel Prize in Physics
Dennis Gabor
Born June 5, 1900, in Budapest, Hungary, and died February 8, 1979, in London, England.
For his invention and development of the holographic method.

Nobel Prize in Chemistry
Gerhard Herzberg
Born December 25, 1904, in Hamburg, Germany, and died March 3, 1999, in Ottawa, Ontario, Canada.
For his contributions to the knowledge of electronic structure and geometry of molecules, particularly free radicals.

Nobel Prize in Physiology or Medicine
Earl Wilbur Sutherland, Jr.
Born November 19, 1915, in Burlingame, Kansas, United States, and died March 9, 1974, in Miami, Florida.
For his discoveries concerning the mechanisms of the action of hormones.

Nobel Prize in Literature
Pablo Neruda, pseudonym of Neftalí Ricardo Reyes Basoalto
Born July 12, 1904, in Parral, Chile, and died September 23, 1973, in Santiago.
For a poetry that with the action of an elemental force brings alive a continent's destiny and dreams.

Nobel Peace Prize
Willy Brandt, né Herbert Ernst Karl Frahm
Born December 18, 1913, in Lübeck, Germany, and died October 8, 1992, in Unkel.
For his efforts to help respect human rights and the total freedom of movement for the people of West Berlin, as well as his role in the creation of conditions for peace in Europe.

The Sveriges Riksbank Prize in Economic Sciences in Memory of Alfred Nobel
Simon Kuznets
Born April 30, 1901, in Kharkov, Russia (now Kharkiv, Ukraine), and died July 8, 1985, in Cambridge, Massachusetts, United States.
For his empirically founded interpretation of economic growth which has led to new and deepened insight into the economic and social structure and process of development.

1972

Nobel Prize in Physics
John Bardeen
Born May 23, 1908, in Madison, Wisconsin, United States, and died January 30, 1991, in Boston, Massachusetts
&

Leon Neil Cooper
Born February 28, 1930, in New York, New York, United States.
&

John Robert Schrieffer
Born May 31, 1931, in Oak Park, Illinois, United States.
For their jointly developed theory of superconductivity, usually called the BCS-theory.

Nobel Prize in Chemistry
Christian Boehmer Anfinsen
Born March 26, 1916, in Monessen, Pennsylvania, United States, and died May 14, 1995, in Randallstown, Maryland.
For his work on the ribonuclease, especially concerning the connection between the amino acid sequence and the biologically active conformation.
&

Stanford Moore
Born September 4, 1913, in Chicago, Illinois, United States, and died August 23, 1982, in New York, New York.
&

William Howard Stein
Born June 25, 1911, in New York, New York, United States, and died February 2, 1980, in New York.
For their contribution to the understanding of the connection between chemical structure and catalytic activity of the active center of the ribonuclease molecule.

Nobel Prize in Physiology or Medicine
Gerald Maurice Edelman
Born July 1, 1929, in New York, New York, United States.
&

Rodney Robert Porter
Born October 8, 1917, in Newton-le-Willows, England, and died September 6, 1985, in Winchester.
For their discoveries concerning the chemical structure of antibodies.

Nobel Prize in Literature
Heinrich Theodor Böll
Born December 21, 1917, in Cologne, Germany, and died July 16, 1985, in Bornheim-Merten.

For his writing, which through its combination of a broad perspective on his time and a sensitive skill in characterization, has contributed to a renewal of German literature.

Nobel Peace Prize
Not awarded.

The Sveriges Riksbank Prize in Economic Sciences in Memory of Alfred Nobel
Kenneth Joseph Arrow
Born August 23, 1921, in New York, New York, United States.
&
John Richard Hicks
Born April 8, 1904, in Warwick, England, and died May 20, 1989, in Blockley.
For their pioneering contributions to general economic equilibrium theory and welfare theory.

1973

Nobel Prize in Physics
Leo Esaki, né Esaki Reiona
Born March 12, 1925, in Osaka, Japan.
&
Ivar Giaever
Born April 5, 1929, in Bergen, Norway.
For their experimental discoveries regarding tunneling phenomena in semiconductors and superconductors, respectively.
&
Brian David Josephson
Born January 4, 1940, in Cardiff, Wales.
For his theoretical predictions of the properties of a supercurrent through a tunnel barrier, in particular those phenomena which are generally known as the Josephson effects.

Nobel Prize in Chemistry
Ernst Otto Fischer
Born November 10, 1918, in Solln, Germany, and died July 23, 2007, in Munich.
&
Geoffrey Wilkinson
Born July 14, 1921, in Springside, England, and died

September 26, 1996, in London.
For their pioneering work, performed independently, on the chemistry of the organometallic, so-called sandwich compounds.

Nobel Prize in Physiology or Medicine
Konrad Lorenz
Born November 7, 1903, in Vienna, Austria, and died February 27, 1989, in Altenburg.
&
Nikolaas Tinbergen
Born April 15, 1907, in The Hague, Netherlands, and died December 21, 1988, in Oxford, England.
&
Karl von Frisch
Born November 20, 1886, in Vienna, Austria, and died June 12, 1982, in Munich, Germany.
For their discoveries concerning organization and elicitation of individual and social behavior patterns.

Nobel Prize in Literature
Patrick White
Born May 28, 1912, in London, England, and died September 30, 1990, in Sydney, Australia.
For an epic and psychological narrative art which has introduced a new continent into literature.

Nobel Peace Prize
Henry Alfred Kissinger
Born May 27, 1923, in Fuerth, Germany.
&
Le Duc Tho, né Phan Dinh Khai
Born October 14, 1911, in Nam Ha province, Vietnam, and died October 13, 1990, in Hanoi.
For their negotiations to end the Vietnam War.

The Sveriges Riksbank Prize in Economic Sciences in Memory of Alfred Nobel
Wassily Leontief
Born August 5, 1906, in Saint Petersburg, Russia, and died February 5, 1999, in New York, New York, United States.
For the development of the input-output method and for its application to important economic problems.

1974

Nobel Prize in Physics
Antony Hewish
Born May 11, 1924, in Fowey, England.
&
Martin Ryle
Born September 27, 1918, in Brighton, England, and died October 14, 1984, in Cambridge.
For their pioneering research in radio astrophysics: Ryle for his observations and inventions, in particular of the aperture synthesis technique, and Hewish for his decisive role in the discovery of pulsars.

Nobel Prize in Chemistry
Paul John Flory
Born June 19, 1910, in Sterling, Illinois, United States, and died September 9, 1985, in Big Sur, California.
For his fundamental achievements, both theoretical and experimental, in the physical chemistry of the macromolecules.

Nobel Prize in Physiology or Medicine
Albert Claude
Born August 23, 1898, in Longlier, Belgium, and died May 22, 1983, in Brussels.
&
Christian de Duve
Born October 2, 1917, in Thames-Ditton, England.
&
George Emil Palade
Born November 19, 1912, in Jassy, Romania.
For their discoveries concerning the structural and functional organization of the cell.

Nobel Prize in Literature
Eyvind Johnson
Born July 29, 1900, in Svartbjörnsbyn, Sweden, and died August 25, 1976, in Stockholm.
For a narrative art, far-seeing in lands and ages, in the service of freedom.
&
Harry Martinson
Born May 6, 1904, in Jämshög, Sweden, and died February 11, 1978, in Stockholm.
For writings that catch the dewdrop and reflect the cosmos.

Nobel Peace Prize
Seán MacBride
Born January 26, 1904, in Paris, France, and died January 15, 1988, in Dublin, Ireland.
For his actions in the fields of human rights, peace, disarmament and freeing Namibia from the rules of South Africa.
&
Eisaku Sato
Born March 27, 1901, in Tabuse, Japan, and died June 3, 1975, in Tokyo.
For his antimilitarism and diplomatic reconciliation, which have contributed to stabilize conditions in the Pacific area.

The Sveriges Riksbank Prize in Economic Sciences in Memory of Alfred Nobel
Gunnar Myrdal
Born December 6, 1898, in Gustafs, Sweden, and died May 17, 1987, in Stockholm.
&
Friedrich August von Hayek
Born May 8, 1899, in Vienna, Austria, and died March 23, 1992, in Freiburg, Germany.
For their pioneering work in the theory of money and economic fluctuations and for their penetrating analysis of the interdependence of economic, social and institutional phenomena.

1975

Nobel Prize in Physics
Aage Niels Bohr
Born of June 19, 1922, in Copenhagen, Denmark.
&
Ben Roy Mottelson
Born July 9, 1926, in Chicago, Illinois, United States.
&
Leo James Rainwater
Born December 9, 1917, in Council, Idaho, United States, and died May 31, 1986, in Yonkers, New York.
For the discovery of the connection between collective motion and particle motion in atomic nuclei and the development of the theory of the structure of the atomic nucleus based on this connection.

Nobel Prize in Chemistry
John Warcup Cornforth
Born September 7, 1917, in Sydney, Australia.
For his work on the stereochemistry of enzyme-catalyzed reactions.
&
Vladimir Prelog
Born July 23, 1906, in Sarajevo, Austria-Hungary (now Bosnia and Herzegovina), and died January 7, 1998, in Zurich, Switzerland.
For his research into the stereochemistry of organic molecules and reactions.

Nobel Prize in Physiology or Medicine
David Baltimore
Born March 7, 1938, in New York, New York, United States.
&
Renato Dulbecco
Born February 22, 1914, in Catanzaro, Italy.
&
Howard Martin Temin
Born December 10, 1934, in Philadelphia, Pennsylvania, United States, and died February 9, 1994, in Madison, Wisconsin.
For their discoveries concerning the interaction between tumor viruses and the genetic material of the cell.

Nobel Prize in Literature
Eugenio Montale
Born October 12, 1896, in Genoa, Italy, and died September 12, 1981, in Milan.
For his distinctive poetry which, with great artistic sensitivity, has interpreted human values under the sign of an outlook on life with no illusions.

Nobel Peace Prize
Andrei Dmitrievich Sakharov
Born May 21, 1921, in Moscow, Union of Soviet Socialist Republics (now Russia) and died December 14, 1989, in Moscow.
For his defense of fundamental principles of peace between men.

The Sveriges Riksbank Prize in Economic Sciences in Memory of Alfred Nobel
Leonid Vitaliyevich Kantorovich
Born January 19, 1912, in Saint Petersburg, Russia, and died April 7, 1986, in Moscow, Union of Soviet Socialist Republics (now Russia).
&
Tjalling Charles Koopmans
Born August 28, 1910, in Graveland, Netherlands, and died February 26, 1985, in New Haven, Connecticut, United States.
For their contributions to the theory of optimum allocation of resources.

1976

Nobel Prize in Physics
Burton Richter
Born March 22, 1931, in Brooklyn, New York, United States.
&
Samuel Chao Chung Ting
Born January 27, 1936, in Ann Arbor, Michigan, United States.
For their pioneering work in the discovery of a heavy elementary particle of a new kind.

Nobel Prize in Chemistry
William Nunn Lipscomb, Jr.
Born December 9, 1919, in Cleveland, Ohio, United States.
For his studies on the structure of boranes illuminating problems of chemical bonding.

Nobel Prize in Physiology or Medicine
Baruch Samuel Blumberg
Born July 28, 1925, in New York, New York, United States.
&
Daniel Carleton Gajdusek
Born September 9, 1923, in Yonkers, New York, United States.
For their discoveries concerning new mechanisms for the origin and dissemination of infectious diseases.

Nobel Prize in Literature
Saul Bellow
Born June 10, 1915, in Lachine, Quebec, Canada, and died on April 5, 2005, in Brookline, Massachusetts, United States.
For the human understanding and subtle analysis of contemporary culture that are combined in his work.

Nobel Peace Prize
Mairead Corrigan (now Mairead Corrigan-Maguire)
Born January 27, 1944, in Belfast, Northern Ireland.
&
Betty Williams
Born May 22, 1943, in Belfast, Northern Ireland.
For their demonstrations of profound conviction that each individual can contribute to peace, through reconciliation and showing the path to resistance, against violence and the abuse of power.

The Sveriges Riksbank Prize in Economic Sciences in Memory of Alfred Nobel
Milton Friedman
Born July 31, 1912, in Brooklyn, New York, United States, and died November 16, 2006, in San Francisco, California.
For his achievements in the fields of consumption analysis, monetary history and theory and for his demonstration of the complexity of stabilization policy.

1977

Nobel Prize in Physics
Philip Warren Anderson
Born December 13, 1923, in Indianapolis, Indiana, United States.
&
Nevill Francis Mott
Born September 30, 1905, in Leeds, England, and died August 8, 1996, in Milton Keynes.
&
John Hasbrouck van Vleck
Born March 13, 1899, in Middletown, Connecticut,

United States, and died October 27, 1980, in Cambridge, Massachusetts.
For their fundamental theoretical investigations of the electronic structure of magnetic and disordered systems.

Nobel Prize in Chemistry
Ilya Prigogine
Born January 25, 1917, in Moscow, Russia, and died May 28, 2003, in Brussels, Belgium.
For his contributions to nonequilibrium thermodynamics, particularly the theory of dissipative structures.

Nobel Prize in Physiology or Medicine
Roger Guillemin
Born January 11, 1924, in Dijon, France.
&
Andrew Victor Schally
Born November 30, 1926, in Wilno, Poland (now Vilnius, Lithuania).
For their discoveries concerning the peptide hormone production of the brain.
&
Rosalyn Sussman Yalow
Born July 19, 1921, in New York, New York, United States.
For the development of radioimmunoassays of peptide hormones.

Nobel Prize in Literature
Vicente Aleixandre
Born April 26, 1898, in Seville, Spain, and died December 14, 1984, in Madrid.
For a creative poetic writing which illuminates man's condition in the cosmos and in present-day society, at the same time representing the great renewal of the traditions of Spanish poetry between the wars.

Nobel Peace Prize
Amnesty International
Founded in 1961 in London, England.
For protecting prisoners against violations of human rights.

The Sveriges Riksbank Prize in Economic Sciences in Memory of Alfred Nobel
James Edward Meade
Born June 23, 1907, in Swanage, England, and died December 22, 1995, in Cambridge.
&
Bertil Ohlin
Born April 23, 1899, in Klippan, Sweden, and died August 3, 1979, in Vålädalen.
For their pathbreaking contribution to the theory of international trade and international capital movements.

1978

Nobel Prize in Physics
Pyotr Leonidovich Kapitsa
Born June 26, 1894, in Kronstadt, Russia, and died April 8, 1984, in Moscow, Union of Soviet Socialist Republics (now Russia).
For his basic inventions and discoveries in the area of low-temperature physics.
&
Arno Allan Penzias
Born April 26, 1933, in Munich, Germany.
&
Robert Woodrow Wilson
Born January 10, 1936, in Houston, Texas, United States.
For their discovery of cosmic microwave background radiation.

Nobel Prize in Chemistry
Peter Dennis Mitchell
Born September 29, 1920, in Mitcham, England, and died April 10, 1992, in Bodmin.
For his contribution to the understanding of biological energy transfer through the formulation of the chemiosmotic theory.

Nobel Prize in Physiology or Medicine
Werner Arber
Born June 3, 1929, in Gränichen, Switzerland.
&

Daniel Nathans
Born October 30, 1928, in Wilmington, Delaware, United States, and died November 16, 1999, in Baltimore, Maryland.
&
Hamilton Othanel Smith
Born August 23, 1931, in New York, New York, United States.
For the discovery of restriction enzymes and their application to problems of molecular genetics.

Nobel Prize in Literature
Isaac Bashevis Singer
Born July 14, 1904, in Radzymin, Poland, and died July 24, 1991, in Surfside, Florida, United States.
For his impassioned narrative art which, with roots in a Polish-Jewish cultural tradition, brings universal human conditions to life.

Nobel Peace Prize
Menachem Begin
Born August 16, 1913, in Brest-Litovsk, Russia (now Brest, Belarus), and died March 9, 1992, in Tel Aviv, Israel.
&
Mohamed Anwar Sadat
Born December 25, 1918, in Mit Abu al-Kum, Egypt, and died October 6, 1981, in Cairo.
For their contribution to the peace agreements between Egypt and Israel, which were signed at Camp David, on the 17th of September, 1978.

The Sveriges Riksbank Prize in Economic Sciences in Memory of Alfred Nobel
Herbert Alexander Simon
Born June 15, 1916, in Milwaukee, Wisconsin, United States, and died February 9, 2001, in Pittsburgh, Pennsylvania.
For his pioneering research into the decision-making process within economic organizations.

1979

Nobel Prize in Physics
Sheldon Lee Glashow
Born December 5, 1932, in New York, New York, United States.
&
Abdus Salam
Born January 29, 1926, in Jhang, India (now Pakistan), and died November 21, 1996, in Oxford, England.
&
Steven Weinberg
Born May 3, 1933, in New York, New York, United States.
For their contributions to the theory of the unified weak and electromagnetic interaction between elementary particles, including, inter alia, the prediction of the weak neutral current.

Nobel Prize in Chemistry
Herbert Charles Brown, né Herbert Brovarnik
Born May 22, 1912, in London, England, and died December 19, 2004, in Lafayette, Indiana, United States.
&
Georg Wittig
Born June 16, 1897, in Berlin, Germany, and died August 26, 1987, in Heidelberg.
For their development of the use of boron- and phosphorous-containing compounds, respectively, into important reagents in organic synthesis.

Nobel Prize in Physiology or Medicine
Allan MacLeod Cormack
Born February 23, 1924, in Johannesburg, South Africa, and died May 7, 1998, in Winchester, Massachusetts, United States.
&
Godfrey Newbold Hounsfield
Born August 28, 1919, in Newark, England, and died August 12, 2004, in Kingston upon Thames.
For the development of computer-assisted tomography.

Nobel Prize in Literature
Odysseus Elytis, pseudonym of Odysseus Alepoudhelis
Born November 2, 1911, in Heraklion, Greece, and died March 18, 1996, in Athens.
For his poetry, which, against the background of Greek tradition, depicts with sensuous strength and intellectual clear-sightedness modern man's struggle for freedom and creativeness.

Nobel Peace Prize
Mother Teresa, née Agnes Gonxha Bojaxhiu
Born August 26, 1910, in Skopje, Ottoman Empire (now Macedonia), and died September 5, 1997, in Calcutta, India.
For her actions favoring children and refugees.

The Sveriges Riksbank Prize in Economic Sciences in Memory of Alfred Nobel
William Arthur Lewis
Born January 23, 1915, in Castries, Saint Lucia, and died June 15, 1991, in Bridgetown, Barbados.
&
Theodore William Schultz
Born April 30, 1902, in Arlington, South Dakota, United States, and died February 26, 1998, in Evanston, Illinois.
For their pioneering research into economic development research with particular consideration of the problems of developing countries.

Selected Profiles of Nobel Laureates

1980–1989

Adolfo Esquivel

For his defense of respecting human rights and feeling of hope when faced with Argentinean military rules.

It is hard to fight for human rights in a country under a dictatorship, and the difficulties only increase when the entire continent leans toward totalitarian regimes. Adolfo Pérez Esquivel struggled through such a situation, expanding his activities from his native Argentina to all of Latin America. In recognition of his important work and undaunted spirit, the Norwegian Nobel Committee awarded him the Nobel Peace Prize in 1980.

Born in Buenos Aires on November 26, 1931, Pérez Esquivel had an interest in the arts from an early age. He studied architecture and sculpture at the Escuela Nacional de Bellas Artes (National School of Fine Arts) and the Universidad Nacional de la Plata (National University of La Plata) before taking up a professorship in architecture. For the next 25 years he taught primary, secondary and university courses in Argentina, but he always had a passion for helping the poor and dispossessed of his country.

In the 1960s he was active in Latin American Christian pacifist groups and became involved in the lobbying begun at a joint conference in Montevideo, Uruguay, to create an organization to oversee all nonviolent movements on the continent. In 1974 he abandoned all other professional activities to dedicate himself full time to coordinating this organization, known as Servicio Paz y Justicia (Service, Peace and Justice).

In 1976 he started an international campaign aimed at pressuring the United Nations into creating a Human Rights Commission. To such an end, a document was drawn up denouncing breaches of human rights in Latin America. In the spring of 1977 Pérez Esquivel was arrested and remained imprisoned — and was tortured — by the Argentinan authorities for 14 months. He was released in May of the following year, but under the condition that he report regularly to the police, among other restrictions. Gradually the pressure was eased, and he was given the opportunity to visit Europe, when he went to Oslo to receive the Nobel Peace Prize. While incarcerated he was also awarded the Pope John XXIII Peace Prize, and in 1999 he received the Pacem in Terris Peace and Freedom Award.

El Servicio Paz y Justicia, of which Adolfo Pérez Esquivel became secretary-general, is now well established. It divides Latin America into three regions, with a central office in each one, and under these are the national organizations. The general coordination is carried out from a central office in Buenos Aires. Servicio Paz y Justicia maintains a Christian perspective and has close contacts with the clergy, particularly with South American bishops, but its principal task is, as always, promoting human, social and economic rights.

In all his activities Pérez Esquivel follows a fundamental principle: the fight can only be undertaken by nonviolent means. He has written a book about his experiences, published in 1995, entitled *Caminando Junto al Pueblo (Walking Together with the People)*.

(1918–2002)

James Tobin

*For his analysis of financial markets and their relations to
expenditure decisions, employment, production and prices.*

The son of a social worker and a journalist, James Tobin was born in
Champaign, Illinois, in 1918. Although he had considered studying law,
on his father's insistence he studied economics at Harvard University and
completed his bachelor's degree in 1939. His studies were interrupted,
however, by World War II, when he became on officer in the U.S. Navy
and served on the destroyer *USS Kearney*. On his return to civilian life he
obtained his doctorate degree in 1947 from Harvard, where he remained
to lecture until 1950. He then transferred to Yale University, where he
remained for the next 38 years.

James Tobin was director of the Cowles Foundation for Economic Research for two
periods, first between 1955 and 1961 and then again between 1964 and 1965. While he was
at Yale Tobin formulated the theories that would earn him the Nobel Prize in Economics; one
of the most significant of these theories shows how the alterations in financial markets, such
as the rise and fall in prices, influence consumer and company costs and investments. He
proved that both families and companies make decisions so as not to run the risk of debt
and that financial investments do not serve only to maximize profit but also to prevent risk.

Tobin was also one of the proponents of the so-called "new economics," based on the
concepts of the British economist John Maynard Keynes. He defended the application of
aggressive governmental policies to achieve social and economic objectives, including
reducing unemployment. To further these objectives he interrupted his academic career
twice to enter politics. Between 1961 and 1962 he was an economic adviser to President
John F. Kennedy, a role he repeated in 1972 at the service of the Democratic presidential
candidate George McGovern, who lost to Richard Nixon. During the 1980s he was highly
critical of President Ronald Reagan's economic policies.

Tobin was awarded the 1981 Nobel Prize in Economics for his contributions in the area
of financial markets and their relationship to expenditure decisions, employment, production
and prices. He demonstrated how national economic policies, above all through variations in
tax rates, influence consumer decisions. Tobin's name also became internationally known at
the end of the 20th century for a proposal he had first made in 1972: called the "Tobin Tax,"
he defended the application of a tax of a 10th of one percent on all monetary transactions as a
means of eradicating poverty in underdeveloped countries.

While he was at Harvard Tobin had met Elizabeth Fay Ringo, whom he married and with
whom he had four children.

**1981 Sveriges Riksbank Prize in Economic
Sciences in Memory of Alfred Nobel**

240

Gabriel García Márquez

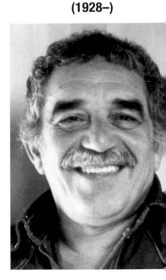

For his novels and short stories, in which the fantastic and the realistic are combined in a richly composed world of imagination, reflecting a continent's life and conflicts.

Gabriel García Márquez was 39 years old when he first came to the world's attention. On a trip to Acapulco in 1965, in a moment of inspiration, he claimed he heard a voice describe how he would write the story he had been carrying around with him for 15 years. He locked himself in a room and, 18 months later, *One Hundred Years of Solitude* was sent to Buenos Aires and published in 1967. For the success of this book and later ones he received the Nobel Prize in Literature in 1982.

Gabriel García Márquez, who is called "Gabito" or "Gabo" by his friends, was born on March 6, 1928, or 1927, according to his father, in Aracataca, Colombia. As his parents were very poor he grew up in his maternal grandparents' home, and they became very influential figures in his life.

He was 8 years old when his maternal grandfather, Colonel Nicolás Márquez Mejia, died suddenly. His grandmother was nearly blind at the time and, as a result, García Márquez went to live with his parents again in Barranquilla. When he was 13 he was accepted as a student at the Colégio São José dos Jesuítas and, a little later, won a scholarship that allowed him to enter a boarding school in Zipaquirá. He later studied law and journalism at the University of Bogotá and Cartagena University, but his attraction to a bohemian lifestyle proved stronger than his will to finish the courses. During this period, while on holiday in Sucre, he met Mercedes Barcha Pardo, aged 13, whom he would marry in 1958.

During his travels García Márquez wrote for various newspapers, sold encyclopedias and was a movie critic and a crane operator, among other things. He lived in various parts of his native Colombia but also went to Europe, the United States, Mexico and Cuba, where he made friends with Fidel Castro. In the 1940s he had several series of short stories published, but in 1952 *The Leaf Storm*, his first novella, was rejected, and Márquez was advised to give up writing altogether.

Despite such criticism he never gave up on his passion. Daily life and politics in Colombia started to exercise a greater influence on his writing, and soon he was known as the leading member of the Magic Realism movement — a group of Latin American writers who combine fantasy and mythology into an otherwise realistic work of fiction. After the success of *One Hundred Years of Solitude*, his previous books also became bestsellers, and even *The Leaf Storm* was published. *No One Writes to the Colonel* (1961), *Chronicle of a Death Foretold* (1981) and *Love in the Time of Cholera* (1985) are just three of the better-known titles from his vast body of work.

Subrahmanyan Chandrasekhar

For his theoretical studies of the physical processes of importance to the structure and evolution of the stars.

Born on October 19, 1910, the third of 10 children, Subrahmanyan Chandrasekhar was first taught at home in Lahore, then part of British India (now in Pakistan), by his parents and a private tutor. His home life was enriching, and he particularly benefited from the intellectual gifts of his mother. At the age of 12, while he was living in Madras, he attended a Hindu school and then entered the Presidency College to study physics. In July 1930 he was awarded a Government of India Scholarship, which allowed him to take his doctorate at Cambridge three years later. In 1936 he was offered the position of associate researcher at the University of Chicago, which he accepted the following year.

He was 20 when he presented his theory that, when they are reaching the end of their lives, large stars collapse and reach an unknown state that is even denser than a white dwarf. It is now known that pulsars and black holes are examples of such states. Chandrasekhar also developed a mathematical theory on the evolution of lower mass stars, such as our sun, and showed that they eventually evolve into red giants. Over the coming years he would also investigate stellar dynamics, the theory of radioactive transfer, the general theory of relativity and relativistic astrophysics.

Among his scientific books are *An Introduction to the Study of Stellar Structure* (1939) and *Principles of Stellar Dynamics* (1943). The last book he wrote was *Newton's Principia for the Common Reader*, which was published a few years before his death. He consciously wrote for people not familiar with scientific terms, allowing a wide audience to appreciate his research.

In 1936 Subrahmanyan Chandrasekhar married Lalitha Doraiswamy, whom he had met during his last two years at Presidency College in Madras. A year later the couple moved to Chicago, and they became American citizens in 1953. Over the coming decades Chandrasekhar developed many important academic friendships and was widely respected; two scientists who deeply credited his influence were Chen Ning Yang and Tsung Dao Lee, Americans of Chinese origin who won the 1957 Nobel Prize in Physics.

In 1983 Chandrasekhar earned his own Nobel Prize in Physics, which he shared with William Alfred Fowler, who won "for his theoretical and experimental studies of the nuclear reactions of importance in the formation of the chemical elements in the universe." Subrahmanyan Chandrasekhar died on August 21, 1995, in Chicago.

William Alfred Fowler also received half of the prize.

The death of a star

The Universe has always been a source of fascination. Successive studies have been carried out to decipher its mysteries. Subrahmanyan Chandrasekhar is a scientist who has worked on this subject and developed the white dwarf theory, for which he was awarded the Nobel Prize for Physics in 1983. This distinction was shared with William Fowler, for his studies into nuclear reactions, which are fundamental in forming the universe's chemical elements.

The formulation and death of white dwarf stars was the basis of a study carried out by astronomers. After 88 weeks of observation, using a system of 10 radio telescopes spread over a continent, the first time-lapse film of a star that was not the sun was produced.

A cloud of dust and gas is pulled by gravity and a rotating disc is formed at its centre

The "prostar" forms when the center collapses under its own gravity

Prostar radiates heat and expels material from its poles

Thermonuclear fusion takes place in the nucleus and the star begins to shine. The disc disperses or forms planets

the size of a star determines the way in which it will die. How a star similar to the sun dies:

When stars use up all their hydrogen, they dilate and become bright red. In this phase, billions of years in the future, the Sun will burn the Earth's atmosphere

Gravity pulls the star's remaining gas, creating a white dwarf star

are of a similar type to visible radiation, but of a larger wave length

This is the event that astronomers have filmed

The star collapses and a nuclear reaction frees its external gases

focuses the radio waves on to the detector

process the signals into images

strengthens the electrical signals

The star's gravity will then pull the gases inwards

The gas doesn't have a symmetrical outward movement and some of the gas has a strange jumping movement both inwards and outwards

In accordance with current theory, the star should send out gaseous shock waves uniformly in every direction

The star behaves just like Mira, a small variable star that shone and oscillated for 80 days

(1902–1992)

Barbara McClintock

For her discovery of mobile genetic elements.

The American geneticist Barbara McClintock acquired enormous fame in the scientific world during the 20th century. She is best remembered for having discovered that genes can change position on chromosomes and consequently affect the behavior of neighboring genes — a finding that proved to be of great importance in understanding heredity processes.

Born in Hartford, Connecticut, in 1902, Barbara McClintock began her career at a time when women were practically denied the right to be prominent figures in the world of science, which makes the biologist and botanist's contributions even more notable. In 1927 she obtained her doctorate from the College of Agriculture at Cornell University, New York, and then devoted herself to the study of genetics.

It is likely that, at least partly because of her sex, her research into gene mobility, which was published in the 1940s and 1950s, was only recognized much later; the fact that little importance was given to genetics when she began working in the field was also a factor. It was only around the time McClintock was born that Mendel's principles of heredity were rediscovered, and even research carried out between 1900 and 1920 was viewed with reluctance by some eminent biologists.

During her university years McClintock decided to take an undergraduate course in genetics at Cornell and was later asked to teach a postgraduate course in genetics. She also attended a course in cytology given by Lester W. Sharp of the Botany Department, whose interest was in chromosome structure and their behaviors. Influenced by her professors and encouraged by the rapidly expanding field, McClintock decided on her future career.

Her scientific life unfolded at many institutions. Besides Cornell University, where she began as an instructor in botany, Barbara McClintock was at the National Research Council, the Guggenheim Foundation, the University of Missouri, the Carnegie Institution of Washington, the California Institute of Technology and the Rockefeller Foundation, among others. She was the third woman in history to be elected to the National Academy of Sciences, and she received many honorary doctorates from American institutions and one, in 1982, from the University of Cambridge. Her awards include the National Medal of Science in 1970 and the Thomas Hunt Morgan Medal from the Genetics Society of America in 1981.

Long after she had published important work in the field of heredity, the discovery of the mobility of genetic elements brought her the 1983 Nobel Prize in Physiology or Medicine. Barbara McClintock died on September 2, 1992, in New York.

The inside of the new DNA chip

The DNA chip is similar to that of a computer chip. It recognizes chemical sequences in the DNA chain. The DNA chip can be used to develop drugs and treatments for genetic diseases.

How a DNA chip detects mutations
Using specialized chemicals, named DNA probes, and weak electrical currents, the chip observes the DNA chain looking for recognized sequences (genes).

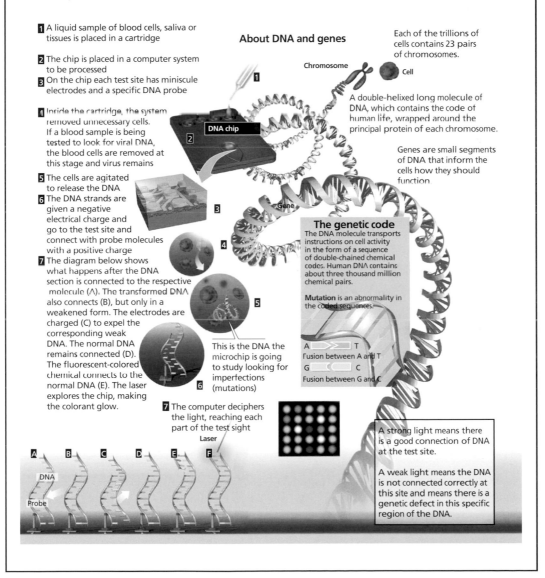

1 A liquid sample of blood cells, saliva or tissues is placed in a cartridge

2 The chip is placed in a computer system to be processed

3 On the chip each test site has miniscule electrodes and a specific DNA probe

4 Inside the cartridge, the system removed unnecessary cells. If a blood sample is being tested to look for viral DNA, the blood cells are removed at this stage and virus remains

5 The cells are agitated to release the DNA

6 The DNA strands are given a negative electrical charge and go to the test site and connect with probe molecules with a positive charge

7 The diagram below shows what happens after the DNA section is connected to the respective molecule (A). The transformed DNA also connects (B), but only in a weakened form. The electrodes are charged (C) to expel the corresponding weak DNA. The normal DNA remains connected (D). The fluorescent-colored chemical connects to the normal DNA (E). The laser explores the chip, making the colorant glow.

About DNA and genes

Each of the trillions of cells contains 23 pairs of chromosomes.

Chromosome

Cell

A double-helixed long molecule of DNA, which contains the code of human life, wrapped around the principal protein of each chromosome.

Genes are small segments of DNA that inform the cells how they should function.

Gene

The genetic code
The DNA molecule transports instructions on cell activity in the form of a sequence of double-chained chemical codes. Human DNA contains about three thousand million chemical pairs.

Mutation is an abnormality in the coded sequences.

A — T
Fusion between A and T
G — C
Fusion between G and C

DNA chip

This is the DNA the microchip is going to study looking for imperfections (mutations)

7 The computer deciphers the light, reaching each part of the test sight

Laser

A strong light means there is a good connection of DNA at the test site.

A weak light means the DNA is not connected correctly at this site and means there is a genetic defect in this specific region of the DNA.

A B C D E F

DNA

Probe

William Golding

For his novels which, with the perspicuity of realistic narrative art and the diversity and universality of myth, illuminate the human condition in the world today.

William Gerald Golding was chosen over the famous novelist Graham Greene, who was considered one of the strongest candidates, for the 1983 Nobel Prize in Literature. This surprising recognition was for his bold exploration of "the darkness of man's heart," particularly for isolated individuals in extreme situations and other spiritual and ethical questions. His first novel, *The Lord of the Flies* (1954), deals with such subjects and is considered one of the most important literary works of the 20th century.

Born on September 19, 1911, in St. Columb Minor, England, William Golding was the son of a schoolmaster and his wife, who both held radical political and social views for the time. Although he had begun to write at the age of 7, Golding was encouraged by his parents to study the natural sciences, which he did at Brasenose College, Oxford. He soon moved to literary studies, however, and his first collection of poems appeared in 1934. A year later he received his bachelor's degree in education.

After graduating, William Golding worked for small theater companies as an actor, producer and playwright, and in 1939 he began teaching English and philosophy at Bishop Wordsworth's School. Unfortunately this work was interrupted by World War II, during which he served as a Royal Navy officer and participated in important battles. The first was in May 1941, when two British vessels confronted what was then the biggest and most powerful ship of the German navy, the *Bismarck*. Near the end of the war Golding was also part of the Normandy invasion in June 1944. Once peace was reestablished in Europe, he returned to writing, his earliest passion, but was deeply affected by his experiences; he later reflected, "Man produces evil, as a bee produces honey."

Although he had published his first collection of poems at the age of 23, Golding later rejected this work and did not consider himself to be a poet. With the *Lord of the Flies* he was definitively launched in the world of literature, but not before the work was rejected by 21 publishers. The book became a bestseller and was filmed by Peter Brook in 1963; the movie was later remade in 1990. With this success he quit his teaching positions and built a legacy of novels, short stories, plays and essays. Similar themes to those in *The Lord of the Flies* appear in his novels *The Inheritors* (1955), *Pincher Martin* (1956) and *The Spire* (1964). He received the Booker Prize in 1980 and eight years later was knighted by Queen Elizabeth II.

William Golding married Ann Brookfield in 1939, and the couple had two children. He died in 1993.

Lech Walesa

For his leadership of the nonviolent movement to achieve the right of free association for Polish workers.

The name Lech Walesa will always be associated with the wave of strikes begun by the Gdansk shipyard workers in 1980. He cofounded Solidarity, the union movement that fought to establish a democratic government in his native country, and later was president of the Republic of Poland between 1990 and 1995.

In December 1970, as tensions increased between workers and the government, Walesa led shipyard protests in which more than 40 workers were killed by riot police. He was arrested and spent a year in prison.

In August 1980 he led a shipyard workers' strike in Poland and reached the historic Gdansk Agreement, with the government, which conferred on workers the right to strike and to organize an independent union, which became known as Solidarity.

Since his Catholicism was a source of inspiration to him, Lech Walesa sought the approval of the Catholic Church and, in January 1981, he was cordially received by his compatriot Pope John Paul II, who was highly influential in Poland at the time.

In 1990 Lech Walesa won the first completely free, open elections and was named the second president of the Republic of Poland. When he was defeated five years later in the next presidential elections he returened once more to the Gdansk shipyards.

Lech Walesa has received numerous honors, including dozens of honorary doctorate degrees, and was named Man of the Year by *Time* magazine (1981), *The Financial Times* (1980) and *The Observer* (1980). He has also received the Presidential Medal of Freedom (1989), the Liberty Medal (1989), the International Freedom Award (1999) and the Pacem in Terris Peace and Freedom Award (2001).

In 2006 Lech Walesa quit the Solidarity movement he had helped to establish, citing that its current administration and their policies had parted from his own views. During celebrations to mark the 25th anniversary of the Solidarity movement he declared, "This is no longer my union. This is a different era, a different people, different problems." He currently lives in Gdansk where he runs a foundation, the Lech Walesa Institute, and continues to speak at organizations, including the United Nations, and at events around the world.

Desmond Tutu

For his work on the South African Churches Council, and also for all the individuals and groups in South Africa who demonstrate human and democratic concerns.

Desmond Mpilo Tutu is one of the most influential South Africans. He has been internationally respected and admired for decades because of his defense of human rights and ferocious opposition to apartheid in his native country. Ordained a priest in the Anglican Church in 1960, he became the first black person to be bishop of Johannesburg in 1985 and the next year became archbishop of Cape Town, thus reaching the highest position in the South African Anglican community.

He was born on October 7, 1931, in Klerksdorp, South Africa, to a poor school teacher and his wife. When Tutu was 12 the family moved to Johannesburg, where he attended Johannesburg Bantu High School. Although he aspired to become a physician, financial realities forced him to train as a teacher at Pretoria Bantu Normal College. He then graduated from the University of South Africa in 1954. For the following three years he worked as a high school teacher.

During this period blacks in South Africa were denied basic rights of citizenship, and the ruling National Party was implementing a system of apartheid, or complete segregation. All citizens were divided into official racial groups and restricted to living in separate areas with their own public facilities; interracial marriage was strictly forbidden. Black South Africans were prohibited from voting in national elections and forming unions and were legally barred from many jobs. Critics of this system were harassed by authorities, placed under house arrest or forbidden to speak in public.

When the National Party initiated an educational program for blacks that was deliberately inferior to that for whites, Desmond Tutu rebelled against this injustice and determined to improve the life of his people in South Africa. Taking the advice of his bishop, he began studying theology and joined the priesthood in 1960. Things only began getting worse, however, as the government began forcibly relocating millions of black South Africans to remote areas of the country.

Between 1962 and 1966 Desmond Tutu lived in England, earning his master's degree in theology. He then spent five years teaching in South Africa before accepting the position of vice-director of the Theological Education Fund of the World Council of Churches in London. Once more in his homeland, in 1975 he became the first black man to be appointed the dean of St. Mary's Cathedral in Johannesburg. The bishop of Lesotho from 1976 to 1978, he was appointed that same year the general secretary of the South African Council of Churches.

During his time in this position, once again the first black man to have the honor, Tutu began his fight against apartheid by advocating reforms in the South African racial-discrimination system while at the same time condemning any type of violence. Although authorities tried to prevent his efforts, even revoking his passport, the government was eventually forced to submit to international pressure.

After the multiracial Republic of South Africa was established in 1994, Tutu returned to his pastoral duties while still being one of the most influential people in the country. One year later he was appointed head of the Commission for Truth and Reconciliation, which was created to investigate crimes and violations of human rights committed by both sides under apartheid. The commission's report, which was published in 1998, contained damning criticisms of the abuses perpetrated by successive governments during the period of racial discrimination while also pointing a finger at the African National Congress, which tried to prevent the publication of the document in court. In the mean time Tutu had retired as the archbishop of Cape Town in June 1996.

Besides the Nobel Peace Prize in 1984, Desmond Tutu has also been awarded dozens of honorary degrees, the Pacem in Terris Peace and Freedom Award in 1987, the Albert Schweitzer Humanitarian Award in 1999 and the Gandhi Peace Prize in 2005. Two compilations of his writings were published in the 1980s, one of speeches entitled *The Divine Intention* (1982) and the other, of sermons, entitled *Hope and Suffering* (1984).

He has been married to Leah Nomalizo since July 2, 1955, and the couple has four children. In 2003 he was elected to the board of directors of the International Criminal Court's Trust Fund for Victims, and he was made a member of a United Nations panel on genocide prevention in 2006. Throughout his career Desmond Tutu has pursued the objective of the creation of "a just, democratic society without racial divisions." Among his fundamental goals are equal civil rights for all, a common education system and world peace.

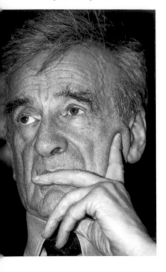

Elie Wiesel

Wiesel is a messenger to mankind; his message is one of peace, atonement and human dignity.

Elie Wiesel was born in the small Jewish community of Sighet in the then Kingdom of Romania on September 30, 1928. His father instilled a deep humanitarian sense in his son, but also encouraged him to focus on secular studies. Elie Wiesel later recalled how his mother represented faith for him and his father reason.

Although Sighet came under Hungarian control during the early years of World War II and was divided into two ghettos, little else changed until 1944, when Nazi forces poured into the area. Along with relatives, Wiesel, only 15, was deported on May 16 to Auschwitz and then to other Nazi concentration and extermination camps. During this time he was starved, overworked and beaten. Of his family only Elie and two older sisters escaped death. He was finally liberated from Buchenwald, a German concentration camp where approximately 560,000 people lost their lives, by Allied troops in 1945.

Although he refused to write anything about his wartime experiences for a decade, his self-imposed silence was finally broken in 1955 with the publication of *Un die welt hot geshvign (And the World Kept Silent)*.

Wiesel acquired American citizenship in 1963. He became a distinguished professor of Jewish Studies at the City University of New York, and since 1976 he has been a professor at Boston University. He spearheaded the building of the Holocaust Memorial Museum in Washington, D.C. He was awarded the Congressional Gold Medal in 1985, and two years later he created the Elie Wiesel Foundation for Humanity.

Throughout his life Wiesel has been tireless in his defense of the vulnerable, specifically those who suffer persecution due to religious beliefs, race or culture. He is always forthright in his speeches and is careful not to be overly optimistic for quick solutions to the world's problems. In a 2006 *Time* magazine interview he said, "My mission has not changed, because I don't think the world has changed. In the beginning, I thought, maybe my witness will be received, and things will change. But they don't. Otherwise we wouldn't have had Rwanda and Darfur and Cambodia and Bosnia. Human nature cannot be changed in one generation." He remains a popular speaker and political activist on a number of topics.

In 1986 Elie Wiesel received the Nobel Peace Prize for his vigorous defense of human rights and dignity. He was presented an honorary knighthood on November 30, 2006, for his work toward Holocaust education. The next year he was attacked in a San Francisco hotel by an anti-Semitic 22-year-old man. Wiesel lives in New York with his wife, Marion Rose, whom he married in 1969; the couple has one son.

James Buchanan, Jr.

For his development of the contractual and constitutional bases for the theory of economic and political decision-making.

In 1986 the Royal Swedish Academy for Sciences decided to award James McGill Buchanan the Nobel Prize in Economics in recognition of his revolutionary work on decision making. While traditional economic theory explains how consumers and enterprises make decisions about the purchase of goods, levels of production, investments and so on, Buchanan developed a parallel theory on decision making in the public sector, which he called the New Economic Policy. Buchanan also transferred the concept of gains, derived from exchanges between individuals, to the domain of political decision-making.

James Buchanan, who was born in Murfreesboro, Tennessee, in 1919, has dedicated himself to economics for nearly 40 years, becoming the most prominent researcher of the theory of public choice. His higher education began at Middle Tennessee State University, and he went on to earn his master's degree from the University of Tennessee in 1941. Seven years later he received his doctorate from the University of Chicago. When he was awarded the Nobel Prize Buchanan was a professor at George Mason University in Fairfax, Virginia, and director of the Center for Study of Public Choice.

In more recent years he has taken the parallels between economics and political decisions even further. It is understood that market behavior is primarily based on voluntary agreements and the exchange of goods and services, which give mutual advantages to the parties involved in the transactions. It is the prerogative of the market system to establish legal mechanisms that protect the rights of those who participate in it. The political system can be understood as a system based on contractual agreements, so Buchanan formulated a theory on the public sector and the making of political decisions based on the principle of unanimity. According to this theory, decisions related to the financing of collective efforts can be interpreted as the result of voluntary agreements between citizens. Each citizen should then, in theory, receive a number of public gains if the value exceeds, in the individual case, what is paid in taxes.

Such theories have been published in numerous books over his lifetime, the most famous of which is *Calculus of Consent*, cowritten with Gordon Tullock, published in 1962.

Sveriges Riksbank Prize in Economic Sciences in Memory of Alfred Nobel 1986

Susumu Tonegawa

For his discovery of the genetic principle for generation of antibody diversity.

Susumu Tonegawa was born on September 6, 1939, in Nagoya, Japan, the second of four children. His father worked as an engineer for a textile company, an occupation that required the family to relocate every few years. Upon reaching adolescence, Tonegawa went to high school in Tokyo, where he developed a passion for chemistry. He took the entrance exam for the Department of Chemistry at Kyoto University, and although he was initially turned down, he finally entered the program in 1959.

He intended to pursue a career in chemical engineering, but he settled on research and teaching. It was at this time that his fascination with molecular biology began. He soon realized that Japan was not suited to his scientific ambitions and moved to the United States, studying at the University of California in San Diego, where he obtained his doctorate in 1968. Tonegawa's research into antibodies started in Basel, Switzerland, at the Institute for Immunology in 1971. Ten years later he would return to the United States and become a professor at the Center for Cancer Research at the Massachusetts Institute of Technology (MIT).

Antibodies are Y-shaped protein-based molecules made up of two chains of combined amino acids. Foreign bodies, known as antigens (bacterial or viral infections, for example), are attacked by antibodies, but only specific antibodies can combat each antigen. It was known at the time that cells called B lymphocytes were responsible for producing antibodies and that these cells had a limited number of genes, but it was unknown why the amount of antibodies produced greatly outnumbers the amount of genes. Tonegawa found the answer, discovering that the genetic material is constantly being reordered and recombined during the growth of B lymphocytes.

For this work received the Nobel Prize in Physiology or Medicine in 1987. He also received numerous other honors, including the Warren Triennial Prize of the Massachusetts General Hospital (1980), the Genetics Grand Prize of Genetics Promotion Foundation (1981), the Louisa Gross Horwitz Prize from Columbia University (1982) and the Bristol-Myers Award for Distinguished Achievement in Cancer Research (1986).

He later wrote, "When I look back on my scientific career to date, I am amazed at my good fortune. At every major turn, I met scientists who were not only at the very top in their own fields, but also gave me insightful advice and generous help." He currently lives with his second wife, Mayumi, whom he married in 1985.

Gene therapy and the immune system

The molecular biologist Susumu Tonegawa, the laureate for Physiology or Medicine in 1987, widened the knowledge of the immune structure within the human body by discovering the genetic principle for the creation of antibody diversity. His contributions have aided the fight against many diseases.

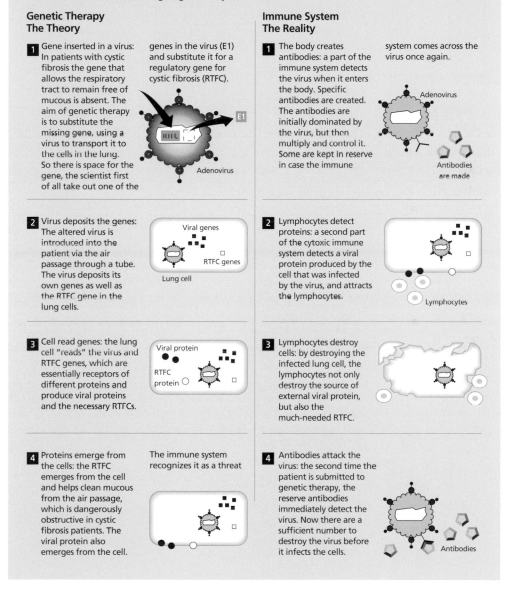

Genetic Therapy
The Theory

1 Gene inserted in a virus: In patients with cystic fibrosis the gene that allows the respiratory tract to remain free of mucous is absent. The aim of genetic therapy is to substitute the missing gene, using a virus to transport it to the cells in the lung. So there is space for the gene, the scientist first of all take out one of the genes in the virus (E1) and substitute it for a regulatory gene for cystic fibrosis (RTFC).

2 Virus deposits the genes: The altered virus is introduced into the patient via the air passage through a tube. The virus deposits its own genes as well as the RTFC gene in the lung cells.

3 Cell read genes: the lung cell "reads" the virus and RTFC genes, which are essentially receptors of different proteins and produce viral proteins and the necessary RTFCs.

4 Proteins emerge from the cells: the RTFC emerges from the cell and helps clean mucous from the air passage, which is dangerously obstructive in cystic fibrosis patients. The viral protein also emerges from the cell. The immune system recognizes it as a threat

Immune System
The Reality

1 The body creates antibodies: a part of the immune system detects the virus when it enters the body. Specific antibodies are created. The antibodies are initially dominated by the virus, but then multiply and control it. Some are kept in reserve in case the immune system comes across the virus once again.

2 Lymphocytes detect proteins: a second part of the cytoxic immune system detects a viral protein produced by the cell that was infected by the virus, and attracts the lymphocytes.

3 Lymphocytes destroy cells: by destroying the infected lung cell, the lymphocytes not only destroy the source of external viral protein, but also the much-needed RTFC.

4 Antibodies attack the virus: the second time the patient is submitted to genetic therapy, the reserve antibodies immediately detect the virus. Now there are a sufficient number to destroy the virus before it infects the cells.

Tenzin Gyatso, the 14th Dalai Lama

[For his] campaign for nonviolence to end Chinese domination in his homeland.

Lhamo Dhondrub was born on July 6, 1935, into a peasant family in the small village of Taktser, northern Tibet. He was only two years old when he was recognized as the reincarnation of his predecessor, the 13th Dalai Lama. He changed his name to Tenzin Gyatso in 1940, the year he became a novice monk and the official spiritual leader of Tibet. The Dalai Lamas are believed to be one of the incarnations of Avalokite vara, a heavenly being that embodies the compassion of all Buddhas, and the succession of these men can be traced back to 1391. Tenzin Gyatso, the Holy Lord, Compassionate, Defender of the Faith, Ocean of Wisdom, has gone on to become both the spiritual and temporal leader of his nation and inspired many more people around the world.

His formal monastic education began at 6, and he completed his final studies in Buddhist philosophy at the age of 25. On the morning of his final exam 30 scholars paid witness to his knowledge of logic, in the afternoon he debated the question of the Middle Path with 15 academics and at night 35 professors tested his knowledge of the canon of monastic discipline and the study of metaphysics. He passed all of his exams with distinction.

On November 17, 1950, however, before he had finished his education, he was called upon to assume full leadership of the state at the age of 15. The People's Republic of China had invaded the nation only a month earlier. Soon the Tibetan people, under military pressure, signed the Seventeen Point Agreement, giving up their autonomy, and the pact was ratified by the Dalai Lama several months later. Successive attempts at a peaceful compromise occurred in the coming years, and in 1954 His Holiness went to Peking (now Beijing) to talk to Mao Tse-tung and other Chinese leaders, but negotiations were unsuccessful. In 1956 he traveled to India to discuss the worsening conditions in Tibet with Prime Minister Nehru.

A failed Tibetan uprising in 1959 put the whole region on edge and, fearing that the Chinese authorities were planning to assassinate him, the Dalai Lama was forced to flee his country. Since 1960 he has lived in Dharamsala, India, the seat of the Tibetan government in exile; 80,000 Tibetans followed him to this new location and have established an agricultural community there.

Over the years the Dalai Lama has repeatedly alerted the United Nations to the injustices in Tibet and led numerous campaigns to increase awareness in the international community of the situation in his country. On his world travels he has established contacts with leaders of almost every nation, and he has visited dozens of countries, including the United States. He outlined a constitution for his nation that would have assured a democratic government, and at the Congressional Human Rights Caucus in 1987 he proposed a Five-Point Peace Plan to begin the resolution of the status of Tibet. The proposals outlined in this plan were: to declare Tibet as an area of peace, stop the massive migration of Chinese into the country, reestablish human rights and freedoms, end production of Chinese nuclear weapons in the country and the dumping of nuclear waste, and begin earnest negotiations on Tibet's status and relationship with China.

Normally referred to as Yeshin Norbu (the wish-fulfilling gem) or Kundun (the presence), the Dalai Lama is the spiritual leader of Tibetan Buddhists, but he has undertaken a crusade for interreligious tolerance, universal responsibility, love, compassion and kindness. He met Pope Paul VI and Pope John Paul II during their reigns and the former Archbishop of Canterbury, Dr. Robert Runcie. At an interfaith service at the World Congress of Faiths he spoke about the necessity for tolerance: "I always believe that it is much better to have a variety of religions, a variety of philosophies, rather than one single religion or philosophy. This is necessary because of the different mental dispositions of each human being. Each religion has certain unique ideas or techniques, and learning about them can only enrich one's own faith."

By awarding the 1989 Nobel Peace Prize to the 14th Dalai Lama, the Norwegian Nobel Committee wanted to "emphasize the fact that the Dalai Lama, in his fight for the liberation of Tibet, has consistently opposed the use of violence. On the contrary, he has always advocated pacifist solutions, based on tolerance and mutual respect, so as to preserve his people's historical and cultural inheritance." Furthermore, those responsible for the choice of the laureate believed that "in the Committee's opinion, the Dalai Lama has put forward constructive proposals with a perspective on the future to solve international conflicts, human rights issues and global environmental problems." While the situation in Tibet has sometimes turned violent, particularly in the run up to the Beijing Olympics, the Dalai Lama has continued to advocate for peaceful solutions based on mutual respect and tolerance. He has received numerous other honors, including the Roosevelt Four Freedoms Award in 1994, honorary Canadian citizenship in 2006 and the United States Congressional Gold Medal on October 17, 2007.

United Nations Peacekeeping Forces

Situated in points of conflict all over the world, it represents the will of the community of nations to achieve peace.

The presence of United Nations peacekeeping forces, commonly known as the "Blue Helmets," can be found around the world today in places like Haiti, Lebanon and Ethiopia. These forces are used by the UN to maintain or reestablish peace in areas of armed conflict between different states, in civil wars or other uprisings. Normally a peacekeeping force is mobilized as a result of a Security Council resolution at UN headquarters, but the General Assembly does, on occasion, order their mobilization. Operational control of the troops belongs to the secretary-general and his secretariat.

A United Nations peacekeeping force acts as an impartial third party that paves the way to resolving the issues that led to conflict. There are two types of peacekeeping operations: the first is unarmed military observers, and the second is lightly armed forces, which, in theory, are only allowed to use their weapons in self-defense. The observer groups collect information for the United Nations about the prevailing conditions where the conflict is taking place. The military forces, on the other hand, have a broader role, such as ensuring opposing parties are kept apart, defending innocent victims and maintaining order for the civilian population.

The Middle East, where it had its first mission, and Africa have been the scenes of most of the United Nations' peacekeeping missions. One of the most famous missions occurred in the Belgian Congo. When it achieved independence in 1960, the country collapsed into anarchy and chaos. A force of about 20,000 soldiers was sent by the UN to help maintain peace and order. The mission of the Peacekeeping Forces was more than this, however, since it also helped prevent a bloody civil war and the province of Katanga from seceding. It was while carrying out the UN mission in the Congo that Secretary General Dag Hammarskjöld, who was posthumously awarded the Nobel Peace Prize in 1961, was killed in an air crash. More than 2,000 other personnel have been killed while on duty. Other important missions occurred along the Indian-Pakistani border and on the island of Cyprus, when civil war broke out between the Greek and the Turkish populations.

Over the years the UN has played a significant role in reducing world conflict and has made strides to eliminate the causes of conflict. The United Nations peacekeeping forces were awarded the 1988 Nobel Peace Prize in recognition of their valuable work.

Nobel Laureates

1980-1989

1980

Nobel Prize in Physics
James Watson Cronin
Born September 29, 1931, in Chicago, Illinois, United States.
&

Val Logsdon Fitch
Born May 10, 1923, in Merriman, Nebraska, United States.
For the discovery of violations of fundamental symmetry principles in the decay of neutral K-mesons.

Nobel Prize in Chemistry
Paul Berg
Born June 30, 1926, in New York, New York, United States.
For his fundamental studies of the biochemistry of nucleic acids, with particular regard to recombinant DNA.
&

Walter Gilbert
Born March 21, 1932, in Boston, Massachusetts, United States.
&

Frederick Sanger
Born August 13, 1918, in Rendcombe, England.
For their contributions concerning the determination of base sequences in nuclei acids.

Nobel Prize in Physiology or Medicine
Baruj Benacerraf
Born October 29, 1920, in Caracas, Venezuela.
&

Jean Dausset
Born October 19, 1916, in Toulouse, France.
&

George Davis Snell
Born December 19, 1903, in Bradford, Massachusetts, United States, and died June 6, 1996, in Bar Harbor, Maine.
For their discoveries concerning genetically determined structures on the cell surface that regulate immunological reactions.

Nobel Prize in Literature
Czeslaw Milosz
Born June 30, 1911, in Seteiniai, Russia (now Lithuania), and died August 14, 2004, in Kraków, Poland.
Who, with uncompromising clear-sightedness, voices man's exposed condition in a world of severe conflicts.

Nobel Peace Prize
Adolfo Pérez Esquivel
Born November 26, 1931, in Buenos Aires, Argentina.
For his defense of respecting human rights and feeling of hope when faced with Argentinean military rules.

The Sveriges Riksbank Prize in Economic Sciences in Memory of Alfred Nobel
Lawrence Robert Klein
Born September 14, 1920, in Omaha, Nebraska, United States.
For the creation of econometric models and the application to the analysis of economic fluctuations and economic policies.

1981

Nobel Prize in Physics
Nicolaas Bloembergen
Born March 11, 1920, in Dordrecht, The Netherlands.
&

Arthur Leonard Schawlow
Born May 5, 1921, Mount Vernon, New York, United States, and died April 28, 1999, in Palo Alto, California.
For their contribution to the development of laser spectroscopy.
&

Kai Manne Börje Siegbahn
Born April 20, 1918, in Lund, Sweden, and died July 20, 2007, in Ängelholm.
For his contribution to the development of high-resolution electron spectroscopy.

Nobel Prize in Chemistry
Kenichi Fukui
Born October 4, 1918, in Nara, Japan, and died January 9, 1998, in Kyoto.
&
Roald Hoffmann
Born July 18, 1937, in Zloczow, Poland.
For their theories, developed independently, concerning the course of chemical reactions.

Nobel Prize in Physiology or Medicine
David Hunter Hubel
Born February 27, 1926, in Windsor, Ontario, Canada.
&
Torsten Nils Wiesel
Born June 3, 1924, in Uppsala, Sweden.
For their discoveries concerning information processing in the visual system.
&
Roger Wolcott Sperry
Born August 20, 1913, in Hartford, Connecticut, United States, and died April 17, 1994, in Pasadena, California.
For his discoveries concerning the functional specialization of the cerebral hemispheres.

Nobel Prize in Literature
Elias Canetti
Born July 25, 1905, in Ruse, Bulgaria, and died August 14, 1994, in Zurich, Switzerland.
For writings marked by a broad outlook, a wealth of ideas and artistic power.

Nobel Peace Prize
Office of the United Nations High Commissioner for Refugees (UNHCR)
Founded by the United Nations on January 1, 1951.
Thirtieth anniversary in defense of refugees.

The Sveriges Riksbank Prize in Economic Sciences in Memory of Alfred Nobel
James Tobin
Born March 5, 1918, in Champaign, Illinois, United States, and died March 11, 2002, in New Haven, Connecticut.
For his analysis of financial markets and their relations to expenditure decisions, employment, production and prices.

1982

Nobel Prize in Physics
Kenneth Geddes Wilson
Born June 8, 1936, in Waltham, Massachusetts, United States.
For his theory for critical phenomena in connection with phase transitions.

Nobel Prize in Chemistry
Aaron Klug
Born August 11, 1926, in Zelvas, Lithuania.
For his development of crystallographic electron microscopy and his structural elucidation of biologically important nucleic acid-protein complexes.

Nobel Prize in Physiology or Medicine
Sune Karl Bergström
Born January 10, 1916, in Stockholm, Sweden, and died August 15, 2004, in Stockholm.
&
Bengt Ingemar Samuelsson
Born May 21, 1934, in Halmstad, Sweden.
&
John Robert Vane
Born March 29, 1927, in Tardebigg, England, and died November 19, 2004, in Farnborough.
For their discoveries concerning prostaglandins and related biologically active substances.

Nobel Prize in Literature
Gabriel García Márquez
Born March 6, 1928, in Aracataca, Colombia.
For his novels and short stories, in which the fantastic and the realistic are combined in a richly composed world of imagination, reflecting a continent's life and conflicts.

Nobel Peace Prize
Alfonso García Robles
Born March 20, 1911, in Zamora, Mexico, and died September 2, 1991, in Mexico City.
For his actions for disarmament and defense of the virtues of patient, methodical negotiation.
&

Alva Reimer Myrdal
Born January 31, 1902, in Uppsala, Sweden, and died February 1, 1986, in Stockholm.
For her efforts for disarmament.

The Sveriges Riksbank Prize in Economic Sciences in Memory of Alfred Nobel
George Joseph Stigler
Born January 17, 1911, in Renton, Washington, United States, and died December 1, 1991, in Chicago, Illinois.
For his seminal studies of industrial structures, functioning of markets and causes and effects of public regulation.

1983

Nobel Prize in Physics
Subrahmanyan Chandrasekhar
Born October 19, 1910, in Lahore, India (now Pakistan), and died August 21, 1995, in Chicago, Illinois, United States.
For his theoretical studies of the physical processes of importance to the structure and evolution of the stars.
&
William Alfred Fowler
Born August 9, 1911, in Pittsburgh, Pennsylvania, United States, and died March 14, 1995, in Pasadena, California.
For his theoretical and experimental studies of the nuclear reactions of importance in the formation of the chemical elements in the universe.

Nobel Prize in Chemistry
Henry Taube
Born November 30, 1915, in Neudorf, Saskatchewan, Canada, and died November 16, 2005, in Stanford, California, United States.
For his work on the mechanisms of electron transfer reactions, especially in metal complexes.

Nobel Prize in Physiology or Medicine
Barbara McClintock
Born June 16, 1902, in Hartford, Connecticut, United States, and died September 2, 1992, in Huntington, New York.
For her discovery of mobile genetic elements.

Nobel Prize in Literature
William Gerald Golding
Born September 19, 1911, in St. Columb Minor, England, and died June 19, 1993, in Perranarworthal.
For his novels which, with the perspicuity of realistic narrative art and the diversity and universality of myth, illuminate the human condition in the world today.

Nobel Peace Prize
Lech Walesa
Born September 29, 1943, in Popowo, Poland.
For his leadership of the nonviolent movement to achieve the right of free association for Polish workers.

The Sveriges Riksbank Prize in Economic Sciences in Memory of Alfred Nobel
Gerard Debreu
Born July 4, 1921, in Calais, France, and died on December 31, 2004, in Paris.
For having incorporated new analytical methods into economic theory and for his rigorous reformulation of the theory of general equilibrium.

1984

Nobel Prize in Physics
Carlo Rubbia
Born March 31, 1934, in Gorizia, Italy.
&
Simon van der Meer
Born November 24, 1925, The Hague, Netherlands.
For their decisive contributions to the large project, which led to the discovery of the field particles W and Z, communicators of weak interaction.

Nobel Prize in Chemistry
Robert Bruce Merrifield
Born July 15, 1921, in Fort Worth, Texas, United States, and died on May 14, 2006, in Cresskill, New Jersey.
For his development of methodology for chemical synthesis on a solid matrix.

Nobel Prize in Physiology or Medicine
Niels Kaj Jerne
Born December 23, 1911, in London, England, and died October 7, 1994, in Castillon-du-Gard, France.
&

Georges Jean Franz Köhler
Born April 17, 1946, in Munich, Germany, and died March 1, 1995, in Freiburg.
&
César Milstein
Born October 8, 1927, in Bahía Blanca, Argentina, and died March 24, 2002, in Cambridge, England.
For theories concerning the specificity in development and control of the immune system and the discovery of the principle for production of monoclonal antibodies.

Nobel Prize in Literature
Jaroslav Seifert
Born September 23, 1901, in Prague, Austria-Hungary (now Czech Republic), and died January 10, 1986, in Prague.
For his poetry, which endowed with freshness, sensuality and rich inventiveness, provides a liberating image of the indomitable spirit and versatility of man.

Nobel Peace Prize
Desmond Mpilo Tutu
Born October 7, 1931, in Klerksdorp, South Africa.
For his work on the South African Churches Council and also for all the individuals and groups in South Africa who demonstrate human and democratic concerns.

The Sveriges Riksbank Prize in Economic Sciences in Memory of Alfred Nobel
Richard Nicholas Stone
Born August 30, 1913, in London, England, and died December 6, 1991, in Cambridge.
For having made fundamental contributions to the development of the systems of national accounts and hence greatly improved the basis for empirical economic analysis.

1985

Nobel Prize in Physics
Klaus von Klitzing
Born June 28, 1943, in Schroda, Poland.
For the discovery of the quantized Hall effect.

Nobel Prize in Chemistry
Herbert Aaron Hauptman
Born February 14, 1917, in New York, New York, United States.
&
Jerome Karle
Born June 18, 1918, in New York, New York, United States.
For their outstanding achievements in the development of direct methods for the determination of crystal structures.

Nobel Prize in Physiology or Medicine
Michael Stuart Brown
Born April 13, 1941, in Brooklyn, New York, United States.
&
Joseph Leonard Goldstein
Born April 18, 1940, in Sumter, South Carolina, United States.
For their discoveries concerning the regulation of cholesterol metabolism.

Nobel Prize in Literature
Claude Simon
Born October 10, 1913, in Tananarive (now Antananarivo), Madagascar, and died on July 6, 2005, in Paris, France.
Who, in his novels, combines the poet's and the painter's creativeness with a deepened awareness of time in the depiction of the human condition.

Nobel Peace Prize
International Physicians for the Prevention of Nuclear War (IPPNW)
Founded in 1980 in Geneva, Switzerland, with its headquarters in Boston, Massachusetts.
For releasing information which arouses concerns as to the catastrophic consequences of a nuclear war.

The Sveriges Riksbank Prize in Economic Sciences in Memory of Alfred Nobel
Franco Modigliani
Born June 18, 1918, in Rome, Italy, and died September 25, 2003, in Cambridge, Massachusetts, United States.
For his pioneering analyses of saving and of financial markets.

1986

Nobel Prize in Physics
Gerd Binnig
Born July 20, 1947, in Frankfurt, Germany.
&
Heinrich Rohrer
Born June 6, 1933, in Buchs, Switzerland.
For their design of the scanning tunneling microscope.
&
Ernst Ruska
Born December 25, 1906, in Heidelberg, Germany, and died May 25, 1988, in Berlin.
For his fundamental work in electron optics, and for the design of the first electron microscope.

Nobel Prize in Chemistry
Dudley Robert Herschbach
Born June 18, 1932, in San José, California, United States.
&
Yuan Tseh Lee
Born November 19, 1936, in Hsinchu, Taiwan.
&
John Charles Polanyi
Born January 23, 1929, in Berlin, Germany.
For their contributions concerning the dynamics of chemical elementary processes.

Nobel Prize in Physiology or Medicine
Stanley Cohen
Born November 17, 1922, in Brooklyn, New York, United States.
&
Rita Levi-Montalcini
Born April 22, 1909, in Turin, Italy.
For their discovery of growth factors.

Nobel Prize in Literature
Akinwande Oluwole (Wole) Soyinka
Born July 13, 1934, in Abeokuta, Nigeria.
Who, in a wide cultural perspective and with poetic overtones, fashions the drama of existence.

Nobel Peace Prize
Elie Wiesel
Born September 30, 1928, in Sighet, Romania.
Wiesel is a messenger to mankind; his message is one of peace, atonement and human dignity.

The Sveriges Riksbank Prize in Economic Sciences in Memory of Alfred Nobel
James McGill Buchanan, Jr.
Born October 3, 1919, in Murfreesboro, Tennessee, United States.
For his development of the contractual and constitutional bases for the theory of economic and political decision-making.

1987

Nobel Prize in Physics
Johannes Georg Bednorz
Born May 16, 1950, in Neuenkirchen, Germany.
&
Karl Alexander Müller
Born April 20, 1927, in Basel, Switzerland.
For their important breakthrough in the discovery of superconductivity in ceramic materials.

Nobel Prize in Chemistry
Donald James Cram
Born April 22, 1919, in Chester, Vermont, United States, and died June 17, 2001, in Palm Desert, California.
&
Jean-Marie Lehn
Born September 30, 1939, in Rosheim, France.
&
Charles John Pedersen
Born October 3, 1904, in Pusan, Korea, and died October 26, 1989, in Salem, New Jersey, United States.
For their development and use of molecules with structure-specific interactions of high selectivity.

Nobel Prize in Physiology or Medicine
Susumu Tonegawa
Born September 6, 1939, in Nagoya, Japan.
For his discovery of the genetic principle for generation of antibody diversity.

Nobel Prize in Literature
Joseph Brodsky
Born May 24, 1940, in Leningrad, Union of Soviet Socialist Republics (now Saint Petersburg, Russia), and died January 28, 1996, in New York, New York, United States. For an all-embracing authorship, imbued with clarity of thought and poetic intensity.

Nobel Peace Prize
Oscar Arias Sánchez
Born September 13, 1941, in Heredia, Costa Rica.
For his work for peace in Central America, efforts which led to the accord signed in Guatemala on August 7 this year.

The Sveriges Riksbank Prize in Economic Sciences in Memory of Alfred Nobel
Robert Merton Solow
Born August 23, 1924, in Brooklyn, New York, United States.
For his contributions to the theory of economic growth.

1988

Nobel Prize in Physics
Leon Max Lederman
Born July 15, 1922, in New York, New York, United States.
&
Melvin Schwartz
Born November 2, 1932, in New York, New York, United States, and died August 28, 2006, in Twin Falls, Idaho.
&
Jack Steinberger
Born May 25, 1921, in Bad Kissingen, Germany.
For the neutrino beam method and the demonstration of the doublet structure of the leptons through the discovery of the muon neutrino.

Nobel Prize in Chemistry
Johann Deisenhofer
Born September 30, 1943, in Zusamaltheim, Germany.
&

Robert Huber
Born February 20, 1937, in Munich, Germany.
&
Hartmut Michel
Born July 18, 1948, in Ludwigsburg, Germany.
For the determination of the three-dimensional structure of a photosynthetic reaction center.

Nobel Prize in Physiology or Medicine
James Whyte Black
Born June 14, 1924, in Uddingston, Scotland.
&
Gertrude Belle Elion
Born January 23, 1918, in New York, New York, United States, and died February 21, 1999, in Chapel Hill, North Carolina.
&
George Herbert Hitchings
Born April 18, 1905, in Hoquiam, Washington, United States, and died February 27, 1998, in Chapel Hill, North Carolina.
For their discoveries of important principles for drug treatment.

Nobel Prize in Literature
Naguib Mahfouz
Born December 11, 1911, in Cairo, Egypt, and died August 30, 2006, in Cairo.
Who, through works rich in nuance — now clear-sightedly realistic, now evocatively ambiguous — has formed an Arabian narrative art that applies to all mankind.

Nobel Peace Prize
United Nations Peacekeeping Forces
Founded in 1948.
Situated in points of conflict all over the world, it represents the will of the community of nations to achieve peace.

The Sveriges Riksbank Prize in Economic Sciences in Memory of Alfred Nobel
Maurice Allais
Born May 31, 1911, in Paris, France.
For his pioneering contributions to the theory of markets and efficient utilization of resources.

1989

Nobel Prize in Physics
Hans Georg Dehmelt
Born September 9, 1922, in Görlitz, Germany.
&
Wolfgang Paul
Born August 10, 1913, in Lorenzkirch, Germany, and died December 7, 1993, in Bonn.
For the development of the ion trap technique.
&
Norman Foster Ramsey
Born August 27, 1915, in Washington, DC, United States.
For the invention of separated oscillatory fields method and its use in the hydrogen maser and other atomic clocks.

Nobel Prize in Chemistry
Sidney Altman
Born May 7, 1939, in Montreal, Quebec, Canada.
&
Thomas Robert Cech
Born December 8, 1947, in Chicago, Illinois, United States.
For their discovery of catalytic properties of RNA.

Nobel Prize in Physiology or Medicine
John Michael Bishop
Born February 22, 1936, in York, Pennsylvania, United States.
&
Harold Elliot Varmus
Born December 18, 1939, in Freeport, New York, United States.
For their discovery of the cellular origin of retroviral oncogenes.

Nobel Prize in Literature
Camilo José Cela
Born May 11, 1916, in Iria Flavia, Spain, and died January 17, 2002, in Madrid.
For a rich and intensive prose, which with restrained compassion forms a challenging vision of man's vulnerability.

Nobel Peace Prize
Tenzin Gyatso, the 14th Dalai Lama, né Lhamo Dhondrub
Born July 6, 1935, in Taktser, Tibet.
For his campaign for nonviolence to end Chinese domination in his homeland.

The Sveriges Riksbank Prize in Economic Sciences in Memory of Alfred Nobel
Trygve Haavelmo
Born December 13, 1911, In Skedsmo, Norway, and died July 26, 1999, in Boerum.
For his clarification of the probability theory foundations of econometrics and his analyses of simultaneous economic structures.

Selected Profiles of Nobel Laureates

1990–1999

(1914–1998)

Octavio Paz

For impassioned writings with wide horizons, characterized by sensuous intelligence and humanistic integrity.

Octavio Paz was born on March 31, 1914, in Mexico City. His father was an active journalist and lawyer who, along with other progressive intellectuals, joined the revolutionary uprisings led by Emiliano Zapata, a leading figure in the Mexican Revolution, which began in 1910. Due to his father's frequent absences, however, Octavio Paz was raised in the village of Mixcoac by his mother, aunt and paternal grandfather, Ireneo Paz, a prominent liberal writer whose extensive body of work and impressive library influenced the young boy.

In 1933, when he was 19, he published his first book of poetry, *Luna silvestre (Forest Moon)*. In his early works Paz deals with Marxism, surrealism, Buddhism and Hinduism; later poems focused on eroticism, religious experiences and his love of modern art. Many of these themes were also approached in his essays; *El laberinto de la soledad (The Labyrinth of Solitude)*, published in 1950, is regarded as a significant comment on Mexican culture and identity.

He studied law at the National University of Mexico, but in 1937 he abandoned law to teach the rural poor in Yucatán. During this period Paz began work on *Entre la piedra y la flor (Between the Stone and the Flower)*, the first of his long poems dealing with the plight of Mexican peasants under the greedy landlords of the day; the poem was published in 1941 and a revised version appeared in 1976. The same year he had arrived in Yucatán, Paz attended the Second International Writers Congress in Defense of Culture in Spain and spoke out against fascism. Upon his return he helped found the avant-garde literary journal *Taller*, which signaled the emergence of a new generation of Mexican writers and a new literary sensibility.

In 1943, while studying at the University of California, Berkeley, on a Guggenheim Fellowship, he was influenced by modernist Anglo-American poetry. Paz then joined the diplomatic service in Mexico in 1945 and was sent to France, where he wrote *El laberinto de la soledad*. In 1962 he was appointed the Mexican ambassador to India. Some of his most important works date from his time as a diplomat, including *El arco y la lira (The Bow and the Lyre)*, published in 1956.

In 1968 he renounced his position as ambassador to protest the government's bloody repression of a student demonstration in Tlatelolco during the Mexico Olympic Games. He continued with his work as an editor and founded two important magazines dedicated to the arts and politics, *Plural* and *Vuelta*. He was also a lecturer at Cambridge and Harvard between 1970 and 1974.

In 1990 he became the first Mexican to receive the Nobel Prize in Literature. He died in Mexico City in 1998.

Edward Thomas

"for their discoveries concerning organ and cell transplantation in the treatment of human disease"

Edward Donnall Thomas is the only son of the second marriage of the general practitioner Edward E. Thomas, who saw his first wife die of tuberculosis and was 50 years old when his son was born in a small town in Texas. It was here that Thomas spent a great part of his childhood and adolescence. At high school he was part of a class of 15 students but failed to distinguish himself academically. Even when he entered the University of Texas, Austin, in 1937, he only passed the first semester with average grades. Thomas's interests in chemistry and chemical engineering, however, soon grew in proportion to the difficulty of his courses.

At the time money was scarce and Thomas had no choice but to move from job to job. One of these was waiting tables in a girls' dormitory but the unglamorous position eventually led to a marriage. On a beautiful and rare snowy day in Texas, he was hit by a snowball thrown by an attractive young woman leaving the dormitory. He decided to avenge this assault on his ego and ran after her to pay her back in kind. Sometime later he married Dorothy Martin and the couple had three children together in the coming years.

In 1943, Edward Donnall Thomas enrolled in the Harvard Medical School, where he received his doctorate three years later. He soon joined the Peter Bent Brigham Hospital, in Boston, where he met the surgeon Joseph Murray, who became a friend and colleague for many years, and the two pursued research on transplants, bone marrow and leukemia.

Throughout his career, Thomas has contributed to the reduction of the painful reaction patients, or hosts, can have to a transplant. He has also demonstrated that bone marrow cells administered intravenously are capable of reproducing marrow and producing new blood cells. Bone marrow transplants can aid or cure serious heredity conditions, including dysfunctions of the immune system such as leukemia and anemia, so these findings have encouraged further research in the field.

In 1990, the Karolinska Institute of Stockholm recognized Edward Thomas's discoveries concerning organ and cell transplantation in the treatment of human disease with the Nobel Prize in Physiology or Medicine; he shared the award with Joseph E. Murray for his contributions in the same area. The work of these two scientists has been crucial for thousands of patients, who can be cured or lead a more dignified life until other more successful methods of treatment appear.

Joseph Edward Murray also received half of the prize.

Available organs

Joseph Murray and Donnall Thomas were awarded the Nobel Prize for Physiology or Medicine in 1990 for "their discoveries in the field of cell and organ transplant in the treatment of human diseases." Advance in this area are ongoing and today the number of organs that can be transplanted has increased significantly. Allied to perfecting surgical techniques is the discovery and development of new drugs that reduce the risk of rejection.

Lungs
A lung transplant can save patients with cystic fibrosis, emphysema or other terminal lung diseases.

Liver
A liver transplant can save patients with terminal liver disease.

Pancreas
A pancreas transplant in a diabetic can eradicate the need for injections of insulin.

Bone Marrow
This transplant can help patients with aplastic anemia and immune system deficiencies and can lead to remission in certain cases of acute leukemia.

Bone
Bone is used in facial reconstructions, limb recovery, in the correction of birth defects, treatments of cancer and oral and backbone surgery.

Cartilage & Tendons
These are used in reconstructive osteo-muscular surgery.

Corneas
These allow the return of sight in blind people suffering from specific diseases.

Heart
This is transplanted to patients with myocardial disease.

Kidneys
A kidney transplant in patients with terminal kidney disease restores the quality of life.

Small intestine
A transplant is a means of treating serious diseases of this part of the digestive system. It permits the re-establishment of nutritional balance.

Muscle membrane
This transplant is used to re-establish support and repair limbs, and defects in the conjunctive fibrous tissue that surrounds the muscles.

Skin
A skin transplant can save the life of a patient with serious burns or accidental losses of tissue.

Veins
These are used in various parts of the body in transplants to re-establish the blood flow.

Georges Charpak

*For his invention and development of particle detectors,
in particular the multiwire proportional chamber.*

Georges Charpak was born to a Jewish family in Dabrovica, Poland, on August 1, 1924. When he was 7 years old his family moved to France, and he received his primary and high school education in Paris and Montpellier. Charpak served in the Resistance during World War II and in 1943 was imprisoned by Vichy authorities. The next year he was deported to Dachau, a Nazi concentration camp, where he remained until liberated by the Allies in 1945.

Returning to Paris he entered the École des Mines, one of the most prestigious schools in the country, and in 1948 he graduated in mining engineering. Six years later he completed his doctorate degree in physics at the College de France. While there he worked in the laboratory of Frédéric Joliot, winner of the 1935 Nobel Prize in Chemistry.

Beginning in 1948 Georges Charpak worked at the Centre National de la Recherche Scientifique (National Center for Scientific Research). In 1959 he moved to Switzerland to become part of the team at the Centre Européen pour la Recherche Nucléaire (European Organization for Nuclear Research), where he remained until 1991; he remains a particularly vocal supporter of nuclear power in France. In 1984 he became a professor at the School of Advanced Studies in Physics and Chemistry and was made a member of the French Academy of Sciences the next year.

Charpak's pioneering work on particle detectors began to be published in 1968, and he soon became regarded as one of the most respected physicists in the field. His creation of various models of particle detectors made it possible for other physicists to focus their interest on the rare interactions between particles. The difficulty with such a study rests in choosing the very few, but exceptionally interesting, interactions among the millions that can be observed. Instead of earlier photographic methods, Charpak used modern technologies and understood the importance of connecting the detector to a computer, which increased the data-collection speed a thousand fold compared to previous methods.

Charpak's ideas were developed over two decades, and he was always at the forefront of this development process. Various types of detectors based on Charpak's original ideas have been used to make important discoveries in the field of particle physics, some of them worthy of the Nobel Prize in Physics before it was awarded in 1992 to the man whose work was fundamental to them. Furthermore, Charpak's detector has been used in other enormously important applications, particularly in the fields of biology and medicine.

Particle detector

The field of Particle Physics developed with the work of Georges Charpak, the laureate for the 1992 Nobel Prize for Physics, for his "invention and development of particle detectors."
Over the years various particles have been detected. Quarks, basic subatomic particles, have aroused much curiosity, above all because they can be divided into various types (known as "flavors").

▶ How scientists study quarks
Physicists study quarks by accelerating protons and anti-protons and measuring the results of the collisions.
Six "flavors" of quark have been identified: "up," "down," "bottom," "strange," "charm," and lastly "top."

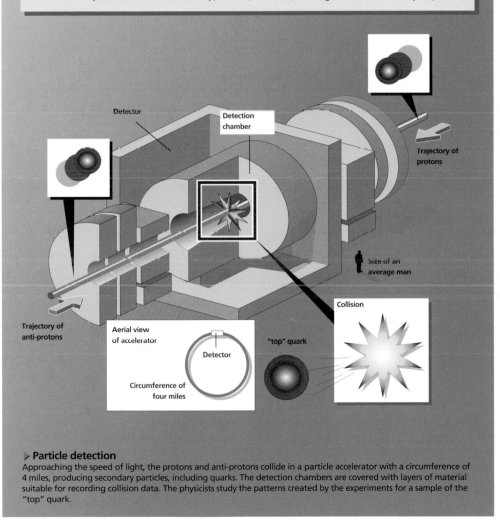

Detector

Detection chamber

Trajectory of protons

Size of an average man

Trajectory of anti-protons

Aerial view of accelerator

Detector

Circumference of four miles

"top" quark

Collision

▷ Particle detection
Approaching the speed of light, the protons and anti-protons collide in a particle accelerator with a circumference of 4 miles, producing secondary particles, including quarks. The detection chambers are covered with layers of material suitable for recording collision data. The physicists study the patterns created by the experiments for a sample of the "top" quark.

Mikhail Gorbachev

For his leading role in the peace process which today characterizes important parts of the international community.

After Joseph Stalin, Mikhail Sergeyevich Gorbachev was the youngest politician to obtain supreme power in the former Union of Soviet Social Republics (USSR). A tireless worker for social, economic and political reforms, Gorbachev was general secretary of the Communist Party of the Soviet Union from 1985 to 1991 and president of his nation from March 15, 1990, to December 25, 1991. At an international level he contributed to the end of the Cold War and officially abandoned the Brezhnev Doctrine, which had allowed former Eastern-Bloc countries to determine their own political affairs. For his central role in resolving European political problems he was recognized with the 1990 Nobel Peace Prize.

Gorbachev was born on March 2, 1931, in Privolnoye, during the brutal reign of Joseph Stalin. Life was extremely difficult during these years, and his paternal grandfather was sentenced to nine years in a Soviet gulag for withholding grain from the collective harvest. The young Gorbachev also worked as a harvester, but with all the restriction peasants experienced, including being denied a passport, he reflected "What difference was there between this life and serfdom?"

Despite hardships, however, at the age of 16 he received the Order of the Red Banner of Labor with his father for bringing in a record crop on their collective farm. This rare honor, combined with his academic talents, particularly in history and mathematics, is thought to have secured his place at Moscow University, where he studied law beginning in 1950. At the age of 21 he joined the Communist Party of the Soviet Union and slowly earned positions of increasing power.

He became a permanent member of the Politburo, or political bureau, in 1980 and was its youngest member. When Yuri Andropov became general secretary in 1982 he acted as a mentor to Gorbachev during Konstantin Chernenko's leadership, which made the young politician even more influential. When Chernenko died in 1985 Gorbachev became general secretary of the Communist Party, and after Andrei Gromiko, chairman of the Presidium of the Supreme Soviet of the USSR, resigned three years later, he also assumed that position.

The period between 1985 and 1990 was crucial in the history of the Soviet Union. By implementing his restructuring program, which he outlined in his 1987 book, *Perestroika: New Thinking for Our Country and the World*, Gorbachev envisaged the economic transformation of his nation; at the same time his pursuit of transparency rather than secrecy in government opened the way for a new political and cultural philosophy. In foreign affairs he was responsible for withdrawing Soviet troops from Afghanistan and for stabilizing relations with China. He was also responsible for signing a series of arms control accords with American presidents Ronald Reagan and George H.W. Bush.

In 1990 the economic situation in the Soviet Union worsened, and food shortages forced the reintroduction of ration cards. Due to the relaxation of censorship and the democratization of the political system, many in the Soviet republics began to voice anti-Russian sentiments and called for independence from Moscow's authority. To deal with the opposition Gorbachev created the office of president, with its greater powers. He was the first and only person to occupy the position, however, and it failed to prevent an August 1991 coup; Gorbachev was placed under house arrest but was released three days later and restored to power.

Meanwhile, Boris Yeltsin had taken advantage of the unrest to increase his political power and had suspended Communist Party activity. Over the coming month Estonia, Latvia, Lithuania, Ukraine, Belarus, Moldova, Georgia, Armenia, Azerbaijan, Kyrgyzstan, Uzbekistan, Tajikistan and Turkmenistan declared their independence. In December 1991, when the member-states voted in favor of dismantling the Soviet Union, Mikhail Gorbachev retired from politics. He was succeeded as head of state by Boris Yeltsin, who had become his political rival.

As a private citizen Gorbachev has remained active in Russian politics. In 1992 he visited the United States and Japan while preparing his book *The August Coup: The Truth and the Lessons* and received the Ronald Reagan Freedom Award. After a failed bid for the presidency in 1996 he established the Social Democratic Party of Russia, which was later dissolved. In October of that same year Mikhail Gorbachev published his *Memoirs*. His wife, Raisa Titarenko, whom he had married on September 25, 1953, died in 1999. Their only child, Irina Mihailovna Virganskaya, currently serves as the vice president of the Gorbachev Foundation.

271

Frederik de Klerk

For their work for the peaceful termination of the apartheid regime, and for laying the foundations for a new democratic South Africa.

In 1993, after Albert Luthuli and Desmond Tutu had been awarded the Nobel Peace Prize for their fight against racial segregation in South Africa, it was Frederik Willem de Klerk's turn to receive the award. He ended 41 years of apartheid and created the outline for a constitution based on the principal "one man, one vote." It was also at his hand that Nelson Mandela was set free in 1990. The two met in Oslo to share the prize.

Born on March 18, 1936, in Johannesburg, de Klerk came from a respected conservative family with a long connection to politics in South Africa. He graduated in law from the University of Potchefstroom in 1958, but he abandoned his legal practice and an invitation to lecture in administrative law at his alma mater to serve as a member of parliament for the National Party in 1969. In the following years he held a succession of ministerial posts.

While minister for education in President Pieter Willem Botha's government he defended segregation in universities, and he was not known for reform initiatives at the time he led the National Party in Transvaal. Things changed, however, and on assuming the presidency of the party in 1989, his first speech as party leader called for a non-racist South Africa and for negotiations concerning the future of the country. In September of that same year he was elected president of the country, thus starting the era that led to the foundations of a new democratic state.

De Klerk began by lifting the ban on the African National Congress and other opposing political forces. He freed political prisoners and in 1991 abolished apartheid, the political policy that had officially been in place since 1950, two years after the National Party had risen to power. With the drafting of a new constitution in 1993, blacks and other ethnic groups were granted the right to vote. The following year fully democratic elections were held. Nelson Mandela was elected president and formed a coalition in which F.W. de Klerk held the position of vice president, although not for long. His image was tarnished when, in 1995, rumors arose about the dubious conduct of security services in the 1980s, which apparently took place with his knowledge. When he gave evidence at the Truth and Reconciliation Commission in August 1996 he assumed responsibility for the disrespect of human rights, although he denied authorizing any crimes.

In 1959 he married Marike Willemse, and the couple had two sons and a daughter together. In 1998 they were divorced and he remarried, to Elita Georgiades.

Nelson Rolihlahla Mandela also received half of the prize.

Toni Morrison

Who, in novels characterized by visionary force and poetic import,
gives life to an essential aspect of American reality.

Toni Morrison was born Chloe Anthony Wofford on February 18, 1931, to
a poor sharecropper family in Lorain, Ohio. At the age of 18 she entered
Howard University, American's foremost black college, in Washington,
DC, where she took a particular interest in drama and read voraciously.
It was also during these years that she changed her named from Chloe to
Toni because she felt too many people had trouble pronouncing it. In 1955
she received her master's degree in English at Cornell University.

Between 1957 and 1964 Morrison was an English instructor at Howard
University, and before that she had lectured at Texas Southern University. At Howard she met
Harold Morrison, a Jamaican architect whom she would marry, and made her initial efforts at
writing fiction. In 1964, the year she divorced, she gave up teaching to be an editor at Random
House in New York.

Six year later her first novel, *The Bluest Eye*, an expanded version of an earlier short
story, was published. Morrison saw *Sula* appear in bookstores in 1973 and *Song of Solomon*
in 1977. This latter work received high critical acclaim, and the success of *Tar Baby* in 1981
cemented her literary fame. After *Beloved*, which won the Pulitzer Prize for Fiction in 1988,
Toni Morrison wrote *Jazz* and *Playing in the Dark: Whiteness and the Literary Imagination*,
both published in 1992. Both books were best sellers. Some of her most recent works are
Paradise (1998), *Love* (2003) and *A Mercy* (2008). She has also produced song lyrics and
since 1999 has co-written several books for children with Slade Morrison, her son.

Most of Morrison's writing tells of the experience of African-Americans, focusing
particularly on women and their position in a racist and male-dominated society. Her
keen perception of the African-American community and its history and the beauty of her
compassionate, poetic language have been widely praised. In recognition of her importance
in the literary community she was made a professor of humanities at Princeton University.

Nelson Mandela

For their work for the peaceful termination of the apartheid regime, and for laying the foundations for a new democratic South Africa.

For 27 years Nelson Rolihlahla Mandela was the best-known political prisoner in the world. His name was the principal slogan in the fight against apartheid in South Africa, and when he was released on February 11, 1990, the event was broadcast live around the world. He jointly received the Nobel Peace Prize in 1993 with F.W. de Klerk, with whom he had established the basis for democracy and racial equality in South Africa. The following year he became the first black president of his country.

Mandela, whose given name was Rolihlahla, meaning troublemaker, was born on July 18, 1918 in Transkei, Eastern Cape, in the Union of South Africa. The son of a former chief and member of the Privy Counsel to the king of the Thembu people and the "third," according to the tribal ranking system, of his four wives, Mandela was himself raised to be a chief. He was the first member of his family to attend school, where, at the age of 7, he was given the English name Nelson, after the British admiral Horatio Nelson, by a Methodist teacher who found his given name difficult to pronounce. He went on to study at Fort Hare University, but he was soon asked to leave because of his involvement in a boycott of university policies by the Students' Representative Council.

After the death of his father when he was 9, Mandela was informally adopted by King Jongintaba Dalindyebo in appreciation of the help the boy's father had given to him during his ascension to the throne. However, when the king arranged a marriage for Mandela shortly after his departure from Fort Hare University, he fled to Johannesburg. There, in 1944, he was instrumental in founding the African National Congress Youth League (ANCYL), along with Walter Sisulu, Oliver Tambo and Anton Lembede. During his early days in Johannesburg, Mandela found temporary work as a security guard for a mine then became a clerk in a law firm, during which time he completed his bachelor's degree through correspondence with the University of South Africa.

After the victory of the white-Afrikaner-dominated National Party in the 1948 elections, Mandela began to be politically involved, opposing the policy of apartheid and racial segregation. In 1952 he was a prominent member of the Defiance Campaign and three years later of the Congress of the People and its adoption of the Freedom Charter, initial steps in the unified rejection of the policies of the National Party. During these years he also offered free or low-cost legal aid to poor blacks who would have otherwise been without representation.

In December 1952 Mandela was put in prison under the application of a law to suppress communism, but his nine-month sentence was suspended. He was forbidden from taking part in meetings or leaving the district of Johannesburg, a situation that continued for nine years but which did not prevent his political activity. In 1956 Nelson Mandela was one of 150 people accused of treason. The trial dragged on until 1961 and concluded with all the accused being acquitted. In the meantime he had married his second wife, Nkosikazi Nomzamo Madikizela, later known as Winnie Mandela, in 1958.

After the Sharpville massacre of 1960, in which 67 blacks were killed by police, the African National Congress and the Pan-African Congress were banned; Nelson Mandela went into hiding. Although initially dedicated to nonviolent methods of political reform inspired by Mahatma Gandhi, in June 1961 the ANC formed an armed faction, the Umkhonto we Sizwe (Spear of the Nation), of which Mandela took command. He traveled across the continent, \received guerrilla training in Algeria and was in London with exiled compatriots. In August 1962, shortly after returning to his country, he was captured, along with other leading members of the ANC. At the trial Mandela represented himself and his companions, all of whom, except for Rusty Bernstein, were sentenced on June 12, 1964, to life imprisonment for planning armed action against the government.

After refusing an offer of conditional freedom made by President P.W. Botha in 1985, he was released in 1990, after President de Klerk had lifted the ban on the African National Congress. Mandela assumed effective leadership and, after difficult negotiations with the government, saw the end of apartheid. In 1994 his autobiography, *Long Walk to Freedom*, was published. That same year, at the age of 77, he was elected the President of South Africa; he retired in 1999 and was succeeded by Thabo Mbeki.

Meanwhile, in 1992 he had announced his separation from Winnie, who had been accused of kidnapping and ordering murders during the 1980s. In September 1996 Nelson Mandela publicly acknowledged his relationship with Graça Machel, widow of the former president of Mozambique, Samora Machel; they married on July 18, 1998, on his 80th birthday. Mandela has a total of six children, four by his first marriage, to Evelyn Ntoko Mase, and two by his second marriage.

Frederik Willem de Klerk also received half of the prize.

Yasser Arafat

For their efforts to create peace in the Middle East.

The Palestinian politician Yasser Arafat was born Mohammed Abdel-Raouf Arafat as Qudwa al-Hussaeini. The date and place of his birth, however, are uncertain; Arafat himself insisted he was born in Jerusalem on August 4, 1929, but according to a birth certificate registered in Cairo he was born there on August 24, 1929.

Yasser Arafat was one of seven children of a Palestinian textile merchant and his wife. When he was 5 years old Arafat's mother died, and he was sent to live with a maternal uncle in Jerusalem, then the capital of the British Mandate of Palestine. After four years he returned to his father in Cairo, but the two were never close; Arafat did not attend his father's funeral in 1952.

While a teenager in Cairo he smuggled arms to Palestine and at 19 left the University of King Fuad I, later Cairo University, to fight in Gaza during the 1948 Arab-Israeli War. In 1949 he returned to Cairo and graduated in civil engineering the next year. Between 1952 and 1956 he served as president of the General Union of Palestinian Students.

When the Suez conflict erupted in 1956 he joined the Egyptian army but never saw action. After the conflict Egyptian President Gamal Abdel Nasser allowed the United Nations Emergency Force to establish itself in the Sinai Peninsula and Gaza Strip; the expulsion of all guerilla fighters, including Yasser Arafat, followed. He attempted to obtain visas from several countries and was finally accepted by Kuwait, where he worked temporarily as a schoolteacher.

As he made connections with other Palestinian refugees, he gradually formed the group that would become known as Fatah. The organization was dedicated to the militant liberation of Palestine and soon became the main military wing of the Palestine Liberation Organization (PLO). During the early 1960s he and companions immigrated to Syria, where they received increased support and membership. After the Battle of Karameh — named after the Jordanian village where the fighting took place — in 1968, when Fatah held its ground against a surprise Israeli attack, Arafat's face appeared on the cover of *Time* magazine, and he received further Arab support.

After being nominated the chairman of the PLO in 1969, Arafat's power continued to grow; four years later the PLO was declared the "sole legitimate representative of the Palestinian people" and became a full member of the Arab League. In November 1974 Yasser Arafat became the first representative of a nongovernmental organization, the PLO, to address the General Assembly of the United Nations.

During the 1970s various subgroups, notably Black September, committed terrorist attacks against Israel. After Israel's invasion of Lebanon, however, Arafat was the target of criticisms from various factions of the PLO, and in the face of this pressure he left his head-quarters in Beirut in August 1982, establishing a new base in Tunisia. In 1987 he left for the Iraqi capital, Baghdad. In time he reestablished his leadership and healed divisions within the PLO.

On April 2, 1989, Arafat was elected president of the self-proclaimed State of Palestine by the Central Council of the Palestine National Congress. It was in this capacity that, four years later, he formally recognized the existence of Israel by accepting the UN Security Counsil Resolution Number 242 and signed, with then Prime Minister of Israel Yitzhak Rabin, the declaration on the autonomy of Gaza and Jericho in Washington, DC. The agreement was later ratified in Cairo in 1994.

In 1994, Arafat was elected president and prime minister of the Palestinian National Authority, which governed the areas of the Gaza Strip and Jericho, and continued negotiations with Israel. Various setbacks and successes occurred in his later years, and although change was gradual and based on compromise, the international community showed him considerable support. He shared the Nobel Peace Prize with his Jewish counterparts, Yitzhak Rabin and Shimon Peres, in 1994 for his attempts at reconciling with Israel and establishing a general peace in the Middle East.

In 1990, at the age of 61, Yasser Arafat was married to Suha Tawil, a Palestinian Christian who converted to Islam, who was less than half his age. Their marriage, which produced a daughter, Zahwa, was widely regarded as a deliberate union between Christian and Muslim Palestinians. Although he survived numerous attempts on his life and various accidents, Arafat died on November 11, 2004, at the age of 75.

Yitzhak Rabin and Shimon Peres also each received one-third of the prize.

Mario José Molina

For their work in atmospheric chemistry, particularly concerning the formation and decomposition of ozone.

José Mario Molina Pasquel Henríquez, known as Mario José Molina, was born to a successful lawyer and diplomat and his wife on March 19, 1943, in Mexico City. From an early age Molina was fascinated by science: he observed amoebas with the help of a rudimentary microscope and, as soon as he could, turned a little-used family bathroom into a laboratory. He first used chemistry sets and later, under the guidance of an aunt who worked in the field, carried out experiments similar to those in freshman courses at college.

Following a family tradition, his parents sent him to Switzerland to study when he was 11. There, however, Molina was disappointed to find that his European colleagues were as uninterested in science as his Mexican friends. Upon returning home he attended the Universidad Nacional Autonoma de Mexico (National University of Mexico), where his lawyer father taught before becoming the Mexican ambassador to Ethiopia, Australia and then the Philippines. On completing his bachelor's degree in chemical engineering in 1965, he decided to proceed with graduate work in physical chemistry.

His took his master's degree from the University of Freiburg in Germany, spent several months in Paris, then applied for admission to a doctoral program in the United States. In 1968, after some time teaching in Mexico, he enrolled at the University of California, Berkeley, where in 1972 he completed his PhD.

In October 1973, some months after marrying his first wife, Molina joined the research group led by Professor Frank Sherwood Rowland.This group sought to prove that common objects such as refrigerators, air conditioning units and aerosols released chlorofluorocarbons (CFCs) that damaged the ozone layer. CFCs, inert industrial compounds, were, at the time, considered to have practically no environmental impact. Three months later, however, Rowland and Molina developed a theory on the depletion of the ozone due to CFCs and concluded that chlorine atoms resulting from the decomposition of CFCs destroyed the ozone catalytically.

The results of this work were published for the first time in 1974, but it took many more years before the international community began to take action. The destruction of the ozone layer and the many problems associated with global warming are far from being solved, but Molina helped us take those initial steps toward awareness. Together with Rowland and Paul Josef Crutzen, Molina received the 1995 Nobel Prize in Chemistry. He is married to Guadalupe Alvarez, and the couple has a son.

Frank Sherwood Rowland and Paul Josef Crutzen also each received one-third of the prize.

The way in which the Earth warms ...

Environmental questions, principally those referring to the increase in size of the hole in the ozone layer, have ignited debates and fed the controversy on the role that man can play in preventing the destruction of the atmosphere. Paul Crutzen, Mario Molina and F. Sherwood Rowland won the Nobel Prize for Chemistry in 1995 for their "work in atmospheric chemistry, particularly concerning the formation and decomposition of ozone."

In science one of the topics that causes the most heated debate is the question of climate change. An international committee has published a new analysis on atmospheric warming.

Some anticipated effects of global warming

■ This map of the world shows the regions where the greatest increase in temperature are expected in the 21st century.

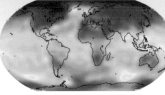

Cooler   Hotter
Relative change in temperature

■ The variations of warming from one area in relation to another is the result of the complexity of climate interaction and climatic variables. A more accurate prediction is hard to make.

THE CONTROVERSY OF GLOBAL WARMING

■ World temperatures normally fluctuate

■ Climatic statistics show that the average temperature is gradually increasing all over the world

Dispute:
There is no consensus among researchers on the speed of warming

New report
The worldwide average temperature will continue to increase.

CONTROVERSY OF THE GREENHOUSE EFFECT

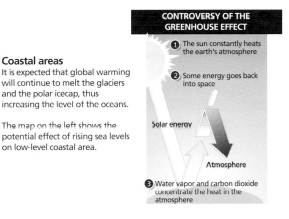

❶ The sun constantly heats the earth's atmosphere

❷ Some energy goes back into space

Solar energy

Atmosphere

❸ Water vapor and carbon dioxide concentrate the heat in the atmosphere

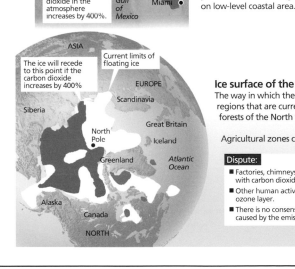

SOUTH EAST

Present coastline

New Orleans

Atlantic Ocean

FLORIDA

The coastline will recede if carbon dioxide in the atmosphere increases by 400%.

Gulf of Mexico

Miami

ASIA

The ice will recede to this point it the carbon dioxide increases by 400%

Current limits of floating ice

EUROPE

Scandinavia

Siberia

Great Britain

North Pole

Iceland

Greenland

Atlantic Ocean

Alaska

Canada

NORTH

Coastal areas
It is expected that global warming will continue to melt the glaciers and the polar icecap, thus increasing the level of the oceans.

The map on the left shows the potential effect of rising sea levels on low-level coastal area.

Ice surface of the Arctic regions
The way in which the ice surface shrinks may cause the ecology of the regions that are currently frozen during the winter to change. The forests of the North will grow more than at the present.

Agricultural zones could move more to the North of these regions.

Dispute:
■ Factories, chimneys and car exhaust fumes are bombarding the atmosphere with carbon dioxide.
■ Other human activities produce methane, another gas that is harmful to the ozone layer.
■ There is no consensus among researchers as to whether global warming is caused by the emissions.

(1937–)

Robert Lucas, Jr.

For having developed and applied the hypothesis of rational expectations, and thereby having transformed macroeconomic analysis and deepened our understanding of economic policy.

Robert Emerson Lucas, Jr., was born on September 15, 1937, in Yakima, Washington. His parents, who inspired Lucas Jr. with their independence and freethinking, were strong Democrats and supporters of President Franklin D. Roosevelt's New Deal.

During World War II the family moved to Seattle, where he attended public schools and in 1955 graduated from Roosevelt High School, which his parents had attended years before. During this time Lucas developed an interest in mathematics and the sciences. He initially planned to attend the University of Seattle and become an engineer, but he then wanted to broaden his horizons. He needed a scholarship to pay for his education and was offered one by the University of Chicago. As there was no engineering department there, Lucas gave up these dreams but, as he later wrote, "I was pretty sure something interesting would turn up."

He began concentrating on mathematics, but exact sciences proved too fastidious for him. He then became fascinated by history and epistemology courses, and he considered an academic career. In 1959 he received his bachelor's degree in history from the University of Chicago, then he was granted a Woodrow Wilson Doctoral Fellowship to study at the University of California in Berkley. Although he enjoyed his time there, he realized he lacked grounding in Greek, Latin, French and German and concluded he wouldn't get far in history. Lucas thus returned to the University of Chicago and took up economics, in which he received his doctorate in 1964. During his studies he was particularly influenced by the work of Paul Samuelson and Milton Friedman. After graduating he taught at Carnegie-Mellon University in Pittsburgh, Pennsylvania, where he developed much of his theoretical work. In 1974 he returned to the University of Chicago, to which he remained connected for most of his academic career.

Lucas has been recognized for developing and applying the hypothesis of rational expectations. His work led to rapid, revolutionary developments in the equilibrium theory of business cycles, provided a better analysis of the difficulties of using economic policy to control economics and argued for the neutrality of money.

In 1959 he married Rita Cohen and the couple had two children together.

Carlos Belo

*For their work toward a just and peaceful solution to the
conflict in East Timor.*

In painful times for the Timorese people he was the voice of those who had
no voice. Carlos Filipe Ximenes Belo, apostolic administrator of Dili, gave
hope and refuge to the Timorese, and with José Ramos-Horta, who battled
in exile for self-determination in East Timor, he received the 1996 Nobel
Peace Prize, a decisive step in mobilizing the support of the international
community.

In 1948 Ximenes Belo was born in Wailacama, and he lost his father
when he was only 2 years old. He attended Catholic schools in Baucau and
Ossu before entering the Dare minor seminary. He left East Timor for Portugal, and while
there he studied at the Salesian College in Estoril, and between 1974 and 1976, back in Timor,
he was a teacher in Fatumaca. In 1975 East Timor declared its independence from Portugal
but was invaded by Indonesia the same year; during the occupation Belo left his homeland
and studied theology at the Catholic University of Portugal for three years, concluding his
ecclesiastic studies in Rome.

In 1980 he was ordained a priest in Lisbon and returned to East Timor the following year.
He once again served as a teacher at the college in Fatumaca, known for its independent and
revolutionary atmosphere, and soon became its director. During this period Ximenes Belo
developed his powerful connection with youth and experienced first hand the pressure and
intimidation techniques used by the occupying Indonesian military forces.

In 1983, following the choice of the Indonesian ecclesiastic authorities, the Vatican nomi
nated him apostolic administrator of the Dili diocese. Five months after he had taken up his
new position Ximenes Belo denounced the Kraras massacre of 1983 during a sermon. As the
Catholic Church was the only institution capable of communicating with the outside world, the
new apostolic administrator of Dili began sending letters and establishing outside contacts.

At a time when the Indonesian occupation was relying increasingly on armed violence,
the Timorese were joining the Catholic Church in increasing numbers. In 1989, shortly
before Pope John Paul II's visit to Indonesia, Ximenes Belo wrote to the secretary-general of
the United Nations and asked for a referendum on East Timor, whose citizens were "dying as
a people and as a nation," be held.

In 1999, thanks in part to Ximenes Belo, Indonesia relinquished control of the country,
and on May 20, 2002, East Timor became the first new sovereign state of the 21st century.

José Ramos-Horta also received half of the prize.

Dario Fo

Who emulates the jesters of the Middle Ages in scourging authority and upholding the dignity of the downtrodden.

The Italian dramatist Dario Fo was born in San Giano, a town in the province of Varese, in 1926. During his childhood the family moved from town to town due to the requirements of his father's job as a stationmaster, but young Dario spent most of his holidays with his grandfather in the countryside. During these summers, Fo traveled the rural roads in a large wagon selling produce with his grandfather, who, to attract customers, told dramatic tales and local news, inspiring the young boy to pursue storytelling himself.

In 1940 the family settled in Luino, and Fo studied at the Brera Art Academy. Near the end of World War II he was conscripted to the army, but he managed to flee and hide for some months in an attic. His parents were both active in the Resistance, including smuggling Jewish scientists and escaped British prisoners into Switzerland. Fo later took come courses in architecture but abandoned the study when he felt a call to the theater. At this time he focused on scenery design but also started to improvise monologues based on the many stories he had heard during his childhood.

He sought out Franco Parenti in 1950 to show him a satirical parable of Cain and Abel he had written, and the Italian pianist and composer immediately invited him to join his company. It was some time later that he met the actress Franca Rame, who would become his constant companion in theater and in life. The couple was married in 1954 and has one child.

During the next decade Dario Fo experienced international success with such plays as *Archangels Don't Play Pinball* (1959), *Isabella, Three Tall Ships, and a Con Man* (1962) and *The Worker Knows 300 Words, the Boss 1,000, That's Why He's the Boss* (1969). In 1962 Dario Fo and Franca Rame wrote and directed the television show *Canzonissima*, which proved to be popular, but after a controversial sketch of a journalist killed by the mafia the couple received death threats and was placed under police protection.

This experience, however, marked just the first of many times that Fo and his family were persecuted. Unafraid to deal with contentious subjects, they have written plays about conflict in the Middle East, state corruption and abuses, Catholic birth control policies and, most recently, the war in Iraq. In 1973, when their theater company produced a play that criticized police, censorship increased, and in March of that year Franca Rame was abducted, tortured and raped by a fascist group commissioned by members of the Italian federal police. In 2006 their political activities culminated in Fo's unsuccessful campaign for mayor of Milan and Rame's successful campaign for the Italian senate.

Günter Grass

Whose frolicsome black fables portray the forgotten face of history.

Of German and Polish descent, Günter Wilhelm Grass was born in the former Free City of Danzig, Germany (now Gdansk, Poland), on October 16, 1927. With the 1959 publication of his critically acclaimed novel *The Tin Drum* he became the literary representative of the generation of Germans who grew up during the Nazi era.

His family owned a grocery store in Danzig, where he received his early education. Grass joined the Hitler Youth in the 1930s and, at the age of 16, was drafted into the German Army. In a 2006 interview he admitted to serving in the Waffen SS, a notorious elite combat unit with a particularly strong commitment to Nazi ideology, during World War II. In 1945 he was wounded and afterward imprisoned in Czechoslovakia.

Upon his release the next year he worked on farms, in mines and as a stonemason's apprentice. Grass entered the Düsseldorf Academy of Art in 1948, studied at the State Academy of Fine Arts in Berlin between 1953 and 1955 and made trips to France, Italy and Spain. At the end of the 1950s he moved to Paris, where he worked as a sculptor, graphic artist and writer. A few years earlier, in 1955, he had become a member of Group 47, the movement created to revitalize the German language after the harm it sustained from Nazi propaganda during the war.

Grass's first poems were published in 1956, and his first play was performed the following year. In 1959 he published *Die Blechtrommel (The Tin Drum)*, a satirical novel on German life in the first half of the century. Its international success was enormous, despite its controversial depictions of the Nazis, and a film version was produced in 1979. *Cat and Mouse* (1961) and *Dog Years* (1963) are its sequels and make up what has been called the Danzig Trilogy, since much of the stories take place in Grass's native city.

In the 1960s Günter Grass became interested in politics and was particularly active in supporting the Social Democrat Party and Willy Brandt, who served as the fourth chancellor of the Federal Republic of Germany. During the events leading up to the reunification of East and West Germany between 1989 and 1990, Grass advocated their continued separation for fear that a unified Germany would once again fall into its former nationalist and militant behavior. Later, much debate and criticism was aimed at *Ein weites Feld (Too Far Afield*, published in 1995), a novel set in East Germany in the years just before the fall of communism and the Berlin Wall. In *My Century* (1999) the author gives his perspective of the century year by year.

Nobel Laureates
1990-1999

1990

Nobel Prize in Physics
Jerome Isaac Friedman
Born March 28, 1930, in Chicago, Illinois, United States.
&
Henry Way Kendall
Born December 9, 1926, in Boston, Massachusetts, United States, and died February 15, 1999, in Wakulla Springs State Park, Florida.
&
Richard Edward Taylor
Born November 2, 1929, in Medicine Hat, Alberta, Canada.
For their pioneering investigations concerning deep inelastic scattering of electrons on protons and bound neutrons, which have been of essential importance for the development of the quark model in particle physics.

Nobel Prize in Chemistry
Elias James Corey
Born July 12, 1928, in Methuen, Massachusetts, United States.
For his development of the theory and methodology of organic synthesis.

Nobel Prize in Physiology or Medicine
Joseph Edward Murray
Born April 1, 1919, in Milford, Massachusetts, United States.
&
Edward Donnall Thomas
Born March 15, 1920, in Mart, Texas, United States.
For their discoveries concerning organ and cell transplantation in the treatment of human disease.

Nobel Prize in Literature
Octavio Paz
Born March 31, 1914, in Mexico City, Mexico, and died April 19, 1998, in Mexico City.
For impassioned writings with wide horizons, characterized by sensuous intelligence and humanistic integrity.

Nobel Peace Prize
Mikhail Sergeyevich Gorbachev
Born March 2, 1931, in Privolnoye, Union of Soviet Socialist Republics (now Russia).
For his leading role in the peace process which today characterizes important parts of the international community.

The Sveriges Riksbank Prize in Economic Sciences in Memory of Alfred Nobel
Harry Max Markowitz
Born August 24, 1927, in Chicago, Illinois, United States.
&
Merton Howard Miller
Born May 16, 1923, in Boston, Massachusetts, United States, and died June 3, 2000, in Chicago, Illinois.
&
William Forsyth Sharpe
Born June 16, 1934, in Boston, Massachusetts, United States.
For their pioneering work in the theory of financial economics.

1991

Nobel Prize in Physics
Pierre-Gilles de Gennes
Born October 24, 1932, in Paris, France, and died May 18, 2007, in Orsay.
For discovering that methods developed for studying order phenomena in simple systems can be generalized to more complex forms of matter, in particular to liquid crystals and polymers.

Nobel Prize in Chemistry
Richard Robert Ernst
Born August 14, 1933, in Winterthur, Switzerland.
For his contributions to the development of the methodology of high-resolution nuclear magnetic resonance (NMR) spectroscopy.

Nobel Prize in Physiology or Medicine
Erwin Neher
Born March 20, 1944, in Landsberg, Germany.
&
Bert Sakmann
Born June 12, 1942, in Stuttgart, Germany.
For their discoveries concerning the function of single
ion channels in cells.

Nobel Prize in Literature
Nadine Gordimer
Born November 20, 1923, in Springs, South Africa.
Who through her magnificent epic writing has — in the
words of Alfred Nobel — been of very great benefit to
humanity.

Nobel Peace Prize
Aung San Suu Kyi
Born June 19, 1945, in Rangoon, Burma (now Yangôn,
Myanmar).
For her nonviolent struggle for democracy and human
rights.

*The Sveriges Riksbank Prize in Economic
Sciences in Memory of Alfred Nobel*
Ronald Harry Coase
Born December 29, 1910, in Willesden, England.
For his discovery and clarification of the significance of
transaction costs and property rights for the institutional
structure and functioning of the economy.

1992

Nobel Prize in Physics
Georges Charpak
Born August 1, 1924, in Dabrovica, Poland.
For his invention and development of particle detectors,
in particular the multiwire proportional chamber.

Nobel Prize in Chemistry
Rudolph Arthur Marcus
Born July 21, 1923, in Montreal, Quebec, Canada.
For his contributions to the theory of electron transfer
reactions in chemical systems.

Nobel Prize in Physiology or Medicine
Edmond Henri Fischer
Born April 6, 1920, in Shanghai, China.
&
Edwin Gerhard Krebs
Born June 6, 1918, in Lansing, Iowa, United States.
For their discoveries concerning reversible protein
phosphorylation as a biological regulatory system.

Nobel Prize in Literature
Derek Walcott
Born January 23, 1930, in Castries, Saint Lucia.
For a poetic oeuvre of great luminosity, sustained by
a historical vision, the outcome of a multicultural
commitment.

Nobel Peace Prize
Rigoberta Menchú Tum
Born January 9, 1959, in Chimel, Guatemala.
In recognition of her work for social justice and
ethno-cultural reconciliation based on respect for
the rights of indigenous peoples.

*The Sveriges Riksbank Prize in Economic
Sciences in Memory of Alfred Nobel*
Gary Stanley Becker
Born December 2, 1930, in Pottsville, Pennsylvania,
United States.
For having extended the domain of microeconomic
analysis to a wide range of human behavior and
interaction, including nonmarket behavior.

1993

Nobel Prize in Physics
Russell Alan Hulse
Born November 28, 1950, in New York, New York,
United States.
&
Joseph Hooton Taylor, Jr.
Born March 29, 1941, in Philadelphia, Pennsylvania,
United States.
For the discovery of a new type of pulsar, a discovery
that has opened up new possibilities for the study of
gravitation.

Nobel Prize in Chemistry
Kary Banks Mullis
Born December 28, 1944, in Lenoir, North Carolina, United States.
For his invention of the polymerase chain reaction (PCR) method.
&
Michael Smith
Born April 26, 1932, in Blackpool, England, and died October 4, 2000, in Vancouver, British Columbia, Canada.
For his fundamental contributions to the establishment of oligonucleotide-based, site-directed mutagenesis and its development for protein studies.

Nobel Prize in Physiology or Medicine
Richard John Roberts
Born September 6, 1943, in Derby, England.
&
Phillip Allen Sharp
Born June 6, 1944, in Falmouth, Kentucky, United States.
For their discoveries of split genes.

Nobel Prize in Literature
Toni Morrison, née Chloe Anthony Wofford.
Born February 18, 1931, in Lorain, Ohio, United States.
Who in novels characterized by visionary force and poetic import, gives life to an essential aspect of American reality.

Nobel Peace Prize
Frederik Willem de Klerk
Born March 18, 1936, in Johannesburg, South Africa.
&
Nelson Rolihlahla Mandela
Born July 18, 1918, in Transkei, South Africa.
For their work for the peaceful termination of the apartheid regime, and for laying the foundations for a new democratic South Africa.

The Sveriges Riksbank Prize in Economic Sciences in Memory of Alfred Nobel
Robert William Fogel
Born July 1, 1926, in New York, New York, United States.
&

Douglass Cecil North
Born November 5, 1920, in Cambridge, Massachusetts, United States.
For having renewed research in economic history by applying economic theory and quantitative methods in order to explain economic and institutional change.

1994

Nobel Prize in Physics
Bertram Neville Brockhouse
Born July 15, 1918, in Lethbridge, Alberta, Canada, and died October 13, 2003, in Hamilton, Ontario.
For the development of neutron spectroscopy.
&
Clifford Glenwood Shull
Born September 23, 1915, in Pittsburgh, Pennsylvania, United States, and died March 31, 2001, in Medford, Massachusetts.
For the development of the neutron diffraction technique.

Nobel Prize in Chemistry
George Andrew Olah
Born May 22, 1927, in Budapest, Hungary.
For his contribution to carbocation chemistry.

Nobel Prize in Physiology or Medicine
Alfred Goodman Gilman
Born July 1, 1941, in New Haven, Connecticut, United States.
&
Martin Rodbell
Born December 1, 1925, in Baltimore, Maryland, United States, and died December 7, 1998, in Chapel Hill, North Carolina.
For their discovery of G-proteins and the role of these proteins in signal transduction in cells.

Nobel Prize in Literature
Kenzaburo Oe
Born January 31, 1935, in Shikoku, Japan.
Who with poetic force creates an imagined world, where life and myth condense to form a disconcerting picture of the human predicament today.

Nobel Peace Prize

Yasser Arafat, né Mohammed Abdel-Raouf Arafat as Qudwa al-Hussaeini
Born August 24, 1929, in Cairo, Egypt, and died November 11, 2004, in Paris, France.
&
Shimon Peres né Shimon Perski
Born August 16, 1923, in Wolozhyn, Poland (now Valozhyn, Belarus).
&
Yitzhak Rabin
Born March 1, 1922, in Jerusalem, Palestine (now Israel), and died November 4, 1995, in Tel Aviv, Israel.
For their efforts to create peace in the Middle East.

The Sveriges Riksbank Prize in Economic Sciences in Memory of Alfred Nobel

John Charles Harsanyi
Born May 29, 1920, In Budapest, Hungary, and died August 9, 2000, in Berkeley, California, United States.
&
John Forbes Nash, Jr.
Born June 13, 1928, in Bluefield, West Virginia, United States.
&
Reinhard Selten
Born October 10, 1930, in Breslau, Germany (now Wroclaw, Poland).
For their pioneering analysis of equilibria in the theory of noncooperative games.

1995

Nobel Prize in Physics

Martin Lewis Perl
Born June 24, 1927, in New York, New York, United States.
For the discovery of the tau lepton.
&
Frederick Reines
Born March 16, 1918, in Paterson, New Jersey, United States, and died August 26, 1998, in Orange, California.
For the detection of the neutrino.

Nobel Prize in Chemistry

Paul Josef Crutzen
Born December 3, 1933, in Amsterdam, Netherlands.
&
José Mario Molina Pasquel Henríquez
Born March 19, 1943, in Mexico City, Mexico.
&
Frank Sherwood Rowland
Born June 28, 1927, in Delaware, Ohio, United States.
For their work in atmospheric chemistry, particularly concerning the formation and decomposition of ozone.

Nobel Prize in Physiology or Medicine

Edward B. Lewis
Born May 20, 1918, in Wilkes-Barre, Pennsylvania, United States, and died July 21, 2004, in Pasadena, California.
&
Christiane Nüsslein-Volhard
Born October 20, 1942, in Magdeburg, Germany.
&
Eric F. Wieschaus
Born June 8, 1947, in South Bend, Indiana, United States.
For their discoveries concerning the genetic control of early embryonic development.

Nobel Prize in Literature

Seamus Justin Heaney
Born April 13, 1939, in Castlesàwson, Northern Ireland.
For works of lyrical beauty and ethical depth, which exalt everyday miracles and the living past.

Nobel Peace Prize

Pugwash Conferences on Science and World Affairs
Founded in 1957 in Pugwash, Nova Scotia, Canada.
&
Joseph Rotblat
Born November 4, 1908, in Warsaw, Poland, and died August 31, 2005, in London, England.
For their efforts to diminish the part played by nuclear arms in international politics and, in the longer run, to eliminate such arms.

The Sveriges Riksbank Prize in Economic Sciences in Memory of Alfred Nobel
Robert Emerson Lucas, Jr.
Born September 15, 1937, in Yakima, Washington, United States.
For having developed and applied the hypothesis of rational expectations, and thereby having transformed macroeconomic analysis and deepened our understanding of economic policy.

1996

Nobel Prize in Physics
David Morris Lee
Born January 20, 1931, in Rye, New York, United States.
&
Douglas Dean Osheroff
Born August 1, 1945, in Aberdeen, Washington, United States.
&
Robert Coleman Richardson
Born June 26, 1937, in Washington, DC, United States.
For their discovery of superfluidity in helium-3.

Nobel Prize in Chemistry
Robert Floyd Curl, Jr.
Born August 23, 1933, in Alice, Texas, United States.
&
Harold Walter Kroto
Born October 7, 1939, in Wisbech, England.
&
Richard Errett Smalley
Born June 6, 1943, in Akron, Ohio, United States, and died October 28, 2005, in Houston, Texas.
For their discovery of fullerenes.

Nobel Prize in Physiology or Medicine
Peter Charles Doherty
Born October 15, 1940, in Brisbane, Australia.
&
Rolf Martin Zinkernagel
Born January 6, 1944, in Riehen, Switzerland.
For their discoveries concerning the specificity of the cell mediated immune defense.

Nobel Prize in Literature
Wislawa Szymborska
Born July 2, 1923, in Kórnik, Poland.
For poetry that with ironic precision allows the historical and biological context to come to light in fragments of human reality.

Nobel Peace Prize
Carlos Filipe Ximenes Belo
Born February 3, 1948, in Wailacama, Portugal (now East Timor).
&
José Ramos-Horta
Born December 26, 1949, in Dili, Portugal (now East Timor)
For their work toward a just and peaceful solution to the conflict in East Timor.

The Sveriges Riksbank Prize in Economic Sciences in Memory of Alfred Nobel
James Alexander Mirrlees
Born July 5, 1936, in Minnigaff, Scotland.
&
William Vickrey
Born June 21, 1914, in Victoria, British Columbia, Canada, and died October 11, 1996, in Harrison, New York, United States.
For their fundamental contributions to the economic theory of incentives under asymmetric information.

1997

Nobel Prize in Physics
Steven Chu
Born February 28, 1948, in Saint Louis, Missouri, United States.
&
Claude Cohen-Tannoudji
Born April 1, 1933, in Constantine, Algeria.
&
William Daniel Phillips
Born November 5, 1948, in Wilkes-Barre, Pennsylvania, United States.
For the development of methods to cool and trap atoms with laser light.

Nobel Prize in Chemistry

Paul Delos Boyer

Born July 31, 1918, in Provo, Utah, United States.

&

John Ernest Walker

Born January 7, 1941, in Halifax, England.
For their elucidation of the enzymatic mechanism underlying the synthesis of adenosine triphosphate (ATP).

&

Jens Christian Skou

Born October 8, 1918, in Lemvig, Denmark.
For the first discovery of an ion-transporting enzyme, Na+, K+-ATPase.

Nobel Prize in Physiology or Medicine

Stanley Ben Prusiner

Born May 28, 1942, in Des Moines, Iowa, United States.
For his discovery of prions — a new biological principle of infection.

Nobel Prize in Literature

Dario Fo

Born 26th of March, 1926, in San Giano, Italy.
Who emulates the jesters of the Middle Ages in scourging authority and upholding the dignity of the downtrodden.

Nobel Peace Prize

International Campaign to Ban Landmines (ICBL)

Founded in October 1992.

&

Jody Williams

Born October 9, 1950, in Putney, Vermont, United States.
For their work for the banning and clearing of anti-personnel mines.

The Sveriges Riksbank Prize in Economic Sciences in Memory of Alfred Nobel

Robert Cox Merton

Born July 31, 1944, in New York, New York, United States.

&

Myron Samuel Scholes

Born July 1, 1941, in Timmins, Ontario, Canada.
For a new method to determine the value of derivatives.

1998

Nobel Prize in Physics

Robert Betts Laughlin

Born November 1, 1950, in Visalia, California, United States.

&

Horst Ludwig Störmer

Born April 6, 1949, in Frankfurt am Main, Germany.

&

Daniel Chee Tsui

Born February 28, 1939, in Henan province, China.
For their discovery of a new form of quantum fluid with fractionally charged excitations.

Nobel Prize in Chemistry

Walter Kohn

Born March 9, 1923, in Vienna, Austria.
For his development of the density-functional theory.

&

John Anthony Pople

Born October 31, 1925, in Burnham-on-Sea, England, and died March 15, 2004, in Chicago, Illinois, United States.
For his development of computational methods in quantum chemistry.

Nobel Prize in Physiology or Medicine

Robert Francis Furchgott

Born June 4, 1916, in Charleston, South Carolina, United States.

&

Louis Joseph Ignarro

Born May 31, 1941, in Brooklyn, New York, United States.

&

Ferid Murad

Born September 14, 1936, in Whiting, Indiana, United States.
For their discoveries concerning nitric oxid as a signaling molecule in the cardiovascular system.

Nobel Prize in Literature

José de Sousa Saramago

Born November 16, 1922, in Azinhaga, Portugal.
Who with parables sustained by imagination, compassion and irony continually enables us once again to apprehend an elusory reality.

Nobel Peace Prize
John Hume
Born January 18, 1937, in Londonderry, Northern Ireland.
&
William David Trimble
Born October 15, 1944, in Belfast, Northern Ireland.
For their efforts to find a peaceful solution to the conflict in Northern Ireland.

The Sveriges Riksbank Prize in Economic Sciences in Memory of Alfred Nobel
Amartya Kumar Sen
Born November 3, 1933, in Santiniketan, India.
For his contributions to welfare economics.

1999

Nobel Prize in Physics
Gerardus 't Hooft
Born July 5, 1946, in Den Helder, Netherlands.
&
Martinus Justinus Godefridus Veltman
Born June 27, 1931, in Waalwijk, Netherlands.
For elucidating the quantum structure of electroweak interactions in physics.

Nobel Prize in Chemistry
Ahmed Hassan Zewail
Born February 26, 1946, in Damanhur, Egypt.
For his studies of the transition states of chemical reactions using femtosecond spectroscopy.

Nobel Prize in Physiology or Medicine
Günter Blobel
Born May 21, 1936, in Waltersdorf, Germany.
For the discovery that proteins have intrinsic signals that govern their transport and localization in the cell.

Nobel Prize in Literature
Günter Wilhelm Grass
Born October 16, 1927, in Danzig, Germany (now Gdansk, Poland).
Whose frolicsome black fables portray the forgotten face of history.

Nobel Peace Prize
**Médecins Sans Frontières
(Doctors Without Borders)**
Founded in 1971 in Geneva, Switzerland.
In recognition of the organization's pioneering humanitarian work on several continents.

The Sveriges Riksbank Prize in Economic Sciences in Memory of Alfred Nobel
Robert Alexander Mundell
Born October 24, 1932, in Kingston, Ontario, Canada.
For his analysis of monetary and fiscal policy under different exchange-rate regimes and his analysis of optimum currency areas.

Selected Profiles of Nobel Laureates

2000–2007

Jack Kilby

For his part in the invention of the integrated circuit.

In 2000 the Nobel Prize in Physics was awarded to three scientists whose work contributed to new information technologies. The American Jack St. Clair Kilby was one of those honored — for having invented the integrated circuit, better known as the microchip, at the end of the 1950s. This work proved fundamental in the development of high-speed computers and digital memory systems. The Russian Zhores Alferov and the German Herbert Kroemer were also recognized for their work on semiconductor heterostuctures, which are widely used in high-speed electronics and fiber-optic networks.

He was born November 8, 1923, in Great Bend, Kansas, where his father ran a small electrical company. He applied to the Massachusetts Institute of Technology (MIT) but failed the entrance examination. He entered the University of Illinois, but his studies were interrupted by World War II, during which he served in the U.S. Army. In 1947, however, Kilby finally received his bachelor's degree in electrical engineering; a year later he married Barbara Annegers. He completed his master's at the University of Wisconsin in 1950. At the time he worked for Globe Union Inc. in Milwaukee, where he developed circuits for electrical products.

It was in the summer of 1958, however, that Jack Kilby made history. While employed at Texas Instruments in Dallas — with only borrowed or improvised equipment at his disposal — he designed and built the first electrical circuit in which all the active and passive components were made from a single piece of semiconductive material, which was the size of half of a paperclip. With the creation of this "microchip" Kilby was responsible for great advances in military, industrial and commercial technology. He led the team that created the first computers and military systems to incorporate integrated circuits and later helped create the pocket calculator and the thermal printer. In 1970 he interrupted his work at Texas Instruments to conduct research on the use of silicon technology to generate electrical energy from sunlight. That same year, long before being awarded the Nobel Prize in Physics, he was awarded the National Medal for Science during a ceremony at the White House.

Between 1978 and 1984 Kilby was a distinguished professor at Texas A&M University. In 1982 he was inducted into the National Inventors Hall of Fame, which includes the likes of Thomas Edison, Henry Ford and the Wright brothers. Two years later the Kilby International Award Foundation was named in his honor.

Thanks to Jack Kilby's contribution, microtechnology has become the basis of the majority of modern technology, from washing machines to personal computers and space probes. He died on June 20, 2005, after a brief battle with cancer and is survived by two daughters.

Zhores Ivanovich Alferov and Herbert Kroemer also each received a quarter of the prize.

Zhores Alferov

For developing semiconductor heterostructure technology.

The work of the physicist Zhores Ivanovich Alferov ushered in the development of such new technologies as fiber optics, CD players and bar codes, and he has improved the lives of many people around the world. A native of Vitebsk, which at the time of his birth in 1930 was a part of the USSR, Alferov was the son of a respected Red Army officer, and the family was moved all over the country during World War II.

After the end of the war Alferov focused on his studies and discovered a love of physics. In 1952 he graduated from the Electrotechnical Institute in Leningrad, and in the following years he worked at the Physio-Technical Institute of the renowned physicist Abram Fedorovich Ioffe. During this fruitful period he worked on a revolutionary semiconductor device used in Soviet atomic submarines and developed semiconductor heterostructure technology for devices including lasers, solar cells and transistors.

In 1969 he traveled to the United States for the first time and was warmly received by the academic community; over the next two years he worked at IBM, Bell Telephone and the University of Illinois laboratories. In 1970 Alferov received his doctorate degree in mathematical and physical sciences from the Ioffe Institute, USSR, and was later asked to be the director of the institute. Two years later he was appointed a member of the Academy of Sciences of the USSR (he later served as its vice president) and was awarded the Lenin Prize. He also served in the Russian Parliament, as a member of the Communist Party of the Russian Federation, and over the years has lobbied for increased financial investment in physics and other fields to prevent scientists from emigrating.

His career reached its high point in 2000, when he was awarded the Nobel Prize in Physics for his work on semiconductor heterostuctures, now widely used in high-speed electronics and fiber-optic networks. The honor was of special significance to Alferov because no Soviet physicist had received the Nobel Prize since 1978, when Pyotr Kapitsa was the laureate. Over the following years he created more than 50 inventions connected to semiconductor technology. Other awards he has received include the Ballantyne Medal from the Franklin Institute in 1971, the USSR State Prize in 1984 and the Kyoto Prize in 2001. He has also been nominated an associate foreign member of the American National Academy of Engineering and the National Academy of Sciences.

Zhores Alferov married Tamara Darskaya and the couple has a son.

Jack St. Clair Kilby also received half of the prize, and Herbert Kroemer received a quarter of the prize.

V.S. Naipaul

For having united perceptive narrative and incorruptible scrutiny in works that compel us to see the presence of suppressed histories.

Vidiadhar Surajprasad Naipaul was born in Changuanas, Trinidad and Tobago, in 1932 to an immigrant family from the north of India. Naipaul moved to England at the age of 18 and attended the University of Oxford on a scholarship. During his time at Oxford he met Patricia Hale, and two years after he received his bachelor's degree in 1953 the couple was married. His wife passed away in 1996, and he has since married Nadira Khannum Alvi, a Pakistani journalist.

Except for a period in the 1950s when he worked as a freelance journalist and broadcaster for the BBC, Naipaul has always been a dedicated novelist and sometime short-story and nonfiction author. He is principally a cosmopolitan writer, mostly because of his heritage. His works evoke a sense of unhappiness about the cultural and spiritual poverty in Trinidad, a complete alienation toward India and an inability to relate to and identify with the traditional values of England, what was once a great colonizing power.

The events of his early works take place in the West Indies. A few years after the publication of his first book, *The Mystic Masseur* (1957), came what many consider to be his best work, *A House for Mr. Biswas* (1961). Largely autobiographical, the story is about Mohun Biswas, a character based on his father, who is in search of his true self and a house he can call his own. Naipaul then widened the social and geographical perspective of his writing to pessimistically describe the impact of colonialism and emerging nationalism in the Third World, particularly in *Guerrillas* (1975) and *A Bend in the River* (1979), which prompted the New York Times to declare "V.S. Naipaul is one of the handful of living writers of whom the English language can be proud."

The novels *The Enigma of Arrival* (1987) and *A Way in the World* (1994) are also largely autobiographical. In the first, Naipaul describes the inner conflicts of a character who identifies more with the metropolis where he lives than the colony where he was born. In *A Way in the World*, a mixture of fiction, memoir and history, Naipaul presents nine independent but interconnected stories in which Caribbean and Indian traditions are combined, an occurrence the author first noticed when he moved to England. In his nonfiction and travel books — such as *The Middle Passage* (1962), for which he received a travel grant from the Trinidad government, and *In India: A Million Mutinies Now* (1990) — Naipaul shares his impressions of the lands of his early youth and those of his ancestors.

Besides the Nobel Prize in Literature, V.S. Naipaul received Booker Prize in 1971 and the T.S. Eliot Prize for Creative Writing in 1986. In 1990 he was knighted by Queen Elizabeth II, and he is generally regarded as the leading English-speaking novelist of the Caribbean.

Kofi Annan

For their work in favor of a better organized, more peaceful world.

Born on April 8, 1938, in Kumasi, Ghana, Annan came from one of the most elite families in his nation: both of his grandfathers and one of his uncles were tribal chiefs. In 1954 the young Kofi Annan was sent to Mfantsipim, a prestigious Methodist boarding school, and during these foundational years he reported learning "that suffering anywhere concerns people everywhere."

Annan went on to study economics at Kumasi College of Science and Technology in his native city, then with a Ford Foundation grant he entered MacAlester College in Saint Paul, Minnesota, from which he graduated in 1961. He joined the United Nations the next year, working for the World Health Organization (WHO), a division of the UN in Geneva, then served with the UN Economic Commission for Africa in 1965.

Returning to his homeland Annan held the post of director of tourism in Ghana between 1974 and 1976. He then went back to the UN, and in New York he took on important positions in human resources (1987–1990), finance (1990–1992) and peacekeeping (1992–1996). The Rwanda genocide occurred while Annan was head of peacekeeping operations, and he was severely criticized by former Canadian General Roméo Dallaire for his passive response to the crisis.

As the UN secretary-general from January 1, 1997, to December 31, 2006), Kofi Annan played a significant part in resolving very delicate political situations. In 1998 he was successful in efforts to make Saddam Hussein accept the return of weapons inspectors to Iraq and oversaw the transfer to civic power in Nigeria. In 1999 he helped resolve the tension between Libya and the international community and organized a response to the violence of the occupying Indonesian forces in East Timor. In 2000 Annan broached the particularly sensitive issue of the Middle East, securing Israel's withdrawal from the south of Lebanon, which was an important step toward peace in the region.

Preserving the environment, the fight against AIDS (which Annan described as "a personal priority") and the fight against poverty and for women's rights in Arab and Muslim countries were some of his other major concerns while in office. In 2005 his *In Larger Freedom* report outlined numerous progressive reforms he desired to see occur to make the UN more effective.

After retiring as secretary-general, Kofi Annan led the new Alliance for a Green Revolution in Africa, was president of the Global Humanitarian Forum and headed a panel to negotiate an end to violence after the 2008 Kenyan elections. In addition to the Nobel Prize he has received numerous honors, including an honorary knighthood by Queen Elizabeth II and the MacArthur Foundation Award for International Justice in 2007.

The United Nations also received half of the prize.

Koichi Tanaka

For their development of soft desorption ionization methods for mass spectrometric analyses of biological macromolecules.

The birth of Koichi Tanaka on August 3, 1959, was followed shortly by the death of his mother. As his father was also in poor health he was raised by an aunt and uncle, who treated him as their own son. In fact, the circumstances of his birth were kept secret from him throughout his childhood. He remembers that he was given values by examples not words: "I have no memory of my parents encouraging me with words like 'study' or 'succeed.' There is no doubt, however, that the values they instilled in me were much more important than those suggested by these words. From my father I learned the importance of working sincerely at the things to which I had committed myself... my mother stressed the importance of working quietly toward achieving my missions in life, without neglecting attention to details."

Although not a particularly dedicated student in his youth, Expo 70, the first world fair held in Japan, had a major impact on him. The exposition showed the future of technology and what life would be like in the coming decades: "I really felt the power of science and technology," he admits, and he committed himself to being a part of that future. In 1978, by then at the top of his class, he entered the Department of Electrical Engineering at Tohoku University. Tanaka found out the truth about his parents during the application process, as it was necessary to register his background officially.

On finishing his studies Tanaka faced the difficult task of finding a good job in Japan. His first attempt was at an electronics company, but he failed the compulsory exam. At the time he decided to expand his focus beyond electrical engineering and, with the support of his mentor, Professor Adachi, he obtained work at the Shimadzu Corporation in 1983. It was in this privileged environment, while focusing on X-ray devices and medical equipment, that he was able to carry out much of the work that earned him the 2002 Nobel Prize in Chemistry.

In 1992 he was temporarily transferred to Kratos Analytical Ltd., a subsidiary company of Shimadzu Corporation, located in Manchester, England. Between 1997 and 2002 Tanaka was posted once again to the United Kingdom.

Yuko Ikegami, a woman from Tanaka's native prefecture, managed to win over the scientist, despite his shyness, and the couple married in 1995.

John Bennett Fenn also received a quarter of the prize and Kurt Wüthrich received half of the prize.

Daniel Kahneman

For having integrated insights from psychological research into economic science, especially concerning human judgment and decision making under uncertainty.

Daniel Kahneman was born to Lithuanian Jewish parents on March 5, 1934, in Tel Aviv, in what is now Israel, while his mother was visiting relatives there. The family had immigrated to France at the beginning of the 1920s, and Kahneman spent most of his childhood in Paris. With the German invasion of 1940, however, the family faced financial ruin, and Kahneman's father, chief of research at a chemical factory, was interned for six weeks in a way station to a concentration camp, before the intervention of the firm secured his release; the family afterward fled to central France.

When asked why he became a psychologist, Kahneman told the following story:

> It must have been late 1941 or early 1942. Jews were required to wear the Star of David and to obey a 6 p.m. curfew. I had gone to play with a Christian friend and had stayed too late. I turned my brown sweater inside out to walk the few blocks home. As I was walking down an empty street, I saw a German soldier approaching. He was wearing the black uniform that I had been told to fear more than any other — the one worn by specially recruited SS soldiers. As I came closer to him, trying to walk fast, I noticed that he was looking at me intently. Then he beckoned me over, picked me up and hugged me. I was terrified he would notice the star inside my sweater. He was speaking to me with great emotion in German. When he put me down, he opened his wallet, showed me a picture of a boy and gave me some money. I went home more certain than ever that my mother was right: people were endlessly complicated and interesting.

In 1946, after the liberation, the family moved to Palestine, where Kahneman received his bachelor's degree in psychology and mathematics at Hebrew University in Jerusalem. In 1954 he served in the Israel Defense Force, mainly in its psychology department. Four years later he moved to the United States, and there he completed his studies in psychology at the University of California, Berkeley, in 1961.

In 2002 he became the first Israeli to win the Nobel Prize in Economics. He is recognized today as the founder of behavioral economics, a branch of study that uses scientific research on human biases, both emotional and social, to understand how financial decisions are made. Since 1978 Kahneman has been married to Anne Treisman, a noted English psychologist who also works at Princeton, and the couple has published several papers together.

Vernon Lomax Smith also received half of the prize.

The Sveriges Riksbank Prize in Economic Sciences in Memory of Alfred Nobel 2002

Jimmy Carter

For his decades of untiring effort to find peaceful solutions to international conflicts, to advance democracy and human rights, and to promote economic and social development.

Jimmy Carter has diligently worked throughout his life to resolve conflicts, promote democracy, improve education, protect human rights and prevent disease. It is for these efforts that in 2002 he became the third American president, after Theodore Roosevelt and Woodrow Wilson, to receive the Nobel Peace Prize.

James Earl Carter, Jr., was born the first of four children on October 1, 1924, in the small town of Plains, Georgia, where he later attended the local school. He came from a long line of Georgia farmers, but his father was also a prominent business owner in the community, and his mother was a registered nurse. Carter distinguished himself academically from an early age, and he went on to study at Georgia Southwestern College and the Georgia Institute of Technology before receiving his bachelor's degree from the United States Naval Academy in 1946. He married Rosalynn Smith the same year, and the couple went on to have four children together.

Carter then served in the Atlantic and Pacific fleets with the U.S. Navy, and he is the only president to have fought in the Korean War. He was particularly interested in the fledgling nuclear submarine program and did postgraduate work in nuclear physics at Union College. Carter's goal was to eventually rise to chief of Naval Operation, but he resigned his commission in July 1953, upon his father's death.

Returning to Georgia he took control of the family's farming business and became a leader in the community, working on education and health boards. A devout Baptist, Carter has always professed the importance of his faith and has served as a Sunday school teacher for most of his life. His involvement in politics deepened, and on January 12, 1971, almost 10 years after being voted to the Georgia Senate, he became the 76th governor of the state. During his term in office he declared that discrimination had no future in Georgia and was one of the first governors in the Deep South to take a public stance against racial inequality. Although he was not well known nationally, Carter announced he was running for the presidency of the United States and overcame all odds to be nominated on the first ballot by the 1976 Democratic National Convention. He was elected the 39th president of the United States on November 2, 1976.

Jimmy Carter's term of office between January 20, 1977, and January 20, 1981, was marked by a series of foreign-affairs successes, including the treaty that relinquished U.S. sovereignty over the Panama Canal, the Camp David Accords signed by Egypt and Israel, the second Strategic Arms Limitations Talks (SALT II) disarmament agreement signed with the

Soviet Union and the reestablishment of diplomatic relations with the People's Republic of China. Domestically, Carter's administration was responsible for creating the Departments of Energy and Education, deregulating the energy, transportation, communication and finance industries and protecting more than 100 million acres (404,685 sq. km) of Alaskan wilderness. Despite this work, several major crises occurred during his presidency, including serious fuel shortages, high inflation, the failed rescue attempt of hostages at the American embassy in Iran and the invasion of Afghanistan by the Soviet Union.

Republican Ronald Reagan beat Carter in the 1980 elections, but this setback did not signal an end to his influence. He returned to Georgia, established the Carter Center to promote human rights and health in 1982 and began a prolific writing career, having published more than two dozen books to date. He and the Carter Center have offered their services to mediate in conflicts in Ethiopia and Eritrea (1989), North Korea (1994), Liberia (1994), Haiti (1994), Bosnia (1994), Sudan (1995), Greater Lagos (1995–1996), Uganda (1999) and Venezuela (2002–2003). The center has also been involved in observing and supervising more than 50 elections in Africa, Asia and Central and South America. Carter remains active and vocal in current politics; in 2007 he joined, with Nelson Mandela, a new humanitarian organization known as The Elders, and he continues to criticize the war in Iraq, the existence of Guantanamo Bay detention center in Cuba and Israel's policies in Gaza, the West Bank and Lebanon.

Both Jimmy Carter and his wife dedicate one week every year to Habitat for Humanity, helping needy people in America and around the world renovate and build their own homes. In a 1991 interview at the Academy of Achievement he explained why it is difficult for us to understand those less fortunate than ourselves: "We care in general about homelessness, or drug addiction, or school dropouts, but we don't know a homeless person, and we don't know a drug addict, and we don't know a school dropout or a teenage pregnant woman. This is not a deliberate discrimination, it's a discrimination by default. We tend to build a plastic bubble around ourselves so that we only have to associate with people just like us."

Besides the Nobel Carter has received dozens of prestigious honors, including the Martin Luther King, Jr., Nonviolent Peace Prize in 1979, the Albert Schweitzer Prize for Humanitarianism in 1987, the Philadelphia Liberty Medal in 1990, the United Nations Human Rights Award in 1998 and the Presidential Medal of Freedom in 1999. He has also received honorary degrees from Oxford, Brown, the University of Pennsylvania, Bates College and many other institutions.

Shirin Ebadi

For her efforts for democracy and human rights. She has focused especially on the struggle for the rights of women and children.

Shirin Ebadi, who in 1974 became the first female Iranian judge, is a human rights activist for whom there is no incompatibility between Islam and a modern, open and just society. She was the 11th woman to receive the Nobel Peace Prize, and the first Muslim woman to win a Nobel Prize in any category.

Born in Hamadan, northern Iran, in 1947, Ebadi grew up in a practicing Muslim family; her father was a lecturer in commercial law and the author of several books. The family moved to Tehran when Ebadi was a year old, and she has remained in the capital ever since. In 1965 she entered the Faculty of Law at the University of Tehran, and became a judge in March 1969.

Ebadi held various positions within the Justice Department, but following the February 1979 victory of the Islamists in the Iranian Revolution, it became official policy that "the legal profession was incompatible with the overly emotional nature of women." Female judges were dismissed, and although they were offered titular positions, Ebadi decided to apply for early retirement in protest. During the following years she published several books and articles in Iranian journals.

The judiciary had been managing the Bar Association since the revolution, and while Ebadi's first application for a lawyer's license was turned down, she was finally granted one in 1992 and established her own practice. She also lectures at the University of Tehran and promotes democracy and liberalization as the solution to many of the problems facing Iranian society today. She continues to fight for the status of women and children in a patriarchal society, leads the Association for Support of Children's Rights and is working to revoke Iranian laws on divorce and succession, which heavily discriminate against women. Nevertheless, she insists that "the fight for human rights is conducted in Iran by the Iranian people, and we are against any foreign intervention."

As a lawyer and activist Ebadi has been involved in many controversial cases, which have led to her being detained, prevented from practicing law for long periods of time and even physically threatened. She explains, "any person who fights for human rights in Iran must live in fear from birth to death, but I have learnt to overcome my fear"; she has also inspired many young people to take a similar stance.

She is a member of the Center for the Defense of Human Rights, which continues to give legal support to the families of intellectuals, journalist and students arrested for their opinions. In addition to the 2003 Nobel Peace Prize, Ebadi received awards from Human Rights Watch in 1996 and the Thorolf Rafto Foundation for Human Rights in Norway in 2001.

Irwin Rose

For the discovery of ubiquitin-mediated protein degradation.

At the age of 78 Irwin Rose was awarded the 2004 Nobel Prize in Chemistry, which he shared with two Israeli colleagues, Aaron Ciechanover and Avram Hershko. Their research, which was begun in the 1970s and mostly carried out in Rose's laboratory in the Fox Chase Cancer Center in Philadelphia, has led to a better understanding of the role of ubiquitin, a chemical marker that is present in all situations of protein degradation by cells. These researchers opened the way for developing more efficient treatments of diseases such as leukemia and cystic fibrosis.

Rose was born in Brooklyn, New York, on July 16, 1926, and demonstrated a remarkable aptitude for sciences from a very early age. He studied for a year at Washington State College before serving as a radio technician with the U.S. Navy during World War II. After peace had been established Rose completed his undergraduate studies. He went on to receive his doctorate degree in 1952 from the College of Chicago, where he had also earned his master's degree when only 26 years old.

He was a member of the Department of Biochemistry at the highly respected Yale Medical School between 1954 and 1963. However, Rose left Yale to begin what would be a long and productive career at the Fox Chase Cancer Center. The center was amalgamated with the American Oncologic Hospital, which was founded in 1904 and was the first institution in America dedicated to cancer patients. The Fox Chase Cancer Center has been responsible for the discovery of vitamin B12, the hepatitis B virus and numerous other scientific discoveries, besides the work done there on the role of ubiquitin. Rose remained connected to the institution until 1995.

In 1979, with a clearly defined career and peer recognition, Rose was elected to the National Academy of Sciences. As part of his research he has also worked in the Department of Medicine at Case-Western Reserve University in Cleveland and the Department of Pharmacology at the New York University.

The love of science is also shared by his wife, the biochemist Zelda Budenstein Rose, who completed her doctorate in 1955, the same year the couple married. Although they both have independent careers, Zelda accompanied her husband to Yale and the Fox Chase Cancer Center. The couple has four children together.

Aaron Ciechanover and Avram Hershko also each received a third of the prize.

Elfriede Jelinek

For her musical flow of voices and counter-voices in novels and plays that, with extraordinary linguistic zeal, reveal the absurdity of society's clichés and their subjugating power.

Novelist, dramatist, essayist and translator, Elfriede Jelinek was awarded the 2004 Nobel Prize in Literature but viewed it as "an enormous personal burden" for having brought her international recognition. She suffers from both agoraphobia and social phobia, anxiety disorders that often prevent her from even leaving her home in Austria. Jelinek sent a video message to the award ceremony instead of attending in person, relating that "I would also very much like to be in Stockholm, but I cannot move as fast and far as my language." She was also reluctant to accept the award because she considers that "when a woman wins a prize, she also receives it for the fact that she is a woman and cannot be limitless in her joy." There was also widespread debate over her selection for the award and Knut Ahnlund left the Swedish Academy, which awards the Nobel Prize in Literature, in protest, declaring her work as "whining, unenjoyable public pornography" and "a mass of text shoveled together without artistic structure." Members of the academy are elected for life so his seat will remain empty until his death.

Elfriede Jelinek was born in Mürzzuschlag, Austria, in 1946; her father was a Jewish chemist of Czech origin who only escaped Nazi persecution because he worked in a strategic wartime industry, and her mother came from an elite Viennese family. Many of Jelinek's relatives, however, were not so fortunate and perished at the hands of the Nazis during World War II.

Although her mother hoped she would follow a musical career and had her study several instruments and even graduate from the Viennese Conservatory with an organist diploma, Jelinek felt called to a different vocation. She studied both art history and drama at the University of Vienna but withdrew from her studies due to her anxiety disorders. Literature, however, allowed her to exercise her talents without direct contact with society and *Lisas Schatten*, her first volume of poetry, appeared in 1967. Jelinek lived first in Rome and then Berlin in the following years, and in 1974 she was married to Gottfried Hüngsberg, after which the couple divided their time between Austria and Germany.

Her work is known for its focus on female sexuality and themes of abuse, aggression and the struggle for power; her later novels and plays deal with social criticism and Austria's inability to acknowledge its Nazi past. English translations of her novels include *The Piano Teacher* (1988), *Lust* (1992), *Women as Lovers* (1994) and *Greed* (2007).

Robert Aumann

For having enhanced our understanding of conflict and cooperation through game-theory analysis.

Robert John Aumann was born into an orthodox Jewish family in Frankfurt on June 8, 1930. In 1938 they abandoned their successful textile business and immigrated to the United States in fear of Nazi persecution.

After attending the Rabbi Jacob Joseph yeshiva school in New York City, Robert Aumann earned his bachelor's degree in mathematics from City College of New York in 1950. Two years later he received his master's from the Massachusetts Institute of Technology (MIT), where he first met John Nash, famed economist and Nobel laureate, and in 1955 completed his doctorate there. During the following years Aumann worked for the Analytical Research Group connected to the Department of Mathematics at Princeton University, and during this time he further studied Nash's work on game theory.

Aumann became an instructor at the Hebrew University of Jerusalem in the fall of 1956 and has remained with the institution ever since. Most of his work has been dedicated to game theory, which seeks to mathematically understand human behavior in strategic situations, whether political, militaristic or economic. Aumann wrote his doctoral dissertation on knot theory, then a more obscure branch of mathematics, which is now employed to help understand the actions of enzymes and DNA. He has also served as a visiting professor at Yale, Stanford and New York University, among others.

Known for his particularly joyful character, Aumann explained his philosophy of life in his Nobel biography: "science is exploration — exploration for the sake of exploration, and for nothing else. We must go where our curiosity leads us, we must go where we want to go. And eventually, it is sure to lead us to the beautiful, the important, and the useful... For me, life has been — and still is — one tremendous joyride, one magnificent tapestry. There have been bad — very bad — times, like when my son Shlomo was killed and when my wife Esther died. But even these somehow integrate into the magnificent tapestry."

Besides the Nobel Prize Aumann received the Harvey Prize in Science and Technology from the Israel Institute of Technology in 1983, the Israel Prize in Economics in 1994, the Erwin Plein Nemmers Prize in Economics from Northwestern University in 1998 and the Von Neumann Prize in Operations Research Theory in 2005. He is also a member of the American Academy of Arts and Sciences, the National Academy of Sciences, the Israel Academy of Sciences and Humanities and the British Academy, and he has received honorary doctorates from several universities.

Thomas Crombie Schelling also received half of the prize.

The Sveriges Riksbank Prize in Economic Sciences in Memory of Alfred Nobel 2005

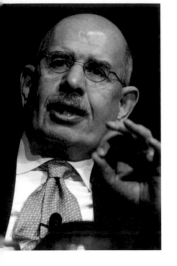

Mohamed ElBaradei

For their efforts to prevent nuclear energy from being used for military purposes and to ensure that nuclear energy for peaceful purposes is used in the safest possible way.

Mohamed ElBaradei was born in Cairo, Egypt, in 1942 and spent his early childhood in that city. His father was a respected lawyer who headed the Egyptian Bar Association and often opposed the policies of the dictatorship of the time. ElBaradei credits his father's work for peace and humanitarian rights as very influential in his own career; in a 2006 Academy of Achievement interview he explained: "I wanted to have a world where people are free to express their views, to have freedom of worship, to have freedom from want, and I saw poverty in Egypt when I grew up. To me, freedom, in the larger sense — to be able to speak, to worship, free from want, free from fear — I think it was a key as to what I thought I would like to do when I grow up."

He distinguished himself academically from an early age and, following in his father's footsteps, entered the University of Cairo, from which he received his law degree in 1962. Two years later ElBaradei entered the Egyptian diplomatic service and was assigned to oversee his country's United Nations missions. During these years he was involved in political and legal affairs but also had his first experience dealing with arms control issues. He concurrently studied at New York University School of Law and earned his doctorate in international law in 1974.

ElBaradei was then appointed special assistant to the Foreign Minister of Egypt and until 1978 served under President Anwar al-Sadat, who abandoned Egypt's close relations with the Soviet Union in exchange for closeness with Western nations. He also worked toward peace with Israel, and during the Camp David peace talks ElBaradei was part of the negotiating team that finally settled on a specific agreement. In 1980 ElBaradei became a senior fellow at the United Nations, in charge of its International Law Program, and between 1981 and 1987 he served as a professor in the same subject at New York University.

He is best known today, however, for his work with the United Nation's International Atomic Energy Agency (IAEA), which he began in 1984. ElBaradei was sent to Iraq in the wake of the Persian Gulf War to destroy the country's nuclear weapons program, and in 1997 he was chosen as the organization's director general for external relations. Saddam Hussein expelled weapons inspectors from his country the following year, but ElBaradei was confident that the IAEA's work had completely destroyed Iraq's nuclear weapons program. After the terrorist attacks on September 11, 2001, he was forced to deal with American insistence that Iraq was pursuing its program once more, but he dismissed key submitted evidence as forgeries before the United Nations Security Counsel. Some have seen his selection for the 2005 Nobel Peace Prize, which he shared with the International Atomic Energy Agency, as a protest to the Bush administration's Iraq policies.

Currently serving his third term as director general of the IAEA, ElBaradei is responsible for ensuring that all UN member-states enjoy the benefits of new science and technology while imposing safeguards that will prevent the proliferation of nuclear weapons. He has also been successful in encouraging the peaceful use of nuclear technology, specifically in radiation therapy, which is being made available to less developed countries around the world. In his interview with the Academy for Achievement he went on to explain that: "We cannot erect walls between the north and the south, between the rich and the poor. We need to make sure that we have an equitable world, where every human being has the right to live a decent life, the right to live a life free from fear, the right to be able to send his kids to have education, the right to have Social Security in their old age. If you do that, I think the insecurities we feel — the extremists that we are seeing — will drop absolutely dramatically."

In addition to the Nobel Prize Mohamed ElBaradei has received the International Four Freedoms Award from the Roosevelt Institute, the Golden Plate Award from the Academy of Achievement, the Human Security Award from the Muslim Public Affairs Council and the Golden Dove of Peace Prize from the president of Italy. He belongs to the International Law Association, the American Society of International Law and has been granted honorary degrees by a dozen universities.

He is married to Aida Elkachef, an early childhood education teacher, and the couple has two children; their daughter, Laila, is currently practicing law. ElBaradei and his wife reside in Geneva, Switzerland.

The International Atomic Energy Agency (IAEA) also received half of the prize.

Al Gore

For their efforts to build up and disseminate greater knowledge about man-made climate change, and to lay the foundations for the measures that are needed to counteract such change.

Albert Arnold Gore, Jr., was born on March 31, 1948 in Washington, DC. His father was a U.S. congressman from 1939 to 1953 and a senator between 1953 and 1971, while his mother, Pauline LaFon Gore, was one of the first female graduates from Vanderbilt University Law School. Gore's family lived most of the year in a hotel in Washington, but during the summer they returned to their large farm in Carthage, Tennessee.

After distinguishing himself at the prestigious preparatory St. Albans School in Washington, Gore entered Harvard University. Studying government, he graduated cum laude in June 1969 after defending a senior thesis on the impact of television on the conduct of a president. Although he opposed the Vietnam War and could have used the influence of friends to avoid service, Gore felt a civic duty to be involved in some way, so he enlisted in the U.S. Army on August 7, 1969. He was first assigned as a military journalist at Fort Dix, and during this time he married Mary Elizabeth "Tipper" Aitcheson; the couple went on to have four children. On January 2, 1971, however, Gore was sent to Vietnam where he served with the 20th Engineer Brigade.

Upon his return he studied journalism and theology at Vanderbilt University and worked part time at *The Tennessean* newspaper. After a year he decided to turn full time to journalism but then attended law school between 1974 and 1976, when he abruptly, and without finishing his degrees, decided to run for a seat in the U.S. House of Representatives. After narrowly winning the Democratic primary Gore thereafter ran unopposed, and at the age of 28 he was successfully elected.

He was reelected in 1978, 1980 and 1982, and in 1984 he ran successfully for a seat in the U.S. Senate. He was extremely active on a number of fronts during the next nine years, but he is particularly remembered for introducing what would later be passed as the High Performance Computing Act of 1991, regarded as a key moment in the history of the internet, and his opposition to the Gulf War.

In 1993 Gore became the 45th vice president of the United States, serving under President Bill Clinton for two terms until 2001. During this time he is credited with developing what he referred to as the information superhighway and contributing to decision making that resulted in economic expansion and low unemployment. He made his first run for the presidency itself in 1988 but eventually dropped out of the race; in 2000 Gore was the Democratic nominee but ultimately lost to the Republican candidate, George W. Bush, but not before a legal debate over the Florida election recount that had to be settled by the Supreme Court. Despite widespread encouragement he was a candidate in neither the 2004 nor 2008 elections, but he has not ruled out the possibility of future political involvement.

According to *The Concord Monitor*: "Gore was one of the first politicians to grasp the seriousness of climate change and to call for a reduction in emissions of carbon dioxide and other greenhouses gases. He held the first congressional hearings on the subject in the late 1970s." His 2006 Academy-Award-winning documentary *An Inconvenient Truth*, which presents evidence of a trend of global warming and its dire consequences, has become the fourth highest grossing documentary in American history and standard viewing in many classrooms. In 2007 he shared the Nobel Peace Prize with the Intergovernmental Panel on Climate Change (IPCC), led by Rajendra K. Pachauri; the IPCC aims to provide decision makers and the world at large with an objective source of information about climate change.

Al Gore has received numerous honors in addition to the Nobel Prize including the Sir David Attenborough Award for Excellence in Nature Filmmaking (2007), a Primetime Emmy Award for Outstanding Creative Achievement in Interactive Television (2007), the Gothenburg Prize for Sustainable Development (2007) and the Dan David Prize for Social Responsibility with Particular Emphasis on the Environment (2008).

Gore also sits on the board for Current TV and Apple Inc., is chairman of Generation Investment Management and an unofficial advisor to Google's senior management. He taught at four universities in 2001, was elected a fellow of the American Academy of Arts and Sciences in 2007 and that same year published his book *The Assault on Reason*, an analysis of electronic media's influence on the marketplace of ideas and its threat to American democracy.

The Intergovernmental Panel on Climate Change (IPCC) also received half of the prize.

Doris Lessing

That epicist of the female experience, who with skepticism, fire and visionary power has subjected a divided civilization to scrutiny.

Doris May Taylor, later Lessing, was born in Kermanshah, Persia, now Iran, in 1919. She spent her early childhood there, where her British-born father worked as a bank clerk. The family made a brief move to Tehran, but in the mid 1920s they spent their life savings on a remote maize farm in Southern Rhodesia, now Zimbabwe. Although the farm failed financially, young Doris enjoyed the wilderness of the landscape and the wildlife that surrounded them. At the age of 13 she dropped out of an all-girls high school in the Rhodesian capital of Salisbury, and two years later she left home and supported herself as a nursemaid.

Although she had no further formal education, Lessing developed intellectually through voracious reading. She moved to Salisbury, where she worked as a telephone operator, in 1937. At the age of 19 she married Frank Wisdom, a civil servant, and the couple had two children together. The marriage, however, dissolved, as she felt that she was becoming trapped in a role that would destroy her, and the two were divorced in 1943.

Soon drawn to politics, she joined the Communist Party of Southern Rhodesia and at a reading group met Gottfried Lessing, a German political activist; they were soon married and had a son together. This period of her life is reflected on in *A Ripple from the Storm* (1958), part of the five-volume series *Children of Violence*. This second marriage failed as well, however, and Lessing then made a permanent move to England with her youngest child in 1949. She also brought with her the manuscript for her first novel, which was published as *The Grass Is Singing* in 1950. Building on its success she supported herself from then on by writing. Her work is largely autobiographical, and she draws heavily from her African experiences.

Following the *Children of Violence* series Lessing wrote *The Golden Notebook* (1962), a narrative experiment that brilliantly reveals the multiple selves of a contemporary woman. In the coming decades she also began to explore inner mysticism, best demonstrated in her 1971 novel *Briefing for a Descent into Hell*, and she also wrote science fiction, such as *Mara and Dann* (1999). Other novels, such as *African Laughter* (1992), deal with later visits to Africa.

Besides the Nobel Prize Lessing has also received the Shakespeare Prize in 1982, the W.H. Smith Literary Award in 1986 and the Palermo Prize in 1987. She turned down an offer to become a Dame of the British Empire because she has always criticized colonialism and the notion of the British Empire. She did, however, accept the title Companion of Honour.

Paul Krugman

For his analysis of trade patterns and location of economic activity.

Paul Krugman was born February 28, 1953, in Albany, New York, and grew up on Long Island. His interest in economics developed at a young age and by 1974 he had graduated with his bachelor's degree from Yale University. Three years later he received his Ph.D. from the Massachusetts Institute of Technology and while studying there had been part of a team sent to work with Portugal's Central Bank. Although Krugman's academic career was impressive, few could have predicted his rapid rise to fame. The *Washington Monthly* has recently named him the most important political columnist in America and *The Economist* has praised him as the most celebrated economist of his generation. He has received numerous awards, including the John Bates Clark Medal in 1991, the Adam Smith Award in 1995, the Prince of Asturias Award, given by the Prince of Asturias, and, of course, the Nobel Prize in 2008.

After receiving his Ph.D., Krugman spent a year working as the senior international economist on President Ronald Reagan's Council of Economic Advisors and held teaching positions at Yale University, M.I.T., Stanford University and University of California, Berkeley. In the year 2000, Krugman joined Princeton University as professor of economics and international affairs and remains a centenary professor at the London School of Economics. He is a member of the Group of Thirty, a body of leading international economists, and a research associate at the National Bureau of Economic Research. As a consultant, he has worked for the United Nations, the International Monetary Fund, the World Bank, the Federal Reserve Bank of New York and for several countries, including the Philippines and Portugal.

Paul Krugman is perhaps best known to the world at large, however, for his column in *The New York Times*. Before joining *The Times*, he wrote articles for *Fortune*, *The New Republic*, *Newsweek* and *Foreign Policy*. He is the author or editor of more than twenty books and hundreds of professional journal articles. Paul and his wife, Robin, have also recently collaborated on two college textbooks dealing with economics. Although his insight and commentary reach into many different topics, the Nobel Prize Committee awarded him their honor because of how he has been able to explain patterns of international trade and how wealth is concentrated by examining economies of scale and consumer preferences.

The Sveriges Riksbank Prize in Economic Sciences in Memory of Alfred Nobel 2008

Martti Ahtisaari

For his important efforts, on several continents and over more than three decades, to resolve international conflicts.

Martti Ahtisaari was born on June 23, 1937, in Viipuri, Finland. When the Soviet Union invaded the country two years later, his family, along with hundreds of thousands of others, was displaced. The Ahtisaaris eventually settled further east in the city of Kuopio but the horrors of the experience left a lasting impression on young Martti. For the last forty five years he has dedicated himself to his job as a civil servant in the Finnish Ministry for Foreign Affairs and the United Nations, drawing on his sensitivity for those who have experienced the hardships of war and displacement.

In 1960, just after graduating from the University of Oulu, Ahtisaari moved to Pakistan to lead the Y.M.C.A.'s physical education training establishment there and soon became active in several non-governmental organizations (NGOs) dedicated to aiding developing countries. Ahtisaari joined the Ministry for Foreign Affairs of Finland in 1965 and by 1971 had risen to become the Assistant Director of its Bureau for Technical Co-operation. The next year he was appointed Deputy Director of the Department for International Development Co-operation and during the early 1970s was also sitting on the Government Advisory Committee on Trade and Industrialization Affairs of Developing Countries. With this impressive resume and a host of personal charms, Ahtisaari found himself made the Ambassador of Finland to the United Republic of Tanzania at the age of 36.

During the mid 1970s he was also accredited to Zambia, Somalia and Mozambique, and served as a member of the Senate of the United Nation's Institute for Namibia between 1975 and 1976. Two years later he moved his family to New York so as to better serve as the U.N. Commissioner for that country, a post he held until 1981.

In 1984, Ahtisaari returned to his native Finland where he served as Under-Secretary of State in charge of International Development Co-operation in the Ministry for Foreign Affairs. Over the next several years Ahtisaari continued to take on more responsibilities, serving as Chairman of the Board of Directors for the Finnish Industrialization Fund for developing countries and Governor for Finland in the African Development Bank, the Inter-American Development Bank, the Asian Development Bank and the International Fund for Agricultural Development.

In 1987, Ahtisaari moved back to New York to serve as the United Nation's Under-Secretary General for Administration and Management, while still maintaining his Special Representative status for Namibia and helping to usher in the independence of that nation. In 1991, Ahtisaari became State Secretary in the Ministry for Foreign Affairs and shifted his attentions to the Balkans.

Finally, after a long and distinguished career with the United Nations and the Finnish Foreign Ministry, in February 1994 Martti Ahtisaari was elected President of the Republic of Finland. He steered his country through economic depression, oversaw its joining the European Union during the six years of his presidency.

In 2000, still wanting to continue his work in international peace mediation and conflict resolution, Ahtisaari founded and now sits as Chairman on the Crisis Management Initiative. His work in recent years has included inspection of old Irish Republican Army arms dumps, sitting on a panel on security and safety for United Nation's personnel in Iraq and, in 2005, facilitating the peace process between the Government of Indonesia and the Free Aceh Movement. Martti Ahtisaari is strongly committed to a united Europe and the possibility of expanding its membership. He currently acts as Chairman of the Independent Commission on Turkey, which examines both the challenges to and possible benefits of extending membership of the European Union to Turkey.

Ahtisaari holds nineteen honorary doctorates from universities all across the world and has received numerous prizes in addition to this Nobel Peace Prize. In 1968, he married Eeva Irmeli Hyvärinen and the couple has a son, Marko, a noted musician and producer.

Harald zur Hausen

For his discovery of human papilloma viruses causing cervical cancer.

Harald zur Hausen was born on March 11, 1936, in the German city of Gelsenkirchen-Buer. His childhood landscape was heavily bombed during the Second World War but all family members survived the conflict and post-war period. Hausen's early schooling was sporadic because of the war and its turbulent aftermath, but he remembers an early interest in natural biology. In 1950, his family moved to Northern Germany where he completed high school with honors.

Deciding to focus on medicine rather than biology, Hausen entered the University of Bonn and continued his studies at the University of Hamburg and the Medical Academy in Düsseldorf. In 1960, he graduated and moved on to medical internship in the hopes of earning his license. Soon, however, Hausen became fascinated with experimental studies and gave up his earlier hopes of becoming a practicing physician. He also realized that post-doctorate positions in post-war Germany were scarce and that it would be to his advantage to emigrate from Germany.

In 1964, Hausen married Ethel-Michele de Villiers, also a scientist, and one year later the couple had their first child. With their newborn son, the Hausens crossed the ocean so Harald could take a position offered to him at the Children's Hospital of Philadelphia. In 1968 they moved back to Germany after an offer to establish his own team of researchers was made to him by the Institute for Virology at the University of Würzburg.

In 1972, Hausen was appointed Chairman of the Institute of Clinical Virology in Erlangen-Nürnberg and it was there that he focused his attentions on papilloma viruses, which he suspected caused cervical cancer. Five years later he was appointed Chairman of the Institute of Virology of the University of Freiburg, where he continued the research that would earn him half of the Nobel Prize. In 1983 Hausen took on the role of Scientific Director of the German Cancer Research Center.

In 2003, after more than 20 years, Hausen retired from the German Cancer Research Center, although he still maintains a laboratory there and acts as Editor-in-Chief of the *International Journal of Cancer*. For his distinguished career in understanding cancer, which will hopefully lead to prevention and therapy, Hausen has received numerous prizes beyond this Nobel, including the Great Cross of Merit in 2004 and the Gairdner Foundation International Award in 2008.

Françoise Barré-Sinoussi and Luc Montagnier also shared half of the prize.

Charles K Kao

For groundbreaking achievements concerning the transmission of light in fibers for optical communication.

Charles Kuen Kao was born November 4, 1933, in Shanghai, China, where he studied Chinese classics with a tutor before entering an international school there where he mastered English and French. Kao's family moved to Hong Kong in 1948, where he graduated from the prestigious St. Joseph's College in 1952. After completing his undergraduate studies in electrical engineering at what is now the University of Greenwich, he obtained his Bachelor of Science degree from the University of London.

He worked for Standard Telecommunications Laboratories in Harlow, England, and it was here Kao began his groundbreaking scientific research. In 1965, he received his Ph.D. degree from University College London. Kao joined the Chinese University of Hong Kong in 1970, where he founded the Department of Electronics. Four years later, he immigrated to the United States and began work at the I.T.T. Corporation in Roanoke, Virginia. By 1982, Kao had risen to be the first Executive Scientist at I.T.T. and he began serving as adjunct professor and Fellow of Trumbull College at Yale University.

Between 1987 and 1996, Kao served as Vice-Chancellor of the Chinese University of Hong Kong, after which he served as Visiting Professor to the same department. In 2000, Kao founded the Independent Schools Foundation Academy in Hong Kong and served as its chairman until stepping down in 2008. During this time he also served as Chairman of Transtech Service Ltd. and I.T.X. Services Ltd.

Over the years, Kao has received many awards for his research but his greatest recognition by far has been the Nobel Prize in Physics awarded for his breakthrough in the field of fiber optics. Charles Kao determined how to transmit light over long distances through optical glass fibers, revolutionizing how societies are networked together and helping to usher in the world we know today. The fiber optic industry that Kao helped develop has facilitated global broadband connections and to show its central role in today's world, more than one billion kilometers of glass fiber optic cable have been laid to date with more produced every day. Kao has been suffering from Alzheimer's Disease since 2004 and currently resides in Mountain View, California, moving from Hong Kong to be closer to his children and grandchild.

Willard Sterling Boyle and George Elwood Smith also shared half of the prize.

Barack Obama

For his extraordinary efforts to strengthen international diplomacy and cooperation between peoples.

Barack Obama was born August 4, 1961, in Honolulu, Hawaii. His mother, Ann Dunham, grew up in Kansas but his father, Barack Obama Sr., was born in Kenya and herded goats there until earning a scholarship to study at the University of Hawaii where Ann was also a student. The couple was married February 2, 1961, and Barack was born six months later.

When he was two, Obama's parents divorced, his father going on to study at Harvard before returning to Kenya and his mother marrying Lolo Soetoro, after which, in 1967, the new couple and the young Barack moved to his step-father's native Indonesia. Obama attended school in Jakarta but his mother, fearing for his safety and education, sent him to live with his maternal grandparents, Madelyn and Stanley Dunham, when he was 10 years old. His mother and sister later rejoined him in America.

Although he excelled in school, from an early age he had to deal with discrimination because of his multicultural background. The absence of his father also left a lasting impression. At the age of 22 his father died in a car crash in Nairobi. After high school, he studied at Occidental College in Los Angles and Columbia University in New York, graduating in 1983 with a degree in political science. After two years working in the business sector, Obama moved to Chicago as a community organizer for low-income residents. During these years Obama joined Trinity United Church of Christ and made visits to relatives in Kenya.

In 1988, he entered Harvard Law School and it was there he met Michelle Robinson, an associate at Sidley & Austin law firm, and the couple soon began dating. Obama was the first African American to be elected editor of the *Harvard Law Review* and graduated magna cum laude in 1991. After completing his studies at Harvard, Obama returned to Chicago to work as a civil rights lawyer and taught at the University of Chicago Law School. In 1992, Michelle and he were married and the couple has since had two daughters, Malia, born in 1998, and Sasha, born in 2001.

His advocacy work led Obama to run for the Illinois State Senate, to which he was elected in 1996. Working with both Democrats and Republicans, he helped draft legislature on health care, early childhood education and programs for the poor. In the November 2004 election, Obama was elected a U.S. Senator from Illinois in the state's greatest landslide victory on record. Soon after being sworn into office, Obama worked on disarmament issues and pushed for alternative energy development and improved veterans' benefits. His second book, *The Audacity of Hope*, was released in 2006 and contained Obama's vision for the future of America, many aspects of which he discussed on the presidential campaign trail.

Obama won the 2008 Democratic presidential nomination after a difficult battle with the U.S. Senator from New York, Hilary Clinton. He defeated Republican nominee John McCain and on January 20, 2009, was sworn in as the 44th, and 1st African American, President of the United States.

Although he inherited a global economic recession, two wars and the nation's lowest international favorability rating on record, Obama rose to the challenge and inspired countless others to believe in America and change itself. In his inaugural speech Obama summarized, saying,"… the challenges we face are real. They are serious and they are many. They will not be met easily or in a short span of time. But know this, America: They will be met."

Obama has demonstrated his intelligence and ability to raise spirits and win support through his personal charm and commitment to multilateral diplomacy. After many years of watching its foreign approval ratings plummet, America has watched its new leader welcomed onto the world stage in an unprecedented manner. The press release for Obama's 2009 Nobel Peace Prize puts it best, "For 108 years, the Norwegian Nobel Committee has sought to stimulate precisely that international policy and those attitudes for which Obama is now the world's leading spokesman."

President Obama donated the entire amount of prize money to charity. The largest amounts went to Fisher House, an organization that provides assistance to families of those being treated in Veterans Affairs medical centers, and the Clinton-Bush Haiti Fund. Among other organizations receiving a part of the $1,400,000 were the United Negro College Fund, the Appalachian Leadership and Education Foundation, the American Indian College Fund and the Hispanic Scholarship Fund.

(1948–)

Elizabeth Helen Blackburn

For the discovery of how chromosomes are protected by telomeres and the enzyme telomerase.

Elizabeth Blackburn was born November 26, 1948, in Hobart, Tasmania, Australia. Both her parents were practicing physicians and Elizabeth quickly demonstrated her aptitude for the sciences. Her family moved to Melbourne, where she attended high school and later the University of Melbourne, from which she graduated in 1970. Blackburn received her Master's degree two years later from Darwin College, Cambridge, followed by her Ph.D. there in 1975. Postdoctoral work was done at Yale University.

In 1978, Blackburn joined the Department of Molecular Biology at the University of California, Berkeley, and in 1990 took on the role of Chair of the Department of Biochemistry and Biophysics at the San Francisco campus, where she continues to work today as Morris Herztein Professor of Biology and Physiology.

She has received honorary doctorates from Yale University, Harvard University, the University of Chicago, the University of Pennsylvania and others. Blackburn was also elected a Fellow of the Royal Society of London in 1992 and a member of both the American Association for the Advancement of Science and the Institute of Medicine in 2000. The list of awards conferred on her by her peers is long but includes the Harvery Prize, the American Cancer Society Medal of Honor and the Meyenburg Prize for Cancer Research. In 2007, *Time Magazine* named Blackburn as one of the Most Influential People of the year.

Elizabeth Blackburn was recognized by the Nobel Committee for her discovery of the molecular nature of telomeres and the ribonucleoprotein enzyme, telomerase. Telomeres are the end portions of eukaryotic chromosomes that function as caps to protect genetic information. Her team has performed numerous groundbreaking studies in this emerging and promising field, drawing attention from all over the world. Some attention connected with her stances on medical ethics has been critical and Blackburn was dismissed from the President's Council on Bioethics, on which she sat from 2002 to 2004, but the world's most prestigious prize organization determined her the most fit recipient in her field only five years later. Elizabeth Blackburn currently lives in California and is married to John W. Sedat; they have a son, Benjamin.

Carol W. Greider and Jack W. Szostak also received one-third of the prize each.

Nobel Laureates

2000-2009

2000

Nobel Prize in Physics
Zhores Ivanovich Alferov
Born March 15, 1930, in Vitebsk, Union of Soviet Socialist Republics (now Belarus).
&
Herbert Kroemer
Born August 25, 1928, in Weimar, Germany.
For developing semiconductor heterostructures used in high-speed- and opto-electronics.
&
Jack St. Clair Kilby
Born November 8, 1923, inGreat Bend, Kansas, United States, and died June 20, 2005, in Dallas, Texas.
For his part in the invention of the integrated circuit.

Nobel Prize in Chemistry
Alan Jay Heeger
Born January 22, 1936, in Sioux City, Iowa, United States.
&
Alan Graham MacDiarmid
Born April 14, 1927, in Masterton, New Zealand, and died February 7, 2007, in Drexel Hill, Pennsylvania, United States.
&
Hideki Shirakawa
Born August 20, 1936, in Tokyo, Japan.
For the discovery and development of conductive polymers.

Nobel Prize in Physiology or Medicine
Arvid Carlsson
Born January 25, 1923, in Uppsala, Sweden.
&
Paul Greengard
Born December 11, 1925, in New York, New York, United States.
&

Eric Richard Kandel
Born November 7, 1929, in Vienna, Austria.
For their discoveries concerning signal transduction in the nervous system.

Nobel Prize in Literature
Gao Xingjian
Born January 4, 1940, in Ganzhou, China.
For an oeuvre of universal validity, bitter insights and linguistic ingenuity, which has opened new paths for the Chinese novel and drama.

Nobel Peace Prize
Kim Dae-jung
Born December 3, 1925, in Mok'o, Korea (now South Korea).
For his work for democracy and human rights in South Korea and in East Asia in general, and for peace and reconciliation with North Korea in particular.

The Sveriges Riksbank Prize in Economic Sciences in Memory of Alfred Nobel
James Joseph Heckman
Born April 19, 1944, in Chicago, Illinois, United States.
For his development of theory and methods for analyzing selective samples.
&
Daniel Little McFadden
Born July 29, 1937, in Raleigh, North Carolina, United States.
For his development of theory and methods for analyzing discrete choice.

2001

Nobel Prize in Physics
Eric Allin Cornell
Born December 19, 1961, in Palo Alto, California, United States.
&

Wolfgang Ketterle

Born October 21, 1957, in Heidelberg, Germany.

&

Carl Edwin Wieman

Born March 26, 1951, in Corvallis, Oregon, United States.

For the achievement of Bose-Einstein condensation in dilute gases of alkali atoms, and for early fundamental studies of the properties of the condensates.

Nobel Prize in Chemistry

William Standish Knowles

Born June 1, 1917, in Taunton, Massachusetts, United States.

&

Ryoji Noyori

Born September 3, 1938, in Kobe, Japan.

For their work on chirally catalyzed hydrogenation reactions.

&

Karl Barry Sharpless

Born April 28, 1941, in Philadelphia, Pennsylvania, United States.

For his work on chirally catalyzed oxidation reactions.

Nobel Prize in Physiology or Medicine

Leland Harrison Hartwell

Born October 30, 1939, in Los Angeles, California, United States.

&

Richard Timothy Hunt

Born February 19, 1943, in Neston, England.

&

Paul Maxime Nurse

Born January 25, 1949, in Norwich, England.

For their discoveries of key regulators of the cell cycle.

Nobel Prize in Literature

Vidiadhar Surajprasad Naipaul

Born August 17, 1932, in Chaguanas, Trinidad and Tobago.

For having united perceptive narrative and incorruptible scrutiny in works that compel us to see the presence of suppressed histories.

Nobel Peace Prize

Kofi Atta Annan

Born April 8, 1938, in Kumasi, Ghana.

&

The United Nations

Founded on October 24, 1945, with its headquarters in New York, New York, United States.

For their work in favor of a better organized, more peaceful world.

The Sveriges Riksbank Prize in Economic Sciences in Memory of Alfred Nobel

George Arthur Akerlof

Born June 17, 1940, in New Haven, Connecticut, United States.

&

Andrew Michael Spence

Born November 7, 1943, in Montclair, New Jersey, United States.

&

Joseph Eugene Stiglitz

Born February 9, 1943, in Gary, Indiana, United States.

For their analyses of markets with asymmetric information.

2002

Nobel Prize in Physics

Raymond Davis, Jr.

Born October 14, 1914, in Washington DC, United States, and died May 31, 2006, in Blue Point, New York.

&

Masatoshi Koshiba

Born September 19, 1926, in Toyohashi, Japan.

For pioneering contributions to astrophysics, in particular for the detection of cosmic neutrinos.

&

Riccardo Giacconi

Born October 6, 1931, in Genoa, Italy.

For pioneering contributions to astrophysics, which have led to the discovery of cosmic X-ray sources.

Nobel Prize in Chemistry

John Bennett Fenn

Born June 15, 1917, in New York, New York, United States.

&

Koichi Tanaka

Born August 3, 1959, in Toyama, Japan.

For their development of soft desorption ionization methods for mass spectrometric analyses of biological macromolecules.

&
Kurt Wüthrich
Born October 4, 1938, in Aarberg, Switzerland.
For his development of nuclear magnetic resonance spectroscopy for determining the three-dimensional structure of biological macromolecules in solution.

Nobel Prize in Physiology or Medicine
Sydney Brenner
Born January 13, 1927, in Germiston, South Africa.
&
Howard Robert Horvitz
Born May 8, 1947, in Chicago, Illinois, United States.
&
John Edward Sulston
Born March 27, 1942, in Cambridge, England.
For their discoveries concerning "genetic regulation of organ development and programmed cell death."

Nobel Prize in Literature
Imre Kertész
Born November 9, 1929, in Budapest, Hungary.
For writing that upholds the fragile experience of the individual against the barbaric arbitrariness of history.

Nobel Peace Prize
James Earl Carter, Jr. (Jimmy Carter)
Born October 1, 1924, in Plains, Georgia, United States.
For his decades of untiring effort to find peaceful solutions to international conflicts, to advance democracy and human rights, and to promote economic and social development.

The Sveriges Riksbank Prize in Economic Sciences in Memory of Alfred Nobel
Daniel Kahneman
Born March 5, 1934, in Tel Aviv, Palestine (now Israel).
For having integrated insights from psychological research into economic science, especially concerning human judgment and decision making under uncertainty.
&
Vernon Lomax Smith
Born January 1, 1927, in Wichita, Kansas, United States.
For having established laboratory experiments as a tool in empirical economic analysis, especially in the study of alternative market mechanisms.

2003

Nobel Prize in Physics
Alexei Alexeyevich Abrikosov
Born June 25, 1928, in Moscow, Union of Soviet Socialist Republics (now Russia).
&
Vitaly Lazarevich Ginzburg
Born October 4, 1916, in Moscow, Russia.
&
Anthony James Leggett
Born March 26, 1938, in London, England.
For pioneering contributions to the theory of superconductors and superfluids.

Nobel Prize in Chemistry
Peter Agre
Born January 30, 1949, in Northfield, Minnesota, United States.
For the discovery of water channels.
&
Roderick MacKinnon
Born February 19, 1956, in Burlington, Massachusetts, United States.
For structural and mechanistic studies of ion channels.

Nobel Prize in Physiology or Medicine
Paul Christian Lauterbur
Born May 6, 1929, in Sidney, Ohio, United States and died March 27, 2007, in Urbana, Illinois.
&
Peter Mansfield
Born October 9, 1933, in London, England.
For their discoveries concerning magnetic resonance imaging.

Nobel Prize in Literature
John Maxwell Coetzee
Born February 9, 1940, in Cape Town, South Africa.
Who, in innumerable guises, portrays the surprising involvement of the outsider.

Nobel Peace Prize
Shirin Ebadi
Born June 21, 1947, in Hamadan, Iran.
For her efforts for democracy and human rights. She

has focused especially on the struggle for the rights of women and children.

The Sveriges Riksbank Prize in Economic Sciences in Memory of Alfred Nobel
Robert Fry Engle III
Born November 10, 1942, in Syracuse, New York, United States.
For methods of analyzing economic time series with time-varying volatility (ARCH).
&
Clive William John Granger
Born September 4, 1934, in Swansea, Wales.
For methods of analyzing economic time series with common trends (cointegration).

2004

Nobel Prize in Physics
David Jonathan Gross
Born February 19, 1941, in Washington, DC, United States.
&
Hugh David Politzer
Born August 31, 1949, in New York, New York, United States.
&
Frank Anthony Wilczek
Born May 15, 1951, in New York, New York, United States.
For the discovery of asymptotic freedom in the theory of the strong interaction.

Nobel Prize in Chemistry
Aaron Ciechanover
Born October 1, 1947, in Haifa, Israel.
&
Avram Hershko
Born December 31, 1937, in Karcag, Hungary.
&
Irwin Rose
Born July 16, 1926, in Brooklyn, New York, United States.
For the discovery of ubiquitin-mediated protein degradation.

Nobel Prize in Physiology or Medicine
Richard Axel
Born July 2, 1946, in New York, New York, United States.
&
Linda B. Buck
Born January 29, 1947, in Seattle, Washington, United States.
For their discoveries of odorant receptors and the organization of the olfactory system.

Nobel Prize in Literature
Elfriede Jelinek
Born October 20, 1946, in Mürzzuschlag, Austria.
For her musical flow of voices and counter-voices in novels and plays that, with extraordinary linguistic zeal, reveal the absurdity of society's clichés and their subjugating power.

Nobel Peace Prize
Wangari Muta Maathai
Born April 1, 1940, in Nyeri, Kenya.
For her contribution to sustainable development, democracy and peace.

The Sveriges Riksbank Prize in Economic Sciences in Memory of Alfred Nobel
Finn Erling Kydland
Born December 1943 in Ålgård, Norway.
&
Edward Christian Prescott
Born December 26, 1940, in Glens Falls, New York, United States.
For their contributions to dynamic macroeconomics: the time consistency of economic policy and the driving forces behind business cycles.

2005

Nobel Prize in Physics
Roy Jay Glauber
Born September 1, 1925, in New York, New York, United States.
For his contribution to the quantum theory of optical coherence.
&
John Lewis Hall
Born August 21, 1934, in Denver, Colorado, United States.
&

Theodor Wolfgang Hänsch
Born October 30, 1941, in Heidelberg, Germany.
For their contributions to the development of laser-based precision spectroscopy, including the optical frequency comb technique.

Nobel Prize in Chemistry
Yves Chauvin
Born October 10, 1930, in Menin, Belgium.
&
Robert Howard Grubbs
Born February 27, 1942, in Possum Trot, Kentucky, United States.
&
Richard Royce Schrock
Born January 4, 1945, in Berne, Indiana, United States.
For the development of the metathesis method in organic synthesis.

Nobel Prize in Physiology or Medicine
Barry James Marshall
Born September 30, 1951, in Kalgoorlic, Australia.
&
John Robin Warren
Born June 11, 1937, in Adelaide, Australia.
For their discovery of the bacterium Helicobacter pylori and its role in gastritis and peptic ulcer disease.

Nobel Prize in Literature
Harold Pinter
Born October 10, 1930, in London, England.
Who in his plays uncovers the precipice under everyday prattle and forces entry into oppression's closed rooms.

Nobel Peace Prize
International Atomic Energy Agency (IAEA)
Founded in 1957, with its headquarters at the Vienna International Centre, Austria.
&
Mohamed ElBaradei
Born June 17, 1942, in Cairo, Egypt.
For their efforts to prevent nuclear energy from being used for military purposes and to ensure that nuclear energy for peaceful purposes is used in the safest possible way.

The Sveriges Riksbank Prize in Economic Sciences in Memory of Alfred Nobel
Robert John Aumann
Born June 8, 1930, in Frankfurt am Main, Germany.
&
Thomas Crombie Schelling
Born April 14, 1921, in Oakland, California, United States.
For having enhanced our understanding of conflict and cooperation through game-theory analysis.

2006

Nobel Prize in Physics
John Cromwell Mather
Born August 7, 1946, in Roanoke, Virginia, United States.
&
George Fitzgerald Smoot III
Born February 20, 1945, in Yukon, Florida, United States.
For their discovery of the blackbody form and anisotropy of the cosmic microwave background radiation.

Nobel Prize in Chemistry
Roger David Kornberg
Born April 24, 1947, in Saint Louis, Missouri, United States.
For his studies of the molecular basis of eukaryotic transcription.

Nobel Prize in Physiology or Medicine
Andrew Zachary Fire
Born April 27, 1959, in Stanford, California, United States.
&
Craig Cameron Mello
Born October 18, 1960, in New Haven, Connecticut, United States.
For their discovery of RNA interference — gene silencing by double-stranded RNA.

Nobel Prize in Literature
Ferit Orhan Pamuk
Born June 7, 1952, in Istanbul, Turkey.
For discovering new symbols for the clash and interlacing of cultures.

Nobel Peace Prize
Muhammad Yunus
Born June 28, 1940, in Chittagong, India (now Bangladesh).
&
Grameen Bank
Begun in 1976 and officially founded in 1983 in Bangladesh.
For their efforts to create economic and social development from below.

The Sveriges Riksbank Prize in Economic Sciences in Memory of Alfred Nobel
Edmund Strother Phelps
Born July 26, 1933, in Evanston, Illinois, United States.
For his analysis of intertemporal tradeoffs in macroeconomic policy.

2007

Nobel Prize in Physics
Albert Fert
Born March 7, 1938, in Carcassonne, France.
&
Peter Andreas Grünberg
Born May 18, 1939, in Pilsen, Czechoslovakia (now Czech Republic).
For the discovery of giant magnetoresistance.

Nobel Prize in Chemistry
Gerhard Ertl
Born October 10, 1936, in Stuttgart, Germany.
For his studies of chemical processes on solid surfaces.

Nobel Prize in Physiology or Medicine
Mario Renato Capecchi
Born October 6, 1937, in Verona, Italy.
&
Martin John Evans
Born January 1, 1941, in Stroud, England.
&
Oliver Smithies
Born June 23, 1925, in Halifax, England.
For their discoveries of principles for introducing specific gene modifications in mice by the use of embryonic stem cells.

Nobel Prize in Literature
Doris Lessing, né Doris May Taylor
Born October 22, 1919, in Kermanshah, Persia (now Iran).
That epicist of the female experience, who with skepticism, fire and visionary power has subjected a divided civilization to scrutiny.

Nobel Peace Prize
Albert Arnold Gore, Jr. (Al Gore)
Born March 31, 1948, in Washington, DC, United States.
&
Intergovernmental Panel on Climate Change (IPCC)
Founded in 1988.
For their efforts to build up and disseminate greater knowledge about man-made climate change, and to lay the foundations for the measures that are needed to counteract such change.

The Sveriges Riksbank Prize in Economic Sciences in Memory of Alfred Nobel
Leonid Hurwicz
Born August 21, 1917, in Moscow, Russia.
&
Eric Stark Maskin
Born December 12, 1950, in New York, New York, United States.
&
Roger Bruce Myerson
Born March 29, 1951, in Boston, Massachusetts, United States.
For having laid the foundations of mechanism design theory.

2008

Nobel Prize in Physics
Yoichiro Nambu
Born January 18, 1921, in Tokyo, Japan.
For the discovery of the mechanism of spontaneous broken symmetry in subatomic physics.
&
Makoto Kobayashi
Born April 7, 1944, in Nagoya, Japan.
&

Toshihide Maskawa
Born February 7, 1940, in Nagoya, Japan.
For the discovery of the origin of the broken symmetry which predicts the existence of at least three families of quarks in nature.

Nobel Prize in Chemistry
Osamu Shimomura
Born August 27, 1928, in Kyoto, Japan.
&
Martin Chalfie
Born January 15, 1947, in Chicago, Illinois, United States.
&
Roger Yonchien Tsien
Born February 1, 1952, in New York, New York, United States.
For the discovery and development of the green fluorescent protein, G.F.P.

Nobel Prize in Physiology or Medicine
Harald zur Hausen
Born March 11, 1936, in Gelsenkirchen, Germany.
For his discovery of human papilloma viruses causing cervical cancer.
&
Françoise Barré-Sinoussi
Born July 30, 1947, in Paris, France.
&
Luc Montagnier
Born August 18 1932, in Chabris, France.
For their discovery of human immunodeficiency virus.

Nobel Prize in Literature
Jean-Marie Gustave Le Clézio
Born April 13, 1940, in Nice, France.
Author of new departures, poetic adventure and sensual ecstasy, explorer of a humanity beyond and below the reigning civilization.

Nobel Peace Prize
Martti Ahtisaari
Born June 23, 1937, in Viipuri, Finland (now Vyborg, Russia).
For his important efforts, on several continents and over more than three decades, to resolve international conflicts.

Nobel Prize in Economics
Paul Krugman
Born February 28, 1953, in Albany, New York, United States.
For his analysis of trade patterns and location of economic activity.

2009

Nobel Prize in Physics
Charles Kuen Kao
Born November 4, 1933, in Shanghai, China.
For groundbreaking achievements concerning the transmission of light in fibers for optical communication.
&
Willard Sterling Boyle
Born August 19, 1924, in Amherst, Nova Scotia, Canada.
&
George Elwood Smith
Born May 10, 1930, in White Plains, New York, United States.
For the invention of an imaging semiconductor circuit – the CCD sensor.

Nobel Prize in Chemistry
Venkatraman Ramakrishnan
Born 1952, in Chidambaram, India.
&
Thomas Arthur Steitz
Born August 23 1940, in Milwaukee, Wisconsin, United States.
&
Ada Yonath
Born June 22, 1939, in Jerusalem, British Mandate of Palestine (now Israel).
For studies of the structure and function of the ribosome.

Nobel Prize in Physiology or Medicine
Elizabeth Helen Blackburn
Born November 26, 1948, in Hobart, Australia.
&
Carol Widney Greider
Born April 15, 1961, in San Diego, California, United States.
&

Jack William Szostak
Born November 9, 1952, in London, United Kingdom.
For the discovery of how chromosomes are protected by
telomeres and the enzyme telomerase.

Nobel Prize in Literature
Herta Müller
Born August 17, 1953, in Ni chidorf, Romania.
Who, with the concentration of poetry and the frankness
of prose, depicts the landscape of the dispossessed.

Nobel Peace Prize
Barack Hussein Obama
Born August 4, 1961 in Honolulu, Hawaii, United States.
For his extraordinary efforts to strengthen international
diplomacy and cooperation between peoples.

Nobel Prize in Economics
Elinor Ostrom
Born August 7, 1933, in Los Angeles, California, United
States.
For her analysis of economic governance, especially the
commons.
&
Oliver Eaton Williamson
Born September 27, 1932 in Superior, Wisconsin, United
States.
For his analysis of economic governance, especially the
boundaries of the firm.

Index